University of Minnesota Press / Minneapolis London

THE UNMAKING OF FASCIST AESTHETICS

Kriss Ravetto

Copyright 2001 by the Regents of the University of Minnesota

Published by the University of Minnesota Press
111 Third Avenue South, Suite 290
Minneapolis, MN 55401-2520
http://www.upress.umn.edu

Library of Congress Cataloging-in-Publication Data
Ravetto, Kriss.
   The unmaking of fascist aesthetics / Kriss Ravetto.
      p. cm.
Includes bibliographical references (p.) and index.
   ISBN 0-8166-3742-3 — ISBN 0-8166-3743-1 (pbk.)
   1. Motion pictures—Political aspects. 2. Fascism and motion pictures.
I. Title.
   PN1995.9.P6 R38 2001
   791.43'658—dc21

                          2001003521

Printed in the United States of America on acid-free paper

The University of Minnesota is an equal-opportunity educator and employer.

12 11 10 09 08 07 06 05 04 03 02 01   10 9 8 7 6 5 4 3 2 1

Contents

Acknowledgments

This study is a product of multiple interactions—between me, the films and the critical thinking that have inspired this work, and the great number of friends and colleagues who have generously offered their time, encouragement, and criticism.

First, I want to acknowledge my deep respect for the intellectual rigor and aesthetic acumen of Pier Paolo Pasolini, Liliana Cavani, and Lina Wertmüller. I also wish to profess my enduring appreciation for my friends and mentors whose guidance and criticism were invaluable. Thanks to Lucia Re, Sande Cohen, Mario Biagioli, Sam Weber, and Margie Waller for engaging my thinking thoroughly, commenting on the various versions of the manuscript, and providing me with a model of scholarly excellence. Special thanks to Randy Rutsky, Ruth Ben-Ghiat, Teshome Gabriel, Peter Wollen, and Geoffrey Nowell-Smith for reading the book in manuscript and providing stimulating remarks. I'm very grateful to the readers' reports from the University of Minnesota Press for their attentive and extremely helpful commentaries. I also want to thank Beatrice Lewin-Dumin, whose careful reading greatly helped me to revise the manuscript. Thanks to Doug Armato for his astute suggestions and for seeing this project through to the end.

My research was markedly facilitated by the generosity of various archives and institutions: in Rome, Cineteca Nazionale, Istituto Luce, l'Archivio di Stato, and Biblioteca Nazionale; in New York, MOMA's Film Archive and the New York Public Library; in Los Angeles, the Getty Center Archive, UCLA Film Archive, and the Academy of Motion Pictures Archive.

Finally, I am indebted to my family, including all of my dearest friends, for their love and support. This book is dedicated to the memory of my father.

Introduction

I was made for love
That is my universe
I can't help it
It is my nature
Love's always been my game
Play it how I may
Men cluster to me
Like moths around a flame,
And if their wings burn,
I know I'm not to blame[1]

—sung by Marlene Dietrich in *The Blue Angel*

How could nazism, which was represented by lamentable, shabby, puritan young men; by a species of Victorian spinsters, have become everywhere today ... in all the pornographic literature of the world, the absolute reference to eroticism? All the shoddiest aspects of the erotic imagination are now put under the sign of nazism.[2]

—Michel Foucault

At the end of the twentieth century, numerous attempts to "settle accounts," "come to terms with," and "work through" fascism, nazism, and the "Final Solution" have garnered public attention throughout both the Western media and the West's high academic circles. For example, recent political and scholarly discourses have demanded that the nations and peoples who fostered and supported fascism acknowledge their

1

"moral responsibility." This question of responsibility has also become a question of "financial accountability" wherein industries like the Swiss banking industry, IG Farben, Deustche Bank, Alliance, and Bertelsmann, to name a few, have not only been accused of profiting from forced labor, the war, and the Holocaust in general, but in many cases have been required to "pay" restitution to the victims and their families. The notion of restitution itself has been justifiably problematized—indeed, how can the victims of forced labor, internment, execution, and the Holocaust be "repaid"? This insurmountable conflict between demands for responsibility and the impossibility of providing fair restitution has led some critics to call for "forgiveness" as a means of resolving such impasses. Whether as calls for "moral responsibility," "restitution," or "forgiveness," such mandates require that the events of World War II be historicized. Yet the very historicization and representation of fascism, nazism, and the "Final Solution" remain ensconced within these contradictory impulses: on the one hand fascism is historicized, represented as contained within an era—1922–1943 for Italian fascism, 1933–1945 for German nazism, and 1938–1945 for the "Final Solution"—and on the other hand it has been dehistoricized, rendered unrepresentable—an unresolvable or unspeakable horror and atrocity that cannot be overcome, only commemorated. Similarly, while fascism and nazism are charged with having promoted the most violent, if not atrocious, ideological practices and policies, they are at the same time considered to have lacked any coherent political and ideological agendas. That is, rather than being grounded on firm ideological convictions, fascism and nazism are instead interpreted as politically inconstant: for Walter Benjamin, fascism did not practice politics but the "aestheticization of politics," and for Philippe Lacoue-Labarthe, nazism did not present an original system but a rhetorical performance of myth ("a myth of a myth"). Hence, at the same time cultural critics and historians treat fascism and nazism as a historical construct divorced from social, ideological, and political systems of postwar Europe and America, these very same intellectuals use fascism and nazism to mark the neutralization of time and history, for example, "the end of history," "the end of poetry," and the "end of man." Rather than address the history of fascism or the history of the Western fascist imaginary (the history of the postwar representation of fascism), the focus of this book will be to address the politics of history itself. It will concentrate on questions such as these: If indeed fascism, nazism, and the "Final Solution" can be clearly separated from the postwar era, why then have they remained at the limits of representation, or the end of history? Moreover, can myth and aesthetics really be divorced from ideology? The trajectory of this study is, thus, to investigate the historiographical interpretations used to construct and situate the coming and going of volatile historical subjects.

Many recent scholarly works argue that it may be too complex to historicize nazism and/or fascism. Nonetheless, countless historians, cultural critics, filmmakers, and television producers continue to disassociate fascism from the present. Fascism presents a disturbance on the smooth surface of narrative history: for Italian philosopher Benedetto Croce, fascism is an ellipsis; for numerous German historians, a stain on humanity or, even, an apocalyptic event; and for conservative ideologues, an aberration of the German or Italian identity. Clearly, the question of how fascism is to be read presents a charged political controversy. For example, debates such as the *Historikerstreit* (historians' conflict in the 1980s over whether nazism and the "Final Solution" can in fact be represented) no longer simply contest historical facts but dispute the politicization of such facts (historicism itself). As a consequence, the terrain of argumentation has shifted from the moral stance of "telling it like it is/was" to the act of selecting what is appropriate for analysis, thereby challenging the traditional role of the historian or cultural critic—whether he or she should be a master or a guardian of the past, a judge or a witness.[3] "Telling it as it is" can no longer be considered an unbiased account of the past. Furthermore, historians and cultural critics such as Saul Friedländer, Zygmunt Bauman, Theodor Adorno, and Jean-François Lyotard question if, in fact, the fascist past can be made sense of, worked through, or mastered. If the events of World War II are unmasterable (they neither pass away nor can be represented or synthesized), then, as William Spanos asks, how can we "analyze and debate the ideological origins and the scope of these appalling Nazi practices?"[4] In his analysis of the *Historikerstreit*, Charles Maier argues that there is an inherent contradiction in the positing of fascism (specifically the "Final Solution") as unspeakable, unmasterable, or unrepresentable. He writes: "the suffering [of the victims] is depicted as ineffable, incommunicable, and yet always to be proclaimed. It is intensely private, not to be diluted, but simultaneously public so that society will confirm the crimes."[5]

Interestingly, what is at stake in the representation of fascism and nazism seems to be outside of histories that restrict themselves to questions of historical context and analyze the specific content of these historical events. As I will argue throughout, the real stakes are set by the politics of memory (not just the victims') and the reconstruction of a legitimate Western European identity and economy in the aftermath of the war. The aim of historical narratives, in respect to Western identity and economic crises, is one of containment—a project of deterrence—as much as it is one of ideological positioning—the reconstruction of a moral ethos. Thus questions have emerged: What constitutes the event of fascism? What are the criteria for representing a historical event? And how is this narrative to be plotted if narrative is indeed determinative? The very attempt to narrativize and moralize fascism translates what is perceived as the object of this moral narrative, the event of fascism as a "lived experience," into representation, which consequently implicates such moral and political representations of fascism in the restaging, stylizing, or aestheticizing of such an event. Representations of nazis as alcoholic bureaucrats (e.g., Steven Spielberg's *Schindler's List*), homosexual torturers (e.g., Wilhelm Reich's *The Mass Psychology of Fascism* and Roberto Rossellini's *Open City [Roma città aperta]*), unmerciful, calculating scientists who use people as test rats for their human experiments (e.g., Hannah Arendt's

Eichmann in Jerusalem and Ingmar Bergman's *The Serpent's Egg*), or a "stain" on the face of humanity (Saul Friedländer's *Reflections of Nazism*) transform the "authenticity" of the event into the theatricality (dramatics) of moral and immoral postures. As a consequence, the nazi and the fascist have by now acquired generalized attributes of evil that slip over into different discourses—alluding to questions of gender and sexuality, religion, hygiene, decadence. Contemporary theorists and writers of all sorts use and borrow from other, equally dubious, conventional aesthetic references, such as the modernists' depiction of man as a machine, Social Darwinists' depictions of racial and sexual inferiority, the fin-de-siècle portrayal of the femme fatale as an emblem of decadence and decadent sexuality, Victorian notions of hygiene and feminine mass hysteria. In this respect, the *Historikerstreit* demonstrated what happens when the more nazism is represented, the more political its connotation becomes.

At the same time numerous historical, documentary, or cinematic projects aim at bankrupting ("unmaking") the efficacy of fascist culture in the postwar period, many histories, documentaries, fiction films, and television series amplify the paradox of representation—the tension between the unspeakable or intensely singular (personal or subjective) experiences of fascism and nazism, and the extremely public (media)

In Giovanni Pastrone's *Cabiria* (1914), the reclining diva, Sophonisbe (Italia Almirante Manzin), represents the decadent and orientalist image of femme fatale circulating at the fin-de-siècle.

obsession with historicizing, aestheticisizing, remembering, commemorating, and interpreting fascism, nazism, and the "Final Solution." In addition, many such representations, whether historical, theoretical, or filmic, apply conventional (prefascist) aesthetic images of evil (sexual perversion, intoxication, madness, disease, decadence, and impurity) to fascism and nazism as a means of expelling them from the present. Friedländer observes that the postwar "attraction [to nazism] lay less in any explicit ideology than in the power of emotions, images, and phantasms."[6] However, the images of perversity, obscenity, inhumanity, and horror that are attributed to fascism, nazism, and the "Final Solution" cannot be exculpated from ideological discourses; they are, indeed, fastened to preexisting moral codes and sexual and racial theories (Darwinism, psychoanalysis, criminology, sexology, and sociology). Therefore, rather than unmake fascist aesthetics, the result of this retrofashioning of fascism and nazism (depicting fascism and nazism as decadent, camp, kitsch, sentimental, or aberrant) attests to the impossibility of disengaging visual and rhetorical constructions from political, ideological, and moral codes. The argument of this book is that contemporary discourses about fascism are not discontinuous with rhetorical, moral, and visual analogies. And these analogies, comparisons, emphases, and reductions testify to our political finagling. In order to represent or keep the past present in our memories—whether that means to write history, bear witness, or visualize—which most cultural critics (aside from those on the extreme right) agree we must do, historians, cultural critics, and filmmakers cannot avoid rhetorical, moral, and visual analogies if we wish to represent at all.

The history of fascism offers an interesting case in historical, aesthetic, and gender politics, drawing on the discourses of impurity and purity and providing only the appearance of stable absolutes of good and evil. This book examines how the disquisition of fascism and the "Final Solution," predicated on the notion of unrepresentability, is in fact overrepresented in such a way as to belie certain historical and historiographic shifts. These shifts range from socialist or Marxist politics in neorealist cinema, psychoanalytic approaches to neodecadent (camp and kitsch) films, to Pier Paolo Pasolini's radical politics of entropy. The approach of this project is both interdisciplinary and critical: it is designed to investigate different theoretical, cinematic, literary, and historical approaches by calling into question past and current models of legitimacy that reinstitute stable concepts of morality, sexuality, and identity from the pre- to the postfascist years; to scrutinize the absolution with which clear moral judgments regarding fascism and the "Final Solution" have been made, and the production of images of radical evil, which in the postwar period support such moral pronouncements. The question is not, however, only one of critiquing the aesthetic coding of morality, but one of disengaging such moral or equally immoral representations from fascist moralism itself. That is, it is also a question of exploring fascism's own complicity with capitalist economic systems and bourgeois social values.[7] I adopt Pasolini's relentless critique of fascism as a mode of criticism that proposes that the gesture of disengagement is itself suspect—that is, discursive and visual disengagement reveals the postwar intellectual, political, and historical culture's vested interest in salvaging bourgeois moralism, the language of absolute righteousness, and capitalist institutions from the stain of fascism.

This notion of "stain" or blemish on history and humanity has served as a point of departure for a series of historical, theoretical, and cinematic accounts of the events of World War II; it justifies its own moral indignation on the principles of religious moralism, binary models of good and evil. Ironically, this model often employs prefascist images and narratives of evil (primarily images of decadence), images that the fascists labeled bourgeois decadence. Hence there is a certain "madness" in attributing the very same characteristics of decadence, evil, sexual perversion, and impurity to the fascists that the fascists once used to demarcate racial, sexual, and political others. In many postwar fictional and historical accounts, the nazi and the fascist become the acme of evil, transformed into symbols of violence, impurity, and immorality; yet these icons are often anachronistically fastened to more generic images of evil. For example, films such as Luchino Visconti's *The Damned* (La caduta degli Dei, 1969), Bernardo Bertolucci's *The Conformist* (Il conformista, 1970), and Bob Fosse's *Cabaret* (1972) present fascism as an amalgam of decadent images, specifically the image of the femme fatale, the transvestite, the sexual pervert, the *Untermensch*, or feminine disease circulating at the turn of the century. While such representations of fascism feminize and sexualize evil (otherness) as a means of critiquing conventional gender roles, they cloak what Janet Staiger calls the "reactionary politics of the new man," who at the turn of the century employed scientific, racial, psychoanalytic, and anthropological models to justify his superiority over his racial, economic, and sexual others.[8]

The fascist deviant represented in the films examined in this book functions as public spectacle while marking a return to the language of purity. In other words, the representation of the *impure* (deviant) is connected to violence performed by the language of purity. Narratives and analytical models from which postwar artists, filmmakers, historians, and theorists construct their own narrative and ideological interpretations reveal de facto encoding of historical events to satisfy present symbolic roles. These symbols (good, evil, pure, impure, etc.) organize the singularity or specificity of a historical event, yet they install the event in a transhistorical model (a moral trying to be a phenomenological model), and to that degree reconstitute a transcendental model. The historic events of World War II have been repeatedly read and reread in terms of contemporary politics, linking "the event" to transtemporal questions of morality and responsibility to the past. How can a universal Western model of moral judgment be designed to reaffirm the present's "responsibility" to historical subjects when it encourages simplistic (polemical) oppositions? What I question is not only the morality but also the "purity and simplicity" that Theodor Adorno insists on in his claim that "[the Jews] are branded as absolute evil by those who are absolute evil, and are now in fact the chosen race."[9] One purpose of this book is to dispute complicity in a binary model that endorses the discourse of absolutes and ensures their symbolic centrality. This type of simplification, the switching of absolute evil from the myth of the Jews as "the menace of humanity" (*Die Drohung des Untermenjuden*) to the sadistic nazis, is one of many that promote a Manichean logic of absolutes, abating or even erasing murkier issues such as the relationship of capital, bourgeois moralism, and gender politics to fascism. The effacing of such issues allows for an exculpation of the "lesser of two evils." The Italian fascist regime and the French Vichy government have been problematized by foregrounding the shift from the spectacle of fascism to nazism that occurs in French and Italian postfascist, neorealist cinematic and literary movements, where the depiction of occupying nazis renders the French and Italians as the victims of war. Thus the Italian and French working classes are recuperated from an abject fascist period as the subject of a new historical discourse, the resistance. This recovery of a legitimate Italian and French national identity, however, returns to a binary economy, that is, it is constructed in opposition to the image of the feminized or excessively cruel nazi, as well as the sexually corrupt or ravaged women (as seen, for instance, in the films *Open City* (1946), *Bitter Rice (Riso amaro,* 1949), and *Two Women* (*La ciociara,* 1960). Such comparisons do not stop at the "relative evil" of the Italian fascists or French collaborators, as opposed to the supreme or exceptional evil

Josef von Sternberg's *The Blue Angel* (1930) produces the infamous icon of Weimar decadence, Lola Lola (Marlene Dietrich).

of the nazis, but further perpetuate "wishful thinking" by disengaging the abnormal (exceptional) evil of Hitler from that of his executioners.

Ironically, at the same time the identity of the victim has been sanitized (purified or cleansed), the victimizer takes on a plethora of characteristics of generic evil, constantly returning to current political events via analogies to fascism or nazism. That is, the threat of the return of fascism is kept alive by constantly displacing what Zygmunt Bauman calls the fascist "truth of modernity" onto what the West considers to be less modern or civilized figures and nations such as Saddam Hussein, Stalin, Serbia, and Cambodia.[10] As a result, fascism and nazism are obsessively historicized and thereby actually dehistoricized. Although they are metonymically linked to the present through current atrocities and political leaders, these very leaders and current events are returned to the past, reinscribed in a predetermined narrative of evil. Similarly, an identification with the victims of fascism, who maintain a certain cultural (contextual) specificity, legitimizes more recent victims at the same time it absorbs their meaning (uniqueness). Auschwitz, as Lyotard argues, has indeed become a model.[11] Hence it is only through identification with the dead and the downtrodden that the scholar, artist, or cultural critic can resurrect a legitimate subject from which he or she can speak. Scholarship's implication in the "politics" of representing fascism and nazism opens onto submerged interconnections of myth and academia's own ideological legitimation in historical narratives and theories of history. Within these recodings, the present is inoculated from the past's extension.

Readings that slip over into national, international, and interethnic politics (who can speak as a victim, who is silenced as a victimizer), and transcendental theories (promotion of good models, from which we can judge right from wrong, good from evil, and the pure from the impure), whether cinematic, narrative, or historical, treat the event of fascism and the "Final Solution" as a model that supports larger conceptual or narrative frameworks. Such idealized models allow historians or filmmakers to play the part of judge or cultural moralist by speaking not only in the name of the victims, the downtrodden, and even the witnesses, but also in the name of truth, as a third party (a disinterested inquiry). This practice of disengagement masks its own violence, its own desire for purity and moral righteousness at the expense of its other—even if it is only an intellectual distance. William Spanos observes that such scholarly acts of disengagement "are inscribed in the [binary] logic that makes the Nazis the absolutized scapegoat of Occidental humanism and thus exonerates the latter—especially the English, the French and the Poles—of its complicity in this event and with racism in general."[12] Although models that read nazism and the "Final Solution" as the product of Western modernism seem to erase "the gray zone" of complicity (relativizing or minimizing the participation of non-nazis), they refuse to sanction the reconstitution of the Western subject as a form of the Platonic good. With the complete discrediting of nazism as both the paragon of absolute evil and the "Final Solution" as the failure (end) of Western humanism (modernism, history, culture), the only salvageable (legitimate, moral) subjective position emerges as that of victims and those who represent them, which includes those who guard against any fascist symptoms.

The discourse of victimization (specifically that of the Holocaust) is, therefore, also fraught with controversies. Many critical thinkers question the discourse of singularity as applied to the fascist state, not for insisting on the uniqueness of the "Final Solution," but for presenting it as only "a Jewish Problem," as well as rendering it as the model of modernity; a model against which all other genocides and public suffering must be measured. Spanos argues that, "given the insistent reference in the planning discourse of official Nazism to 'judeobolshevism' as the essential enemy of Germany, isn't the Nazis' extermination of an untold number of civilian Slavs not to say other 'inferior' peoples, a part of the discourse of the Holocaust?" (*Heidegger and Criticism*, 243). Similarly Maier asks: "Do Armenians and Cambodians also have a right to publicly funded Holocaust museums ... [we relativize other persecutions] Biafra was only hunger, Cambodia was only a civil war, the destruction of the Kurds was not systematic; death in the Gulag lacked national identification marks" (*The Unmasterable Past*, 165–66). While Bauman notes the singular nature of the Holocaust, "the fact that the Jews had been marked for total destruction," he states, "even so, the Holocaust was not simply a Jewish problem." Making the "Holocaust the property of the Jews, ... reduce[s] the Holocaust to a private trauma and grievance of one nation," (*Modernity and the Holocaust*, ix–x). The battle over who has the right to speak as a victim, or who is the "purest" victim, determines who has the right to present political subjectivity, yet this also, as Omer Bartov points out, "must not be made into the focus of Jewish existence, for it is a black hole that sucks everything beautiful and hopeful into its void."[13] Within the discourse of uniqueness the act of historizing (making analogies, establishing a continuous narrative) is equated with relativizing or neutralizing the non-narrative or radically traumatic experience of the victim. Consequently, it has been argued that such readings reduce not only the Holocaust but Jewish identity to a private trauma. Moreover, any comparison of the genocide of the Jews (1940–1945) to that of the Armenians (1894–1896 and 1915–1923), Cambodians (1971–1972), Rwandans (1995–1996), Native Americans, and others opens itself up to apologetics and therefore historical relativism—arguments that attempt to depict the Holocaust as just one event among many. Yet this controversy over relativizing the Holocaust itself exhibits a series of enigmas: on the one hand, any comparison of other genocides to the "Final Solution" might relativize its uniqueness, thereby downplaying the true horror of nazi and fascist atrocities; on the other hand, the very insistence on presenting the "Final Solution" as a radical break in human history obscures the suffering and uniqueness of victims of other wars and genocides or other victims of nazism and fascism (Slavs and Gypsies, for instance). Therefore this book questions the presentation and representation of fascism modeled on Eurocentric generational classifications in which one's identity is determined by one's relation to the events of

In Luchino Visconti's *The Damned* (1969), Martin von Essenbeck (Helmut Berger) gives a campy performance of Dietrich in drag as the Reichstag burns.

World War II. For example, Jürgen Habermas argues that the "period between 1933 and 1945 is the horizon or the point of departure for identification." Hence Habermas distinguishes generations of German men (and possibly women) on their conscious-ness of guilt or the lack thereof, locating the fixed image of Western twentieth-century history on the "unloading ramp at Auschwitz." And then, in an almost biblical ges-ture, he turns this identification into an original sin, "a traumatic refusal to pass away from a moral imperfect past tense that has been burned into our national history."[14] It is not only an insistence on clear boundaries and borders that he returns to histori-cize, but also the empowering and securing of nazism as world historical event—a symbolic point of departure and, more importantly, an inescapable traumatic point of rupture—tactics of representation that point to their own political agenda, subse-quently maintaining the Occident as a negative model—one of failure that dwarfs all histories, economies, and differences. It is precisely this process of silencing difference by reducing the discourse to that of binary opposites, failed desires, and identifications that has led Jean-François Lyotard to claim that "one does not dare think out nazism because it has been beaten down like a mad dog, by a police action, and not in con-formity with the rules accepted by its adversary's genres of discourse (argumentation for liberalism, contradiction for Marxism), [therefore,] it has not been refuted" (*The Differend*, 106). The very site of this silence is marked by an aura of the forbidden and thus empowered as what Primo Levi calls "una malattia morale o un vezzo estetico o un sinistro segnale di complicitá" (a moral sickness or an aesthetic veil or a sinister sign of complicity.)[15]

In order to highlight and contest ideological or narrativizing projects (memory politics), this text will apply Nietzsche's genealogical method, a process of uprooting the origins (motives) of dialectical thinking (conservative, liberal, and leftist) and test-ing the sanctity of its moral legitimations, especially that of the good model itself. Accordingly, the first chapter begins by situating postwar cinematic representations of fascism, nazism, and the "Final Solution" in relation to historical, theoretical, and moral models, shifting (in the second chapter) to cultural and aesthetic references of these cinematic representations; the last three chapters explore Pier Paolo Pasolini's *Salò* (1975), Liliana Cavani's *The Night Porter* (1974), and Lina Wertmüller's *Seven Beauties (Pasqualino settebellezze*, 1976), films that critically work through a series of historical, theoretical, moral, and aesthetic models. This book sets out to problema-tize theoretical and cinematic projects that aim at either distancing scholarly, histori-cal, aesthetic, or political discourse from fascism, nazism, and the "Final Solution" in order to reaffirm a positive national, subjective identity for the survivors (as in the case of neorealist cinema), or to submerge criticism of fascism in what Sande Cohen calls "passive nihilism"—"the logic of affirming the least negative choices"—or what Nietzsche calls "self-narcotization"—indulging in the aesthetics of excess and the hedonistic-pessimistic pleasure of failure or cruelty (as in the case of neodecadent cinema).[16] While all of the films of the postwar period addressed in this book con-demn fascism, each critical mode of representation (neorealism, neodecadentism, and the films of Pasolini, Cavani, and Wertmüller) expresses its own political and ideological agenda, even if it is nihilistic or anti-ideological. Neorealism returns to the narrative mode of tragedy, assigning the victim to the role of protagonist in order to restore legitimate political subjects and national identities in the immediate postwar period (from 1945 to the early 1950s). Neodecadent cinema, on the other hand, explodes bourgeois moral models by examining the postwar fascination with sexualization and eroticization of fascism and nazism, that is, popular culture's rendering of fascism and nazism as sublime. As Andrew Hewitt argues in *Political Inversions*, neodecadent constructions of fascism are deeply influenced by the Frankfurt School's "psychopolitical writings [wherein sexuality] is pathologized as a potentially fascistic fascination with the erotics of power, and that fascism, in turn, is presented as a psychosexual manifestation of homosexual narcissism."[17] Instead, *Salò, The Night Porter*, and *Seven Beauties*, expose various fascistic economies that extend beyond historical fascism—reaching into the discourses of victimization, gender difference, capitalism, and bourgeois moralism.

I question neorealism's curious resuscitation of the binary model of moral positions (identification with the victims and condemnation of the victimizers), given its awareness of the failure of such a moral model under fascism. This restitution of moral positions is reflected in the repetition of prefascist aesthetic codes, in the more ambiguous positions of the femme fatale and the homosexual (both male and female), who remain associated with pure evil, even after their exclusion (and even in some cases extermination) by both fascists and nazis. While such aesthetic codings of evil clearly mark the neorealists' attempt to distantiate themselves from fascist politics in the immediate postwar period—presenting the Left as a legitimate (antifascist, moral) political ideology—the very rehearsal of these aesthetic codes implicates not only Marxist politics but also realist aesthetics in "fascistic tactics." As the neodecadent cinema of Visconti, Fosse, and Bertolucci suggests, binary thinking necessitates the "fixing" of a site of "illegitimate sexuality" in order to reinforce or solidify its own concept of legitimacy. Hence neodecadent representations of nazism and fascism, which arose after the economic boom years in Europe (the late 1950s through mid-1960s), questioned the Left's ability to sanitize European history and politics by providing the resistance as an alternative history to that of European fascism. The neodecadent reexamination of fascism focused less on political ideology and more on a psychoanalytic examination of self, particularly the fascist psychosexual self. As a result, depictions of nazis and fascists were often sexually pathologized. Yet the sexually subversive figures appearing in many neodecadent representations tended to destabilize unequivocal ideological and symbolic constructions such as human nature, both "good and evil," and national subjects besides the obvious concepts of gender and hierarchical family and state structures. In this case, the recurrent images of the prefascist and fascist periods foregrounded the limits of a discourse of purity by manifesting these sexually ambiguous images as both erotic and repugnant. However, neodecadent cinema itself

Liza Minnelli plays the role of Sally Bowles in Bob Fosse's *Cabaret* (1972), recalling the famous Dietrich posturing as she sings "Cabaret."

continued to reinscribe the femme fatale in the filmic imaging and reimaging of fascism and nazism.

Unlike neorealist cinema, neodecadentist cinema projects a pessimistic prognosis as to whether postwar society can unmake or work through fascism, yet it also resigns itself to what Nietzsche calls "the voluptuous enjoyment of eternal emptiness, art 'for its own sake' and 'pure knowledge' as narcotic states of disgust with oneself" (*The Will to Power*, § 29). Michel Foucault implies that the condition for eroticizing nazism is that there remain an uncertain threat, a potential menace that operates as the ultimate sign of transgressive sexuality. Thus the neodecadent resituating of the nazi as the locus of subversive sexual attraction and the subsequent equation of nazism with sexual transgression not only conflate sexuality with pure evil and pure violence, but also reduce sexuality to a narrative of repression, thereby abstracting sexuality and installing it within the reactionary or "dubious discourse of the symptom," to use the words of Paul de Man. In his critique of the mechanisms of historical and psychoanalytical modes of interpretation, de Man argues that "the analogy with psychoanalysis underscores the epistemological complexity of the historian's task. Both analyst and historian point to cognition that, for reasons variously identified as psychological, epistemological, or in the case of Heidegger, ontological, is not available as an actual presence and therefore requires a labor of interpretation or of reading prior even to determining whether it can ever be reached."[18] The concern about neodecadentism is precisely in the mechanism of interpretation and its reading of cognition in relation to a historical event, thereby giving it reason or making it readable. In relation to neodecadent cinema, I underline the evasiveness of what is called a symptom, its adherence to the predetermined logic of failure (the inability to transform because of its own indulgence in or resignation to the pleasure of displeasure).

What distinguishes films like *Salò*, *The Night Porter*, and *Seven Beauties* from *The Damned*, *Cabaret*, and *Lili Marleen* is that they attempt to disrupt both the feminizing and moralizing method of historicizing fascism, as well as the reliance on binary models to ensure the separation between purity and radical evil. Rather than respond to the failure of the 1968 student protests (against U.S. involvement in Vietnam, the complicity of major European political figures with fascism and fascist practices, and the growing discontent over the Left's capitulation to the politics of liberal humanism) to induce radical change, Pasolini, Cavani, and Wertmüller neither surrender to the politics of cynicism (passive nihilism) nor relinquish criticism's radical potential to reevaluate values. Instead, they relentlessly deconstruct binary models and their cultural permutations, neofascism and neocapitalism. While agreeing with the neodecadentists that fascism persists in the postwar period in the form of moralism and the repressive state and economic apparatuses, Pasolini, Cavani, and Wertmüller genealogically trace the transition of the "old fascism" of Hitler and Mussolini, predicated on the cult of the hero, to "neofascism," which has replaced the hero with the moral model. They decodify the fascism of Hitler and Mussolini by unearthing the network or alliance of power under fascism, exposing the inextricable connections of bourgeois morality, technological modernization, and capitalist socioeconomic structure plugged into fascist regimes.[19] In an attempt to go beyond good and evil, beyond the fascist system of Mussolini and Hitler, they configure a new strategy of resistance. However, this resistance does not imply that they dissociate postwar Italy and Italians from fascist Italy and its intellectuals (nor Germany and Germans from nazism), as the neorealists did. Rather, they renounce the insidious disassociations from fascism, since these narrative and historic disengagements turn fascism into an event (singular and unified) while maintaining its ideological apparatuses—its moralism, its worship of technological weapons of production and destruction, its modernizing process, its binary economy, and its creation of new evils, new enemies, cold wars, class wars, and race wars.

Because Cavani and Wertmüller follow Pasolini's understanding of neofascism or contemporary society as a networking of repressive forces, capitalism, moralism, Catholicism, bourgeois culture, and patriarchal hegemony, I read them alongside Deleuze and Guattari's *Anti-Oedipus* and *A Thousand Plateaus*, since it is in these texts that fascism is presented not as a political ideology nor a totalitarian organization but as an agency of desire—a "desiring-machine," a "war machine" that infects every level of social desire with the desire for repression and abolition. Thus, in an attempt to disarm neofascism and to salvage desire (a process of becoming other or different), Pasolini, Cavani, and Wertmüller scandalize all ideological determinations that they see conforming to a model of purification. Their films expose the logic of disengagement, revealing the impossibility of recuperating (narrating or historicizing) a "pure" or legitimate historical subject, even that of victims, since this would imply that their death and suffering can be reabsorbed into historical thinking through some sort of sacrificial logic. More importantly for Pasolini, Cavani, and Wertmüller, this identification would mean that those who speak in the name of the victims would have to disassociate themselves radically from the logic (morality) of the system of victimization/fascism—bourgeois moralism and neocapitalism. Rather than reaffirm this critical distance, or the comfortable distance of the spectator, they problematize the intersecting discourses of nazism and sexuality by returning to the discourse of intimacy—an imposed intimacy on the victimizer.

Unlike numerous other films made on this subject, *Salò*, *The Night Porter*, and *Seven Beauties* focus on the relationship of the victim and the victimizer, exploring the implication of the victims with the perpetrators, a participation that Bauman sees as a "crucial condition [for] the success of [SS] bureaucrats."[20] For example, while Pasolini is primarily concerned with the dehumanizing forces of the perpetrators (bourgeois fascists/capitalists), their systematic devaluation of moral considerations in favor of a sadistic rationality of excessive self-indulgence (the rabid consumption of all otherness), Cavani and Wertmüller examine how the act of seducing as well as being seduced causes the subject(s) to become other; they focus on the spectacle of seduction as a product of an enigmatic intimacy between victim and victimizer. In the films of Cavani and Wertmüller this "dangerous" intimacy transforms the fixed economy of master/slave (situating the audience as a voyeuristic onlooker) to a more liquid economy whereby the victim and victimizer repeatedly exchange roles, forcing the audience to identify with undesirable characters and situations.

Although Pasolini, Cavani, and Wertmüller are equally implicated in the sexualization of the figure of the nazi, as Marguerite Waller puts it, they are "insistently ambiguous and open, [they] offer too many possible readings of figures, actions, images and sequences."[21] They confuse and constantly transmute the "revival" theater of fascist sadomasochism where the feminine is forced into two contradictory positions: one of the victim par excellence, and the other of the absolute sadistic victimizer. While Pasolini presents both capitalism and fascism as codependent, antierotic forms of supreme rationalism (a ferocious force of consumption and contamination), Cavani estranges the notion of the "pure" victim by reintroducing the eroticism of masochism, and Wertmüller replaces the image of the nazi as a sadistic feminized man with an equally sadistic masculinized woman. These filmmakers attempt to disrupt the traditionally engendered subject/object relationship, refusing to render their films knowable or recoverable. That is, they resist cultural cooptation by disappointing the conventional narrative and aesthetic expectations, exaggerating fascism's antiaesthetic, if not grotesque, characteristics and its anti-idealistic forces that make it unconsumable.

This treatment of what has otherwise been considered a taboo subject (the intimacy of the victim/victimizer relationship, the sexualization of nazism, the representation of neocapitalism as codependent on neofascism, and the questioning of legitimate subject positions) has not only caused film critics, historians, and cultural theorists to renounce these films, labeling them "immoral," "pornographic," and "depraved," but also to jettison analytical readings. Recently critics have returned to analyze these films, yet many readings continue to marginalize what they consider their scandalous rendition of fascism, nazism, and the "Final Solution". The object of this book is to read these films in terms of radical thinking—that is, to place them in the tradition of radical criticism that tests the sanctity of all value judgments, moralisms, and subject positions and does not transpose one ideological model for another but rather seeks to question the projection of models of interpretation onto all human experiences and events. This form of radicalism comprises what Jean Baudrillard calls a fatal strategy: a theory whose strategy is ironic, designed to deconstruct the institutionalization of transgression—the institutionalization or globalization of fascistic desires for repression and abolition. Because Pasolini, Cavani, and Wertmüller understand fascism to have permeated every social desire with a fatalistic desire for repression, consumption, and destruction, they do not provide for a new subjective identity to emerge from their narratives; rather they call for an implosion of moral and social values. Their strategy is to mimic the language of fascism itself, to replicate its gesture of destabilizing the position of subjectivity, which does not allow for the re-creation of moral positions but in fact confronts them as totalizing discourses. This strategy of radical criticism that seeks to undermine dominant discourses

In Lina Wertmüller's *Seven Beauties* (1976), Shirley Stoler plays the nazi commandant whom Pasqualino tries to seduce.

leaves no space, not even a critical one, as a viable subjective position. Thus this strategy manifests itself as a lethal antibody, which is no longer designated to restore the Platonic model of the good to health but to corrupt the simulated, inauthentic replications of that model in order to expose the radical depravity of its progeny, the system of "normal" morals and meaning itself. As a consequence *Salò*, *The Night Porter*, and *Seven Beauties* force spectators to become conscious of the fact that they cannot interpret the films in terms of traditional Western narratives or histories recording both gender politics and the Holocaust.

Salò, *The Night Porter*, and *Seven Beauties* scandalize the politics of identity and identification, which hinge on the assembling of communities whose pedigree is either sanctioned or renounced by an appeal to "history." Much has outraged critics and spectators of these films: first, these three directors' repudiation of a facile identification with certain types of one-dimensional narratives; second, their exposure of the couching of politics (sexual, ethnic, national, economic) in historical modes of representation; and third, their refusal to participate in what Lyotard calls a "dialectic of redemption." These moralistic types of narratives can be seen in, for example, the tragic feminization of victims such as those found in George Stevens's *The Diary of Anne Frank* (1959) and Alan Pakula's *Sophie's Choice* (1982); the romantic masculinizing of antifascists as depicted in Josh Waletzky's *Partisans of Vilna* (1986) and John Huston's *Victory* (1981); the tragic-romantic narratives of resistance appearing in Andrzej Wajda's *Ashes and Diamonds* (1958), Gillo Pontecorvo's *Kapo* (1960), and the Taviani brothers' *Night of the Shooting Stars* (1982); the moralistic antifascism of Rossellini's *Open City* (1946) and Michael Verhoeven's *The White Rose* (1983); the salvageable good (nazi) venture capitalists exemplified in Steven Spielberg's depiction of Oskar Schindler (*Schindler's List*, 1993), the good German soldiers as opposed to bad nazi soldiers in Sam Peckinpah's *Steiner* (a.k.a. *The Iron Cross*, 1977), or the moral Austrian family characterized by Robert Wise in *The Sound of Music* (1965). At stake in these righteous, and therefore cathartic, renditions of tragic victims of fascism and heroic martyrs of the resistance is not only a desire to cleanse the postwar period of the disease of fascism—to isolate it or contain it—but also a determination of who will be able to claim the so-called copyrights to historical figures, and for what political ends.

While resembling, by often citing, previous incarnations of decadence, representations and interpretations of fascism and nazism, in order to render visible the ambiguous constructions of sexual politics, *Salò*, *Seven Beauties*, and *The Night Porter* foreground the artificiality of building a moral conscience from the ruins of historical subjectivity. They reintroduce what Primo Levi calls "gray zones," referring to both the impossibility of representing authentic sensual experience and the inability to model historical representations on a discourse of purity, as a form of the tragic-romantic narrative.[22] Instead of presenting sexuality as a feminine disease that weakens or afflicts the pure masculine body, these films undermine the tired metaphors of sexual difference and call into question the disingenuous binary economy and its symbolic ordering.

Rather than reinstating a cathartic cleansing process, these films disavow the moralistic reading as well as the location of a legitimate subjective position. They point to the misleading separation of a sense of historical righteousness from the sublime fascination with evil and moral transgression. It is precisely this erotic fascination with fascism—not only within textual representation but also in the theoretical reflection and situation of these films—that problematizes the process of abjection as a process of symbolic separation. Each of the last three chapters here provides an exegesis of key representations of fascism, uncovering the mechanics of repositing and reimaging of the historical consciousness of fascism, which are accompanied by a moral conscience. These films foreground the subjective "presence" of interpretation in each historical revision and question the construction of a dialectical narrative as a means of perpetual separation of the subject of history from what is considered abject. They scandalize this process of othering (disengaging, abjecting, etc.) by presenting scandal itself as a political gesture.

In sum, this book is about the impossibility of applying "normal" criticism, "conventional" historical interpretation, and "cathartic" cinematic representations of the past without engaging in the theatrics of political and moral side-taking. The political use of the socially sanctioned role of the good or the pure masks present political agendas under the guise of history, morality, or value judgments. Hence the aim of my text is to expose the logic and conjugation of engagement and disengagement—with the other, with evil, with even the present—as a duplicitous gesture, one that is more spectacular than critical. In short, the appropriation of victims, the innocent dead, or a hermetically sealed (detached) intellectual discourse is treated as itself embedded in a series of cultural, aesthetic, social, ideological, and historical illusions.

1. Between Remembering and Surviving

In my opinion the ambiguity of human nature and therefore historical ambiguity is the necessary point of departure in understanding different obsessions with the past. In fact, it is the analysis of "ignorance" in response to the events of World War II that may be examined if we are to better understand the ignorance allowed during the war, that allowed for the rise of the dictators. There is a reason to scandalize this Milanese notion of surviving: the world does not want to know! It does not want go forward only to fall back into this ambiguity.... My film is not liberating like some political films. These political films make it easy for the public to identify themselves with righteous characters: it is interesting to think about how the audience will bring themselves to identify with my protagonists: they might feel very embarrassed. Is it possible to identify oneself with an ambiguous character? To recognize oneself in him?[1]

—Liliana Cavani

"Use me," and this means: There is no me.... The question of passivity is not the question of slavery, the question of dependency not the plea to be dominated. There is no dialectic of the slave, neither Hegel's nor the dialectic of the hysteric according to Lacan, both presupposing the permutation of roles on the inside of a space of domination. This is all macho bull shit. "Use me": a statement of vertiginous simplicity, it is not mystical, but materialist. Let me be your surface and your tissues, you may be my orifices and my palms and my membranes, we could lose ourselves, leave the power and the squalid justification of the dialectic of redemption.[2]

—Jean-François Lyotard

Since *The Night Porter* (1974), *Salò* (1975), and *Seven Beauties* (1976) were produced during Europe's volatile and politically unstable "anni di piombo" / "die bleierne Zeit"

21

("the leaden years," 1972–1980), they enter into the politics of rethinking fascism and nazism in a period when the issue of remembering (especially memorializing the Holocaust) was finally beginning to be addressed in Europe, together with a growing concern over the popularity of neofascist and neonationalist parties and their deep-seated involvement in covert political actions and organizations. The renewed interest in the events of World War II set off the "fascist-debate" among primarily intellectuals of the Left. Yet these debates were embroiled in the factioning of the Left into splinter groups, stemming, mainly, from the student revolts of 1968. On account of its participation in the "Great Historical Compromise"—the European Left's concession to the American- and British-backed Italian center-Right party the Democrazia Cristiana (DC) in 1946–47, and the German center-Right party the Christliche Demokratische (CDU)—and a litany of other such compromises, movements such as Rote Arme Fraktion (or Baader-Meinhoff Gruppe), Lotta Continua, Il Manifesto, Brigate Rosse, Collettivi Politici Metropolitani, and Action Directe argued that the Partito Comunista Italiano (PCI), the German Sozialdemokratishe (SPD), and the Parti Communiste Français (PCF) were not revolutionary enough to succeed in changing the existing (prototypically fascist) sociopolitical system.[3] Thus, at the same time the radical Left denounced their "fascist fathers," they declared enmity with the traditional Left (the Italian PCI, the German SPD, the French PCF) for capitulating to the governance of the DC and its German (the CDU) and French (the RPF under de Gaulle) equivalents, which they considered to be neofascist and complying with the armed suppression of the student/worker alliance's political activities (most notably those of Rote Arme Fraktion or Baader-Meinhoff Gruppe, Lotta Continua, Autonomia Operaia, and the Brigate Rosse).[4] Thus the framework within which this examination of fascist history opens in Europe is primarily established on a certain notion of distance, a generational distance for some, and ample time for emotional detachment for others; and secondarily, an era of pronounced political and economic crisis, when predominant politicians and intellectuals seemed incapable of coming to terms with some of the more transgressive cultural shifts, such as student revolts, the militant movements of the radical Left, the women's movement, and gender and sexual politics.[5] The prevailing interest in fascist history unfolded as both a distant memory and a renewed political threat.

Fascism occupied the unique (if not contradictory) space of a historical past and a political present. As a result, the debates regarding the meaning of fascism focused on questions such as, Was fascism a point of departure (can it be relegated to the absolute past)? or, Is fascism continuous with the present? Films like *The Night Porter* and *Seven Beauties*, and Sidney Lumet's *The Pawnbroker* (1965) reflect the shift from the 1940s and 1950s calls for justice for nazi and fascist war crimes throughout Europe, the vindication of the dead, and the deification of the martyrs of the resistance—as seen in many Soviet and Eastern European social-realist, Italian and French neorealist, and Hollywood films of the 1940s and 1950s—to the 1960s and 1970s attempts to "come to terms" with nazism and the "Final Solution"—what the Germans call *Vergangenheitsbewältigung*, mastering or coming to terms with the past. *The Night Porter*, *Seven Beauties*, and *The Pawnbroker* attempt to bridge the divergent cultural and historical perspectives on collective and personal memory by focusing on memory as both an intermediary and immediate sensation—focusing on the duality of memory, its simultaneous sense of distance and one of presence. Consequently, these films reflect the psychological, political, and cultural anxiety produced by such disjunctive memories. The memories of the survivors depicted in these films challenge historical narratives that strive to vindicate the dead or romanticize the heroes of resistance: they present the memory of the living as neither heroic nor coherent, that is, they disavow such justifications. Primo Levi illustrates the difficulty of justifying or making sense of the past when he writes that survivors are "deprived the solace of innocence.... The worst survived, that is, the fittest" (*I Sommersi e i salvati*, 687–89). Within these films, memory is presented, like Freud's theory of trauma, as disrupting narrative and historical identifications rather than providing historical or narrative resolutions. Hence they reveal the disjuncture between collective (national, historical, narrative) and personal (singular experience) methods of "coming to terms with the past."

In Bernardo Bertolucci's visually stylized film *The Conformist* (1970), Marcello (Jean-Louis Trintignant) makes the roman/fascist salute. This act of conformity will be mirrored in his subsequent condemnation of fascism once the war has been lost.

The anxiety caused by "coming to terms with" the fascist past primarily affected the credibility of the existing political parties that identified themselves as the progeny of the alleged heroes of the resistance (with the exception, of course, of the Movimento Sociale Italiano [MSI] and other neofascist parties). This revival of *defascistizzazione/Entnazifizierung* (defascisization/denazification) signaled the demise of certain cultural convictions relative to the formation of national identities, contemporary politics, and the history of the representation of fascism. While, in 1974, Enrico Berlinguer (the then-head of the PCI) petitioned for reassembling the "historical" alliance of the antifascist forces created in the years 1943–1947 in an attempt to circumvent a permanent shift of Italian politics to the right (as in the case of Chile), the European Right consistently reacted to entreaties such as *defascistizzazione* and a need to remember, or to reassemble, "historical" antifascist coalitions, by stressing their policy of forgetting and mastering the past. A similar policy can be seen operating in President Ronald Reagan's justification for accompanying German Chancellor Helmut Kohl when he visited Bitburg in 1986 (the cemetery where so many Waffen-SS troops were buried). Reagan declared his solidarity with the policy of forgetting at the same time he articulated a new approach to the question of responsibility, universal victimhood. He stated: "I think that there is nothing wrong with visiting that cemetery where these young men are victims of Nazism also, even though they were fighting in German uniform, they were drafted into service to carry out the hateful wishes of the Nazis. They were victims, just as surely as the victims in the concentration camps."[6] Such comparisons give political credence to "revisionary" historical commentators, for example, Andreas Hillgruber, who, like Reagan, claims that "ordinary" Wehrmacht soldiers were "victims" of Russian atrocities.[7] Although reactions to the call for *defascistizzazione/Entnazifizierung*, by both the Left and the Right, were predictable, these divergent strategic approaches to "history" emphasized that "history" had become an essentially politicized construct. Given the political instability of historical discourse,[8] the politics of memory became not only a central concern for leftist intellectuals and artists, but also a political gesture, a challenge to the credibility of existing political systems (including the Left) that wished to present themselves as both moral and pure—that is, untarnished by, or at least not responsible for, fascism. Even in the 1998 election for German chancellor, the new chancellor, Gerhard Schröder, usurped Kohl's claim to be blessed with a late birth ("die Gnade der späten Geburt"), since unlike Kohl he was "truly" born after World War II, which is to say, he cannot even be associated with the generation of the Hitler youth.

On the other hand, those who advocated a policy of forgetfulness, historicization, or mastery of the past (as for instance the leader of the French National Front, Jean-Marie Le Pen[9]) were the same individuals and groups who were increasingly involved in a series of ongoing conspicuous scandals linking "democratic parties" to neofascist parties, paramilitary groups, and supranational intelligence and secret-service agencies (for instance, the "Rosa dei Vento"). These and other embarrassing links problematized the overwhelming desire, on the part of Europeans, to bury the past. Critical examinations, which associated the Right's policy of forgetting under the auspices of "progress" and "democratization," ascribed neocapitalist politics to neofascist strategies—covert terrorist actions whose sole purpose was to maintain the hegemony of a capitalist political economy—and linked democratic leaders to neofascist projects—the clandestine reinstallation of neofascist figures within the sociopolitical infrastructure. Cinematic representations of fascism registered these cultural debates in terms of an aesthetic recoding of the representation of fascism. Italian, French, and German cinema in particular radically broke away from the sentimental and melodramatic aesthetics of neorealism. As opposed to lauding the resistance, films such as Marcel Ophuls's *The Sorrow and the Pity* (1970) seriously impaired the "popular memory" or legend of the French resistance by disclaiming its alleged feats. While this attack on "popular memory" or national identity caused historians such as Saul Friedländer to comment that "*The Sorrow and the Pity* marked a further stage in a more *authentic* perception of collaboration and of the resistance," but it enraged critics like Michel Foucault, who exemplifies the gravity of this debate over representation when he insists that "it is vital to have possession of this memory, to control it, to administer it, tell it what it must contain."[10] This conflict over how representations of antifascist resistance movements are to be treated coincides with the aesthetic shift from the cinema of neorealism, which affirmed a political commitment to antifascism, to what Friedländer calls the "new realism" (authenticity) of *The Sorrow and the Pity*, which undermines the accomplishments of the resistance as relatively insignificant in relation to the numbers of people who did not resist fascism and nazism. By presenting the people's commitment to the antifascist resistance as both romanticized and often misleading, films such as *The Sorrow and the Pity* impede attempts to identify with the resistance as well as to renew antifascist politics in the postwar period. In addition, such "authentic," deromanticized representations of the resistance question the historical legitimacy of postwar European governments—de Gaulle, De Gasperi, and Adenauer—by representing postwar political institutions as themselves built on an exaggerated if not mythic alliance to "historical" antifascist resistance movements. For example, films such as *The Sorrow and the Pity* contest not only the historical and political validity of linking postwar European institutions and governments to antifascist movements (those that predate the end of the war), but also their appropriation of the rhetoric of the resistance, at least in the case of France and Italy. This overidentification of postwar governments with antifascist ideology and resistance movements, according to Ophuls, covers up the more disturbing (antiheroic) public and political "passivity," or worse, public desire for fascism.

While nazism and fascism have been read (represented in historical narratives, fiction, film, and television) within a historical context, the representation of the "Final Solution" remains part of an ongoing debate as to whether it can be represented, because of its uniqueness and the problems involved in speaking for the victims or speaking in the name of the dead. Claude Lanzmann's *Shoah* (1985) illustrates the enigma surrounding the representation of the victims. While *Shoah* "documents" the testimony of the survivors of the "Final Solution" through fictionalized accounts, it distinctly refuses to use nazi footage of the concentration camps (often used in documentaries of the "Final Solution" to evidence the atrocities committed).[11] For Lanzmann, the question of representation goes beyond that of fictionalizing the lives of the victims and the events of World War II; it is also a question of framing those events, memories, and victims. He asks if it is possible to make sense of the "Final Solution" through the eyes (cinematic gaze) of the nazis, the "objective" point of view of a third party, or even someone, for instance, like Steven Spielberg. As a consequence, the "Final Solution" has often been extricated from the context of nazism and fascism and treated separately by historians and philosophers of the postwar period. That is, while historians and cultural critics localize fascism in "the past" (e.g., disengaging it from the present), the "Final Solution" is not relegated to a "common past" but is ascribed to the discourse of experience and memory, which is both past and present, "uncommon" (radically singular), subject to both change (mutation and forgetting) and traumatic effects (it does not pass away). What emerges from these debates is a serious scrutiny of the status and use-value of historical narratives, including the influence of the media on popular memory of World War II and the "Final Solution," since the popular media (film, television, narrative fiction) seems to be one of the only places where these types of representations converge. However, films such as *Shoah* also bear the distinct marks of a transformation in modes of representation: from the emphasis on an "objective history" (as in the case of neorealism) to a subjective testimony or confession. The shift from an objective to subjective point of view parallels certain trends in the historians' debate over the representations of fascism (1970s) and the 1980s' *Historikerstreit* over the representation of the Holocaust, concerning what constitutes historical representations given the discrepancies in interpreting evidence and inscribing such controversial themes into representational narratives.

In his analysis of the shift from "authentic" historical narratives in neorealism to the authenticity of testimonial discourse, Thomas Elsaesser argues that "while memory, especially when contrasted with history, has gained in value as a subject of public interest and interpretation, history has become the very signifier of the inauthentic, merely designating what is left when the site of memory has been vacated by the living."[12] Aware of such aesthetic and polemic distinctions between fact and meaning, the films of Pasolini, Cavani, and Wertmüller do not attempt to expose the past as in a factual or documentary historical account, such as Alain Resnais's *Night and Fog* (1955) or Marcel Ophuls's *Hotel Terminus: The Life and Times of Klaus Barbie* (1988). Instead they investigate the politics of memory as a product of the mass media. Their cinematic style of narration emphasizes the fictivity of the subject matter; not only are the mannerisms of the characters reminiscent of certain popular attributes, but the fragmentation of the narratives and their integration of documentary footage, dreamlike sequences, opera, or pop music point to their artificiality. By emphasizing artistic style they analyze more subtle complexities of memory, trauma, and survival—

not of the Jewish victims of the Holocaust but the non-Jewish survivors, including victims, collaborators, and fascists. Accordingly, they foreground the artificial devices involved in representation. Their project is to scrutinize what had previously been considered the unspeakable or the impossible, what had been reduced to the binary economy of good and evil.

By inscribing their films within preexisting aesthetic codes (camp, kitsch, S-M, decadence), Pasolini, Cavani, and Wertmüller reveal that discursive forms of representing fascism have undergone a series of transformations tantamount to what Michael Geyer terms, "a kind of secular morality play"—consistent with the racial and sexual theories of Cesare Lombroso, Max Nordeau, and Otto Weininger. Although, as Geyer explains, the evil "that resulted from certain ideologies, attitudes and behaviors [was to be laid open] in such a way that it could no longer be thought of without their attending historical consequences; memories were not summoned up by an individual and interior process of self-examination, nor were they subjected to a tribunal of conscience in a culture of guilt. The televised articulation of the past set the individual free."[13] Because, as Geyer ascertains, the politics of memory took hold through film and television and therefore implicated no one in particular (other than, perhaps, figures like Hitler, Mussolini, and Himmler), Pasolini, Cavani, and Wertmüller question the production of digestible visualizations of Italy's and Germany's fascist past. By digestible I mean that protagonists are either heroes, victims (narratives are either romantic or tragic), or, in the case of Federico Fellini's *Amarcord* (1974), benign children, thus allowing audiences, even in lieu of their own irreconcilable memories of past events, to identify with the victims, heroes, or adolescents of these televisual or filmic narratives. Pasolini, Cavani, and Wertmüller investigate the highly politically charged territory of compliance, compromise, and survival—a territory disliked by culturally sanctioned factions of both the Left and the Right, since it offers no clear moral perspective.

Films such as *The Damned (La caduta degli dei,* 1969), *The Conformist (Il conformista* (1970), and *The Marriage of Maria Braun (Die Ehe der Maria Braun,* 1978) no longer documented or dramatized antifascist protagonists. Instead they explore the territory of "the enemy within"—a subjective or psychological approach to fascism, challenging older and contemporary representations of fascism and nazism, specifically neorealist renderings of fascism as a "parenthetical degeneration of progressive history" or as the product of "the crisis of modernity." These films, along with *The Night Porter* and *Seven Beauties,* investigate issues of class in connection with collaboration, sexual perversion, and the fascination or eroticization of nazism and fascism. Furthermore, they problematize notions of singularity (the exceptionality of the "Final Solution," signaling "the end of history" and "the end of man") by reinscribing the "Final Solution" within the context of nazism and fascism as well as theories of human nature, gender, and sexual politics. Such revisualizations of the fascist or nazi past contribute to the disavowal of a historical mastery over the past, depicting the permeation of nazism and fascism into the postwar period. This bleeding of ideological or historical boundaries, resonating in narratives such as *The Night Porter* and *Seven Beauties*, points to the ambiguity of discerning what is past from its effects (the real from the imaginary, the pure from the impure).

While such ambiguities have been interpreted by historians including Omer Bartov and Saul Friedländer and cultural critics including Bruno Bettelheim and Primo Levi as abusing the experience or memory of the victims, the morally, sexually, and historically ambiguous images that appear in films like *The Damned, The Conformist* and *Lili Marleen* eschew endeavors to depict "what really happened," responding instead to the resurfacing of nazi and fascist images in the postwar period. Hence these films are more historiographical than "historical." Their aim is not to represent historical events but to analyze the relationship of official history to representations of popular culture, concentrating specifically on how this relationship continues to articulate current political problems as endemic to the system of meaning itself. Thus they question the "historical correctness" of realist narratives (both historical and cinematic) that, as Bartov describes, "set out to prove both the existence of the Holocaust as an historical event and as one that still lives on in the memories of all who were involved in it" (*Murder in Our Midst*, 128). Rather than yield to the conventional or what has been presented as the "morally responsible" aesthetic style of realism ("telling

Amarcord (1974) visualizes what Federico Fellini called the "prolonged adolescence" of fascism. Here fascism is seen through the "romantic" dreams of a heartbroken schoolboy.

it like it is"), these films explore the complex aesthetic and ideological recodings of fascism appearing in historical, popular, and subcultural accounts. By incorporating and juxtaposing multiple and often disparate references to other "histories" of fascism (neorealist, psychohistorical, Marxist, feminist, etc.), these historiographical films criticize all "historical" projects for participating in the aestheticization of fascism. Rather than simply exhibiting what Bartov calls a "detached, amoral, nonjudgmental, complacent, and highly dangerous morbid curiosity about extremity," these films analyze the cultural obsession with extremity (*Murder in Our Midst*, 128). By exposing the intricate networking of images—fascists, nazis, mad scientists, evil doctors who are likened to femmes fatales, sadists, masochists, homosexuals, and drag queens—films like *Salò*, *The Night Porter*, and *Seven Beauties* reveal how the appearance of such sexual, immoral stereotypes mix aesthetic styles (realist, decadentist, expressionist, modernist, camp, and kitsch) and thus confound the contexualization of fascism itself. This hyperreferencing present in films like *The Damned*, *The Conformist*, *Cabaret*, *Salò*, and *Seven Beauties* demonstrates how fascism and the cultural obsession with fascism transcend both national and historical boundaries, entangling traditional styles and national myths, placing fascism out of context (out of time), and muddling the ideological discourses that have been used both to support and condemn it.

While most of the films I address are made by Italian filmmakers I do not consider them to be Italian per se; rather they comprise what I call composite cinema: they confound notions of context, national cinema, and national history by referring to intertextual, intercultural, and international images of fascism. For example, they point to the decontextualization and transfiguration of decadent images and narratives of the fin-de-siècle, Weimar Germany, and the Hollywood dream factory, fascist aesthetics of both Italian modernism and neoclassicism, the nazi propaganda cinema of Leni Riefenstahl, and violent cultural and political images of the late sixties. Because these films seek to address the historiography of fascism (they take the cultural obsession with fascism as their subject), rather than represent histories of fascism (historical specificity), they become much more difficult to locate in terms of traditional categories. Instead of belonging to a national cinema, these examples of composite cinema become transnational, referencing German, Italian, French, and American history, theory, and film: German expressionist and new objectivity cinema of the 1920s and 1930s; American or Hollywood cinematic style and glamour of the 1940s and 1950s; Italian neorealism; psychoanalytic theory; British modernism; Italian futurism; French surrealism; French existentialism, and so on. In addition, most of these films were coproduced by Italian, French, and German or English companies. This transnational quality is reflected in each director's choice of actors. In *The Night Porter*, which was filmed in English, Cavani casts two British actors in the leading roles (Charlotte Rampling and Dirk Bogarde) and French, Italian, and German actors in the supporting roles; in *Seven Beauties*, shot in both Italian and German, Wertmüller uses both Italians and Germans in the leading roles (Giancarlo Giannini and Shirley Stoler); similarly *The Damned* and *Lili Marleen* were shot primarily in English then dubbed into German and Italian. In these films Visconti and Fassbinder mix German, English, and Italian actors and German, English, and Italian languages. Moreover, instead of attempting to focus on moral issues, with the intent of reestablishing national narratives and national heroes, these films address larger theoretical questions concerning whether it is possible to contain and thereby unmake fascism and maintain prefascist, and even in some cases fascist, moral, racial, and sexual identifications in the postwar period.

What distinguishes *Salò*, *The Night Porter*, and *Seven Beauties* from the films of Visconti and Fassbinder is that they treat the renewed interest in fascism as continuous with traditional gender, racial, sexual, and even national biases. They focus on problematizing conventional constructions of sex and gender that are "re-absorbed" into moral and ideological models vis-à-vis an appeal to history or "pastness." For this reason, Pasolini, Cavani, and Wertmüller question whether such constructions are an effect of history or an effect of the aesthetic representations of history. More than any other films of the 1970s or even films produced in the 1980s and 1990s that often adopted conventional aesthetic styles and narrative agendas—realistic yet redemptive "telling it like it is/was," as for instance Markus Imhoof's *The Boat is Full* (1981), Agnieszka Holland's *Europa, Europa* (1990), Steven Spielberg's *Schindler's List*, and

In *The Damned,* Sturm Abteilung debauchery serves as a sign of the hidden homosexuality of nazi Germany, allegedly leading up to Die Nacht der Langen Messer (Röhm Putsch), in which SA leader Ernst Röhm, along with one thousand other SA, were murdered under the direction of Heinrich Himmler.

Francesco Rosi's *The Truce (La tregua,* 1998); or the passive nihilism of stylized neodecadent cinema in, for example, François Truffaut's *The Last metro (Le dernier métro,* 1980), Rainer Werner Fassbinder's *Lili Marleen,* István Szabó's *Mephisto* (1981), and Lars Von Trier's *Zentropa* (1991)—*Salò, The Night Porter,* and *Seven Beauties* challenge "historical" frameworks, hierarchies of good and evil, feminization of sexual perversion, the (mis)placing of images of seduction and sexual subversion onto the repressive images of fascism and nazism, and the redemption of "normalized" bourgeois morality. Thus it is no wonder that, until recently, they have been dismissed as "morally ambiguous"; as Bartov claims, they "*exploit* our *mean instincts,* and seem to blame us for possessing them" (*Murder in Our Midst,* 128, my emphasis). Yet in the process of denouncing these films, Bartov and other critics reveal not only their own aesthetic bias for realism (historical representation over historiographical questioning of representation itself) but also their desire to define the historian/cultural critic as moral authority, someone who can translate complex or ambiguous historical events into "simplistic, unambiguous images." For this reason, *Salò, The Night Porter,* and *Seven Beauties* menace current historical forms of representation, recent debates including the *Historikerstreit,* and the questioning of the "moral" agenda of historical relativism and deconstructive criticism.

History, Relatively Speaking

Because the films of Pasolini, Cavani, and Wertmüller clearly challenge conventional moral discourses that are fastened to cultural and sexual politics, they excite a certain moral panic. Dominick LaCapra explains that "when the security and self-certainty of pure oppositions are placed in doubt, distinctions become more rather than less important, and their ethical and political bearing is of crucial significance. In addition, more hangs on certain distinctions than on others."[14] Although LaCapra impugns historical approaches that dismiss critical theory for not addressing how historical research is interpreted, he does not sanction the deconstruction of such moral categories but instead reaffirms the "centrality" of the distinction between perpetrators and victims in the Holocaust, reading one as evil and the other as innocent ("not perpetrators or collaborators in any *significant* sense"). He suggests that "even to compare these distinctions may be symptomatic of a crisis in judgment."[15] Just as the testimony of the victims of the Holocaust had been silenced for almost thirty years, the analysis of nazism and fascism is also marked by an aura of foreboding—one must not "know" fascism or nazism because knowing, in the case of evil, always involves tasting some forbidden fruit, that is, it is perceived as a process of contamination. Yet although the "symbolic capital" of surviving, or affiliation with the survivors of the Holocaust, ordains a certain political credibility (what Bauman calls the position of sanctity), the association with nazism and fascism performs the exact opposite in terms of global politics (this does not necessarily hold true for local politics).[16] For example, the prewar writings of Martin Heidegger and the postwar writings of Paul de Man have been discredited (in certain intellectual circles, primarily among liberals and neo-humanists) because of their affiliation with fascism, as well as the nazi party itself, as in the case of Heidegger.[17] This affiliation is read as thoroughly corrosive, sanctioning not only the condemnation of Heidegger's antihumanist discourse and de Man's deconstructive mode of analysis—reading fascism and nazism as permeating all of their work, even the pre- and postwar writings—but more importantly, the condemnation of their critical frameworks, censuring all theoretical discourses and critical thinking that contest moral and historical truths. That is, all deconstructive discourses that dispute humanist and historical truths are dismissed as apologetic, revisionist, and, therefore, fascist. Because of its seemingly binary or absolute moral classification, "history" and the appeal to the "history" of World War II creates new moral criteria. History, as Nietzsche foresaw, has become a surrogate for religion, distinguishing the damned from the saved. For instance, while Bartov argues that historians "must adjudicate who was responsible [that is,] the historian cannot escape the responsibility of acting as a judge in this context," Carlo Ginzburg insinuates that the historian performs the function of both detective and judge, and LaCapra believes that history should be a form of catharsis, effectively rendering the historian a therapist.[18]

Whether as judge or therapist, the historian claims staunch rights to wield the authority of representation. Historical copyrights, therefore, serve as political weapons. Because of history's overdetermined political nature, employing historical narratives demonstrates that historical communities are configured and reconfigured (confirmed and denied) on the basis of mobile alliances. For example, Josef Stalin has undergone a series of transformations: from the antidemocratic and antifascist figure-head of Bolshevism or communism, perceived by Western countries as a vociferous international threat to interfuse class politics into global politics, to a coconspirator in the parceling-up of Eastern Europe, to "uncle Joe," a comrade in arms fighting against nazi Germany and fascist Italy during World War II, and finally to a fascist, a power-hungry expansionist, a dictator, as well as a mass murderer. The embedding of real (or present) political events in predetermined ideological discourses (conservative Marxist, feminist, psychoanalytic, etc.), is identical to, as Sande Cohen criticizes, "a displacement of thinking through the unstable hierarchy that frames lexia . . . These [discursive] frames are already condensed stories . . . [that] establish story pertinence and deintellectualize other narrative frames. . . . [And as] pure determinants of narration, they can be thought of as repressions of semantic contention."[19] Cohen points out that demands for moral frameworks slip over into demands for deintellectualization (repression of contention), appeals to simplification, to mediation and interpretation by historians and cultural critics, which are designed to combat ambiguity and complexity in favor of reifying preordained categorical and moral imperatives.

However, the effect of referencing historical singularities (the uniqueness of each historical event) and the "subjective" memories of the survivors of the war and the Holocaust means, as Hayden White's work points out, the creation of certain ambiguities. First, the meaning of events themselves remains ambiguous, owing to their consignment to a past that is either unreachable, and thus unrepresentable, or only reachable through memory, which is often embellished with and filtered through present cultural and political issues. By the same token that events are considered singular, they also are regarded as unrepresentable in terms of historical discourse (a narrative that attributes certain ideological meanings to specific events). As White attests, "the victims of the Holocaust cannot be simply forgotten and put out of mind, but neither can they be adequately remembered; which is to say, clearly and *unambiguously identified.*"[20] And second, the significance of the continuing effects on current societies and generations that did not experience such events, while attesting to a certain importance, cannot be clearly measured nor understood. "Among those effects," White suggests, "must be listed the difficulty felt by present generations of arriving at some agreement as to their meaning. . . . In other words, what is at issue here is not the facts of the matter regarding such events but the different possible meanings that such facts can be construed as bearing."[21] The multiplication of "historical interpretations" of fascism, nazism, and the Holocaust only points to the relativity and political nature of historical discourse. Yet the question of relativity is highly contested among historians, especially in the historicization of the Holocaust, since deeply embedded within the discourse of the Holocaust is a question of morality that has been taken for granted by historians as a common structure: nazism is immoral. By invoking historical relativism I am not insinuating any practice of "assassinating the memory of the victims" nor what has often been confused with historical relativism, the practice of historical revisionism—a denial of the facts, as in the case of the French "historian" Robert Faurisson.[22] What I am concerned with are questions of responsibility that are inconsistent with models of historical truth.

In reaction to more relativist approaches to the "Final Solution" that do not question the "facts" (as would a revisionist) but rather the installing of the "Final Solution" into Manichean moral and ideological paradigms, historians including Perry Anderson, Amos Funkenstein, Omer Bartov, and Carlo Ginzburg relegate relativist approaches such as White's to historical revisionism, which is to say, neofascism. Bartov illustrates this confounding of historical relativism with historical revisionism when he writes, "relativism lacks commitment to truth and morality and does not allow choice, it contains an element of cynicism; and while humanity is based on choice, relativism makes any argument allegedly possible" (*Murder in Our Midst*, 134). Here "lack of commitment to truth" skips over the fact that "truth" itself is the very site of dispute (in addition to human truth and free choice) and slips readings that point to "truth" as relative to the speaking subject into absolute fictions (validating any reading). This political gesture, the accusation of relativism as participating in revisionism, is designed to secure a singular moral paradigm, and more importantly to secure the credibility of the historical profession against what Anderson describes as "the reduction of history to rhetoric."[23] What is at stake here is not only certain ideological understandings of truth and their moral paradigms but a question of historical modes of representation.

Since it is impossible to separate historical events from popular memory, which has already been deeply influenced by popular culture, for Pasolini, Cavani, and Wertmüller there is no authentic history, or cognitive authority (official story). But this does not imply that they become what Vidal-Niquet calls "assassins of memory," because, as Lyotard explains,

> Whenever one represents, one inscribes in memory, and this might seem a good defense against forgetting. It is, I believe, the opposite. Only that which has been inscribed can, in the current sense of the term, be forgotten, because it could be effaced. But what is not inscribed, through lack of inscribable surface, of duration and place for the inscription to be situated, what has no place in the space nor in the time of domination, in the geography and the diachrony of the self-assured spirit, because it is not synthesizable—let us say, what is not material for experience because the forms and formations of experience, be they unconscious, are inapt and inept for it—cannot be forgotten, does not offer a hold to forgetting, and remains present "only" as an affection that one cannot even qualify, like a state of death in the life of the spirit (*Heidegger and "the jews"*, 26).

This process of inscription seems to be accelerated when popular memory is infused with sexual politics, because the aesthetic linkage of nazism and fascism to sadomasochism, impurity, degeneration, decadence, femininity, and homosexuality overwrites the image of the nazi or the fascist with the image of woman and the sexual deviant. The process of forgetting is also an aesthetic practice whereby the image of the nazi or fascist is decontextualized from the "official history" and transformed into various icons of popular culture through a metonymic process. Since the nazi and the fascist stand for supreme evil, they are embellished with various other "attributes" of evil. Nazism epitomizes the model of evil at the same time it becomes part of other discourses—those of sexuality, gender, and aesthetics. This process of metonymy thus serves a dual purpose, first as a process of dissemination, and second as a process of dilution/effacement. Nevertheless, "historical" communities as well as "historical" discourse have shaped as much as they are shaped by images of history. The commonplace of metonymic linkages of the nazi or the fascist to images of sexual deviance even in "official" accounts of nazism—as for instance the widely accepted view that the nazis are antimoral, antibourgeois, and sexually perverse—attests to the reliance of "official" representation on icons of evil emerging from popular culture. Yet these images of popular culture do not necessarily stem from official history; rather, they refer back to popular culture and its aesthetic coding.

Ironically, while the (allegedly objective) history of the "Final Solution" and the rise of nazism remains irrefutable, the image or visual representation (allegedly subjective) has become the terrain of current critical contention regarding the moral and ideological implications of nazism and the "Final Solution." Take for example LaCapra, who in *Representing the Holocaust: History, Theory, Trauma* (1994) hesitates to critique the significance and centrality of cultural paradigms modeled on historical and cultural representations of the Holocaust, yet in a subsequent article in *Critical Inquiry* criticizes Lanzmann's *Shoah* for expressing the presence rather than the *pastness* of the trauma of the Holocaust.[24] While criticism over the representation of the real becomes increasingly more difficult—given the reservations about the ability of historical narrative to account mimetically for the events of the past without recoding this pastness in political terms and the current skepticism regarding the authority of historical discourse to speak for the silent and the dead—historical inquiry has shifted focus, from representations of the real (the creation of a historical narrative) to cultural criticism of the public image of nazism and fascism manufactured through cinema, television, and newsreel footage. Thus historians such as Saul Friedländer, LaCapra, and Jürgen Habermas explore cultural studies in order to pronounce judgment on whether the media is faithful to "historical truths" and how the media has psychologically (historically) affected its viewers.

Justice Deferred

Pasolini, Cavani, and Wertmüller expose a certain type of political correctness that deters critical inquiry; a historical retrofitting that is codependent on duplicitous moral imperatives used to displace real political problems concerning the way global economies, gender, sexual preference, race, and ethnicity are aesthetically coded, intellectualized, and spun into highly politicized narratives. What I mean by the displacing of highly politicized issues is that metonymic linkages to nazis, fascists, Stalinists, victims or survivors of the Holocaust, antifascists and conformists, pure Aryan women and unhygienic femmes fatales, bourgeois moralists, and sexual perverts are used to determine who will die, who will starve, who will be put in their proper place, and who will be redeemed in places like the Middle East, the former Yugoslavia, the former Soviet Union, the Swiss banking industry, blue- and white-collar workforces, and even suburban households. The politics of reading present sociopolitical impasses in terms of predetermined "historical events," as well as historical name-calling (labeling someone a "Hitler," "Duce," "nazi," "fascist," or evoking "Auschwitz," "concentration camps," "racial or ethnic genocide"), serves first to distance current predicaments, setting them in the absolute past where they have already been judged (sanctioned or condemned), and second to install figures like Saddam Hussein, Bosnian Serbs, Israelis on the West Bank, Iranian fundamentalists, and so forth, into an ontology of radical evil.[25]

This gesture of diegetically situating present political events in terms of prepackaged historical models functions to reduce the reading, and thus meaning, of political/cultural economies to binary models of pure good and absolute evil. As a consequence, the position of good is purged of evil. And as Etienne Balibar explains, this type of humanist model (based on free choice and universal rights of man) "sets itself up as a diagnosis of the normal and the pathological and ends up echoing the discourse of its own object, demonizing Nazism which itself demonized its enemies and victims."[26] For Balibar, humanism and fascism are not mutually exclusive, since certain forms of humanism also partake in the suppression of the inhuman (or all too human). For instance, as Dominick LaCapra argues, historians' casting of Auschwitz as what Adorno called the "extremity that eludes the concept" and, therefore, the ultimate challenge to all representation has manifested the "Shoah as 'symbolic capital' by Israel as well as the entire Israeli-Palestinian conflict and the marked opposition to Israeli policy."[27] Or as William Spanos argues, "the (ab)use of the discourse of the Holocaust by the state of Israel in its effort to repress the legitimate claims of the Palestinian people makes clear, it has also lent itself to onerous political purposes" (*Heidegger and Criticism*, 234). On the other hand, evil is deprived of its own history, its own sense of community (cultural context); it becomes a "stain" on humanity. As Saul Friedländer elaborates, "Nazism was the damned part of Western civilization, the symbol of evil. Everything the Nazis had done was condemned, whatever they touched defiled; a seemingly indelible stain darkened the German past, while preceding centuries were scrutinized for the origins of this monstrous development" (*Reflections on Nazism*, 12). Nazism is stripped of all ideology, all humanity, culture, and history in order to become a permanent prop in the historical clearinghouse of icons of repudiation and moral malfeasance. Though nazism and fascism not only intersect with but succor conservative moral, sexual, scientific, technological, and national issues, they stand for only one thing, evil, while their victims (specifically the genocide of six million European Jews) come to represent the paragon of purity and innocence. In no way am I suggesting that nazis and fascists be unaccountable for the crimes they committed, yet I do reproach the binary economy that allows for such practices as demonizing the nazis or fascists in order to redeem one's identity, beliefs, ideology, and actions as a lesser evil. Maurice Merleau-Ponty's recollection of the occupation of France by the nazis (1939–1944) illustrates this reduction of identification to reactionary ultimatums: choosing to identify or being identified with the nazis automatically makes one inhuman, rejecting nazism (albeit a private as opposed to public resistance) equates to the salvaging of humanity. He posits that the rise of nazism presented Germans with a dilemma: they had "a choice between their humanism and their government, a choice by which they would have lost their respect either for themselves or for their country. [And he resolves this dilemma by deducing that] there was only one solution to their inner debate: a German victory."[28] This ex post facto solution, however, determines an irrefutable (a priori) alliance with the state whereby all self-identifying Germans were incidentally enlisted in the state's nationalist, racist, or colonial agenda. Yet such arguments that disengage humanism from the state's colonial enterprises or nationalistic politics quell examinations of not only humanism's own moral discourse, its unanimity with nazism or fascism, but also the production of historical meaning. Since it is precisely this humanist ethos that will be used to justify the survival of people like Merleau-Ponty (to liberate him from the nazi dictum that "no one is innocent"), it must be above suspicion, it must become metahistorical.

The process of making historical subjects safe to identify with (what Bauman calls the "sanitizing of the Holocaust") for those obsessed with an acute need for purity is contingent on what Jacques Rancière calls "the neutralization of the *appearance of the past*," that is, the translation of uncertain, unstable, amoral events into an ontological modality.[29] The act of disengaging or extricating one historical subject from another exposes the dialectic of redemption as a reactionary form of justification, a slippery process subject to many linguistic tics and twists. Within this dialectical model, the affirmation of one's own historical community depends on the negation of an other as the greater evil. It functions as a process of shifting blame, disengaging the subject from the discourse of power, therefore liberating it from the politics of responsibility via particular appeals, such as: I may have collaborated but I wasn't a fascist, I may have been a fascist but I wasn't a nazi, I may have been a nazi but I didn't know about the "Final Solution," I was just following orders, I am not Hitler (most notably Eichmann and Höss). In response to this logic of deferral, Cavani exclaims, "nessuno voleva sentir parlare di colpa. . . . È sempre colpa del funzionario che sta sopra e cosí la colpa passa di testa in testa fino ad Hitler. Solo Hitler sarebbe dunque colpevole"

Marcello (Jean-Louis Trintignant) passes before a series of neoclassical monuments in *The Conformist.*

(nobody wants to talk about responsibility.... It is always the responsibility of the functionary [the bureaucrat] who was a superior, thus, responsibility is passed from head to head finally reaching Hitler. Therefore, it must only have been Hitler who was guilty/responsible [*The Night Porter*, x]). Accordingly, Hitler, Eichmann, Goebbels, Mussolini, Pétain, and Himmler do not have any exchange value; instead they are deeply embedded within a fixed economy. These figures have taken on mythological or epic proportions, they have become out of this world—bestowed with absolute and resolute evil they become superhuman. Although often situated as radical evil within the heart of Europe, these mythic figures perform as emblems of extreme otherness, thus providing the groundwork for a dialectical and moral model or a model of deferral, one that silences responsibility in favor of differences, complexities, and ambiguities yet still plays upon notions of absolutism: absolute evil in this case.

This characterization of Hitler, Mussolini, Eichmann, and others as one-dimensional or epic antiheroes (if not pure forces of evil), does not, however, comply with the observation that Auschwitz represented a radical break from Enlightenment notions of morality. Many attempts to understand Auschwitz, nazism, and fascism by postwar intellectuals, historians, and filmmakers continue to rely on strict binary models of morality, yet at the same time they realize that this binary model itself has also been used as a means of justification for Eichmann, Mussolini, and Hitler. Critical thinkers including Hannah Arendt (who maintain Enlightenment models and morals) are outraged by the fact that Eichmann can quote Kant's humanist ideals, defending his "acts of state" (the murder of hundreds of thousands of captured Jews, Gypsies, and Slavs) at his trial in Jerusalem. It was Eichmann's conviction of his innocence on the grounds that he was "just following orders"—what Arendt calls his "uncompromising attitude toward the performance of his murderous duties"—that damned him "in the eyes of the judges more than anything else."[30] More than the failure of Enlightenment or humanist ideals, it is the radical indifference to human suffering and the turn toward moral relativism in order to account for such events and sentiments (or lack thereof) that torments thinkers like Arendt. What disturbs so many of those who demand justice for nazi atrocities is that justice (exercising the law) can only be done as a form of corporal punishment. The law cannot purge the racial, gender, and political theory of the extreme Right. Sande Cohen argues that "it is doubtful whether Nazism is reducible to criminality, a category of law.... Notions of criminality are not the issue and signify, in fact, an agenda of nostalgia ... Nazism made law irrelevant; it showed law to be an ambiguous formation within modernity."[31] Eichmann's (as many others like him) lack of self-recognition as an antagonist in narratives or ontologies of radical evil—his inability or unwillingness to express remorse—and his conviction that he acted as a good citizen—abiding and upholding the law—undermines what Croce called "il senso politico" as predicated on both profound moral intent and noble ideals. Although Eichmann admitted to the crimes he had committed, he had no guilty conscience; rather, he insistently referred to his "duty," as other former nazis had insisted on their obligation to the "advancement of science." While constructions of responsibility—responsibility to the law and to the pursuit of scientific knowledge—are absolutely incriminating within the context of nazi Germany, such appeals to Kant, practical reason, purity, duty, and high ideals damn, as well as these former nazis, the belief that knowledge, culture, progress, moral purity, and social consciousness are inherently good or pure in a Platonic sense.

Questioning the Project of Rehumanizing

No matter how hard postwar intellectuals attempt to salvage "the project of Enlightenment," Adorno suggests that these "events made a mockery out of immanence as endowed with a meaning radiated by an affirmatively posited transcendence," and I might add they made a mockery out of the postwar legal and ideological discourse that attempted to keep separate its moral authority from that of the former nazis (*Negative Dialectics*, 361). For example, even though Stanley Kramer's film *Judgment at Nuremberg* (1961) concludes by presenting the triumph of the moral integrity of the American legal system, which is faced with political pressure to acquit former-nazi judges, the postscript to the film undermines this very "judgment." It claims that by the time the film was made, ten years later, not one of the ninety-nine convicted former-nazi officials continued to serve his sentence. *Judgment at Nuremberg* expresses an internal critique of power politics that answers to the changing political climate, not to high moral ideals. An effect of eclipsing postwar demands for justice by cold war politics is the belief that these former nazis got away with murder.[32] While the labeling of nazi and fascist war crimes as "crimes against humanity" (universal) rather than inhuman acts (singular) serves to reaffirm Western notions of democracy—human rights that are ensured by a legal system that reaches beyond the illegitimacy or aberration of the German nation-state under Hitler—the privileging of the security of Western capitalism over the desire to avenge these "crimes against humanity" makes the justice system appear suspect, or at least beholden to political influences (which also questions the legitimacy of a legal system based on "natural and universal rights"). Teresa de Lauretis explains that "if Europe had to be rebuilt with the help of U.S. capitalism to serve as a bastion against Communism, not all ex-fascists and Nazis could be done away with—certainly not their major support institutions, the bureaucracy, the courts, and the church"—and, I might add, the economic infrastructure.[33] As a result, Germans came to be considered a part of Western democracy, allies in the war against Soviet expansion. Yet *Judgment at Nuremberg*'s critical poignancy rests in its presentation of former-nazi officials and American army and government officials sharing the same ideological beliefs, antibolshevism, and political strategies, which Herr Hans (one of the former-nazi judges) explains were also the beliefs of Adolf Hitler. Thus the American military and the American government are linked to (if not dependent on) former nazis and even a political agenda put forward by Hitler. This "judgment" on American politics, of course, can be read as almost apologetic for the former nazis, who like the Americans sacrificed justice to power politics. It also suggests that denazification or *defascistizzazione* was a complete failure.

Pasolini, Cavani, and Wertmüller observe that both good and evil have become relative terms. Yet it is precisely the notion of moral relativity that causes a crisis of representation by calling into question the notion of progress and the grounds for asserting moral law. As Andrew Hewitt writes, "The privative notion of evil in turn creates a void of meaning, a representational 'numbness'; the lack of a representation is felt as the lack of any bodily sensation of Auschwitz."[34] Many depictions of concentration camp victims repeat this nazi logic, treating the other (Jewish, Gypsy, Slav, homosexual) as lacking in representation, as dehumanized and faceless. Hence filmmakers like Steven Spielberg and Roberto Benigni have attempted to resolve this crisis of meaning and identity by returning to the discourse of humanism/relative good (in Spielberg's *Schindler's List* and Benigni's *Life Is Beautiful* (*La vita è bella*, 1997). Rather than conform to the traditional representation of the anonymous, dehumanized tragic victim of the nazi death camps, the protagonist in *Life Is Beautiful*, Guido, is humanized through his sense of humor and his imagination, even if he ultimately ends up with the nameless dead, while Oskar Schindler is humanized through his guilt and compassion for his Jewish laborers. Whereas *Schindler's List* has been lauded for its humanist message, Benigni's film has been severely criticized for using humor in its depiction of the Holocaust. Contrary to Ella Taylor's reading of Benigni's film as "making the Holocaust more palatable ... as to convince any naive observer that Auschwitz was a slightly unsavory boot camp whose minor discomforts could be hurdled with a little ingenuity and sunny outlook," *Life Is Beautiful* does not claim to be historically accurate. It aims rather to confront countless other interpretations of the Holocaust where the victims simply disappear, leaving the survivors to bear the guilt of living in their place.[35] Unlike Benigni, who returns to humanism as a means of identifying the Jewish victim (and subsequently dehumanizing the Italian fascists and the German nazis), Pasolini, Cavani, and Wertmüller choose less politically charged figures, distinctly non-Jewish characters—Cavani's protagonist is the daughter of a socialist, and Wertmüller's is an Italian army deserter who is captured and placed in a concentration camp. Pasolini, on the other hand, chooses to focus on Italian fascists rather than German nazis. Instead of canonizing humanistic or heroic images of resistance, such as Rossellini's Manfredi and Francesco or the Taviani brothers' Galvano, which Millicent Marcus points out are "designed to galvanize a legitimate postwar society," Cavani and Wertmüller debunk such moral allusions by shifting the focus from the partisans—those who can speak in the name of "duty" and "responsibility" to an abstract ideal (freedom, democracy, morality)—to the collaborators and the survivors, more specifically to the interaction of resisters and survivors with fascists, nazis, and collaborators.[36] Unlike Pasolini, who allows his audience to identify only with fascist perpetrators and their neofascist incarnations (i.e., the position of absolute evil), Cavani and Wertmüller create protagonists who are victims (but not *pure* victims), collaborators, and perpetrators.

While maintaining what LaCapra has called "crucial distinctions," identification with the protagonists of these films is not a question of right and wrong; instead it involves various levels of incrimination. For instance, Cavani's portrayal of former nazi SS men draws from such examples as Eichmann, Barbie, and Priebka only to satirize moral convictions espoused by them. In the process of undermining the self-proclaimed redemption of these dubious figures, she also implicates psychoanalytic readings of nazism and the Holocaust that promulgate therapeutic models, designed to purge the subject of any symptom of guilt. As Hans (one of the former-nazi characters in the film) declares, "We need to defend ourselves, the war is not yet over, we need to cleanse ourselves so we don't suffer from guilt complexes." These former nazis perform their own therapeutic process, allowing them to purge themselves of any sign of guilt that could possibly be used to identify them as blameworthy of participating in nazi war crimes. While Cavani personifies former nazis as extremely synthetic and adaptable—adopting images and discourses of authority or legitimacy—her characterization of the concentration camp survivor (Lucia) reveals the opposite. She undermines that very authority or legitimacy, since Lucia's very presence points to both the hypocritical reestablishment of former nazis to "legitimate" authorial roles within Austrian society and the continuity of their allegiance to their nazi identities and ideological beliefs. Cavani constructs the character Lucia from disparate sources: accounts of Italian socialist women imprisoned by the nazis during World War II, who express a certain compulsion to return to the past, both physically to the concentration camp site and hypothetically in terms of memory; and in response to aesthetic and ambivalent sexually charged images, such as Marlene Dietrich and Helmut Berger performing Dietrich in *The Damned*. Thus she fuses the politics of memory with the aesthetics of nazism and fascism, in an attempt to reveal the radical inconsistencies of the two forms of representation.[37] What Cavani delves into is a more personalized or internalized politics of memory: while the former nazis want to survive the burden of the past by distancing themselves and purifying their conscience (as well as the evidence that links them to the events of the past), the so-called survivors cling to memory (demanding that we remember), yet this memory compromises their own survival as well as their own "therapeutic" ridding themselves of the drastic guilt of being spared.

An examination of the terms of survival is also a central concern for Wertmüller. Like Cavani, she represents survival as a certain form of "necessary" compromise, even if the character she uses to express such a compromise (Pasqualino, an aspiring mafioso) seems to have no real moral conviction. By juxtaposing Pasqualino to more "noble characters," who die in the name of humanistic values of Western culture, Wertmüller questions the upholding of these very values in the context of the concentration camp. She echoes the thinking of Eli Pfefferkorn, who argues that "in the death camps, death was never a triumph. What might have elevated the recalcitrant inmate to the status of martyrdom or heroism in the eyes of his fellow inmates was an act that supported them in their struggle to get through another day's suffering."[38]

Dying in the name of humanity is not necessarily a heroic act, especially if the repercussions to such an act meant the death of fellow prisoners.

Reacting to Ambiguity

For Pasolini, Cavani, and Wertmüller what has triumphed is the desire of those who do not want to know, who want to remain ignorant. It is a victory for the process of "dumbing down" complex cultural and historical issues to simplistic political decisions, which in turn overshadow the "gray areas"—the ambiguity created when high humanist ideals are applied to fascist politics. By confronting appeals to history as a means of identification with historical and moral ambiguities, Pasolini, Cavani, and Wertmüller question the process of making sense out of nazism, fascism, and the Holocaust by means of what Nietzsche would call an "eternal return" to a moral model, a dialectic of redemption and damnation.

Because they do not offer a final solution or make sense out of nazism, fascism, the obsessive historicization of World War II, the fetishization of the nazi as a sadomasochist, or the fixation on remembering the Holocaust, the films of Pasolini, Cavani, and Wertmüller frustrate their critics and their audiences. Rather than reading Pasolini's reference to the city of Marzabotto, where a real massacre of resistance fighters took place, as a gesture of solidarity with the principles of antifascism, Italo Calvino berates Pasolini for using such a reference, as if referring to a real massacre would somehow soil the now tragically romanticized memory of the victims by incorporating them in an ironic narrative whose subject is sadism and neofascism.[39] Similarly, Naomi Greene contends that "*The Night Porter* and *Seven Beauties* polemically reduce fascism to sadomasochistic theatrics."[40] Demands for consolatory visualizations of antifascists when confronted with complex if not repugnant visualizations of corruption and being corrupted communicate a certain compulsion to "neutralize the appearance of the past" by enframing it within stable systems of meaning and rigid ethical codes. My question is, how could such disturbing, grotesque (especially in the case of *Salò* and *Seven Beauties*), and radically de-eroticized films be considered "pornography of the Holocaust?"[41] Many critics of these films express their hostile reaction to them as a contradiction in terms. For example, at the same time Pauline Kael calls *The Night Porter* a "porno Gothic," she argues that "this spin-off of *The Damned* doesn't get you hot; the sex is full of self-disgust, and it makes you cold [which] probably has a lot to do with the horror-film, ugly-sex atmosphere." And she adds, "[Charlotte] Rampling is an emblem of contamination."[42] Unknowingly, Kael points to the very aspect of these films that "gets under the skin of its viewers," that is, the ambiguity caused by images that are considered both seductive and "dirty." This seduction that is an infection or a contagion fulminates the distinctive play of attraction and repulsion; it no longer can be considered dangerously sexy; instead it is disruptive of a certain voyeuristic enticement. These films perform as a contagion, defying genre boundaries (love story, horror film, nazi cult, psychological drama), sexual boundaries (female or male homosexuality, masochism, sadism), boundaries of self and other (whose point of view is the story told from, the victim's or the former nazi's), and moral distinctions (between good and evil).

In addition to their questioning the political and moral purpose of memory and its intrinsic relationship to survival, both Cavani and Wertmüller contextualize (or visualize) their films within the aesthetic discourse of camp—visually referencing the masculinized if not transsexual image of Dietrich and the campy repetition of that image in films such as *The Damned, Cabaret,* and *Lili Marleen.* The intertextual reference to Dietrich reveals the traces of her iconic metamorphoses from her own ambiguous, yet distinctly voluptuous sexuality, to becoming a model for drag queens, and finally the return of this fatale image to the feminine body—a body that is aged and withered in *Salò,* emaciated in *The Night Porter,* and obese in *Seven Beauties.* By inscribing this overdetermined aesthetic image of nazism and fascism into the context of the concentration camp, the films challenge the sexual politics of camp as well as psychoanalytic exposés of fascism and nazism as an outbreak of psychosexual perversion and of the Holocaust as a desire to purify the self by annihilating the other. In particular, they explore the political implications of popular culture's conflation of sexual politics with representations of nazism and fascism. Probing the limits of certain intersections—the sexualized aesthetics of nazism within the context of the "Final Solution," the victim as both martyr and collaborator or survivor—Pasolini, Cavani, and Wertmüller reveal how binary models cannot adequately account for such moral and ideological ambiguities.

By questioning this interconnection of memory, desire, and aesthetics, they analyze what Lyotard calls the mise-en-scène of the "space of domination," revealing that its mysterious or mythic powers remain intact in the dialectic of absolutes—absolute evil and absolute power. For Pasolini, Cavani, and Wertmüller, like Lyotard "this is all macho bull shit": it is a capitulation to the squalid dialectical politics of heroes and martyrs. These films affront not only the moralizing apparatus that codifies and segregates good and evil, pure and impure, real and fantasy, promoting a bourgeois (fascist) moral economy, but also the discursive disciplines that configure and reconfigure these moral judgments in terms of historical subjects, victims and victimizers, fascists and antifascists, and so on. In particular, they inveigh against the dependency of moralism on the processes of historical legitimation and the subsequent visualization of politics that effectuates not only sexual politics (both gender politics and those of sexual preference) but the construction of communal as well as ethnic and class politics. These films work toward what Baudrillard calls "the vanishing point of discourse itself,"[43] whereby all totalizing systems of knowledge collapse into ideological propaganda.

For Pasolini the historical, theoretical, and cinematic discourses of fascism can no longer be confined to a debate over whether it was an effect of modernization or caused by reactionary traditionalism. Neofascism (neocapitalism) operates with contradictions and in fact feeds off of and synthesizes contradictions: it is both repetitive—it repeats generalized myths of national heroism, collectivism, and bourgeois moralism that operate against an unspecified, and even arbitrary, enemy—and modernizing—it worships scientism, translating technological advancement into the defining principle of mastery. Roland Barthes describes this contradictory nature of the bourgeoisie as a dynamic interchange between myth and the technological means to power: "The petite-bourgeois class is not liberal (it produces Fascism, whereas the bourgeoisie uses it): it follows the same route as the bourgeoisie, but lags behind."[44] Yet for Pasolini this alleged gap has closed. Modernism and traditionalism, once considered as diametrically opposed, converged in modern warfare and the modern-war or cold-war economy. For example, in *Porcile* (1967) the traditional or nationalist desire to purge society of all forms of otherness (impurity), which was manifested in the technologically inspired genocide and mass murder, unilaterally transformed the compulsion for destruction into one of control and consumption. In *Porcile*, Herdhitze, the former-nazi doctor, consolidates his button manufacturing company with the neocapitalist Klotz's sausage company.[45] This unification of former nazis with neocapitalists presents the ability of capitalism and nazism to mutate and adapt to new models of control and legitimacy, thereby perpetuating the insidious economy of neofascism in the form of capitalism and the bourgeoisie. Herdhitze and Klotz serve as allegorical figures: as individuals they represent the merger of captains of industry with fascist leaders, and as representatives of corporations they allude to such German companies as Mercedes, Krupps, IG Farben, Braun, and Volkswagen, and such Italian companies as FIAT, RIV, Olivetti, Pirelli, and Finsider, which not only profited from the nazi and fascist war economies (producing weapons and means of mass destruction, human testing, etc.) but also continued to prosper in the postwar years.[46] By recalling archetypal models of capitalism's final modulation from the fascist war economy to neofascist cold-war economy, which maintained not only production but also the same captains of industry and scientists (fascist leaders), Pasolini inculpates the global bourgeoisie for their complicity not only in the cultural and social politics of fascism but also in their violent disassociation from fascism, shifting the blame to those who gave the orders.[47] Theo Angelopolus's *The Traveling Players (O Thiassos,* 1975) directly links Italian fascists to German nazis, the British army, the secret police, the Greek royalists, and the postwar international capitalists as well as the CIA, reinstituting mythopoetic heroes, but Pasolini offers no such position of tragic purity, no disengaged identifications from the bourgeoisie. His imaging of modernity is purely bourgeois and purely fascist. In *Porcile,* as in *Salò,* Pasolini makes it very clear that the bourgeoisie are both the forefathers and the inheritors of fascism.

The transition from Hitler and Mussolini's spectacle of fascism to the specter of fascism is marked by the transfiguration of symbolic manifestations of power—staged invasions of territories, imperialist conquering of peoples, mass movements of armies and heavy artillery—into deterritorialized forms of power—the conquering and control of markets by means of indirect violence, whereby survival is exchanged for speculation. Thus the racially determined, territorialized new order of Hitler and

Mussolini is reconfigured in the deterritorialized (a supposed equal opportunity) code of the new world order—a term coined by Woodrow Wilson in reference to the League of Nations, echoed by Adolf Hitler, and evoked more recently by George Bush when he described the function of the United Nations and NATO as global "peace-keeping" or policing forces. This rhetorical teleology of new orders not only simulates an image of mastery of the new or emerging shifts of global power and capital; it also mandates new economies of control. The permeation of the war economy into all forms of global and local economics—conventional warfare, economic warfare, cultural warfare, the war against drugs, price wars, the war against inflation, class war, race war, germ warfare, the war against cancer, etc.—amounts to the reconfiguration or erasure of international, interpersonal, and intrapersonal relations. The culture that emerges from this age of global capitalism becomes a by-product of consumption and (cold) war economies.

And so, rather than single out fascism and nazism from the discourses of capitalism and bourgeois moralism (Oedipalism), Pasolini relentlessly restores them to modernity's ambiguous, yet collective, myths of continuum and continuation. For example, the continued influence of the fascists and neofascists in the case of the Christian Democrat Fernando Tambroni, whose coalition government allied the DC with the MSI (1960), provoking enormous popular reactions, first in Genoa, and then in the South. (These protests were then repressed by the police of the interior minister, Mario Scelba). In addition, the involvement of the SID (Servizio Informazioni Difesa, Italy's secret service) in covert actions with neofascist terrorist groups marked the advent of what the Left called "Strategia della Tensione," a strategy designed to scare the public into believing the *teoria degli opposti estremismi* (that extreme Left and Right were the same) and, most of all, to reinforce the political stability of the DC.[48] The growing popularity of the extreme Right—new movements such as Ordine Nuovo, Avanguardia Nazionale, Terza Posizione, Ordine Nero all connected one way or another to the MSI—amounted to the MSI gaining popular votes in the 1972 election. Subsequently Italy's most right-wing coalition government since the war (under Andreotti) was formed. Fascism stopped being a monster of the past, and the intellectuals (almost all on the Left) became more and more engaged in an antifascist struggle. Finally, the scandal of the "Rosa dei Venti" (the "Weathervane") took place one year before the making of *Salò*. Like the "Strategia della Tensione" this scandal also involved both the extreme Right and the secret service that coordinated acts of terrorism. Yet this organization was linked to an international secret service organization established by NATO, thus implicating the Western capitalist powers in the politics of neofascism. Hence Pasolini regards the repetition of fascism and its counterparts (bourgeois capitalism and consumerism) as a nexus (neocapitalists with neofascists and the military-industrial complex) that incessantly reproduces not just "society as spectacle" but societies under control of commercially designed desires, whether political or material.

Waxing Fatale

While Pasolini challenges these official and popular "histories" through an exegesis of neocapitalism (neofascism) as a virus that infects all levels of society with the desire for repression, and more importantly the desire for abolition in the form of consumption, Cavani and Wertmüller repudiate the return to a binary moral model of identification (self/other, good/evil, masculine/feminine) in the postwar period. What Cavani and Wertmüller have in common with Pasolini is a certain relentless attempt to deconstruct fascism from within, a strategy that involves collapsing the referents of official or legitimate historical communities (survivors, resistance fighters, bourgeois humanists, moral values, capitalists) within popular culture or aesthetic representations of illegitimate communities (fascists, nazis, mafiosi, sexual perverts, femmes fatales). Consequently, this critical mimicry of conventional aesthetics of fascism or nazism illustrates Cavani's and Wertmüller's own distinct fatal strategies. Yet rather than staging fascism as a sign of an apocalyptic end of all social relations, they stage the death of the image of evil seduction as manifested in the icon of the femme fatale—an icon of impurity and immorality.

In contrast to Pasolini's reincarnation of the image of the femme fatale as a dusty undesirable parody of necrophilia, Cavani restores the femme fatale to an icon of kitsch erotic sexuality, while Wertmüller places her within the aesthetics of the grotesque (satirical camp). Unlike other reincarnations of the "imaginary" nazi sexual politics, *The Night Porter* and *Seven Beauties* disrupt the continuity of the misrepresentation of the image of the femme fatale. Yet, as in Pasolini's film, they undermine the economy of purity as a discourse that divides and sorts out claimants in terms of sex, race, and sexual practice. All three filmmakers explode binary notions of desire (as either "normal" or illicit) by concentrating on repressed desire as a return of something unrecoverable. Yet they do not escape the predicament of eroticizing nazism. In fact they indulge in excessive visualizations of sexuality. Although Pasolini, Cavani, and Wertmüller are equally implicated in the sexualization of the figure of the nazi or the fascist, they exhaust the aesthetics of the sublime. Therefore they elude any possible return to the confines of "straight" politics or the stylistic campiness and kitsch of other films. By placing the "sexual deviant" in the position of the nazi and by "re-spectacularizing" the feminine body as a masculinized body or a satirical body, these seminal films become expressions of desire that utilize what Irigaray or Bhabha would label a mimetic strategy—a repetition of moral and ideological models only to haunt them with visions of their own inhumanity, their own violent repression of the other. The function of mimicry is twofold; first, it reveals the violence inherent in the process of disengagement, and second, it foregrounds the inability of the moral or ideological model to reabsorb the "repressed." Therefore the mimetic mode of disruption recalls the slippage between high ideals and inhuman practices (i.e., the continual othering or condemnation of deviant sexuality, homosexuality, and female sexuality).

In the cases of Cavani and Wertmüller these spectral images of abject sexuality

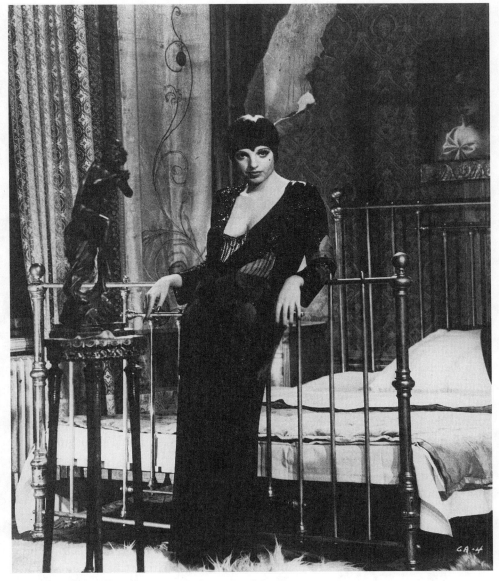

In *Cabaret*, Sally Bowles (Liza Minnelli) poses as a rather parodic sex symbol.

cannot fall into clear categories of good and evil nor victim and victimizer. Instead they express a certain desire to seduce moral positions, and thus they become tools of diffusion and multiplication of meanings. In addition, this multiplication of references counters projects that attempt to periodize fascism; by focusing on the contemporaneous and enigmatic presence of fascism in memory and in contemporary society, it implicitly criticizes the conflation of fascism or nazism, in previous re-representations, with current gender politics. In order to situate these films' critical reading of the convergence of sexual politics with fascist aesthetics, I read them against the grain of Bertolucci's, Visconti's, and Fosse's framing of fascist sexual transgression within the binary politics of moral absolutes. Rather than indulging in the aesthetics of evil and decadence as a means of establishing an antifascist aesthetic, Cavani and Wertmüller reject the categorical distinctions of good and evil, since already embedded within such a binary economy is a notion of purity that is also gendered masculine.

Unlike this unambiguous masculine figure, the femme fatale marks a site of ambiguity: she cannot be reduced to a single subject but in fact persists as extranarrative. She signifies a range of contradictory positions: the parody of heterosexual male aggressive sexuality and aggressive female sexuality; homosexuality, both male and female; an overdetermined spectacle of female sexuality; questions of identity, racial purity, and finally feminist politics. The numerous revisions of the femme fatale form a series of synecdoches—mythical temptresses (Circe, Sirens, Salome); reclining decadent femmes fatales of the fin-de-siècle (vampires, degenerates, pale consumptives; i.e., sickness incarnate); modern vamps and cabaret singers (the feminized machine of Fritz Lang's *Metropolis*, the libertine flapper of G. W. Pabst's *Pandora's Box* [*Die Beuchseder Pandora*, 1929], the sadistic cabaret singer in von Sternberg's *Blue Angel*); black widows of forties and fifties film noir; postwar hyperbolas of the fatal figure in pornography (the sadomasochistic dominatrix performed by both sexes); kitsch feminizations of male beauty (Luchino Visconti's effeminate aristocrats, aesthetes, and nazis; Bernardo Bertolucci's fascists; Bob Fosse's drag queens; and Liliana Cavani's transsexuals); and the campy, grotesque women of Lina Wertmüller, Federico Fellini, and Pier Paolo Pasolini. Her symbolic meaning is invariably transferred into new aesthetic codes, new icons of deviance, by a process of repeating her mode of dress and comportment. The very form of the femme fatale, her/his theatricality and image (created by fetishistic dress codes), produces a visual and literary effect of consistency, played out through the genres of film noir, camp, and the filmic reimaging of the fascist period.

This consistency, however, does not render the fatal image localizable in terms of a chronological development, nor in terms of sex; instead she/he becomes recognizable by her pure appearance, her artificial codes—her song, the masculine tone of her voice, the way she walks, takes off her gloves, holds her cigarette, or wears her anklet or her hat. Although this fatal figure transcends film genres and their intricate use of intertextual references, it maintains a narrative position (that of an evil force that pulls the strings). The femme fatale functions as a negative double for morality and legitimacy; marking the collapse of the discourses of historical representation, sexual politics, and ideological formations of identity and purity. That is, the femme fatale performs as a cipher (a historical fetish) receiving the marks of prefascist and fascist decadence and at the same time concealing her own dubious constructions under the sign of feminine sexuality. The very delimiting of this sign sanctions the collapse of borders: affirmative feminine desire is emphatically represented (especially in nineteenth-century anthropology, criminology, and scientism) as aggressive feminine sexuality (prostitution), feminized masculinity, homosexuality, transsexuality, the unnatural, and the abnormal. This delimitation of feminine desire, however, continues to be characterized by filmmakers, historians, and psychoanalytic cultural theorists as a degenerative force, putrefaction, specifically not a process of interruption, but one of contagion. Thus the reduction of feminine sexual pleasure by the symbol of the femme fatale enables the violent affirmation of a preexisting symbolic order—the "proper" masculine hegemony of purity and legitimate moral authority—and the negation of historical, sexual, and representational ambiguities. For this reason, the recitation of the femme fatale, from her fin-de-siècle incarnations to her Dietrichesque model of coldness and cruelty and finally to her postfascist multiplication in the role of a nazi dominatrix, constitutes a negative continuity—as evil and impurity embodied in the feminine and her homosexual surrogates. The persistent referencing and repositioning of the femme fatale as a cipher of social evils promotes a binary model that distinguishes purity and impurity as an exclusively sexual discourse, yet the "seductivity" of the discourse itself disrupts its own confinement to a binary economy. While the femme fatale serves as a negative pole in the binary model of purity/impurity, her "seductivity" functions as a process of subversion—a blurring of the boundaries of the impure or absolute evil. Thus at the same time she represents "impurity" she evokes a desired transgression or "egression" from the very site of purity, hence she presents a disruption of the location of both morality and chronology.

Neorealist and neodecadent representations of fascism reify prefascist and fascist discourses of "purity," which allows for the consistent marginalization of feminine sexuality to be unproblematically reconfigured as (or equivocated to) homosexuality and/or sadomasochism, and the contemporary repetition of that model among cultural critics. The framing of the impure reveals, consequently, its nontranscendental linkage to the production of a fascist moral ethos, where, as Jean-François Lyotard puts it, the "[fascist] hero is alive and well. Under other names 'Nazism' persists in the West."[49] Fascism persists not only in the reimaging of the masculine hero but also in critical models that continue to promote notions of purity, under the auspices of an ideal, law, aesthetic, new order, which in effect gives rise to the radical suppression of otherness (the impure).

Films like Rossellini's *Open City*, Visconti's *The Damned*, and Bertolucci's *1900* evoke the misogynist fin-de-siècle theories of Otto Weininger, Cesare Lombroso, Max Nordeau, and Sigmund Freud. Feminine sexuality is envisioned as a disease (Lombroso), a form of degeneration (Nordeau, also Darwin's social theory), an expression of lack or nothingness (Weininger), and a dangerous force to be controlled and mastered (Freud). Otto Weininger exemplifies this positioning of woman as man's negative double when he writes "women have no existence and no essence: they are not, they are nothing . . . woman has no share in ontological reality."[50] Ironically, his binary thinking, which not only collapses woman into the image of the femme fatale but relegates her to the big nowhere, reappears, not merely in Freudian psychoanalysis but also in Lacanian and post-Lacanian cinematic and linguistic theory, where woman is said to lack any visible or at least coherent traces of desire. Whether idealized or demonized, the femme fatale is embedded in a discourse of otherness, where she becomes a cipher and an empty signifier for what Jacques Lacan and Slavoj Žižek term a "determining negativity." As a negative double, this hyperbolic fatalistic woman stands in for everything evil, yet she is no-thing. The disavowal of woman's agency or desire conceals a real political agenda, a self-fulfilling prophecy in which man discovers and reinstalls woman into all narratives as a metaphor for everything that is other than man. In other words, woman becomes man's therapy, his means of cleansing and purging himself of all those characteristics that threaten his ability to identify with his ideals.

Paradoxically, both Wertmüller and Cavani have been included in the ranks of femmes fatales by their critics, especially the Holocaust survivors Bruno Bettelheim and Primo Levi, who have accused them of seducing the spectator by presenting "un film bello e falso" (*I Sommersi e i salvati*, 685). It is precisely the focus on nazism as a site of sexual politics that has caused this reaction. Yet what is overlooked in this criticism is that Wertmüller's and Cavani's films distort the reality of the event itself, since they refer less to the historical question of the rendering of the event than to the fetishization of the event in established sadomasochist cult followings. By incorporating references to more "legitimate" filmic or historic accounts of nazism and fascism, Cavani's erotic and Wertmüller's grotesque representations of sexuality and nazism question the viability of emplotting nazism or fascism within a romantic or tragic narrative. Rather they demonstrate the problem of representing the historic "event" by pointing to the act of remembering as itself an act of differentiation.

Whereas the films of Visconti, Bertolucci, and Fosse represent the return of the repressed as a continuous sadistic repression of the sexually marginalized, Pasolini, Wertmüller, and Cavani problematize the conflation of discourses of nazism and sexuality. *Salò*, *Seven Beauties*, and *The Night Porter* defy hetero- and homosexual filmic conventions. The films converge in their disruption of the engendered subject/object relationship and in their refusal to produce univocal readings. This instability of subjective positioning does not allow for the recreation of moral positions nor the reestablishment of a transcendental narrative but in fact confronts them as totalizing discourses that mimic the language of fascism itself. As representations of cinematic otherness *Salò*, *The Night Porter*, and *Seven Beauties* confound spectators' ability to interpret the films in terms of traditional Western narratives, heroes or histories regarding the emplotment of both gender politics and the Holocaust.

Even though these films display a critical consciousness regarding the impossibility of representing the past, they also participate in the ongoing revisualization—in popular memory—of nazism, fascism, and the "Final Solution." However, it is the hyperpresence of textual referentiality and an ironic intertextual play that "endlessly reproduces" polemical readings of these films. For example, the Dietrich role is mimicked in *The Night Porter* as Max's fantastic memory of Lucia's singing—mimicking both Dietrich's style and costume for an audience of nazis. Critics who reject this image of Dietrich (most notably Rex Reed and Pauline Kael) as a seedy or ugly version of Dietrich or as camp neglect the changing ideal aesthetic image of the female body, which no longer is defined as the voluptuous body of the movie star but instead the anorexic body of the model. By placing a sex symbol within the context of the concentration camp, Cavani questions the aestheticization of the female body, especially the reimaging of the female body in 1970s media, since it was there that the female body was produced as a waif image, one of starvation and weakness. Rather than read this image as a debased version of Dietrich, I see an implicit critique of the reconstruction of the female body and its sexual appeal—a transformation from figurative contours of the female body to the angular androgyny of a more generic body, a masculinized, yet by comparison markedly weakened, body. Moreover, Lucia (who we learn was Max's "favorite" prisoner) recalls the narrative emplotment of Pontecorvo's *Kapo* (1960), in which the young Jewish girl (the Kapo) prostitutes herself to the nazis in order to ensure her survival. However, Lucia lacks a sense of agency; she does not choose (hence one cannot find fault with her) but instead is Max's chosen "little girl." Yet in her performance as Dietrich she becomes a little boy instead of an excessive female, dressed not as Dietrich but as an SS officer, which, ironically, gives her the appearance of both a sadistic dominatrix and an effeminate nazi. In addition, this scene is complicated by the aesthetic reference to prewar Weimar Berlin cabaret, specifically the lowest type of cabaret (that of Dietrich's *Blue Angel* performance, the *Tingletangle*)[51] along with the set and costume design that recall the artistic style of German Expressionism (i.e., what the nazis labeled *Entartete Kunst*, degenerate art). In the case of *Seven Beauties*, Dietrich is evoked by the costuming and the bodily positioning of the nazi commandant. The commandant straddles a chair, much like the stage performance of Sally Bowles in *Cabaret*—where Sally is also dressed in men's clothing and also sings in German to her audience—and assumes the cold expressionless look of Dietrich or Garbo, but unlike the classic femme fatale she is not the seducer, rather she is the object of Pasqualino's seduction. These depictions are far less transparent and more ironic than the campy transvestite or lesbian transformations of Dietrich appearing in the films of Visconti, Bertolucci, and Fosse, since they challenge the aesthetic rendering of fascism, thereby engaging in a line of questioning that problematizes both historical and psychological readings of fascist sexual politics and the Holocaust.

2. Feminizing Fascism

Kinder, heut' abend, da such ich mir was aus
Einen Mann, einen richtigen Mann
Kinder, die Jungs hang mir schon zum Hals heraus
Einen Mann, einen richtigen Mann.
Kinder, heut' abend such' ich mir was aus—

Children, tonight I look for someone real
A he-man, the right kind for me.
Children, the young are a pain in the neck!
I want the real man, the right kind for me.
Children, tonight I look for someone real—

—sung by Marlene Dietrich in *The Blue Angel*[1]

The femme fatale is never fatale as a natural element, but as artifice, as seductress or as the projective artifact of male hysteria. The absent woman, ideal or diabolic, but always fetishized, that constructed woman, that mechanic Eve, that mental object, scoffs at the difference of the sexes. She scoffs at desire and the subject of desire. . . . Through her, it is sex which denies difference, it is desire itself which lays a trap for itself, the object which takes its revenge.

—Jean Baudrillard, *The Perfect Crime*

Almost no one speaks of Mussolini anymore, not even to curse him.[2]

—Benedetto Croce

This chapter explores differences and similarities between postwar and fascist encoding of the relationship between political ethics and sexuality. Although the object of this chapter is to look specifically at postwar films that follow their neorealist predecessors in transforming the fascist construction of sexuality from an image of excessive masculine virility to one of excessive feminine or feminizing degeneration, such aesthetic feminizations and sexualizations recall various discourses circulating at the fin-de-siècle, which are anchored to the image of the femme fatale. Therefore, in order to understand the implications of such aesthetic and discursive references to fin-de-siècle notions of feminine sexuality, it is necessary to explore the sustained interconnections of the image of the femme fatale with the "gendered" discourses of science, psychoanalysis, and racial, liberal, and progressive theories. Fin-de-siècle representations of femininity, which are inextricably tied to notions of hygiene, evolution, sexual difference, and biological and social determinism, continue to politically and socially imbue current representations and theoretical understandings of feminine sexuality with the attributes of decadence and evil. For example, while *Species* (Roger Donaldson, 1995) and *Alien* (Ridley Scott, 1979) present the female body as both violently visceral and putrid, galvanizing fears of contamination, reproduction, and consumption by femininity, *Basic Instinct* (Paul Verhoeven, 1992), *The Last Seduction* (John Dahl, 1994), and *Black Widow* (Bob Rafelson, 1986) return to the image of femmes fatales as cold and cruel, depicting women who lure their victims through sex, squander their resources, and destroy them; and *Die Sehnsucht der Veronika Voss* (Rainer Werner Fassbinder, 1982) and *Zentropa* (Lars Van Trier, 1991) reuse the image of the femme fatale in the context of fascism as a metaphor for the seduction of evil. Hence I take issue with the continual recycling of the femme fatale as a generic category of evil, abjection, and seduction, by examining the inconsistencies in such multiple uses of her image in early silent film, cinema of the fascist period (1922–1943), neorealist cinema, neodecadent as well as the more experimental cinema of the 1970s, and more recent cinematic representations of fascism. The cultural obsession with the image of the femme fatale as an emblem of decadence, the cult of death, vampirism, lack (in the Freudian and Lacanian sense), evil incarnate, feminine weakness, drag queens, and sexual and racial impurity indicates that this figure has not been "worked out": she remains a figure of ambiguity, a foil for a series of disparate yet related discourses. While the generic ur-fatale represents a range of evils, the inscription of this image in specific discourses (criminology, anthropology, psychoanalysis, etc.) and historical contexts (fin-de-siècle, Weimar Germany, fascist Europe, postwar America, etc.) absorbs and carries with it a variety of allusions that corrode the very discourses in which it is embedded. As a consequence, these multiple appearances debilitate what Marshall McLuhan calls the "cool culture of the screen"—a reproduction of generic images that invoke a sense of visual pleasure producing the effect of "placation"—and therefore incites, as he argues, "a furious fill-in or completion of the senses that is sheer hallucination."[3] The inconstancies and complexities of these furious attempts to saddle the femme fatale with such generic evils (nazism, horror, perverse sexuality, evil incarnate, social malaise) return her to the status of a cultural hallucination.

While many postwar representations of fascism (cinematic, cultural, and theoretical interpretations) are highly critical of fascism, asserting an antifascist stance, they often disregard the sexual politics of the very images and rhetorical tropes they choose to identify with fascism itself. Such images and rhetoric of difference, however, recall not only binary models of good and evil but also models of sexual, racial, ethnic, and social differences. For example, neorealist cinema, which for the most part identifies itself with working-class politics and neo-objectivity, often frames the fascist or nazi as perversely sexual (homosexual, sadistic, and effeminate), degenerate, and bourgeois. Neodecadent cinema, on the other hand, likens fascism to both postwar and fin-de-siècle elite decadence, capitalism, and bourgeois culture yet adopts a similar process of "othering" fascism in terms of sexuality and subjectification of evil. While neorealist projects clearly advocate a historical rupture with Europe's fascist past—disengaging the image of Italians from effeminate, bourgeois models of fascism—the object of neodecadent cinema is to come to terms with fascist sexual appeal by embracing the abject. The neorealists inscribe their protagonists and heroes in a narrative of opposition to fascism (fatal feminism), declaring fascism as radical evil, while the neodecadents reject the binary model that positions fascism as absolute evil and antifascists as absolute good, yet at the same time they embrace the image of evil as a seductive image. Although both projects are strategically and politically divergent, as are their aesthetic modes of representation, their sociopolitical critique of fascism is met and often undermined by their tenacious use of feminine sexuality and homosexuality as integral with the aesthetics of evil.

The feminization of impurity and homosexuality (as the replacement of the nazi as a deviant feminine, male homosexual), as well as the stigmatization of particular sexualities, reemerge in modern films, ranging from the established tradition of conservative sanctions (as, for example, Roberto Rossellini's neorealist masterpiece, *Open City*) to the more disruptive interpretations of Liliana Cavani, Pier Paolo Pasolini, and Lina Wertmüller. The framing of the impure reveals, consequently, its nontranscendental linkage to the production of a fascist moral ethos, thereby provoking such questions as Pasolini's: "Did nazism ever die? Weren't we crazy to believe it was just an episode? Wasn't it nazism which defined the petite-bourgeoisie as 'normal' and doesn't it continue to do so? Is there some reason why mass racist massacres must be finished with their concentration camps, their gas chambers etc.?"[4] According to such thinking, fascism persists not only in the reimaging of the masculine (bourgeois) hero but also in critical models that continue to promote notions of purity—under the auspices of an ideal, law, aesthetic, new order, which in effect gives rise to the radical suppression of otherness (the impure).

This representation of "the other" as "the impure" collapses the distance between discourses (film, literature, and theory) of and about fascism. It is my concentration on the sexualization of "the other" that leads me to trace the vicissitudes of the femme fatale, since she supplements the discourse of "the other" in her inscription in the metaphorical transference of sexual impurity from the prefascist to the fascist and finally to the postfascist models of interpretation of filmic, literary, and theoretical texts. By associating the femme fatale with her predecessors, these texts install her in a metonymic chain: her emergence from the context of the fin-de-siècle and Weimar Germany, her displacement in nazi Germany, and her subsequent incorporation in a moralizing binary ideology. Within this dynamic of purification of the "normal," feminine sexuality consistently remains a metaphor for moral and political perversion. Through the binary model, which has been operative in the sociological definitions of both race and gender, the prefascist and fascist moral deployments infect postwar representations of fascism and nazism. Thus, while not particular to fascism, the rhetoric of purity rests on an act of foreclosure, a contingency that necessitates the constant repudiation of a predetermined defining negativity (the impure, evil, illegitimate, racial, national, and sexual otherness).[5] This contingency renders the binary model of purity/impurity a circular operation whose significance derives from an appearance of separation, even if the feminine only serves as a defining negativity (as in the case of psychoanalytic and dialectical theories).

Subjective singularity (the good fascist, the evil socialist or communist, the pure Aryan, the impure Jew, and their postwar reversals) functions as discursive and iconic illusion of separate images representing the singular position of an affirmation (having the power to represent itself as a derivative of the pure) that defines itself in opposition to that which it repudiates. Such a "dialectical" process sanctions the pure or legitimate subject (both fascist and antifascist) to constitute its own logic and consequently erects ontological, hierarchic, and territorial apparatuses: law, master narrative as well as a counternarrative (i.e., victimization by the impure), sexual difference, and truth-value. The process of legitimation is primarily a process of identification that hinges on the act of negation as much as it rests on a promised transcendence: for the fascists the negation of liberalism and socialism will make way for the "Third Way," a so-called return to the narrative of imperial sovereignty, while the postwar antifascists draw on the master narrative of resistance in order to "return" to the ontological narrative of liberalism or socialism. Dialectical narrativizing eliminates opposition by means of discrediting the transcendental model and, more importantly, dehumanizing the identity of the opposition. In this equation liberals, Marxists, and socialists are pictured as feminine, Jewish, homosexual, and flabby by the fascists, while the fascists are framed as sadistic, homosexual, feminine, and bureaucratic by postwar antifascists. Thus the ontological economy of purity/impurity grounds itself in the logic of singularity, as well as in the strategy of infinitely engaging in a dispute for the territory of "historical representation" as exclusive property in such ontological struggles. These processes of "othering" amount to the creation of a site of pure evil that threatens to infect "normal" or "legitimate society." The interest of the pure lies in the ideological systemization of negative absolutes and the repetition of this modus operandi from its prefascist constructions to fascist Italy and nazi Germany to the postfascist politics "after Auschwitz" in which the nazis replace the Jewish people, the femme fatale, the Bolsheviks, homosexuals, and Slavs as absolute evil.

Images of impurity (femmes fatales, political, ethnic, and sexual barbarians) often serve to camouflage political stakes: as Charles Maier argues, the *Historikerstreit* is, in part, politically motivated by the reunification of Germany and reflects a desire on the part of many German historians (most notably Ernst Nolte and Andreas Hillgruber) to "master the past," which has translated into the rerepresentation of German soldiers and citizens as victims of World War II, specifically victims of the Russian "orgy of revenge."[6] Furthermore, Omer Bartov points out that Hillgruber's depiction of the Red Army in *Zweierlei Untergang* bears striking similarities to the representation of Bolshevik women by many members of the Freikorps outlined in Klaus Theweleit's study of the post–World War I era, *Male Fantasies*. Hillgruber, like the commanders of the Freikorps, affixes the image of the Red Army to sexual barbarity, the mass Asiatic hordes who embody an all-consuming feminine sexuality that acts like a disease.[7] The image of woman is reconnected to not only the crowd (Le Bon) and sexual deviance (Lombroso, Nordau) but also to disease and the *Untermenschen* (Weininger). Unlike Bartov, I seek not to judge whether such metaphors are "historically" justifiable but to question the allusion to the femme fatale as seductress, rapist, sexual barbarian, *Untermensch*, and object of revenge. Such representations of sexual anxiety foreground the rhetoric and trespass of borders by aestheticizing that which threatens the very demarcations of the pure (as either a seduction or rape by the impure) as well as the subsequent moral and legal significances that valorize such distinctions. It is this obsessive process of purification in a system of representation, predating and postdating fascism, that consistently attributes to its "other(s)" a pronounced erotic decadence. The eroticism of these others—the femme fatale or the fascist—however, maintain a subversive power, the dark power of transgressive pleasure.

Acting and Reacting Fatale

The femme fatale who epitomizes an economy of decadent or hedonistic seduction also serves as a metaphor for multiple transgressions of sexuality and morality. In other words, as a metaphor the femme fatale offers man a line of escape—a means for transgressing the confines of conventional romantic and moral narratives. Yet this desire for transgression is never attributed to the femme fatale, who is cast in the mold of permanent disgrace (absolutely empty, resolutely evil). She becomes a vehicle for man's calculated (willful) fall from grace, his falling out with existing order. As a consequence, the femme fatale emblemizes a transcendental movement: she is the negation of a repressive order. But her inscription within the discourse of the abject does not allow her dialectically to transcend her aesthetic or ideological roles. Her fixed position as hedonistic, evil, and abject, therefore, bars her from the aesthetics of the sublime as well as any ontological struggle designed to overcome existing strife. She signifies only a force of negation. It is rather her victim who transcends the femme fatale, through the suffering he or she endures. Thus the femme fatale remains a one-dimensional figure who embraces a plethora of undesirable interpretations of absence, abjection, sadism, masochism, excess, and of course violence and a violation of nature.[8] Although she is already coded by a variety of deviant discourses, the metonymic process that configures and reconfigures the femme fatale neglects her disruptive gesture in its hasty attempt to recycle her as an emblem of evil. She defies attempts to circumscribe her in a unified discourse of evil by seducing those who censure her, catching them in a double-binding gaze: first a glare of violent disavowal; yet this generalized moral remonstrance is closely followed by a more intimate glance, a longing look that expresses a desire to find in her some promise of escape or transcendence. Thus at the same time she excites a moral panic—the fear of being infected and consumed by evil—she provokes a desire to transgress those very moral categories. Yet the trajectory of desire of the femme fatale remains ambiguous. It is precisely this ambiguity, whether transgressive or transcendental, that fascist and postwar cinema and history (specifically neorealist cinema) react against and neodecadent cinema seeks to exploit.

The enduring ambiguity that manifests itself in the cultural imagery of the femme fatale appears where Victorian virtues of woman as household saint are turned into vices—domestic angels are demonized as sickness incarnate—and when women's cultural identity is turned against her—the emancipated woman, the feminist, is turned into a woman of easy virtue, a whore or degenerate.[9] While each embodiment of the femme fatale (whether a domestic image of infirmity or a siren of decadence) complicates and contradicts her original articulation, the profusion of sadistic and seductive images of Circe, Medusa, Pandora, Judith, and Salome in the art of Gustav Klimt, Otto Friedrich, Gustav Moreau, and Aubrey Beardsley; the representation of desire for feminine purity as a form of necrophilia, decadentism, and vampirism in the literature of Gabriele D'Annunzio, Oscar Wilde, Charles Baudelaire, Frank Wedekind, and Bram Stoker; and the depictions of the female parasite, feminine nothingness, mimicry, impurity, and passivity in the "scientific discourse" of Otto Weininger, Cesare Lombroso, Charles Darwin, Gustav Le Bon, Max Nordau, and Sigmund Freud attest to the unprecedented dread of female sexuality and the hysteria over its perceived homicidal power. Riddled with extreme hostility toward feminine sexuality, the political and social climate of the turn of the century coincided, as Sandra Gilbert and Susan Gubar point out, with "aggressive male avant-garde movements that emerged on the scene simultaneously with the rising demands for women's suffrage and women's rights, and the subsequent feminist incursions. In this period of sexual antagonisms, as depicted by Bernard Shaw, Henrik Ibsen, and Friedrich Nietzsche (1847–1920), intellectuals responded to women's suffrage struggles in Europe and modernist movements with masculine aggressivity."[10] Already installed in the discourse of aestheticism as what Wilde called the "more decorative sex," or Nietzsche called "God's second mistake," the decadent figure of woman became the rallying point for the male intellectual elite's political, cultural, and aesthetic agenda. The affirmation of modern man's virility and vitality was predicated on the negation of femininity as a sign of decadence, weakness, disease, and impotency.

Although many cultural historians and theorists argue that this antifeminine sentiment arose in response to the emergence of women's rights movements and the refashioning of woman as the "new woman"—who is no longer dependent on men for survival and protection and refuses to be treated as a child, as in the case of Ibsen's character Nora in *A Doll's House*—prominent intellectual figures (primarily social scientists) such as Darwin, Le Bon, Lombroso, Nordau, Weininger, and even Freud do not attempt to reform the social role of woman but make her disappear altogether.[11] The tension between the sexual or seductive woman and the saintly woman is no longer treated as a binary opposition but collapsed into one form of feminine degeneration: while the representation of the femme fatale as a vamp, a social parasite who feeds off men and lives on conspicuous consumption, may certainly be interpreted as a political response to woman being targeted as the addressee of consumer culture and to the emergence of women's rights movements, the enframing of feminine sexuality as infirmity comes from scientifically determinist or essentialist arguments that are deeply connected to racial, genetic, and hygienic (contamination) theories.

Bartolomeo Pagano as strongman Maciste and Italia Almirante Manzin as the decadent femme fatale Sophonisbe in *Cabiria*.

Despite the more liberal façade of such pseudoscientific theories (for example, Freud's and Weininger's espousal of a primary sexual ambiguity, bisexuality or polymorphous sexuality), within these theories woman is designated as "nothing" but a receptacle for numerous male inscriptions, genetic codings, and cultural influences.[12] Weininger, whose theoretical premise is based on sexual difference, illustrates this misogynist logic and reactionary thought designed to attack all cultural constructions of femininity. He insists that woman is nothing: on the one hand, woman simply imitates man's virtue, that is to say, she is merely a simulation of man's desire for his own goodness, purity, and honesty; and, on the other hand, when she presents herself as equal to man in intelligence and capacity, she is thereby at best already biologically constituted as a man. Thus woman, he claims, does not exist. Such theories result in what Misha Kavka calls "the male hysteria of the cult of educated masculinity, exposing it[self] as cultural pathology." ("Misogyny and [Male] Hysteria in Otto Weininger," 129). Pathological obsessions, steeped in the discourse of hygiene, produce a variety of contradictory positions, from the fear of contact with the feminine to the fear of tumescence, proliferating more violent attitudes toward sexuality and women, which can be seen in modernist and avant-garde fantasies of the "bachelor machine" (Marinetti's *Mafarka il futurista*, Wyndham Lewis's *Human Age*, Fritz Lang's *Metropolis*, etc.) and in the rhetoric of Adolf Hitler (fraught with images of disease, infection, infestation, putrefaction, pestilence; for example, he compared Bolshevism to syphilis and labeled Jews vermin or a virus).

The work of Weininger, like that of Lombroso, Nordau, Freud, and Le Bon, becomes the center of many antifeminist (and anti-Semitic) debates, most notably among the avant-garde of the early twentieth century, for example, Wyndham Lewis, Ezra Pound, D. H. Lawrence, Karl Kraus, August Strindberg, and Gabriele D'Annunzio. Debates over women's rights, questions of femininity, and race appear in avant-garde periodicals like *La Voce*, *Lacerba*, and *Blast*, alongside, and often in unison with, debates over nationalism, colonialism, interventionism in World War I, anti-Semitism, the *Action Française*, and avant-garde and modernist art. In movements such as futurism, vorticism, modernism, nationalism, and in emerging schools such as psychoanalysis and criminology, the figure of the femme fatale is positioned as the icon of literary and artistic decadence as well as a social threat that must be combated. These masculinist discourses slip over into misogynist models of gender politics that situate the feminine body as not only the site of a gender battle but also a dumping ground for a stock of images considered abject or undesirable to the fluctuating masculine position. The understanding of feminine sensuality as an infectious disease exceeding the limitations of the body via a series of synechdoches is replaced by the unhygienic feminine body that threatens to contaminate and castrate the male spirit or vital force; for the futurists, woman threatens "La nostra nuova concezione della vita, le forme d'igiene spirituale" (Our new conception of life, the form of spiritual hygiene).[13] Woman remains the site of negativity in a masculine dialectic.

Many avant-garde agendas set out primarily to disempower the femme fatale (as a metaphor for all women) of her seductive allure by reducing femininity to less than a reproductive function and illogically conflating the feminine with the colonized, the *passatista* (pacifist), *parlamentarismo* ("parliamentarism"), *decadentisti* (decadents). As a consequence, this overdetermined analogizing not only engenders all relationships but also assimilates social relations to sexual interaction, where the masculine position repeatedly represents itself as sadistic. For example, Marinetti transforms the helpless feeling of dread, when coming into contact with the feminine sexuality, into an act of violence, yet also one of self-expression: he writes, "Possedere una donna, non è stronfinarsi contro di essa, ma penetrarla! . . . Abbasso le diplomazie delle pelle! viva la brutalità di una possessione violenta e la bella furia di una danza muscolare esaltante e fortificante" ("to possess a woman is not to rub yourself against her, but to penetrate her. . . . Down with the diplomacy of the skin, long live the brutality of a violent possession and the beautiful fury of the dance of exalted and fortified muscles").[14] Furthermore, all metaphors for the feminine—nature, colonies, passivity, otherness in general—are treated in a similar fashion in futurist writings. The futurists' self-fashioning as mythic synthesis of man and machine also attempts, however, to usurp the "power of seduction" in an effort to master symbolic meaning traditionally attributed to femininity.[15] The reaffirmation of masculinity in the form of "the unitary virile body" is contingent on the "defeat of the danger of feminine involutions."[16] As a result, the futurists, like many other modernist and avant-garde intellectuals, degrade the spectacle of an alluring fluid feminine subject as well as the cinematic cult of the diva (most notably Elenora Duse in theater and Lydia Borelli and Francesca Bertini in early cinema) and replace the decadent spectacle with the theatrics of superhuman and supersexual masculine machines, which fashion themselves the new icons for a cult that desires the modern, worships male youth, and promotes industrialization, and institutionalized warfare.[17] This transformation of the sexual imaginary serves to create an erotics of violence, an aesthetics of aggressive male sexuality—a hysteria of objective visibility that aims at the destruction of intimacy, emotions, and secrets. The politics of the futurist movement are circumscribed by the social spectacle of aggressive heterosexual masculinity that bridges the reactionary stance to the then-emerging gender antagonisms with the mounting entreaties by Italian nationalists for colonial enterprises and intervention in World War I.

The celebration of the destructive potential of technology, war against all pacifists, the colonial wars, and the globalization of capital instantiated the need for both an Italian and a German identity as a rallying point for political mobilization. The fascist regimes readily appropriated this mechanical concept of total mobilization attributed to modernity as a promise of solidarity, albeit based on another myth: the connection of modern Italy to imperial Rome—as seen in films such as Guazzoni's *Quo Vadis?* (1913), Pastrone's *Caberia* (1914), Gallone's *Scipione l'Africano* (1937)—and modern German to legendary Nordic myths—depicted in Fritz Lang's *Die Nibelungen*

(1924), Leni Riefenstahl's *Das blaue licht* (1932) and later *Triumph of the Will* (*Triumph des Willens*, 1934)—through which not only analogies with patriarchy and empire could be made but also the application of social-Darwinist theories of "racial" and "historic" superiority. Although Emilio Gentile argues that avant-garde movements such as futurism must be distinguished from fascism with respect to its more violent antitraditionalist, individualist, antimoralist, and anti-Catholic agenda, he states, "the futurists [and modernists] participation in fascism when in power took place with a full awareness of what fascism was, and the regime never suggested its totalitarian politics were in conflict with their conception of culture, with their idea of modernity, or with their vision of the destiny of the nation."[18] I do not wish to underrate the differences of the two movements nor the difference between German nazism and Italian fascism, which both separately and concurrently underwent a series of political, cultural, and aesthetic transformations. My focus, rather, is on shared representations of gender that coalesced around the politics of nationalism and the subsequent construction of the myth of *Italianità* and *Blut und Boden*—the belief in the "regeneration" of a "new Italy" or a "new Germany" and a "new man" diametrically opposed to the provincialism of the Giolitti era and the decadent liberalism of Weimar. Mussolini's and Hitler's simulation of the avant-garde concept of national regeneration and the revolutionary figure of the new man emerges from the "new man" heralded in the avant-garde movements of the turn of the century (antiauthoritarian, militaristic, violent, and self-righteous), but also from the popularization and massification of what Raymond Williams has called "cultural Darwinism" and Guy Debord the "society of the spectacle."[19] The mobilization of the spectacle in popular culture or mass politics permitted and thrived on what Williams argued are the "ambiguities between revolution and carnival." Prefascist and fascist rhetorical strategies focused on excoriating the "despicable" effeminate qualities of their political opponents, exaggerating the failures of liberal reformism, especially its inability to suppress mass working-class movements.[20]

Prefascist movements like the Italian *squadristi* or the German Freikorps and later the fascists usurped the leftist territory of revolutionary discourse for their own rightist revolution and competed for mass audiences and the mastery of popular culture. These groups used the means of violence to crush their political opponents (primarily socialists for the *squadristi*, and Bolsheviks, socialists, and women for the Freikorps, who were responsible for the assassination of Rosa Luxemburg, an unpunished crime that was followed by a series of notorious femme-murders).[21] Masculinist groups such as the Freikorps, the *squadristis*, futurists, vorticists, the dominant scientific and intellectual community shared not only the dread of being infected by fatal feminism but reacted to such a fear by projecting violent male fantasies into the theater of mass culture, legitimizing these violent reactions through politics, science, law, and mass spectacle. Such violent masculinist agendas did not come without social consequences: in her study of sexual murders in Weimar Germany, Marie Tartar observes, "When the victims are prostitutes—women marked with the signs of corrupt and corrupting sexuality—the killer is not infrequently judged to be a normal person provoked to an act of violence or his victims are seen as complicitous in their murders.... is it, then, any wonder that many sexual [racial] killers perceive themselves to be guardians of a higher moral order, ridding the world of polluting influences?" (*Lustmord*, 54).

The New Woman of Weimar Cinema

While the famous fin-de-siècle actress Eleonora Duse functioned for the Italian futurists as an icon of decadentism, Marlene Dietrich's portrayal of Lola Lola provided the fatal icon of wild, decadent, adulterous woman of the 1920s Weimar Berlin. Dietrich's embodiment of the femme fatale is "spectacularized" not as a nostalgic woman infected with tuberculosis but as a "new woman," an excessively sexual yet sterile woman (*Berlinerisch*). This "masculine woman," who is known for her sexual aggressivity and her ability to cross-dress, appropriates the charge of the seducer. Her possession of agency, as opposed to passivity, along with her emotionless facial expression, destabilizes the traditional heterosexual romantic narrative and confounds another set of inculcated gender barriers.[22] Indeed the sexual ambiguity of Lola Lola (including her spin-offs) and the duality of the figure of Lulu in *Pandora's Box* and the cyborg/vamp of *Metropolis* render them easy targets for reactionary politics.

Yet what distinguishes Dietrich as the ideal vamp is her equivocal composure as a mixture of stereotypical masculine and feminine attributes that cannot be returned to a traditional version or vision of femininity (as they can in the case of Mae West), as well as her deployment in an ironic narrative in which she cannot be morally or socially redeemed (cleansed or purged) through an Aristotelian concept of catharsis or traditional narrative paradigms.[23] Rather, the iconic figure of Lola Lola maintains the masculinized feminine position not only via her ambiguous self-fashioning but also by the fact that it is she who desires beyond the "institution" of marriage, who seduces and abandons, and who supports her mate, while her husband (Professor Immanuel Rath/Dr. Unrat) is forced to dress in aprons and don a chicken costume only to be publicly humiliated, and ultimately he commits suicide.[24] Dietrich reforms the mastery of seduction from what Baudrillard labels the "hot" feminine or intimate seduction of the decadents to the coldness and cruelty of the movie star on the screen, which, as he claims, emerges from the "intersection of two cold mediums, the image and the masses" (*Seduction*, 95).

The Blue Angel alters the original narrative of its source (Heinrich Mann's 1905 novel, *Professsor Unrath*) that was known for its criticism of the vices of bourgeois society and focuses more on the dark side of seduction.[25] Kracauer attributes the success of the film to Marlene Dietrich's "new incarnation of sex"—"with her provocative legs and easy manners, [she] showed an impassivity which incited one to grope for the secret behind her callous egoism and cool insolence.... The other reason for the film's success was its outright sadism."[26] This sadistic "impassivity," however, is constantly questioned by Lola Lola's interest in lovemaking, which plays on nostalgia as much as on promised pleasure; callous coldness is played off desire for a romantic experience (nostalgic) and at the same time an unknown pleasure (futuristic). The film sustains the prospect of a romantic outcome by "suspending" the satisfaction that conventional narrative desires; even though Dietrich appears cold and cruel, she still alludes to the conventions of sentimental love. Her melancholic songs of longing and unfulfilled love, as well as her role-playing as the *hausfrau* who makes the professor breakfast and dresses him for work, promise to satisfy as much as they parody male fantasies of sexual conquest and domestication of the new sexual woman. Despite the obvious social contradictions in this fantasy of conquest and domestication, the professor responds to the game of seduction by attempting to translate sexual passion and pleasure into sentimental love; he brings Lola Lola flowers, defends her honor, buys her a ring and vows to marry her.

Gaylyn Studlar attributes this type of seduction (mixing sexual desire and romantic love) of the audience to a masochistic pleasure whereby the visual pleasure of Dietrich "does not involve mastery of the female but submission to her body and her gaze"; it is a giving in, a losing of control (*In The Realm of Pleasure*, 29). This loss of control is made evident by the juxtaposition of Lola Lola's song "einen Mann" with "Üb'immer Treu und Redlichkeit," a popular German tune devoted to the praise of loyalty and honesty, which usually accompanies scenes of the professor in the classroom, since it is his song that fades out and hers that lingers, not only in the film but in our cultural memories. Professor Rath relinquishes not only his own bourgeois ideals (honesty, loyalty, respect) but his status (title, place) within the social structure for the promise of pleasure, his allusion of romantic love. He renounces his own social standing to become the *einen Mann* (the one man) or the *richtigen Mann* (the right man) whom Lola Lola claims to desire. It is not until the end of the film that the meaning of *einen Mann* becomes clear as *any* man or every man, rather than one man. While the film clearly identifies the professor's own "weakness" as the cause of his "social" downfall, it does not clarify whether Lola Lola is directly responsible for his ruin. Although she is implicated in humiliating and cuckolding her husband, her indifference toward love diffuses her intent—it is unclear whether she decidedly seduced Professor Rath or whether he blindly pursued her, attempting to incorporate her into his own fantasy of love.

This process of seduction reveals that it is also a process of misreading the subject's own desire into and onto his or her object—a misreading of the self's imagined pleasure in the other's gesture. Yet this subjective desire must confront the more ambivalent desire of the other that offers himself or herself up as an object. It is the initial attraction compulsion that confuses both who desires and the registers of power implicit in the seduction process itself. Because the seducer explicitly plays with a stacked deck, the game of seduction never presents itself as a game of chance. As a result, both players in the game of seduction cannot identify themselves as pure victims (dupes) nor completely naive, rather they reveal their fascination with the other's seductive power as an attraction to violence.

Although not explicitly, Italian cinema of the 1930s was greatly influenced by the films of German Expressionism; the numerous recitations of the image of the cabaret vamp (Lola Lola) were realized in, for example, Renato Castellani's characterization of Zazà (1943), a seductive cabaret singer. Yet this depiction of the femme fatale, as well as many others like her, is re-encoded into a moral system by the depiction of her punishment, her humiliation, and ultimately her destruction. While Zazà appears to be a typical vamp—singing songs with sexual innuendoes, hiding behind veils, displaying her legs, removing her glove and leaving it with her future lover—unlike Lola Lola, she secretly desires to be loved in a conventional manner. This desire is made apparent when she meets her lover's daughter and is shamed into leaving his home, realizing that she has no place in this "reputable" existence. In the end, her lover, Dufresne, is restored to his family, while Zazà realizes that her licentiousness has stigmatized her and can only bring her empty sexual encounters, not real love (as embodied by the family and all its respectable trimmings: house, children, wealth, etc.). Without hope, she not only ends up alone but takes her own life.

Characterizations of the femme fatale made during the fascist period were emplotted in three different narratives, none of which are identical to that of *The Blue Angel* or *Blonde Venus*. The narrative was often resolved by the character's "coming to" moral consciousness, which either redeemed her as an asexual woman, a woman who by having a child out of wedlock must suffer a series of tragedies and humiliations before she can return to her mother, as exemplified in Amleto Palermi's *La Peccatrice* (1942), or drove her to commit suicide, as in *Zazà*. Alternatively, she is represented as a victim of male desire (rape or deception); impure, she necessarily dies as a sacrifice to the healing or cleansing of society, as in the case of Goffredo Alessandrini's *Le nozze di sangue* (1942), where the innocent bride is seduced by her husband's enemy, believing, all the while, that her seducer was her betrothed; and Max Ophuls's *Signora di tutti* (1934), in which the protagonist falls in love with the son and is seduced by the father, taking the father away from his ailing wife. Or she is represented as pure evil and accordingly must ultimately die or be stripped of her social codings, as in Mario Camerini's *Il grand'appello* (1942), where the protagonist's lover is a Spanish mercenary selling guns to the enemy; and Vittorio De Sica's *I bambini ci guardano* (1942), whose antagonist leaves her husband and son, causing the husband to commit suicide and the son to refuse to acknowledge her as his mother.

These films use the discourse of purity or goodness both to legitimize conventional sex roles and to justify racial, sexual, and political hatred. From the binary stance of moral legitimacy, fatal feminism, racial otherness, and political opposition parties became inseparable ideological enemies of the "good Italian people," consequently becoming the focus of conventional morality's crusade against a subversive image (yet also scapegoat) threatening traditional modes of power. Instead of utilizing the double, which John Orr describes as a "ubiquitous shadow [that] usually signifies rebellion by the bourgeois hero against his/her middle class role and its forms of sexual constraints," the double in Italian cinema of the thirties is vanquished by the

In Renato Castellani's *Zazà* (1943), Isa Miranda, acting in the title role, plays a decadent cabaret singer who seduces a married man.

son's vengeance against the father's impropriety and the femme fatale's seductivity, as in *Sotto la croce del sud* (1938), *Il grand'appello* (1936), and *Lo squadrone bianco* (1936), where women not only symbolize racial otherness but moral and ethical otherness, decadence and illicit desire.[27] Yet while the feminine is no longer treated within the public forum as a waste product, annihilated as such, it is used as an example of immoral behavior, and in many cases the degenerate woman is juxtaposed with a glowing example of righteous behavior. Thus the evil twin of the "good" woman (usually a matronly figure), in order to be exonerated, must become conscious of her fall into disgrace and suffer the humiliation of being outside legitimate social boundaries.

Images that did not conform to conservative social roles (mother, sister) were automatically labeled whorish by nazi and fascist pietism.[28] In many films, in fact, unmarried women are perceived as possible threats to the social order, and in Germany, where unmarried women were not considered citizens, this fear was given legal credence. The legacy of the unknown and thus "aggressive" sexuality of the "new woman" (along with her desired departure from the sexually neutralized roles of mother and sister) posed a threat to fascist regimes that relied on bourgeois morals and family values as a point of reference in their nationalist discourse and agenda. The "biological politics" of the fascistic regime were epitomized by the dictum "fate figli, molti figli, [perché] il numero é potenza" ("have children, many children, because there is strength in numbers)."[29] Victoria de Grazia concludes that this type of sociosexual disciplining was "easily fused with anti-feminism and anti-Semitism."[30] The "new woman" was interpreted only in terms of sexual licentiousness and reduced simultaneously to the object of erotic desire and a potential menace to male sexual mastery and self-mastery. Accordingly, in terms of the evolving racial and nationalist discourse, the "new woman" was spectacularized in the rhetoric of racial purity as the site or dumping ground of the impure. Within fascist narratives, both Italian and German, the sexual female symbolized an imminent death of the male hero by consumption or castration—an antiheroic death, a feminine death of decay. The hyperbolized figure of excessive female sexuality makes manifest, as Klaus Theweleit claims, the male fear of dissolution in the overflowing waves of feminine fecundity (losing the "self" in the liquid female body), or as Linda Mizejewski argues, the fear of male impotence.[31]

Films made during the fascist period that focus on moral punishment and humiliation of the femme fatale resemble Fritz Lang's depiction of the vamp in the machine, who is the enemy/double of the good Christian mother Mary figure, Maria (*Metropolis*, 1926), and George Wilhelm Pabst's innocent yet hedonistic Lulu (*Pandora's Box*, 1929), whose fatal(e) mistake is to seduce and prostitute herself to a sadistic misogynist (Jack the Ripper) instead of her other or "usual" masochistic "victims."[32] That is, *Metropolis* and *Pandora's Box* lend themselves to morally complicit interpretations of sexuality by obeying conventional narrative forms of resolution. *Metropolis* not only reinforces the binary positioning of women (Madonna/whore) but also the split of thinkers from workers, where the working-class revolt fails but the workers are saved or delivered by the aristocratic son of the city's master/owner. However, the parody of the "new woman" as what Andreas Huyssen calls "the vamp in the machine" is not a simple image of evil; she is also an agent of class warfare, a metaphor for the modern city, a "working girl" who is fashion-conscious, exotic, and sexually wild (seducing the sons of masters). At the same time she is a robot (like the workers for whom she has been created to mislead) and a Marxist revolutionary who stirs the workers to rebel, to destroy the machines that torture them (hence she speaks the language of Leninism). She therefore slips between roles: the robotic agent of capitalism and a sexual threat to the established order. This constant slippage makes her role more ambiguous than that of her religious motherly (domesticated) counterpart. Although she is the progeny of science and industrialism, she cannot be simply reduced to an analogy for the bachelor machine or a siren of the modern city, for she also bears the signs of commercialism (the sleek fashion of the machine, Art Deco), colonial possession (her costume and dance are reminiscent of Josephine Baker in *Princess Tam-Tam*, and a variety of Orientalist images of sexuality), and the insatiable desire of feminine sexuality and rabid capitalism. Although diametrically opposed to Freder (the male protagonist in *Metropolis*), the vamp is also a mediator between the divided worlds. She can cross the barriers between the luxurious city above ground and the nightmarish factory world below. When compared to Freder, she recalls the Nietzschean articulation of the paradox of "Alexandrine culture, [which in order] to be able to exist permanently, requires a slave class, but with its optimistic view of life it denies the necessity of such a class, and consequently, when its beautifully seductive and tranquilizing utterances about the 'dignity of man' and the 'dignity of labor' are no longer effective, it gradually drifts toward a dreadful destruction."[33] The "uneasy" resolution of the film— Freder's appeasement of the workers through mediation of industry's and workers' demands—does not ameliorate the disempowerment of the working class, who are still represented as barbarians (similar to H. G. Wells's mole people in *The Time Machine*), resorting to violence, destroying machinery, burning the false Maria (the vamp), and almost drowning their own children. Here Lang replicates the prevailing paranoia concerning a possible socialist or proletariat revolt. He returns to the image of Christianity (the church, spirituality, prayer) as man's salvation from this social tension; only the image of Christianity that remains unsullied by this class struggle. Randy Rutsky argues that in *Metropolis* Lang anticipates fascist aesthetics, creating a sense of fascist wholeness by unifying technology with mysticism: nazi wholeness, according to Rutsky, "involves a mediation of repressive modernity, with a repressed 'eternal' spirit—the spirit of Germany. What the leader-mediator offers, then, is a restoration of this ancient spirit: a re-spiritualization, a 're-enchantment,' that will 'reanimate' a 'dead,' technologized modern world."[34] As a consequence the vamp, who is a product of modernization, technology, and capitalism, must be purged from this order as an unwanted by-product, since she is the only element that is "soulless" and therefore an enemy of the German spirit.

Pabst instead emulates Weiningerian social theory and equates feminine seduction to a "Pandora's box," where his character Lulu, a Jewish femme fatale, represents polysexuality. Yet Lulu, as well as the Countess Geschwitz, her lesbian admirer, and Schigloch (all of whom possess a certain avarice) return the discourse of sexuality and seduction to a racial discourse, where Jewish characters perform as the corrupters of legitimate social order. Lulu, who is also a threat to this masculine German spirit, ruins her respectable German admirers—accidentally killing her husband in a struggle over the gun after he attempts to kill her, and after his death becoming his son's lover, only to squander away all of his money. Like Lang's vamp, Lulu's own wildness, decadence, and corruption lead her on a path to self-destruction, but this time she is destroyed by someone who is like her, both sadistic (fatal) and Semitic. As Nancy Harrowitz and Sander Gilman point out, Jack the Ripper in Frank Wedekind's text, *Pandora's Box*, is a Lombrosian sadist, that is, "a caricature of the eastern Jew."[35] Harrowitz explains that what surfaces in this image of Jack "is a cultural theme of blood, vampirism, cannibalism, and sexual perversion all linked to the antisemitism prevalent at the time" (*Anti-Semitism, Misogyny, and the Logic of Cultural Difference*, 55). *Pandora's Box* not only reflects the femme-deaths (serial murders) occurring in 1920s Germany; it also legitimizes the murder of the protagonist under the rubric of *Lustmord*, what Tartar attributes to the violent reaction against feminine decadence, degeneration, and anti-Semitism. Although Jack, like the serial killer Bruno in Robert Siodmak's *The Devil Strikes at Night* (*Nacht wenn der Teufel kam*, 1957), is himself a degenerate (insane), his choice of victims (sexual women, prostitutes) reflects more culturally sanctioned hatred of sexual women rather than expressing his own individual insanity or moral corruption. While Siodmak criticizes the logic of such thinking by demonstrating how depictions of impurity were turned into social threats—symptoms of a diseased society—dovetailing with nazi justifications for purification, eliminating *Untermenschen*, Pabst fuels representations of decadence, feminine sexuality, and deceit as symptoms of social corruption. Lulu, along with Countess Geschwitz and Schigloch, who plays a parasitic father figure, embody a variety of social vices, sexual perversity, greed, and insensibility, and also reemphasize the deep-seated connection of the femme fatale to racial abjection and Victorian notions of hygiene (racial and sexual purity).

The Blue Angel, on the other hand, offers no moral resolution, thus remaining morally ambiguous. The antibourgeois and specifically amoral performance of the couple deflects interpretive moral oversimplifications; it leaves the complexity of seduction as an enigma confounding spectators' ability to identify with the characters. Dietrich's performances in *The Blue Angel* and *Blonde Venus* serve as textual references for her reinscription in postfascist films, where she becomes not only an icon of subversive sexuality but also an icon of camp.[36] Here I refer to Susan Sontag's definition of the spectacle of camp as the "love of the unnatural: of artifice of exaggeration" and Andrew Ross's "power in decline."[37] It is not the image of Dietrich that is re-cited but instead the bloated, campy spectacularization of that image. This satire of the femme fatale "respectacularizes" the feminine body as a masculinized body or a satirical body;

she then becomes an icon mimicked in postfascist cinema as both the lesbian sadist and the transvestite masochist. The figures of Lola Lola and the Blonde Venus herself have acquired the definitive cultural signification of theatricality and sexual fantasy, yet one in the postwar period that points more toward the repudiation of effeminacy rather than the spectacle of seduction. These "new" cult icons have been reencoded in the site of sexual ambiguity, that is, the intersection of masculine aggressive sexuality (sadistic) with feminine infectiousness and also passive sexuality (masochistic) and feminine capriciousness. The infinite reproduction or recitation of the Dietrich roles and images encompasses a range of deviant sexual identities, from the Sadean woman, to the masochistic dominatrix, to the hyperbolized feminine as acted by a male transvestite, to the lesbian, to a perpetual exchange of cross-dressing and role-playing. Therefore it is not surprising to find Dietrich-like icons of decadence ("Sadean women") turn into distorted forms in Rossellini's *Open City*, Visconti's *The Damned*, Fosse's *Cabaret*, Bertolucci's *The Conformist*, Pasolini's *Salò*, Cavani's *The Night Porter*, and Wertmüller's *Seven Beauties*.

Ironically, what has been considered antifascist cinema displaces the aggressive

In *The Blonde Venus* (1932), Dietrich performs the cabaret act "hot Voodoo," referencing both the image of the Venus Hottentot and the theories of social Darwinism.

sexuality of Marlene Dietrich's portrayal of Lola Lola from the context of the Weimar Republic only to put it into place once again, but this time as a "modern" cultural icon of fascist sexual politics. Lola Lola is reinscribed in a sadomasochist play, dressed in nazi regalia. Films such as *The Damned*, *Cabaret*, and *The Conformist* revise nazism as the "idealized" theater of a morally reprehensible sexuality, staging both voracious sexual consumption and, at the same time, violent sexual control and torture. Linda Mizejewski elucidates this intrinsic contradiction in the revision of the cabaret vamp, arguing, "Antifascist productions end up duplicating the fascist politics they strive to condemn, reproducing the homophobia, misogyny, fascination for spectacle, and emphasis of sexual difference that characterize German fascism."[38] The process of transforming the decadent into the fascist and vice-versa is a synechdochic repetition, maintaining the aesthetic form, emptying it of its former historical index, but still installing this mutated form into an ideological and moral framework. I agree with Michel Foucault's questioning of this permutation: how could nazism, which fashioned itself on its own model of blood purity and masculine mastery, become the ultimate sign of decadent erotic sexuality? More specifically, how could the nazi and the fascist come to be identified with the same "impure" icons (feminized sadists, femme fatales, etc.) they once used to demarcate external (Bolshevik, Slav, African) and internal (Jew, homosexual, mentally disadvantaged, Gypsy) others?

In addition to the unproblematized exchange of the attributes of the other, surprisingly, this fascination with fascism has drawn several homosexual filmmakers, as well as theoreticians, to present nazism and/or fascism as ultimately rooted in homosexuality itself. The dynamic revision of fascism as homoerotic serves simultaneously to offer queer politics (by association with a sublime, powerful sign of abjection) an attractive means of threatening heterosexual politics and to return this means of transgression to a moral repudiation of the preestablished social abjection of homosexuality. Through the guise of the symptom, an otherwise aggressive male sexuality is mistakenly framed as homosexual, collapsing the homosexual into the homosocial. Consequently, I want to underscore that politics of visual identity present in both neodecadent and neorealist films erases its own genealogy, its connection to discursive positions, so as to emphasize only its relation to artifice and the unnatural. That is, neodecadent cinema and neorealist cinema treat fascism in the aesthetic of camp— as power in and of decline. Although neorealist and neodecadent filmmakers project similar images of nazism and fascism, their political agendas diverge radically: while the neorealists used representations of fascism to reaffirm an antifascist Italian national identity, neodecadent filmmakers question such a break with fascism, by suggesting that fascism aesthetically maintains a seductive appeal. Further, the figure of the femme fatale, with all her allusions to the artifice of Art Nouveau, Orientalism, German Expressionism, and film noir, undermines "realist" approaches to representing fascism. Hence, the femme fatale or vamp acquires her own political agenda, one that does not acquiesce to the romantic, tragic narrative of neorealism, nor does it surrender to the "passive nihilism" of neodecadentism's ironic narratives.

Feminizing Fascism

In opposition to the fascist promotion of the masculinization and vindication of a nationalist moral ethos—as exemplified in the numerous images of Mussolini, including, for example, the well-known 1932 documentary *Mussolini Speaks*, where he is extolled as a "modern Caesar"—neorealist and neodecadent films dissolve the image of the Duce and the futurist rhetoric of masculine vitality by replacing it with the image of the effeminate fascist. Bertolucci's *The Conformist* and *1900*, Visconti's *The Damned*, and Rossellini's *Open City* present the image of the nazi and the fascist as an expression of radical evil; however, rather than characterize evil as aggressively masculine, they feminize it through sexualization.[39] The threat of radical evil is, then, reconfigured as a feminine sexual threat. Yet the menace of evil is not directed toward women, as emblems of the *Patria* or *Blut und Boden*, but toward men, who in the postwar period have been stripped of their "masculine models" of identification.

During and following the reconstruction in Italy, in order to resuscitate political legitimacy Italian political figures and institutions have had to disavow fascist models of authority, law, virility, and nationalism. Although identification with the resistance became a prerequisite in reestablishing moral and political credibility, the same resistance that seemingly unified Italy (after the fall of Mussolini in 1943) against a common enemy radically decentralized authority, and, with it, legitimate models with which men could identify. Resistance movements were far from homogenous; they split along party lines into a multiplicity of political factions: communist, socialist, Christian Democrat, and Catholic parties. And because they all vied for political dominance, they all projected their own image of a new Italy and the new Italian man. As a consequence, the only common ground that unified resistance movements was the creation of a negative image, a generalized discourse of vindicating innocent victims. However, this historical common ground, antifascism, a form of intraclass alliance, has recently been subjected to more conservative reinterpretations, specifically in Germany, Italy, and France, where the political climate of the 1990s decidedly shifted to the right. Accordingly, the notion of innocent victim has undergone significant changes: for example, Silvio Berlusconi, the prime minister of Italy (leader of the Forza Italia Party), suggested after his election in 1994 that many fascists were also victims of unjustified partisan acts of revenge and so deserved to be remembered along with partisan heroes. Leonardo Paggi interprets such polemical statements as attempts to revindicate the Right's historical mandate in contemporary politics; he writes, "by shifting to the right, the moderate center seems to wish to cancel or forget the 'plebeian' component of postfascist democracy [in favor of] reestablishing a national continuity, a major issue of both Italy and Germany since the mid-1980s."[40] Although these appeals to history and national identity require a good deal of historical revision (if they are not completely arbitrary, they are wildly selective), what has remained consistent in these discursive practices is the rhetorical model that divides good from evil and the pure from the impure.

Cold War politics, however, are largely responsible for eclipsing postwar demands for justice by redirecting attention away from the collaborators toward another enemy, the threat of communism. Films such as *Judgment at Nuremberg* and *The Traveling Players* demonstrate how Western social ideals (justice, democracy, freedom) were met with political cynicism (letting former fascists go unpunished, demolishing liberation movements if they moved too far to the left, etc.), thereby suggesting that Europe was never denazified; the former fascists and former nazis not only returned to prestigious positions within their nations' capitalist institutions (Agnelli, Olivetti, IG Farben, Krupps, Volkswagen, etc.) but also became important figures in the military industrial complex. They informed the OSS and CIA regarding communist activities and so returned to combat their wartime enemies, the Left. In the name of expedience and preservation of the bourgeois-capitalist infrastructure, the allies contributed to the legitimization of the most conservative interlocutors (such as the Savoy monarch, marshal Badoglio, the German judicial system, the former military secret intelligence and the capitalist cartel of industrialists) even though they were tarnished with twenty years of fascist support. This exoneration of the bourgeoisie from its historic role in fascism was designed to recuperate the political and economic support of an international bourgeoisie, especially given the then-reemerging threat of communism (in Italy, Greece, Yugoslavia). Pier Paolo Pasolini argues that the acceptance in postwar Italy of previously fascist figures—among them De Gasperi, Elio Vittorini, Curzio Malaparte, Roberto Rossellini, and the Agnelli family—and in postwar Germany of industrialists implicated in manufacturing death camps "provided the bourgeoisie with an alibi behind which to hide its own poor conscience, giving it a right to citizenship in Italy, by presenting themselves as 'committed,' and it was precisely the bourgeoisie that wanted and accepted these figures."[41] Yet the question is not whether one resisted fascism; it is why a certain cultural production and technological progress were given immunity from what was later to be thought of as the impurity or immorality of fascism.

It was the desire to preserve conventional notions of "normal" or "legitimate society" that paved the way for the reidentification of legitimate society itself with monumental resistance heroes who opposed the decadent or sadistic enemies of bourgeois moralism. Paggi explains that at the same time the "antifascist political discourse had tended to outline a patriotic epic, centering on the figure of the male combatant hero and martyr, the upshot of this portrayal is a highly selective historical memory, in which complex and ambiguous situations that fit uneasily, if at all, the basic premise of heroic armed conflict have been conveniently swept under the carpet."[42] While neorealism focuses on the plebeian component of antifascism, it reinstalls postwar icons of evil in the form of fin-de-siècle icons of feminine decadence and degeneration, reproducing the cultural and ideological coding in which these images were previously inscribed. At the same time the femme fatale resurfaces she elicits a hypochondriac compulsion to quarantine her, allowing man once again to buttress the walls of his own being. By disavowing the image of the fascist hero, this alleged new man redefines himself. Even films that seek to question the emergence of a new man modeled on an old image of purity and heroic manliness return to the structural logic of othering when they use the image of the femme fatale in the place of supreme evil. Although as Robert Kolker writes, "Neorealism is a pivot, a break [from] the fascist politics of melodrama and spectacle, its emotional excess, demand for sacrifice and apotheosis of death," this break between postwar and wartime European aesthetic and cultural politics continues to harbor a similar structure of disengaging with otherness, that is, neorealism distinguishes itself in opposition to what it considers to be impure. Such a clear breakage, as Zygmunt Bauman argues, reveals the flawed logic of treating fascism, nazism, and the Holocaust as an aberration rather than "the legitimate product of civilization . . . the truth of modernity rather than a possibility it contains" (*Modernity and the Holocaust*, x). Hence, notions of breakages often attempt to isolate nazism or fascism by reading it as a part of the mystery of human psychology rather than working through the social, cultural, sexual, and political mechanisms that produce(d) it.

While Millicent Marcus claims that "Neorealism became the repository of partisan hopes for social justice in the postwar Italian state," she proceeds to argue that "for many critics, Neorealism is first and foremost a moral statement, 'una nuova poesia morale' whose purpose is to promote a true objectivity."[43] Yet the neorealist self-identification as a cinematic "repository" of historical consciousness and moral conscience functions simultaneously as a device of separation, via the processes of obsessively historicizing the themes of fascism and the war and of continuously detaching itself from its recent past through a strategy of ethical indignation—all of course ex post facto. The ideological restructuring of the collective Italian conscience (transforming the history of fascism into a tragic narrative of deceit against the Italian people) legitimized the deliberate disassociation of neorealism from what Rossellini acknowledges as its "less immediate precursors," namely, fascist filmmakers such as Blasetti and Camerini. Both directors were contemporaries and teachers of many neorealist filmmakers (including De Sica, Zavattini, Zampa, Antonioni, Fellini, and Rossellini himself) at Cinecittà during the years of the fascist regime. Yet Rossellini contends that neorealism arose "*unconsciously* as dialectical filmmaking, and then acquired a *conscious* life in the heat of the human and social problems of wartime and the postwar years" (*My Method*, 34, my emphasis). Furthermore, André Bazin distinguishes neorealism from its "less immediate predecessors" by arguing that "the real revolution took place more on the level of *subject matter* than of style. Is not neorealism primarily a kind of *humanism* and only secondarily a style of filmmaking?"[44] This purported consciousness provided a new paradigm of representation and a so-called social objectivity, spontaneously making neorealism political and lending it what Lucia Re terms "a renewed sense of urgency." Political urgency to represent an Italian hero/protagonist (often tragic or pathetic) allowed neorealism to recontextualize itself in what has been perceived as a historic rupture with its fascist past.[45] This strategic maneuver leads to the simplification of otherwise extremely complicated political

struggles of the late fascist period, as well as distracts attention from the allied involvement that stymied the resistance (in order to prohibit the empowerment of the Italian socialist and communist parties).[46] This is not to say that all neorealist films repeat
simplistic notions of heroism; indeed, they often reveal a lack of heroism, focusing on
human failures rather than triumphs. In their adamant rejection of fascist aesthetics
and politics, they reify an ethical attitude toward human behavior that is not easily
distinguishable from wartime or prewar sentiments. By focusing on individual or
human issues, films such as *Open City*, *Paisà*, and *Bitter Rice* return to questions of
morality, on a personal or psychological basis, presenting fascism itself as a social disease, a moral corruption, rather than a product of modernity. Yet this disease is often
represented through images of decadence and excess (wealth, violence, indifference,
cruelty, evil), which continue to be inculcated by the antifeminist image of the femme
fatale, thereby recalling Victorian notions of hygiene, including racial hygiene.

The neorealists recreate a discourse of political consciousness based on a moralistic model that is designed to exclude textual ambiguities—any obfuscation of the
separation of good from evil—yet that often promotes the same (prewar) misogynist
and homophobic representations of evil itself. Hence neorealism, which Marcia
Landy identifies as "the cinema of demystification," appropriates Marxist discourse,
while remythifying preexisting (even fascist) sexual constructions, which functioned
historically to endorse the representation of sexual purity.[47] In an attempt to deterri-
torialize the image of the Italian nation and its national hero from the fascist, bourgeois decadence of political power and to reterritorialize the natural simplicity and
honesty of the proletariat, the neorealists simultaneously repositioned the fascist and
the nazi as the locus of endless impurity—both sexually and ideologically. Thus in
Rossellini's *Open City* and Bergman's *The Serpent's Egg*, fascism and nazism become a
sign of total abjection. In his analysis of *Open City*, Peter Brunette posits that for
Rossellini, "sexual inversion is the signifier par excellence for decadence" elucidating
"the struggle between good and evil in clear, uncomplicated black-and-white terms."[48]

Neorealism's repetition of this residual, dialectical model functions as an inverse
form of imitation of fascist moralism, where the model of moral rectitude is simply
replaced from one political group (fascists) to another (antifascists), keeping intact
the sexual and metaphysical dimensions of the model itself. Within this simplistic
dynamic of good versus evil, women are hypersexualized as a buttress for evil, while
the masculine hero is desexualized in order to separate him from what the neorealists deem attributes of the weak or the impure, namely, promiscuity. According to
Angela Dalle Vacche, "the neorealist body of Roberto Rossellini's cinema is frail and
transitory," in comparison to the "marble heroes of fascist cinema," suggesting the
transitory nature of individual agency in comparison to the historiographic project
and projections of fascism.[49]

Indeed, unlike the social realist films from the Soviet Union and Yugoslavia, or
even French films such as Jean Pierre Melville's *L'armées des ombres* (1969) or Rene
Clément's *La Bataille du Rail* (1946) that return to glorify historiographic projects—

to monumentalize the resistance and the political ethos attatched to specific heroes, "comrades or partisans"—Italian neorealist films that are aware of Italy's fascist past cannot indulge in such romantic narratives. Instead, Italian filmmakers like Rossellini and De Sica, who made films under the fascist regime, resort to making antifascism a moral duty by presenting fascism as a corrupting or morally debilitating agency, yet one that is associated with sexual and material improprieties (avarice and greed). This feminizing of "weakness" undercuts some of the more critical references in films such as Rossellini's *Open City* and *Germania anno zero* and De Sica's *Two Women*, where they problematize moralizing the agency of manhood. Characters who espouse the rhetoric of resistance, communism, socialism, or any other form of antifascism are also depicted as weak, even in respect to their own ideological passion. For instance, the communist partisan in *Open City*, Manfredi, who is betrayed by his lover, Marina, is portrayed as inhuman—married only to political ideals rather than the society or people for whom he fights. Yet the pedagogical weakness causing the ultimate downfall of characters like Manfredi is presented as symbolically more profound or tragic than the death and rape of feminine characters. Although Manfredi is clearly not represented as infallible, Rossellini stages his death as a modern crucifixion, mimicking Christian iconography.

While the male protagonists possess both political agency and moral symbolism, the female characters are continually reduced and exploited as a rhetorical body. *Open City*, *Paisà*, *Two Women*, and *Kapo* stitch the feminine body into an emblematic site, a battleground, where the body generates a series of metaphors: ranging from the terra firma of survival—even if this means collaboration, as in the case of Rossellini's Marina and Pontecorvo's *Kapo*—to political guilt as sexual guilt—"sleeping with the enemy," as exemplified in *Kapo*—to the traces and inscriptions of foreign invasions and subjugation of the body, as in *Two Women*, revealed by Cesira and her daughter Rosetta: first by the fascists (as a sexual threat), second by the Germans (who coldly kill young Italian men), and ultimately by the allies (whose victory over the fascists allows for their Moroccan counterparts to gang rape Italian women). In neorealist cinema, women's sexual purity, like Italy's innocence, is always at stake, and tragically lost. The proverbial *she* is left once again seduced and abandoned, only now she takes on the vanquished form of war-torn Italy. The feminine figures who do not represent promiscuous bodily corruption (addictions to drugs, power, or material wealth) or sexual violation become sacrificial victims to the Italian national rebirth (e.g., Rossellini's Pina, who will not see the promised spring of the resistance). The humiliation and fall of Italian masculinist politics transforms the notion of a national idol (or ideal) from the statuesque masculinity of the Roman and fascist heroes to the violated body of the virgin and the mother that hosts (cinematically) the alien virus of fascism, thus collapsing fascism and nazism into an epidemic of sadistic decadentism that permeates the membrane of an always already effeminate body. This reterritorialization of sexuality as effeminate and unchaste, as an illness that corrupts the flesh, realigns the hermeneutic circle to include the nazi as the incarnation of pure evil or absolute impurity (as in the case of *Open City*, where nazis are either effeminate homosexuals who torture and kill not only heroic partisan communists but also partisan priests, or lesbian seductresses and drug pushers who corrupt what could have been otherwise "normal" Italian women).

Images of femininity as well as female characters are often used metaphorically to emblemize the "ruined map of Italy," which is itself often presented as reduced to prostituting itself to the West—evidenced in the writings of Curzio Malaparte, specifically *La pelle*, as well as in Wertmüller's *Seven Beauties*, Pasolini's *Accattone*, and Fellini's *Nights of Cabiria*. Peter Brunette claims that

> Rossellini's men are often larger-than-life figures who fight for causes that are vaguely defined, but nevertheless transcend their own meager individual selves. They are the initiators of all the action; the women, on the other hand, both good and bad, are seen as acted upon, rather than as actors in their own right. Pina takes action, to be sure, but, again, her action is motivated by natural "womanly instinct" in the defense of her man. The only woman who is depicted as an active force is Ingrid, and she is seen significantly as a lesbian, and thus thoroughly masculine. (*Roberto Rossellini*, 50)

Although Ingrid (a nazi officer) seduces Marina (the lover of a partisan organizer), she, like Marina, is merely an instrument used by Major Bergmann, head of the Gestapo, to attack other men. The image of Bergmann, who Millicent Marcus likens to "a composite of Gestapo chief Herbert Kappler and Nazi commander Eugen Dollmann," however, symbolizes the source of feminine (deceptive and seductive) power, since it is he who orchestrates not only the seduction of Marina but the deception of Manfredi (*Italian Film in the Light of Neorealism*, 37). In fact, Rossellini presents both Marina and Ingrid as objects of exchange; even as they represent vehicles for disseminating fascist power, by collecting information and patrolling the public, they are also implicitly attached to commodities. Ingrid seduces Marina not simply with money but with liquor, a luxurious apartment, and finally a fur coat (her payoff for helping trap her lover Manfredi). All of the accoutrements in Marina's apartment, the liquor, drugs, jazz music, and her profession as a dancer and cabaret singer suggest that she is not just a "bad woman" but a modern woman, who is urbanized according to what Rossellini believed to be American standards. Rossellini implies a certain complicity of nazism and fascism with bourgeois decadence (capitalism), specifically the seductive allure of urban pleasures and commodity fetishism. However, Marcus points out that "Rossellini does not allow us to ascribe Marina's complicity to any bourgeois decadence, nor to a lifelong dependence on luxury, but instead to *personality weakness* that makes her succumb to the seduction of drugs, fur coats, and lush surroundings" (*Italian Film in the Light of Neorealism*, 38). Thus, at the same time that the moral distinction between the two characters (Pina and Marina), who have the same economic and social backgrounds, is made in almost black and white fashion, the class distinction is removed and qualified as purely a moral issue—an issue of choice.

Yet the aesthetic coding of Marina suggests otherwise. She appears to be fashioned on the image of the femme fatale, particularly the diva lying on a white bed, shot in soft focus, reminiscent of the reclining ladies of Art Nouveau and depictions of the two-faced woman, whose public face is that of the beautiful femme fatale, but whose private face is that of death. Like the femme fatale described by the aestheticists, futurists, and fascists, she is a mask for a multiplicity of evils. She consequently alludes not only to the decadence of the fin-de-siècle associated with the bourgeoisie but also to the decadent subjectivity that serves as a negative image or counterdiscourse to the themes of *Open City*. For instance, Marina challenges notions of national and class hegemony by moving beyond the parameters of class. Rossellini links her "weakness of personal character" to the social weakness of the bourgeoisie, which, in his analysis of Georg Lukács, Andrew Hewitt describes as "the decadent self-liquidation of the bourgeoisie."[50] It is her rupture with her class identification that seems to lead her astray. Her willingness to sell herself and betray her lover for luxury items and drugs may seem utilitarian, but her main flaw is her lack of faith—her inability to love and be loved. Pina, on the other hand, maintains her identity as both what Marcus calls a *populana* and a model of feminine social defiance, an image of purity, dignity, and morality. Yet as a model of resistance and the fight for freedom, she, like Manfredi, must be

Marina (Maria Michi) receives a mink coat from Ingrid (Giovanna Galletti) as a reward for spying on her boyfriend for the nazis in Roberto Rossellini's *Open City* (1945).

sacrificed so that a new Italy can be born. She dies in an attempt to save her future husband, Francesco. Thus, as Bram Dijkstra argues, "death became a woman's ultimate sacrifice [gift] of her being to the males she had been born to serve. To withhold from them this last gesture of her exalted servility was, in a sense, an act of insubordination, of self-will."[51] In contrast to this saintly yet servile image of Pina, Marina does not sacrifice herself so that Manfredi can live (so that Italy can reunify against a common foe, nazism); thus she signifies not only "insubordination" but selfishness and deceit.

Rossellini refines what the fascists coded as the aesthetics of *strapaese*—the romanticization of the peasants and rural life as more pure, mystical, organic, and authentic—as opposed to *stracittà*—the urban, secular world of the department store—replacing the rural peasants with the urban poor.[52] He reinstalls the aesthetics of neorealism into what Pierre Sorlin calls "puritanical, not to say misogynist," discourse.[53] This puritanism, however, entails a glorification of asexuality, a return to gender roles of real men, who fight for high ideals (freedom, humanism, moral values) and resist evil, and real women, who embody purity and strength. Yet the concerns of women are always secondary to those of their male counterparts. Furthermore, sexuality itself becomes feminized; in the case of *Open City*, Marina, Ingrid, and Lauretta (Pina's decadent sister) are the only sexualized figures. That is, they seem to have no male counterparts other than Lauretta's one-night stand, Fritz, and Major Bergmann, who is implicitly homosexual. Thus, while moral or good characters are married to ideals, even if they lack compassion, bad or evil characters are radically sexualized, pointing to both their moral ambiguity and their ability to seduce and therefore infect moral society. However, these characters' ability to seduce seems to be largely ineffective; therefore, evil seems less the effect of seductivity and sexuality, than seductivity and sexuality appear to be aftereffects of an ambiguous (unidentified) source of evil. Although sadistic nazis, mercenary women, and illicit sexuality are clearly represented as evil, other characters such as Manfredi (whose own dogma belies any compassion or love he could have had for Marina) and Don Pietro (who reminds the audience that every Italian was responsible for fascism) are not necessarily presented as good; rather, they redeem their evils (failure to overcome fascism) by becoming sacrificial victims of the rebirthing/cleansing of Italy. It is only the children partisans, led by Romolleto (literally "little Rome," playing on the ancient myth of Romulus), who will see the promised spring of a new Italy—that is, it is the image of a group of young boys, who after witnessing the execution of Don Pietro by a nazi functionary walk off into the city, with the Vatican as a backdrop, that will embody Rossellini's hopes for a new Italy.[54]

Decadent Histories

Carlo Emilio Gadda's 1957 *Eros e Priapo* offers a good example of the revision of fascism as an obsession with pure male physicality and a renewed revulsion with the feminine body. However, Gadda alters the game of seduction from a desire for evil to a craving for violence. He returns vehemently to represent what the Italian philosopher

Benedetto Croce claims has all but disappeared—the figure of Mussolini. Similar to the hyperbolic style in the representation of Mussolini in Fellini's *Amarcord*, Gadda's reading of the seductive and cinematic physique of Il Duce as the body politic is "en-gendered" as a feminized homosexual body whose pornographic allure ironically procures only the misogynistic violence of the narrative that constantly imagines the laceration and penetration of his subjugated figure. Gadda's linguistic method of surrounding the textual or metaphorical anatomy with a series of graphic adjectives that probe and cut through its membrane replicates a misogynist's (serial killer's) desire to massacre the feminine body. Hence the parody in Gadda's homoeroticization of fascism is accompanied by the nullifying presentation of the body as always already feminine, prurient, and carnal. Here Gadda opens up the hypermasculine physique of Mussolini for speculation, feminizing not only his body but his strategy of seduction of the masses in the process. Gadda's textual strategy of parodic mimicry as a form of violation and rupture, however, as Barbara Spackman points out, turns a presumably antifascist parody into misogynist discourse, which, she explains, "is doubly malicious, for the novel is a critique of fascism not only through an idiosyncratic psychoanalysis but also through a figuration of the receptive masses as woman, and a subsequent attack upon those masses through a not-so-idiosyncratic misogynist discourse."[55] Thus what Homi Bhabha names the "slippage between the mimic man [in this case, text] and the model" reproduces in *Eros e Priapo* a preexisting ambivalence, not toward fascist authority, since it parrots that authorial violence, but toward a manifestation of a paralysis of desire, reducing or dismissing the erotic to the realm of hysteria, and sexuality to the act of rape.[56] The act of mimicry, in this case, acts as a form of repetition—not in the Deleuzian sense, where the very act of repeating is difference, but in the Lacanian sense, where desire retreats into reproduction rather than otherness. Gadda's own act of parody is itself entrapped in the very model it seeks to undermine.

The radical sexualization of nazism and fascism in *Eros e Priapo* as well as in neodecadent films germinates the bloating of fascism and nazism as idealized spectacles of the sublime (in this case a potential violence). While Gadda's antiaesthetic representation of fascism, for example, vulgarizes the historic memory of fascism by rendering it impure, the neodecadents (neoaestheticists) utilize a mimetic style of representation in order to subvert the traditional intolerance of sexuality by exploding the discourse of repression into the politics of camp, thereby idealizing nazism and fascism as the ultimate expression of the sublime (as a pure form of erotic violence). The strategy of mimicry present in *Cabaret*, *The Conformist*, and *The Damned* functions both to augment the tension between bourgeois morality and the heterosexual and homosexual masquerade of femininity and to return nostalgically to a decadent code of gay identity.[57] Thus the neoaestheticist representations of Visconti, Bertolucci, and Fosse provide an exegesis of the neorealist postwar "poesia morale" establishing a complex code of iconicity in terms of a Baudrillardian cinema of hyperreality and total simulation.[58]

Such interpretations of fascism and the sexual appeal of fascism defy the terms of periodicity and reflect on modern analogies that use fascism and nazism as their point of departure—a departure from the historic event. Here I make a distinction between two theoretical approaches: the first directly confronts nazism and/or fascism as its object of analysis, as in the case of Klaus Theweleit's *Male Fantasies* (volumes one and two), Maria Antonietta Macciocchi's *La donna nera*, and George Mosse's *Nationalism and Sexuality*. These texts provide interpretations and explanations of the attraction of fascism to the masses and analyze this mass appeal of fascism in terms of sexual politics, thereby giving rise to the second approach: an examination not of nazism or fascism itself but the cultural recodification of nazism in the realm of cultural aesthetics and a spectacular expression of sexual politics (a sadomasochistic economy). My interest is primarily in this second approach, what Friedländer calls the recurrent "obsession with nazism in the contemporary imagination, [and] . . . the birth of a new discourse that ceaselessly elaborates and reinterprets [its own sexual fantasy in the nazi cult of the visual]."[59] Although I focus on the latter of the two approaches, I am also compelled to explore the theoretical intersections of the two fields of study along with the vehement criticisms leveled against Cavani and Wertmüller by Primo Levi and Bruno Bettelheim.

Contemporary theoretical approaches that note the difference between homoeroticism and homosexuality nonetheless tend to blur the lines between the two when it comes to fascist sexual politics. Mosse proposes, like Theweleit, to examine fascism as a sexually repressed discourse, one that is explicitly misogynist and homophobic and implicitly homoerotic. This mode of inquiry mimics Wilhelm Reich's "analysis" of Mussolini, along with Napoleon, as belonging to the "phallic-narcissistic-sadistic" character type, according to which "homosexuality lies at the root of [self] addiction [and is] likewise the result of phallic frustration." Hence, according to Reich's perspective, phallic exhibitionism overcompensates for having "anal homosexual impulses" and having identified with woman "at the phallic stage."[60] Both Theweleit and Mosse rehearse this notion of nazism as both overtly homosocial and secretly homosexual. The slippage, or even the convergence, between identification (with men) and desire (for women) creates what Eve Sedgwick calls a homophobia, which, she claims, derives from the confusion of the identification of men with men and their desire for women.[61] This reading of fascism and nazism as surreptitiously homosexual complies with Fosse's rendering of Christopher Isherwood's text, *Berlin Stories*, into its filmic version, *Cabaret*, and Bertolucci's cinematic rendering of Alberto Moravia's *Il conformista* as well as Visconti's revisioning of nazism in *The Damned*. Although films like *The Damned, The Conformist, Die Sehnsucht der Veronika Voss*, and *Cabaret* use the aesthetics of camp to criticize (parody, hyperbolize) fascism and its sexual appeal, they present fascist sexual politics as a veil for repressed homosexuality. *The Damned*, the most explicit and excessive of the these films in terms of representations of sexual deviance, equates nazism and fascism with not simply repressed homosexuality but a host of practices deemed perverse—promiscuous sexuality, cross-dressing, transvestitism, pedophilia, adultery, and the rape of a mother by her son. Each act of perversion not only climaxes in the death of the feminine but also in man's assumption of feminine power. Pleasure is recoded, as Baudrillard postulates, as "cool cold pleasure, not even aesthetic in the strict sense." [62] The enjoyment of violence aestheticized in the cinema of Visconti, Bertolucci, and Fosse recalls aestheticism's banalization of evil in the form of ennui or the decadent boredom of the fin-de-siècle.

At the same time that these cool (in McLuhan's sense: beautiful, enchanting, and numbing) ironic revisions of fascism that appeal to aggressive if not sadistic masculine aesthetics uncover certain critical subtexts of fascist aesthetics, rather than explore the linkages of fascism to aggressive masculinity, they turn fascist sexuality into an effeminate, homosexual, campy aesthetic of death, decay, and fatal feminism. This, in effect, only serves to confirm the very site of masculinity that they attempt to subvert as a symbolic ideal, even if it is only phantasmatic. By mimicking fascism and nazism as expressions of degenerate sexuality, camp productions return to models of (feminine)

Anna (Dominique Sanda) imitates masculine postures, while Giulia (Stefania Sandrelli) plays the part of the gullible woman, as the two become a spectacle of ambiguous sexuality in *The Conformist*.

negativity and also reproduce desire as loss or lack (deferring again to the phantasm of masculine sexuality or the nostalgia of power in decay), thus revealing their debt to psychoanalytic models of thinking. Although I do not concur with feminists who argue that the aggression, ridicule, and cruelty of camp practice and commentary are just misogynist attacks on women, I maintain that these campy productions are still deeply embedded in the logic of exclusion (otherness, abjection, sexual difference).[63] While I agree with Caryl Flinn and Judith Butler that camp is not directly an attack on masculine or feminine sexuality but rather a parody of the notion of an "original normalizing fiction of gender identity" (an attempt to reveal the arbitrariness of gender constructions), I do not support the theory that camp decontexualizes human subjectivity, identity, and the body. Rather, I concur with Sande Cohen, who argues that camp's parody of sexuality contains within it the very foreclosure or law (castration, normalizing gender constructions, sexual antagonism) that it might be said to exceed (*Passive Nihilism*, 115–16). That is, by the very fact that such attempts to "suspend foreclosure" are made on, as Cohen writes, "symbolic identity based on gendered negations (the overvaluation of any sexual position)," these excessive parodies foreclose themselves within the very limitations they seek to negate. As a result, what Andrew Ross calls "necrophiliac tendencies of camp"—the "sick fascination with the link between glamour and death"—pass into what Cohen has termed cultural nihilism—the culture of failure. Furthermore, the linking of fascism, nazism, and the "Final Solution" to camp not only rearticulates the rhetoric of exclusion but also binds the discourse of nazism, fascism, and the "Final Solution" to that of the abject, a defining negativity: "the end of history" (Friedländer et al.), "the end of poetry" (Adorno), "an incommensurable trauma" (LaCapra), or "the point of departure for identification" (Habermas).

Because many postwar re-representations of the femme fatale, nazism, and fascism dovetail with psychoanalytic theory, it is necessary to explore the linkages of neodecadence to psychoanalytic interpretations of nazism and fascism. My objective is to examine the recoding of nazism and fascism as what Wilhelm Reich describes as "the distorted and diverted *homosexual* and *sadistic* feelings created by fascism," to what Freud observed as the "pleasure of being beaten," and the neodecadentists' visualization of such sadomasochistic economies.[64] However, by focusing on the resistance to bourgeois moralism or puritanism, the neodecadentists reveal that desire in psychoanalytic theory is configured as a desire for evil, one that is directed against the law, yet also in the name of the law. This desire for evil comes as a by-product of a dialectical model of interpretation that operates on the most rigid moralism (the sacrificial logic of desire) and the most rigid discipline—demanding the repression first of sexual desires, then of social desires, and finally constituting desire as a desire for repression. According to psychoanalytic theory, this repression does not come without side effects; I refer here to the later theoretical writings of Freud, in which repression recodes the original articulation of desire as a form of acting out. Since we cannot make sense out of presence (desire for the other, becoming other), we detach ourselves from it or repress the fact that we are always within it (always desiring the other, always unable to grasp the present), in order to master it. Thus the desire for the other is sub-limated into desire for power. This project, of course, as Freud posits in *Civilization and Its Discontents*, is a complete failure, since the more we try to control the other the more it withdraws. According to Freud, this results in a lashing out at all those figurative metaphors we have chosen to represent presence, desire, and otherness. The problem here seems to be that the only relationship that psychoanalysis avows between the representation, desire, and the real is first a sadistic desire to consume it, and second the reactionary desire to destroy it. The cycle of the repression of desire churned into the lust for knowledge kills in turn the objects it is fascinated by. As a consequence the neodecadent filmmakers and theorists transform all sexual relations into masochistic and sadistic enactments, all conflicts into hysterical or psychotic out-breaks, and all desire into a desire for control over the feminine (as the figure of the real), which amounts to the suppression of more radical and revolutionary renderings of culture. In the context of such thinking, nazism and fascism are read as an outbreak of excessive femininity.

In postwar neodecadent films this vision of man fighting to preserve the form and hygiene of his body from what appears to be the danger of dissolving into femi-ninity, therefore, returns him to the role of a moral victim in a play of good against evil. The femme fatale, whom Jean Baudrillard calls "the projective artifact of male hysteria," is now dressed up as a nazi, is reinstalled in a binary economy, a Manichean vision of the world. She is once again reduced to what Lacan calls a "symptom of man," that is, she marks the site of abjection, reflecting all the undesirable qualities that man wishes to expel from himself—violence, sexual perversion, sexual ambigu-ity, homosexuality, bad history, and bad faith. Yet, because she operates within a logic of attraction/repulsion, she represents the unsymbolizable, man's attraction to the products of his own abjection, as well as a sense of presence that always escapes him. Thus the femme fatale finally serves to mask the site where binary economies collapse. She marks the limit of desire, the point at which desire "schizes" into a desire for con-trol and a desire to transgress all social and moral orders—a desire to become other and at the same time consume otherness.[65]

The films of Rainer Werner Fassbinder provide an example of this attempt to transgress models of control (dominant male discourse and patriarchal institutions) by submitting oneself to conventional modes of seduction, enchantment, subversion, and bourgeois decadence. Often for Fassbinder, the desire for transgression that is projected onto the femmes fatales represents a failed desire—the male protagonists in *Veronika Voss, Lili Marleen, The Marriage of Maria Braun, Lola,* and *The Station Mas-ter's Wife* emblematize this image of failure; they are impotent, duped, seduced, and abandoned, yet the fatale figure, like Lola or Maria Braun, discovers that, as Anton Kaes puts it, "she was never more than an object of exchange in a transaction between two men."[66] Despite the rather traditional depiction of the femme fatale in these same films (their mimicking of Dietrich's low voice, her singing off key, her blonde hair, and her cold indifference), Fassbinder draws attention to the fact that the cultural obsession with Dietrichesque femmes fatales disrupts notions of historical context or periodicity. By repeating the image and glamour of the prewar femme fatale in the context of the war and the postwar period, Fassbinder establishes a chronological nexus between the time depicted in these films—from prewar Germany to postwar and even contemporary politics. By substantiating such aesthetic and political continuities he questions historical projects that set out to disengage fascism from the present. Critics like Saul Friedländer contest that such films mythologize history, turning it into kitsch melodramas, and therefore, according to David Bathrick, miss the point of Fassbinder's representation of German history in the light of Hollywood spectacle. Referencing 1920s and 1930s European adaptations of Hollywood aesthetics, Fassbinder restores German history to capitalist (fascist and bourgeois) modernism and, more importantly, problematizes what Bathrick calls the "mythical historical divide, [by refusing to present] history as having a clean break with the hegemonic structures of the fascist everyday."[67] However, in his questioning of German *Kulturpolitik*, especially as it relates to coming to terms with Germany's nazi past, woman functions as a vehicle for male desire, driving these films to their tragic conclusions. Because women become the means through which one man can seduce another, they bear the marks of failed desires, betrayal, and corruption. Although the figure of the femme fatale in Fassbinder's films exemplifies the disempowerment of women (Germany and feminine sexuality), the femme fatale continues to function as a form of fatal feminism.

In order to establish themselves as "il sublime spirituale e l'eroico," nazi and fascist rhetoricians necessitated the construction of their others. This is not to say that nazism and fascism created identical discourses of otherness; however, women, Jews, and homosexuals were principal among these. However, nazi and fascist rhetoricians also share a paternal signifier that accompanies their self-inscription in a tragic-romantic narrative (*il sublime spirituale e l'eroico*), which depends on the invisible conspiracy of the other. Slavoj Žižek articulates this conspiracy as "a mysterious power of Jews to manipulate events, to pull the strings behind the scenes."[68] Women and Jews were deposited in the site of pure evil (of negativity) as the corrosion of the social fabric, the loss of identity in the tide of communism and Freudianism (the feminine mass), the loss of a monumental (historical) point of reference, dissolving a cultural identification and its romantic narrative. However, it is not enough simply to see this process of othering in operation: as Žižek concludes, the "function of [this] ideological fantasy was to mask the inconstancy, the fact that society [or the national social] did not exist [as a unified entity both racially and culturally], and thus compensated ... for its failed identification."[69] The national imaginary necessitated the "big Other," the big evil or the big myth in order not only to project its own paranoia (of its own impotence or impurity) but also to serve as a border from which it could draw itself in opposition. According to Jean-François Lyotard:

If there is a terror in Nazism, it is exerted internally among the "pure," who are always suspected of not being pure enough. They cleanse themselves of suspicion by exempting themselves from all impurity, through oaths, denunciations, pogroms, or final solutions: the Jews and others are not suspect, they are already judged.[70]

I want to distinguish Lyotard's logic from that of Lacan or the neo-Lacanian theory of Slavoj Žižek, who argues that "It should be clear, now, precisely how anti-Semitism and Fascist corporatism form the two sides of one and the same coin. In its repudiation of Judeo-democratic 'abstract universalism,' as opposed to the notion of society qua harmonious organic place, corporatism is inspired by the very insight that many a democrat prefers to shirk."[71] Although both Lyotard and Žižek critique nazism for predicating communal identification on some shared guilt or, more precisely, on the fetishistic disavowal of this guilt, while Lyotard inveighs against the binary model of pure/impure, Žižek suggests the omnipresence of this model, namely, that it is fundamental to the formation of all communities, which means that all communities are intrinsically fascist. What distinguishes Lyotard from Žižek is that, for Lyotard, fascism is an ongoing process that needs to be combatted, while Žižek posits that fascism is a universal model that will inevitably be repeated. The very theoretic model (fascist constructions of desire and processes of identification) that Lyotard sees as complicit with fascism, capitalism, and the negation of desire is the same model that Žižek protects as universal (the threat of castration which thereby enslaves men and women to a fear of their own potential failure or loss, turning us all into the modern Oedipus). This law is simply one that justifies a preexisting hierarchy, by which I mean capitalist or fascist modes of legitimization. What is at stake here is not simply the feeling of having a proper place, of having an investment or claim in the community; it is the undermining of critical and creative discourses for the purpose of maintaining the structure of the symbolic law of repression. In fact, this universal Oedipalization renders us impotent onlookers in our own cultural and political interactions. The real truth behind the modern Oedipus is that he serves as a means of internalizing the law of submission and repression and the relinquishing of desire, so as not to upset the order of things. Moreover, Zygmunt Bauman points out that primitivist models (utilized by both Freud and Žižek, e.g., primal hordes, primitive communities) are inefficient as tools for understanding modern genocide.[72] Models that are predicated on the hatred for or resentment of the other interpret political mechanisms in terms of human individual psychology, rather than delegitimizing the role of repression in the social engineering of such mass annihilations, exposing the connection of repression to moral drives, humanist discourses, civilizing processes, and their radical indifference toward otherness. Lyotard explains that this disjuncture of discursive identifications operates outside of any common law or language (whether Oedipal, primitive or otherwise). He writes: "My law kills them who have no relevance to it. My death is due to their law, to which I owe nothing. Delegitimation is complete, it confirms the suspicion cast upon the we that supposedly assures the linking of the prescription onto the norm, namely, that it is a fiction"—an Oedipal lie that masks the violence of capital, mass slaughter, and senseless repression (*The Differend*, 101).

Masquerading Marlene

Unlike Ettore Scola's *A Particular Day* (*Una giornata particulare*), which attempts to be historically correct by representing the repudiation of homosexuality and the reduction of the role of women to a biological function during the fascist period, the films of Bertolucci, Visconti, and Fosse treat fascism psychologically, returning to a discourse of role reversals, as well as to the historical discourse of the exceptionality of nazism, fascism, and the "Final Solution." As a consequence, the spectator is liberated from any association or identification with the representation of the fascist or nazi; yet these aestheticized visualizations of nazi and fascist sexuality seduce the spectator, drawing him or her into a sadomasochistic libidinal economy. Here the attraction is not ideological but aesthetic: fascism is turned into a violently beautiful fashion show. This retrofitting or recycling of the image of fascism or nazism, as Baudrillard argues, "has taken over and imposed its own immanent ephemeral logic; an immoral logic without depth, beyond good and evil, beyond truth and falsity; a logic of the extermination of its own referent, a logic of the implosion of meaning in which the message disappears on the horizon of the medium" (*Evil Demon of Images*, 23). This aestheticizing or eroticizing of the image renders the relationship of victim to victimizer unclear. In fact, it shifts the model from a discourse of good versus evil to one of self versus other, inscribing this revised relationship, of course, into a libidinal economy—either masochistic or sadistic. The problem with this sexualization of fascism is that it always returns to a psychoanalytic model, which normalizes perversity even as it advances repression as an antidote to violence.

Yet, while these cinematic forms of decadence disrupt the filmic discourse of authenticity (they no longer attempt to mimic the real event), they maintain a modicum of critique by debunking moral humanism. They implicate bourgeois or moral humanism in what is portrayed as secret homosexual, sadistic, and incestuous desires. In effect, this aestheticization of nazism and fascism allows for extreme violence to become the preeminent form of magnificence, transforming the neorealist identification with the victims (whether pure or impure) into the visualization of the victimizer, the nazi, the fascist, the sadist, the torturer, and so forth. What is assumed as a subversive position with respect to bourgeois politics and moralism, via its ambiguous physical representations of gender boundaries, turns into the fetishization of the nazi. The spectacular fantasizing and mimicking of the "degenerative" tendencies of women, the femme fatale in particular, amounts to fetishizing the feminine man dressed in nazi regalia. The satire of feminine sexiness in *The Damned* and *Cabaret* reconstructs the feminine as an exaggerated performance of seduction: the masquerade of Helmut Berger as Marlene Dietrich, whose performance seduces only his own mother, and the campiness of Joel Grey (embodying feminine masculinity), who acts out a fictive marriage with an ape—referring simultaneously to Darwin's theory of evolution in collaboration with the racial discourse of Weininger, Goebbels, and Lombroso—recalls only the perversity and role-changing of Dietrich in the *Blonde Venus*: her masculine drag performance, her performance as a helpless woman, and her costuming as an ape. Hence this association of the feminine with nazism and fascism as a means of both destroying its extremely masculine image and empowering feminine seduction, as Freud argues, "makes women [or men dressed as women] acceptable as sexual objects," yet only in order, as Luce Irigaray responds, to "desire itself through the other."[73]

In usurping the position of feminine sexuality, the effeminate fascist male can be read as a disavowal of the law of castration (an alleged form of masochism). But his schizophrenic identification with the femme fatale, as a drag queen, a lesbian, a transvestite, or an effeminate male homosexual, radically strips sexiness from the female body. He reduces the body to an artificial parameter in order to coopt her seductivity for himself. In fact, it is the feminine double who is consistently eliminated from the narrative: in *The Conformist*, Anna, who represents Marcello's desire to express his homosexuality, is assassinated by the fascists in his place. Similarly, Visconti's Martin literally forces his mother to commit suicide. The suicide immediately follows an Oedipal scene signifying his rebirth as replacement of the mother. In "Good-bye Berlin," as Mizejewski notes, "the apparent hetero-sexuality and promiscuity of the Sally Bowles character is sent into a spin through a variety of displacements and repressions" (*Divine Decadence*, 86). What has otherwise been read as a masochistic process of identifying with the mother in the place of the father, therefore transmutes into a form of sadism, defeating the masochist's desire itself. Sexuality is thus reduced to a symptom of masochistic mothering and sadistic Oedipal fathering; this process amounts to not only the nullification of the mother but also, as Lyotard explicates, "the concomitant destruction of every eloquent emotion [especially that of feminine pleasure]."[74]

The Damned reflects an amalgamation of aesthetic styles (Wagnerian opera, kitsch, cabaret, and decadence), monumental postures, and images of decadent sexuality. Yet rather than representing a nostalgic lament for the demise of the aristocracy, high culture, and high humanism, it is more damning of these cultural codes. As the Italian title implies, it depicts the fall of the gods; however, it does not replicate the monumental tragic myth of the German *Götterdämmerung*—the last of Wagner's Ring Cycle, in which the fate of the gods is sealed—rather it presents this fall as a form of decline, or degeneration. The film begins with the mimicry and mockery of both Lola Lola and her song "Kinder, heut' Abend such' ich mir was aus" and the image of Marlene Dietrich as she appeared in *Blonde Venus*, via the character Martin Von Essenbeck, who performs in drag for the family on the occasion of his grandfather's birthday (supposedly occurring while the Reichstag burns). The drag scene itself presents a multiplicity of contextual and intertextual significations, introducing the topic of the "feminization" of the "up"-coming generation of Germans and also the male attraction to the *richtigen Mann*—as Helmut Berger expresses this desire for *einen Mann*. Martin (played by Berger) redefines the meaning of the song once again, turning it into a campy parody of Hitler's SS as well as of Dietrich's sexual appeal. Martin's flagrant decadence marks the degeneration of ("German") morals of the "third" generation of Germans. Visconti's rendering of the three generations of von Essenbecks delineates the "progressive" allegorical breakdown of Germany. The "historical" allegory is mirrored in the (de)generation of the von Essenbeck family: the old aristocratic "head" of the family, the industrial capitalist, Joachim von Essenbeck (whose name reflects his historical "Germanness"); his son, Baron Konstantin (the last emperor), who is a supposed leader of the SA; Martin, the third generation, the nazi or SS prototype. The first generation is presented as Kaiser-like, aristocratic, and family-oriented. The second generation is presented by Joachim's second oldest son, Konstantin, who appears as politically aggressive, lecherously decadent, yet excessively masculine even though he is bisexual and transvestite. Konstantin embodies the values of the SA and their violent takeover of the state and private industry. The third generation (or Reich), represented by Martin, is effeminate, sadistic, yet clandestinely violent. Martin is depicted as a troubled child who is in constant psychological turmoil. Both the second and third generation of von Essenbecks masquerade as women (the masquerade of the feminine), which culminates in the fatalistic sacrifice of the image of the feminine: the members of the SA are slaughtered at an "orgy" where they parade as women; Elizabeth (the daughter of Joachim) dies in Dachau because of her husband's affiliation with the socialist party; Liza (a little Jewish girl who lives in an apartment where Martin rents a room) commits suicide because she has been "defiled" by Martin; and Sophie (resembling the photographs of Dietrich hanging on Martin's wall) and her lover are forced to commit suicide. Visconti's "confused" homosexual (third Reich) character is feminized as a transvestite, an androgynous pedophile, an (Oedipal) rapist, and also as a nazi. Martin, who inherits not only the family fortune and industry but also the image of the nazi, changes costume from that of Marlene Dietrich to that of the SS officer without changing his sexuality. Visconti suggests that it is the military uniform that "covers" up this femininity.

It is in this masquerade of the homosexual (transvestite) economy that the feminine is satirized as a place of perversity, excess, defilement (as in the case of the little Jewish girl), and most of all death. Woman is a defiled or discarded victim, and the homosexual sadist is all that persists in her stead. This parody of woman as excess constructs female sexiness as masochistic performance, "divine decadence." According to Mizejewski, "the parodic drag symbolizes the dread of female biology" (*Divine Decadence*, 85). Ironically, the transvestite is placed in the site of liberation, the liberation from motherhood, which Mizejewski criticizes as a displacement of a misogynistic discourse. Martin cross-dresses and mimics the image of his own mother, displacing her from the role of motherhood, the "biological dread," to that of the sterile and fatal femme. For Visconti's Sophie, sex is a means of manipulating others and empowering herself, even at the expense of her son and her lover. She seduces Martin just as she would Friedrich (her lover); when she states, "I know Martin's desire," she essentially confirms her ability to control him via sexual blackmail. This disassociation from the role of motherhood allows Martin to break the Oedipal taboo by forcing his "excessively sexual mother" to satisfy his Oedipal desire, and then once he has "defiled his place of origin" he does not blind himself in horror, but rebirths his "self" as a nazi—a feminized yet misogynistic order.

Unlike Visconti's Martin and Fosse's (Isherwood's) Brian Roberts, who "actively" engage in sexual politics, Bertolucci's (Moravia's) Marcello remains a spectator of the "sexual act," not only of the primal scene but also of the reenactment of this scene symbolized by Anna's affair with the fascist official. As Angela Dalle Vacche explains, "Marcello's yearning for statue-like immobility grows out of the need for a heterosexual façade, perhaps as a symptom of deep horror for the heterosexuality of parents seen in sexual intercourse" (*Body in the Mirror*, 85). This statuelike image derives from Marcello's desire to emulate the icons of heroic fascism and the subsequent fascist or bourgeois ethical values (which he essentially perceives as the same) as well as from a profound disgust for heterosexual intercourse as unclean. This spectacle of monumental purity—which is constantly being put into question by Marcello's "illicit" sexual desires—directly contrasts the feminine uncleanliness that can be seen in the

Martin (Helmut Berger) oversees the marriage of his mother, Sophie (Ingrid Thulin), to her lover, Friedrich (Dirk Bogarde), just before he forces them to commit suicide in *The Damned*.

confusion of "il grido" (as the feminine vocalization of sexual pleasure) with that which Marcello translated to a discourse of pain, "ammazzare un gatto" (killing a cat). This diametric opposition is repeated in the rendering of Marcello; as Dalle Vacche points out, Marcello's gestures are confined and resemble "the straitjacket position assumed by Marcello's father in the asylum," in contrast to the sensuality and dancing feminine bodies of Giulia and of Anna, who also mimics Dietrich in her gestures and alludes to a certain sexual promiscuity in which Marcello will not participate but only watch (*Body in the Mirror*, 87–88). Although I subscribe to Dalle Vacche's interpretation of Anna's scream against the window of Marcello's car as a reference to the face of Medusa, I do not read this stare as that which reinforces male monumentality (turning men into graven images), nor one that invokes male fear of castration, but as the covering of feminine pleasure. The face of Medusa covers up the "ethical" male's "dread of feminine biology" and sensuous sexual pleasure. Thus sexual pleasure is read as both feminine and nefarious. Marcello relinquishes his homosexual proclivity to the monumental (sadistic) law of fascism. However, Marcello's sexual desire is metaphorically expressed through Anna's sexuality; and Marcello participates (vicariously) in Anna's sexual confusion—both illicitly heterosexual and lesbian (or homosexual in the case of Marcello)—and its allegorical refraction in her political "engagement." Because she submits to fascism (while he prostitutes himself to "normalcy," against both his rearing and sexual impulses), her political conviction (liberal or socialist) is repudiated as sterile by the filmic emplotment. While Anna's stance is presented as sterile, like her marriage to Professor Quadri, Marcello's fascist and masculinist discourse is refigured as a masochistic disguise for homosexual desire.

In *The Conformist* this process of doubling, which traditionally serves as a device of othering or projecting the "darker" nature of one character onto another, operates where Anna becomes the scapegoat, suffering the consequences for Marcello's desired sexual transgression. Her death marks his failed line of escape. But Marcello reacts by squelching his homosexuality, thus regenerating this passion into reactive sadistic politics. For Marcello (and the fascist man), women function as an outlet for the expression not only of his (man's) desire, but also for his homosexual desire, while he (man) remains passive and secretly homosexual. Maria Macciocchi argues that the "impotenza dell'omosessualitá la propensione pederastica dei nazisti e la fame di donne (che non fossero mogli e madri)" ("impotence of homosexuality manifests itself in the pederastic propensity of the nazis and the hunger of women who were not wives and mothers").[75] Ironically, it is the image of woman and all her sensuous aspects that must be destroyed in order to return man to an order where fascist ideals and homosociality still prevail.

Although in Fosse's *Cabaret* the male homosexual is presented as protagonist (Brian), identification with the character positions the spectator as viewing female sexuality through the specific homosexual milieu. Within this sexual role playing, the feminine is cast in the role of the sexual deviant and impure, yet she symbolizes the decadence of the homosexual community. Unlike identification with Marcello, which involves a guilty self-hatred, Brian symbolizes, according to Mizejewski, the "moral (normal) witness to nazism" (*Divine Decadence*, 220). Hence the antifascist message is intellectualized and articulated through the eyes of a homosexual male. The only failure in placing Brian as the "hero" is, in fact, his homosexuality. *Cabaret* itself begins as a montage of Liza Minnelli (Sally Bowles) singing "Mein leiber Herr" to a transvestite, Joel Grey. This carnival of role reversals directly recalls the cabaret scene in *The Blue Angel* and its mimicry in *The Damned*. Yet here Minnelli appears as controlling sexual authority, upstaging the other male transvestite performers who parody her own feminine sexuality: her masculinized handsomeness as well as her costume recall the previous performances of the sadomasochistic mise-en-scéne as acted by both Dietrich and Berger, only to decontextualize them. Fosse turns the Dietrich role not into a confused and resentful lesbian (as in the case of *The Conformist*) but instead a parody of excessive feminine sexuality; she no longer looks for the *einen Mann* but falls in love with a homosexual (Brian) who pronounces her as "fatal as an after dinner mint," thus neutralizing if not delegitimizing her portrayal of sexual authority. The role of the femme fatale is re-represented as a sham, and in this misogynist discourse male love for men becomes a profound ideal, where aesthetic beauty belongs to man

Marcello (Jean-Louis Trintignant) watches, impotently, as Anna (Dominique Sanda) pleads for her life after witnessing the execution of her husband, Professor Quadri, in Bernardo Bertolucci's *The Conformist*.

as both the object and subject of desire—and the feminine plays the role of a foil or an aestheticized fool mocking her own lack (and grotesqueness) in terms of this "campy" sexual economy. As Mizejewski notes, the aesthetics of camp are antifeminine. In fact this satirical feminism operates on the concept that Sontag elaborates in "Notes on Camp":

> What is most beautiful about men is something feminine, what is most beautiful in women is something masculine, woman [is seen] as a "big-playing-role" [hence] the taste for androgyny [the feminized SS officer] merges with excessive femme [fatal], in the articulation of gesture and pose. (279)

However, the role-playing is a spectacle in which men dress as women, and women are dressed as Sadean dominatrices and in monkey suits, directly referring back to *Blonde Venus*, where Dietrich's cabaret act requires her to emerge from a monkey costume. But *Cabaret* shifts the referent from the "savageness" of Dietrich to a pseudo-Darwinist narrative that links women to Jews and to homosexuals in a discourse of inferiority and impurity. Hence the Blonde Venus, the feminine, the Jew, and the monkey converge as symptomatic expressions of impurity (racially, sexually, and "scientifically"). *Cabaret*'s musical numbers signify the nazification of society, from "*Willkommen*," to "*Mien lieber Herr*," to the most chilling song, "*Tomorrow Belongs to Me*," where ordinary people join in with the Hitler Youth. This last song evokes a certain authenticity of nazi pageantry, as opposed to the complete artificiality of the cabaret. This "sublime" scene, however, is followed by Joel Grey's parody of nazism—his dabbing on of some mud to imitate Hitler's mustache before he sings, "If you could see her through my eyes—she wouldn't look Jewish at all." The juxtaposition of the two songs marks the sexual, racial, and moral purity of the young Aryan boy who moves a crowd of people to sing "*Tomorrow Belongs to Me*" as contrasted with the seedy decadence of the Kit Kat Klub. Fosse suggests that this image of purity (sexless nazis) is far more seductive than the overdetermined lewd sexuality and sensuality of the club—the sound of the communal voice of "*Tomorrow Belongs to Me*" becomes viscerally seductive, while the words "life is a cabaret, old chum," sung by a group of goose-stepping dancers in drag, is presented as lewd satire. The figure of woman, however, is returned the grotesque (a site of decay), while men become sexualized and romanticized by usurping feminine sensuality—beyond the spectacle. Therefore the male homosexual replaces the sexual desirability of the feminine and reduces the threat of feminine dread (carnal entrapment) to nothingness, by eliminating her (and her other role as mother) from the sexual economy.

Indeed, these neodecadent interpretations of the sexual politics of fascism and nazism adopt a Sadean model. While seemingly choosing a feminine (masochistic) model of feminine excess as a line of escape, they attempt to evade the logic of the law, yet they ultimately return to it as the embodiment of sadism, cannibalizing the feminine. That is, the celebration of the decadent, sterile woman dovetails with the

In *Cabaret*, Liza Minnelli and Joel Grey sing a very campy version of "Money Makes the World Go Around" at the Kit Kat Klub.

project of sadism. Within the Deleuzian understanding of the Sadean economy, it follows that men belong to nature only via "social conservatism" and are subject to sadistic violence only insofar as they depart from their "essential" anarchic nature, while women become the sadistic victims par excellence since they are victimized for upholding their "true nature."[76] By deterritorializing the feminine body only to reterritorialize the masculine power of transgression and seduction, they return the visual and sexual pleasure of sadism by consuming the other—infinitely returning woman to a pulp fiction.

One of the most disturbing aspects of Visconti's, Bertolucci's, and Fosse's reading of nazism, fascism, and feminine sexuality is that it does not allow women any means of subjective identification, not even traditionally through the male subject position. Women are returned to the economy of sexual and social stratification, where power is determined by the implementation of pure agency, causing the object through which power affirms itself to disappear. This indifference for the object, which empowers the self's pure agency, is illustrated in Freud's translation of orgasm into a discharge of tension, which thereby effectuates the disappearance of the object of desire. It is the installing of desire into the logic of singularity (the construction of a bounded individual) that heightens the self as the sole agent of desire who acts on objects, thus reducing desire to object relations. Here the psychoanalytic model tips over into sadism. Similar to de Sade's institutionalization of power, the nazi conspicuously makes the law, as well as reason, serve his ends. And this illustrates the cynical resolution of all three films: *The Damned*, where Martin rapes and murders his mother and his mother's husband as a means of exerting his own power; *The Conformist*, where Marcello turns on his only friend, accusing him of being a fascist; and *Cabaret*, where Sally not only stays in nazi Germany but also tailors her performance to a more conservative model, transforming the sexually implicit song *"Mien leiber Herr"* to *"If They Could See Me Now."* In effect these films, designed to demythify bourgeois moralism and its compliance with fascism and nazism, reproduce decadent images of fascism and nazism, which relocate the spawning of fascist desire in the upper classes. In addition, they reproduce the feminized image of decadence and perversity and imply that fascism and nazism can be read in terms of an Oedipal economy—within the sexual drama of the family. By Oedipalizing fascism, these films suggest, like psychoanalysis itself, that desire can only be expressed as a form of sadism or masochism, and that fascist meaning, like all meaning, must be predicated on sexual difference. And since fascism is considered an aberration, or a form of social perversity, it must also express itself as sexually perverse. This insistence on sexualizing fascism not only keeps fascism alive in the hearts and minds of popular culture and its sexual imaginary; it also squelches more radical critiques of both sexual politics and fascist political economies (such as those of Pasolini, Cavani, and Wertmüller) in favor of the structural apparatus of repression. The scandal of camp (its flamboyant satire of bourgeois models of aesthetic beauty, icons of sexuality, and sublime desires), similar to the initial scandal of psychoanalysis (its scandalizing Victorian notions of sexuality, and sexual desire), is paradoxical: at the same time that camp and psychoanalytic theory posit biological polymorphism, social stereotyping, and an all-pervasive social impurity, they produce uncompromisingly rigid formulations of masculinity and femininity, thereby collapsing strategies of fascism and antifascism. That is, the real scandal of camp and psychoanalytic theory extends beyond its criticism of bourgeois (Victorian) notions of sex, gender, hygiene, symbolic language, and humanity and reinstates what it perceives as repressive (fascistic) apparatuses at the very heart of humanity, language, and social and sexual relations.

3. *Salò*: A Fatal Strategy

The worst aspect of the sufferings of the inmates is not the pain endured but the pain furiously desired by others. Pain resulting from sickness or accidents does not seem as horrible; the depth of horror is in the will of those who command it. A world in which many individuals suffer great pain but in which the common goal was to fight pain would be soothing. Degradation, ignominy, cowardliness multiplied—destroying little by little the fortress that reason is at the root of the civilized world—disturb us more violently than does raw suffering.[1]

—Georges Bataille

What makes fascism dangerous is its molecular or micropolitical power, for it is a mass movement: a cancerous body rather than a totalitarian organism. . . . Only microfascism provides an answer to the global question: Why does desire desire its own repression, how can it desire its own repression? The masses certainly do not passively submit to power; they do not "want" to be repressed, in any kind of masochistic hysteria; nor are they tricked by an ideological lure. [Yet this danger is also] turning to destruction, abolition pure and simple, the passion of abolition.

—Gilles Deleuze and Félix Guattari,
A Thousand Plateaus

Released weeks after Pier Paolo Pasolini's brutal murder on 2 November 1975, *Salò* remains shrouded by the spectacle of his death. Because it was his final film, *Salò*'s posthumous release elicited an array of biographical readings, ranging from that of Rocco Mangia, the defense lawyer for Pino Pelosi (Pasolini's alleged murderer), who used the film as evidence of Pasolini's so-called sadistic intent toward his client, to that of Italo Calvino, who likened Pasolini to "the perverted gentlemen of the court of

Salò," since, like these gentlemen, "money conditioned [Pasolini's] relationship to the subproletariat youth."[2] Lifetime friends such as Giuseppe Zigaina considered *Salò* Pasolini's last will and testament.[3] According to his many critics, *Salò* was symbolic proof of Pasolini's moral depravity (that he was a sadist), and to his sympathizers it was a sign of his suicidal despair (that he was a masochist). Enzo Siciliano, Pasolini's biographer, even went so far as to ask, "Was his murder a suicide by proxy?"[4] And, as Maria Antonietta Macciocchi reflects: "Society took its revenge in the same manner in which [his murder] was committed, [it was] a public execution carried out in a spectacularly bloody manner so that all might see and understand."[5]

Yet what remains questionable, if not dubious, is the practice of understanding or making sense of his death in light of his work. The violent spectacle of his disfigured body, which appeared on the front page of almost every European newspaper, became the model for misreading Pasolini's private and intellectual life. This excessive biographical interpretation of *Salò* by critics and biographers reveals an obsessive search for the "truth" of Pasolini's sexual desire, or sexual practice as it was inscribed in his films. What strikes me as sinister about such readings (did he deserve it? did he ask for it?) is that underneath these moral judgments lies the tendency to eroticize the sadistic violence of *Salò*, and the violent circumstances of Pasolini's death. The sexual scandal of Pasolini's homosexuality and even the violent circumstances of his death have been used to obfuscate the more radical implications of Pasolini and his work. As a consequence, the anxiety caused by Pasolini's "disturbing" representation of fascism as sadism becomes foreclosed. Rather than acknowledge Pasolini's scrutiny of the limits of neocapitalism—its antihistorical, immoral, asexual, and inhuman mechanisms—moral condemnations of Pasolini's sexuality evade critical engagement with his work, by turning Pasolini (and with him all of his work) into an aberration, a monster (abnormal and abject). Georges Bataille exposes the logic of this type of mechanism when he writes: "In judging so violently, one subtracts the monsters from the possible. One implicitly accuses them of exceeding the limit of the possible instead of seeing that their excess, precisely, defines this limit" ("Reflections on the Executioner and the Victim," 19). This relegation of Pasolini's body of work to the abject removes his ideological derivations from the ranks of legitimate Italian political and cultural analysis.

Pasolini's dislocation from institutions and their ideological framework has posed a problem for critics who wish to situate him in terms of preestablished political discourses. The impulse to codify Pasolini's work in ideological models (Marxist, Freudian, feminist, conservative, etc.) has often resulted in the analysis of Pasolini ad hominem. Beverly Allen writes, "Pasolini insists on his own marginality," and Giuseppe Zigaina reflects that "Pasolini always and invariably wrote about himself."[6] Similarly, Millicent Marcus declares, "He was a narcissist caught in the bind of trying to lose himself sexually in another," and William Van Watson labels him one of the "self-destructive bourgeoisie, not an Oedipus, but a Laius figure, a man with power," while Alberto Moravia returns Pasolini to politics, yet the debased (emotional and personal) politics of "comunismo sentimentale."[7] Whether narcissistic, masochistic, or marginal, these interpretations of Pasolini (the man) castrate Pasolini's intellectual work and his intellectual thinking, reducing him, as Paolo Valesio suggests, to a symptom of his class, his power, or his sexual desires.[8] I wish to read Pasolini against his critics and to reposition *Salò* within the context of Pasolini's ideological and political commitment to revolutionary politics and, most importantly, his radical critique of moral and political complicity.

Pasolini, the monster, the heretic, the *scrittore scomodo* (discomforting writer), and the filmmaker of *cinema impopolare* (unpopular cinema), haunts the institutionalization of the scandalizing process, casting doubt on narratives of transcendence (progress and hope). Instead of repeating the spectacle of scandal as a moralizing gesture, Pasolini ironically mimics the gesture of scandal so as to interrupt its moralizing effect. For Pasolini, morality, in the age of neocapitalism, is scandalous. When asked by Philippe Bouvard if *Salò* would scandalize, Pasolini answered, "I believe to give scandal is a duty, to be scandalized is a pleasure, and to refuse to be scandalized is moralism."[9] His haunting aesthetic of scandal cannot be reduced to a symptom of his sexual anxiety, as I would argue it is in the neodecadent films of Visconti, Bertolucci, and Fosse. Unlike *The Damned, The Conformist, 1900,* and *Cabaret,* where transgression is represented through the return of the repressed, *Salò* renders the act of transgression as institutionalized. Pasolini's cinema as well as his intellectual writings scrutinizes the integrity of self-contained disciplines (literature, film, history, politics), histories (bourgeois, fascist, colonialist, capitalist), discourses (Marxist, psychoanalytic, Nietzschean, semiotic, feminist, Sadean, mythic), and binary economies (good and evil, Western and non-Western, pure and impure, affirmative and negative) by recuperating the violence of disassociation, the process of cutting out; that is, he decodes constrictive narrativizing projects. While theoretical discourses of Marxism, postcolonialism, feminism, psychoanalysis, and semiotics have often been considered distinctly separate if not conflicting, Pasolini pirates some of their critical perspectives and deterritorializes them via a strategy of juxtaposition. Thus his particular version of pastiche does not constitute a synthetic model of heterogeneous ideas and disciplines—a weaving of textual and theoretical discourses into a multicultural, feminist, or Marxist movement of transcendence. Rather, his endless referencing and dissimulating of myths, icons, and historical narratives generates a narrative or ideological *spargamos*, it induces a process of spontaneous combustion that produces a hermeneutic explosion. If one follows the logic of his texts rather than impose preexisting and ad-hominem ideological models on them, Pasolini's filmic presentations of mythic narratives emerge as radical refusals of paradigms of transcendence.

Pasolini's constant decoding of fascism, however, also deterritorializes its spaciotemporal limits, uncovering its incestuous links to capitalism (fraternal) and moralism (paternal, Oedipal). This radical deterritorialization delimits fascism and reopens the fascist networking of disciplines of power. For Pasolini, like Deleuze and Guattari, fascism is not a self-contained totalitarian state apparatus but a war-machine, an assemblage of desire that infects every discipline it encounters. Driven by desire for radical purification, fascism expresses itself as unlimited destruction.[10] And for Pasolini this cancerous force persists in the "desire for repression, the passion for abolition." Many critics, however, have accused Pasolini of inflating fascism as a referent for all social evil, an analogy for not only modernization but also bourgeois moralism, neocapitalist consumerism, and sexual politics after the "sexual revolution." But detractors of Pasolini's representations of fascism, like Franco Ferrucci, who accuses Pasolini of "applying the term fascism to everything that he doesn't like, yet always placing the bourgeoisie as the origin of all evil," and more sophisticated arguments, such as James Roy McBean's critique of Pasolini for failing to establish his "well-intended progressive intellectual schema" in *Salò* and *Teorema*, neglect both Pasolini's radical critique of neocapitalism and his reproach of "progressive" discourses of resistance.[11] In spite of the new Italian constitution (1946–48), predicated on *defascistizzazione*, the process was never really completed. Many fascist laws and codes that contradicted the premise of the new constitution were never repealed, including the Latern Pact—a concordat between the fascists and the Catholic church that proclaimed Catholicism the official religion of the state and made its education compulsory

In Pasolini's *Salò* (1975), the kidnapped victims are forced to behave as dogs, begging for their supper. Here they are led by the fascist collaborators.

in state schools. Furthermore, despite the foundation of the Italian Republic on the basis of the antifascist resistance, as evidenced in article XII of the constitution—*Articolo delle norme finali di appendice*, where it is written, "è proibita sotto qualunque forma l'apologia o la ricostituzione del disciolto partito fascista"—there were movements such as the MSI (*Movimento Sociale Italiano*), whose chief was a former fascist officer of Mussolini's Republic of Salò (Giorgio Almirante) and "L'Uomo Qualunque" (a.k.a. the *qualunquista* or the common man's movement) mostly composed of former fascists and modeled on the French "boulangistes" of the thirties.[12] In the first election held in the newly formed Italian Republic (1948) these movements gained public recognition and political credence by winning seats in the parliament headed by the Christian Democrat Alcide De Gasperi (who would remain prime minister from the fall of Parri until 1953). Pasolini, as many other Italians on the Left, believed the PCI (Partito Comunista Italiano, under the leadership of Togliatti) to be partly responsible for this victory (of the Right and its industrial sponsors and benefactors), since it was Togliatti's party that compromised the most powerful weapon of the Left (working-class militancy) in the course of deliberations within the antifascist coalition with the Christian Democrats—lasting until 1947 when the Left was expelled from the government by De Gasperi.[13]

Although it was through the ideology of the Italian antifascist resistance movement and, in particular, The Partito Comunista Italiano (which was both anticapitalist and antibourgeois) that Pasolini developed his politics of resistance, he also inveighed against the discrete, self-contained representations of the Left—its moralism and its narrative disengagement from fascism, that is, its disassociation from that which it deemed undesirable, impure, or immoral. In his relentless resistance to the disciplines of power, Pasolini does not endorse any form of complicity with purity, for it is always this desire for rigid purity, in his eyes, that perpetuates the fascist dissemination of power. Instead, he challenges postwar narratives and self-representations by the Left, asking, is it possible to resist fascism by using its own weapons (rigid moralism and rigid discipline); is it possible to resist a force that is in its very nature destabilizing (defies representation, constantly invades other territories)? Finally, in a self-reflective and self-critical mode, Pasolini asks, is it possible to transgress when transgression itself becomes institutionalized?

For Pasolini there are as many points of departure from fascism as there are bottlenecks, intersections with capitalism, bourgeois sexual politics, Catholic morality, and returns. Fascism serves as both a symbolic point of departure, from which he develops lines of escape, and points of inescapable return, in which all lines of escape are themselves lines of destruction and exhaustion. Pasolini distinguishes the fascism he resists or escapes (the old fascism of Mussolini and Hitler) from the new fascism of neocapitalism (an inescapable consumption, the cannibalization of all forms of resistance). This shift from "old fascism," "the decadent Hitlerian period," to "neocapitalist fascism," the neodecadentism of consumer capitalism, reflects the shift in the ordering principles of capitalist economies that Gilles Deleuze outlines as the replacement of what Michel Foucault labeled "disciplinary societies" by "societies of control."[14] The distinction between these two social economies is that in fascist capitalism (disciplined economies) the disruption or explosion of disciplines is still possible, leaving an opening for alterity, whereas with capitalist fascism (economies of control) there is no outside of the confines of dominant culture. The only model of resistance is implosive. For Foucault the separation of prisonlike disciplinary powers is rigid, therefore, the separation or discontinuity from one institution to the other provides the opportunity for resistance or transgression—a falling between the cracks, creating fissures, disruptions—but societies of control are much more fluid. Within these societies power mutates to conform to the flow of capital and exchange.

The first actualization of the fascist war-machine is a network of disciplines (a prison system) whose aim, as Michel Foucault argues, is "to derive the maximum advantages and to neutralize the inconveniences (thefts, interruptions of work, disturbances and cabals) as the forces of production become more concentrated; to protect materials and tools and to master the labour force" (*Discipline and Punish*, 142). This rigid penal system functions as a network of monopolies—enclosed disciplines, enclosed spaces, and disciplinary institutions (factories, schools, hospitals, bureaucracies, states, armies, nuclear families). Here Pasolini anticipates what Baudrillard calls *duopolies*, "a system constantly transcending itself in a perpetual crisis and self-challenge" (*Simulations*, 136). What marks the disappearance of these disciplinary societies, for Pasolini, is the disappearance of the margins caused by the normalization and modulation of individuals who are then transformed into what Deleuze calls "dividuals, and masses, samples, data, markets, or banks" ("Postscript on the Societies of Control," 5). Pasolini's inability to find a utopian space or, for that matter, any place that is untouched by consumerism leads him to believe that modernization is immanent, and that inevitably it will cannibalize all forms of life. Deleuze describes this transformation as the passing of one animal to another, the mole to the serpent; the burrowing network of accumulations (the factory as prison) giving way to the model of the corporation, an infinite modulation. As opposed to the assembled and ordered space of societies of discipline, Deleuze argues "control is short-term and [operates in] rapid rates of turnover, but [it is] also continuous and without limit, while discipline was of long duration, infinite and discontinuous. Man is no longer man enclosed, but *man in debt*" ("Postscript on the Societies of Control", 5). Thus, while the first model is one of a network of disciplines—a moving from one enclosed space to another—the second is that of a virus—"metastable states of universal deformation." Fascism, therefore, permeates the boundaries of all discourse becoming an unlimited process, a pestilent or snakelike corruption.

I trace the metamorphosis of Pasolini's radical critique of fascism and neocapitalism through his distending aesthetics of scandal. Accordingly, I follow Pasolini's scandalous aesthetic turn toward erotic Dionysian otherness (homosexual, transsexual, maternal, subproletariat, animistic). This aesthetic is accompanied by a strategy of juxtaposition in which the mere appearance of sacred otherness upsets disciplinary societies' reactionary desire to devour its difference and, therefore, disrupts the disciplinary mechanics of digestion of difference, homogenization, and historicization, that is, those forces that neutralize anything that threatens to tear down their retaining walls. Yet the transmutation of disciplinary societies into societies of control causes the disappearance of this Dionysian force (as well as its potential to rupture the fascist war-machine). The strategy of conquest in societies of control supersedes the confrontational politics of discipline—the direct violence of slavery, colonialism, genocide, imprisonment, forced labor, exile—with its politics of commercializing difference. This strategy of radical deterritorialized consumption operates on the indirect violence of merchandising, selling otherness (exoticism, tropical tans, foreign lands) and fashioning itself as difference (radical chic, revolution rock, guerrilla girls, modern primitives, gangsta rap). Yet what remains crawling under the skin of this multicultural global economy is the corporate mergers, hostile takeovers, United Fruit companies and the OPEC nations, and, bigger still, the massive debt that constantly reminds us of our responsibility in the form of an installment check.

The fascist organization of society into disciplinary institutions, therefore, transforms from what Paul Virilio labels "the materialization of the war machine" to "materialized war."[15] The neofascist war economies become economic warfare over markets and materials, rather than territories and sovereignty. In the age of postindustrialism or neocapitialism, capital no longer depends on the fascist war-machine to secure its political, economic, and cultural form because as capital keeps growing, war becomes increasingly what Deleuze and Guattari call a "war of matériel" in which "the human being no longer even represents a variable capital of subjection, but is instead a pure element of mechanic enslavement" (*A Thousand Plateaus*, 466). As a consequence, for Pasolini, scandal in the age of controlled societies (mass debt) becomes what Baudrillard names "the scandal effect." This effect simulates artificial oppositions—it repeats conventional binary oppositions—that "always pay homage to the law, by concealing that there is no difference between the facts and their denunciation" (*Simulations*, 26). Within this system scandal is purely theatrical. The real scandal for Pasolini is that a moral gesture itself promotes an immoral economy: "Capital doesn't give a damn about the idea of the [moral] contract which is imputed to it—it is a monstrous unprincipled undertaking, nothing more" (*Simulations*, 29). Pasolini responds by transforming his aesthetic from scandalous otherness to a form of scandalous mimicry. He mimics the spectacular interplay of neocapitalism and moralism, in an attempt to dissimulate neocapitalism from its moral superstructure. And finally in *Salò* Pasolini employs irony as the trope of scandal. The Sadean scandal of *Salò* is beyond the consciousness of the discontinuity between moral ideals and capital gains, beyond what de Man calls the "social language [moral, legal] that dissimulates the inherent violence of the actual relationships between human beings."[16] In *Salò* all social relations become an ironic hyperbole of a system of violent consumption and control that cynically maintains the gesture of symbolic authority (law, patriarchy, wealth, high culture) and its transgressive muse or siren (the femme fatale, albeit an aged, excessive image). This extremely controlled society no longer necessitates morality (internalized order). Instead it operates on what Sande Cohen calls "cold blooded terrorism," an "extermination of possibles, reducing all other modes of becoming, and binding language to an economy without expanding things to say" (*Academia and the Luster of Capital,* 74).

Tout Est Bon Quand Il Est Excessif—Marquis de Sade

In *Salò* Pasolini escalates his fatal strategies, responding to the Italian political and cultural shift to the right and the growing "tolerance" for neofascist parties such as the MSI. Pasolini's fatal strategy is one wherein he delimits historical narratives about fascism, presenting fascism as a proliferation of the desire to consume that spirals into the vertigo of a violent consumer frenzy. *Salò* visualizes the fatal strategy underlying the logic of late capitalism, its entangled circuitry of consumption, destruction, reason, scientific method, control, and purification that become life in extreme: pure war, pure fascism, self-interest, masculine sexuality, contamination, pure disappearance. In *Salò* there is no longer any possibility of resisting indoctrination by the system, nor of subverting or undermining its authority, as there is no outside of neocapitalism or its neofascist policing forces. Radical interiorization of all social relations is achieved by capital's delegitimation of stable or fixed narrative or discursive identities in favor of what Lyotard calls an arbitrary (alienated) "egalitarian institution of pleasure," yet one that upholds the value of exchange and expenditure at the expense of desire (*Libidinal Economy,* 141). For Pasolini, neocapitalism's networking of bourgeois moralism to neofascism to societies of control triggers a chain reaction in which meaningful identifications linked to epistemological metanarratives and ideological constructions of reality collapse.

The replacement of the binary model (a system of opposition, of boundaries between good and evil) by the network model allows for the coexistence of contradictory discourses such as a moral realism, deterritorialized capital, and neofascist control. The coexistence and intersection of conflicting narrative and ideological discourses as well as modes of representation (historical, cinematic, literary, documentary, etc.) challenges not only the sanctity of historical and cultural discourses but also their ability to draw lines of closure. Pasolini's strategy in *Salò* is to jam up systemic classifications of historic events by emphasizing that the overuse and overcoding of images, icons, and narratives of good and evil (of fascism and capitalism, bourgeois moralism and decadentism) produces an economy of frantic revision. Such economics of revision point to the permeability or instability of cultural references—national identities, historical narratives, narratives of resistance, moral narratives, etc. The constant mutation of cultural identities in the media as well as in intellectual circles, and the simulation of historical narratives, undermine the credibility of the process of revising, resulting in the questioning of the validity of such discourses as history and morality. These questions, when combined with the history of fascism, evoke the modern "historians' debate" over the limits of representation—specifically the intellection or historicization of the Shoah.

While Pasolini does not directly engage in this debate, his convergence of discourses (Sade, fascism, modernism, capitalism, bourgeois moralism) is politically charged by the debate, yet in juxtaposition to the *Historikerstreit*, *Salò* precipitates its own unique critical cogency. The *Historikerstreit* confronts the conundrum of establishing a stable Western identity (a credible historical subject) in the aftermath of nazism and fascism. Historians and other intellectuals have attempted to reconcile the demand that we *never forget* (a constant reidentification of the Western traditional ethos with the victimizer) with a good model that declares *never again* (one that identifies with the victim in order to deter the possibility of repetition). For Pasolini, the romantic narratives (subjects) of Western history—the enlightened imperialist narrative of the white man's burden or the civilizing mission, the triumphant narrative of the scientific revolution that promises modernization and technological advancement, and liberal narratives of gradual progress—are epitomized by Hitlerian and Mussolinian fascism. However, these narratives do not need Hitler and Mussolini as their protagonists: in fact, the deposing of Hitler and Mussolini cathartically cleanses these narratives, allowing the bourgeois family man to disassociate himself from his previous role in the narrative of fascism, and therefore to revise his narrative as well as his image within the discourse of Western European reconstruction (neocapitalism). Thus neofascism has modulated itself from the monumental spectacle of Hitler and Mussolini to the spectacle of banality.

For Pasolini, the fascist has changed his point of reference from the mythic superman (Maciste/Mussolini) to the bourgeois Everyman (the individualist, the libertine). Rather than representing fascism as lying dormant (thus creating a need for perpetual deterrence), Pasolini sees the continuation of bourgeois capitalism as an indication that neofascism comprises the dominant social system. Hence, for Pasolini, neofascism itself participates (as did its predecessor) in the demand for boundaries between pure and contaminated, truth and lie, victim and victimizer, good and evil. Instead of engaging in the debates that argue for an ethical obligation to represent the Holocaust so as to deter both a recurrence and a return to prenazi, prefascist narrative identifications, Pasolini refuses to validate any moral or ethical position that speaks in the name of the victims at the same time as it promotes neocapitalism. Pasolini's referencing images of fascism, nazism, and the Holocaust engage in the politics of the *Historikerstreit*, not at the level of historical or mimetic representation, but in the problematizing or wounding of speculative discourses—Enlightenment, scientism, metaphysics. He pursues the logic of Adorno's *Negative Dialectics*, in which Adorno argues that there can be no poetry after Auschwitz, that is, there can be no art or transcendental historical or ideological models after the Holocaust. According to Lyotard's reading of Adorno, history and art after Auschwitz signify an "endless repetition of bad infinity." He explains, "we wanted the progress of the mind, we got its shit" (*Differend*, 87). Yet, in his analysis of Adorno's *Negative Dialectics*, Lyotard demonstrates that "for Adorno,

'Auschwitz' is a model, not an example. . . . The 'Auschwitz model' would designate an experience of language that brings speculative discourse to a halt" (*Differend*, 88). Although Pasolini emulates Adorno's distrust of speculative discourses, unlike Adorno and his followers he does not consider fascism a model of limitation; instead he presents it as a contagious assemblage of desire. In doing so he rejects historical narratives that attempt to compartmentalize fascism, as for instance Croce's narrativizing fascism as a parenthetical lapse in liberal history. For Pasolini there can be no after Auschwitz; as Lyotard explains, "annihilation has not happened once, sometime ago, at Auschwitz, but, by other means, apparently totally other, it is happening now in the 'administered world,' in late capitalism, the technoscientific system whatever name one gives to the world in which we live, in which we survive" (*Heidegger and "the jews,"* 44). Rather than constituting a model, Auschwitz and the cultural obsession with representing Auschwitz become another aspect of the cannibalistic economy underlying neocapitalism.

Thus it follows that Pasolini would choose the extremely rationalist logic of Sade as a means of disclosing neofascism's own fatal strategy. For Pasolini, Sade provides a line of pure destruction that will escalate "the end"—an implosion caused by the emulation and exaggeration of neofascism's own logical model. Yet this fatal strategy does not just emerge out of Pasolini's reading of Sade but from his understanding of the following scholars' postwar interpretations of Sade: Roland Barthes, *Sade, Fourier, Loyola*; Maurice Blanchot, *Lautrèamont e Sade*; Simone de Beauvoir, *Faut il brolee Sade*; Pierre Klossowski, *Sade mon prochain*; and Phillip Sollers, *L'écriture et l'experience des limites* who appear on a title card that precedes the opening credits of *Salò*. If, as the film suggests, these references can be used to enhance our understanding of *Salò*, then they clearly indicate a set of philosophical problems that Pasolini sets out to address. More than simply adopt or recite some of these philosophical readings of Sade, Pasolini responds to these works: he questions their ability to read our understanding of, or coming to terms with, fascism through Sade. Even as he engages certain aspects of these postwar interpretations of Sade, he challenges their use of Sade as a critical model. Pasolini's attraction to Sade can be seen as responding to Klossowski's question, "Pourquoi Sade n'a pas recherché une formulation conceptuelle positive de la perversion?" ("Why did Sade not seek a positive conceptual formulation of perversion?") even if it is precisely the factor of outrage (*l'outrage*) that sustains the reiteration of transgression. Here Klossowski explains that if Sade had treated perversion as a model of outrage or subversion "le Sadisme même ne serait alors qu'une idéologie utopique parmi d'autres" ("Sadism itself would then be just one utopian ideology among others").[17] What constitutes Pasolini's position, as well as Sade's and his reader's, as antiutopian and antisystemic is that in order to take flight from cultural hegemony (neofascism, neocapitalism) one must adopt a fatal strategy (a parodic gesture that ends in self-consumption).

By representing fascism and capitalism as antisystemic (radically antiutopian) he also enters into the discussion between historical relativism and historical revisionism (categories that have been analogized by thinkers such as Terry Eagleton and Carlo

Ginzburg). Pasolini responds to this ideological politicking via the discursive practice of analogy by seeing all discourses that use what he considers to be completely exhausted ideological models—Western enlightenment and cultural modernism—as historically revisionist. He therefore reverses the criticism of historical idealists and Marxist theorists who metonymically link historical relativism to historical revisionism to fascist history itself under the rubric of lack of a moral perspective.[18] Like many other critical thinkers who cannot consciously or ethically align themselves with the neoepistemologists nor their apologetic metadiscourses (Marxism, feminism, liberalism, conservatism, revisionism), Pasolini sees radical narrative criticism as the last remaining gesture for defying neofascism. Consequently, radicality in *Salò* is presented as what Klossowski terms Sade's deciphering of the "mystery of being" as the "possibility of evil and nothingness."

Salò denaturalizes what has been presumed as common sense, that is, the achievement of Western science, progress, and humanism, yet it does so in such a way as to emphasize the impossibility of escaping this unnatural system. But Pasolini does not stop with critiquing ideological models; he takes on critical models as well, questioning the veracity of modernist criticism. In *Salò* Western high culture is portrayed as the propriety of the fascists, as their sacred object of self-affirmation used to legitimize notions of racial, ethnic, and cultural superiority. It is the libertines, the "bourgeois fascist fathers," who discuss symbolist poetry and Nietzschean and Sadean philosophy, quote Proust, Pound, Baudelaire, and Lautrèamont, and surround themselves with the works of Léger, Sironi, Severini, Duchamp, and so on. That is, it is the fascist bourgeois fathers who master the discourses of radical and revolutionary opposition; they discuss anarchic philosophy and modernist literature, they buy avant-garde art. Pasolini exposes the enigma facing liberal, leftist and postmodernist intellectuals who wish to reclaim the radicality of modernism and avant-garde and experimental art and yet to disassociate the aesthetics and radical nature of these movements from the impurity and political and moral stigma of fascism (Adorno, Habermas, Jameson). What distinguishes the insurrection of the libertines from polemical strategies of opposition (revolutionary or confrontational politics) and subversion (the politics of implosion and hybridity) is that traditional political conflicts promulgate the same "democratic way." Inasmuch as these radical discourses fashion themselves in terms of permanent opposition, they enrage the republican government (Sade) or the capitalist system (Pasolini) by demanding universal subjection to "just authority"—demanding the total disciplining of society, the conformism of the will. Although the libertines maintain a homogeneous identity (based on a set of rules or laws and high cultural identifications), their avowal of that identity is contingent upon their neutralizing of those elements that threaten to discipline their antisystemic model.

In contrast to the libertine principles, liberal, revolutionary, minority, and feminist discourses operate on a sacrificial logic wherein the subject must spurn desires that do not comply with the narrative programming of the ideal citizen. Yet many fashionable or illusory forms of diversity (tolerance) ironically identify with and continue to materialize intolerant measures—demanding just suppression, for example, the right to life, capital punishment, anti-immigration policies, antigay laws, political correctness, legalized diversity, "just causes," and "just" wars. Neocapitalism incorporates this "unlimited accusative" economy in order to simulate a tension between the forces of homogeneity and heterogeneity (disintegration), allowing for neocapitalism's constant modulation and reassertion in opposition to the forces of evil. Unlike disciplinary societies that squelch resistance (attempting to isolate and imprison opponents), neocapitalism absorbs (cannibalizes) resistances, aligning and thus rejuvenating itself by incorporating new principles or by squelching new forms of conflict. What is so insidious about deterritorialized power is its ability to metamorphose, to commercialize or overcode images of resistance, and therefore to neutralize or decodify revolutionary discourses.

In *Salò* Pasolini delineates the integral relationship of the politics of singularity (the level of frenzy, the pursuit of self-fulfillment), domination (a demand for a disciplined assimilation to a homogeneous model) with the neocapitalist politics of controlled diversity (a latent fatal strategy that identifies with the other only in the aftermath of its death) as three contemporaneous discourses and logical systems that form a symbiotic process. While the opposition between victor and vanquished

At the end of *Salò,* two of the fascist guards dance while the libertines perform their finale of carnage.

(subject and object, active and passive, etc.) is ironically maintained, the "other" disappears into the spectacle of history—the other is repeatedly killed off via its endless reinscription in narratives of victimization. As a pure victim the other serves as an icon for reactionary politics. Consequently, instead of discrediting discourses of power, the other legitimizes power's "just causes." This transappropriation of the other allows it to pass into the aesthetic dimension where it produces an iconic shift that reforms the offensive image of the conqueror into the defensive image of the protector (father, priest, lawyer, governor, financier, the roles held by Pasolini's libertines), subsequently translating the discourse of invasion into treaties of deterrence, security, and policing. Thus the ideology of domination no longer needs to bloat its own image in response to its own "fascisizing paranoia." While this social spectacle positions itself with and against "just causes," impure enemies (i.e., images of absolute evil), it no longer engages solely in the politics of purity, strength, and monumentality. Rather than engaging in the fascist politics of the *squadristi* that Bertolucci's character Attila defines in *1900* by killing the "pussycat" (which he has chosen to symbolize the "disease of communism") with his sheer brute strength, neofascism also employs the strategy of its opponent—"the playing on human feelings," utilizing the politics of victimization. Neocapitalism incorporates the politics of victimization into its own rhetoric of persuasion, which then implicates the victim in a political agenda serving neocapitalism's own reactionary and binary apparatus. By calling for retribution the victim reveals his or her own inculcation in the paranoid reactionary politics of domination (demanding purification, the annihilation of absolute enemies, whether physically, morally, or psychologically). The victim's demand for justice, according to Sade, is always an appeal to a law that is not only already institutionalized but is defined only in terms of an abstract notion of the good (Plato), a purity that itself defines the good (Kant), or by punishment, retribution, and repression (Hegel). Roland Barthes explains: "In Sade the victim desires law, wants meaning, respects the paradigm; the libertine, on the other hand, strives to broaden transgressions (incest/parricide), the libertine will do anything to join the terms (to be both incestuous and a parricide, and especially to force someone else to commit the same transgression), the victim will do anything to resist, raise the narrative as a sacred object of assembly."[19] Yet Pasolini discerns that the rhetoric of power oscillates between the discourse of the victor (the conqueror, the fascist) and the discourse of the victim, reflecting a readjustment of the neocapitalist system as the process of aestheticizing both positions. Therefore, rather than undermine the moral authority of the system, the rhetoric of power selectively disables the process of identification with that moral authority. What *Salò* represents is the one-dimensionality of this seemingly multifaceted system. In this hyperrationalized and hypercontrolled world, politics—liberal (Enlightenment), radical, and identity politics—as well as social relations disappear, leaving only an extremely internalized economy driven by a fanatic desire for self-affirmation.

Aside from some of the graphic images, what disturbs the audience is that *Salò* does not allow the victims any means of subjective identification—they are forbidden to engage in any form of worship, to possess any pictures, to have any sexual relations except for those imposed on them by the libertines. The victims are returned to the economy of sexual and social stratification, where power is determined by the implementation of pure agency, causing the object through which power affirms itself to disappear. This indifference for the object that empowers the self's pure agency is illustrated in Freud's translation of orgasm into a discharge of tension that thereby effects the disappearance of the object of desire. It is the installing of desire into the logic of singularity (the construction of a bounded individual) that heightens the self as the sole agent of desire who acts on objects, thus reducing desire to object relations. Pasolini demonstrates the extinction of desire as a result of the process of overinterpreting desire, by primarily psychoanalytical (masochistic, sadistic) and progressive (liberal Marxist) analytical methods. Remaining faithful to the logic of Sade (and critical of Freud, who presents sadism and masochism as a complementary articulation), Pasolini embraces the logic of sadistic subversion in its extreme form, hence he refuses to moralize or resolve his cinematic projects vis-à-vis a method of transcendence, transference, or catharsis. He questions the mechanisms involved in the persistent discursive process of identification with the wronged other (historical, ethnographic, aesthetic, postcolonial) that cling to a re-representation of the murderous extermination of otherness in an attempt to recover the discourse of the outside or otherness. Ironically these discursive, theoretical practices seek to legitimize the living subject in terms of a sacrificial logic—extermination or negation itself (as in the case of Pasolini's *Medea* and *Il Vangelo secondo Matteo*).

Yet this siding with the victim must always be incomplete and ultimately, for Pasolini, disingenuous. The alliance of the myth of the good or pure, dead subject with those who live in memory of that historical subject creates its own fatal strategy, wherein the repetition of the sacrificial logic of purification (martyred witnesses) disappears in the process of aesthetization or, as Jean-Luc Nancy argues, in the "horror [which] has no access, no appropriation, only revelation, infinite, or rather, indefinite [silent witnesses]."[20] In the very act of remarking the site of the subject's death (an identification with the cadaver), the site of speaking vanishes or is constantly deferred back onto the event, and the site of annihilation returns as a medium of deterrence, thus negating the subject's presence and delimiting the confines of the event. Since those who speak in the name of the victims or fashion themselves as inheritors of the burden of victimization cannot count themselves among the dead (what Lyotard calls a "pure victim") nor even speak as victims, they cannot escape being internalized by the system. Rather they fatally sacrifice themselves to the promotion of the politics of nostalgia for the idea of a just society, a mechanism of diversion inherent to neocapitalism's advertising campaign. The radical subject of opposition disappears in the vertigo of nostalgia for the event (which must always be determined ex post facto), offering him- or herself up as an object, yet one that cannot be read in terms of sacrifice, since this would involve the validation of some sinister type of logic. Reinhart Koselleck illustrates this illogic in his analysis of the representation of the Holocaust:

"those destroyed are deprived of a final meaning, that of being a sacrifice; [as a result, nonsense or] absurdity becomes an event."[21]

Hence Pasolini's shift in strategy from a cinematic resistance to neocapitalism to the "unpopular cinema" of scandalizing parody perplexes the attempt on the part of political correctness to identify with the victims (whether in World War II, global colonization, or Oedipalization). It is not the victim per se that he inveighs against, but the use of the victim to perpetuate the same project of transcendentalism already installed in hegemonic power. As a consequence he relentlessly refuses to engage in the resubjectification of the victim. He offers only the subjective point of view of the libertines, forcing the audience to realize their own internalization of this sadistic (fascist) bourgeois libidinal economy. By presenting the subject as already radically internalized in societies of control, Pasolini collapses dialectical constructs (self/other, good/evil, moral/immoral), and with them the production of meaning that is predicated on such a binary model. In *Salò* even the meaning of death is abrogated by the indifference of the system. Enzo Sicilano gives an example of this replacing of cathartic empathy for the tragic hero by radical indifference: "The kind of bodies Pasolini presents in *Salò* are gray, beautiful, well proportioned, but annihilated, canceled out by their own beauty, raped of their existence in the hell in which they are subjected."[22] It is not only the multitude of the victims, the pure mass, which causes them to disappear as subjects, but the fact that their appeals to the protection of the law or to God are met with laws that are designed only to destroy them—to ridicule them in their constant self-objectification. *Salò* thus represents the legitimation crisis of the law, its disengagement from its addressee (the people, the mass). Instead of warranting "justice" (the promised recompense of moral law), the victims' self-identification as victims categorically reduces them to the sublime, to aesthetic images or objects of suffering. Yet once the sublime can no longer elicit a spiritual aura (once it is secularized, demythologized, or demystified), the image of pathos loses its moral implications as well as its cultural significance (catharsis). If it is only the law that provides the victim with the means to secure his or her "rightful place" and "meaningful" identity within the capitalist system or bourgeois culture, then without access to its means of punishment he or she has no means to identify him- or herself outside of being a pure victim, a body, an object to be inscribed upon, consumed, and eliminated.[23] It is with this in mind that the Avvocato (the Lawyer, one of the libertines) declares that not only are the libertines the unequivocal masters of the state, "ma noi fasciti siamo i veri anarchici" ("but we fascists are the real anarchists"). Hence the law, as well as its institutionalization, unfolds as a schizophrenic economy whereby the power that manifests itself in the most deterministic form is at the same time driven by the most riotous desires. The law is thus reduced to its pure form, its pure instrumental propensity.[24]

Given the precarious positioning of the law, that is, subject to modulation in accordance with neocapitalist economics and neofascist politics (the whims of the libertines), Pasolini represents victims (the followers of empire and upholders of the laws of domination) as serving only to reproduce libertines' (neocapitalism's own) means of self-exertion. However, as the libertine's act of affirmation (in the form of transgression) necessitates the destruction of the victim, self-assertion disappears immediately upon completion of the act of transgression, thus it must be infinitely repeated. It is the production and reproduction of transgression that conforms to the model of consumer capitalism, perpetuating the frenzy of consumption (destruction), an affirmation whose only means of definition is through violent negation.[25] The libertines exemplify the "nonexistence" of their victims when they address them as "deboli creature incantenate, destinate ai nostri piaceri" ("weak enchained creatures, destined for our pleasure") just prior to their entrance into the villa, which marks their accession into the first *girone* (*le manie*/manias) where they will be forced to live out the destiny the libertines have devised for them. In this declaration of authority, the libertines literally pronounce the death of their victims: "spero che non vi siate illuse di trovare qui la ridicola libertà concessa dal mondo esterno, voi siete fuori di campi di ogni legalità, nessuno sulla terra sa che voi siete qui, per tutto quanto, riguardo al mondo, voi siete già morti" ("I hope you don't expect to find here the ridiculous freedom granted by the outside world, you are beyond the reach of any legality, no one on earth knows you are here, with regard to the rest of the world you are already dead"). Yet the repercussions of this relentlessness of crime—the complete disavowal of the other (object-victim)—result in the transcendence of nothing, the inability to overtake what is lost. The libertine produces only an expenditure of energy, and economy of waste and self-negation.

States of Evil

The frenzy of commercialized consumption subjugates desire and its expression to a rational or scientific model that thereby denaturalizes and exorcises the intimacy (and otherness) of desire. In an attempt to expose the inherent violence in a "rationalized" economy of consumption, Pasolini pursues Sade's parodic deconstruction of Enlightenment thinking, specifically social contract theory together with such notions as the state of nature and its utopian social order, since according to Sade these philosophical, political, cultural, and scientific thoughts emanate from an undisputed a priori construction of the law. While this law is conceived as diametrically opposed to all illusions (primarily religion, but also metaphysics), it is also grounded on disputable territory, fact, and reason.[26] What Sade recognizes and Pasolini replicates is the absurdity of erecting moral law on reason, because reason displaces as much as it deconstructs morality and the illusions implicit in such actions as "self-mediating activity" or the transformation of the will into self-censorship.[27] Here reason, identified only as a force of negation, takes itself as its own object (objective) acting for itself (a narrative of self-fulfillment) and in itself (a nonnarrative hyper-self-reflective analysis). Yet what remains ungrounded (illegitimate) is the embodiment of the subject of the law in figures (the legislator, the patriarchal father, the governor, the fascist, the priest, the bourgeois capitalist) that already represent social inequality.[28]

This extremely sadistic perspective of Enlightenment politics, the terrorism of a system that rationalizes control and its violent means to stabilize power, is achieved through what Klossowski outlines as the "arrival of Reason at atheism," that is, an extinction of faith which renders reason autonomous from God, liberty, fraternity, equality, common will (Rousseau), or civil society (Hegel) (*Sade mon prochain*, 20–21). Lack of faith subsequently disables reason's power to affirm a moral model. Radical secularization of reason debilitates its enlightened (progressive, productive, positive) identification and arrests the dialectical procedure of disengaging from a discursive double, perverse, or nihilistic reason. Reason thus ferociously decodes its own moral referent—the *thing-in-itself,* the transcendental subject, humanist ideal, scientific advancement, natural rights, universal law, equality—restoring the simulated transparencies of rational motivations to their reactionary origins. It is this appeal to the law (reason), the demand for purification, which kills in the name of political correctness (a transcendental good). Yet Pasolini's, as well as Sade's representation of the failure of Enlightenment thinking does not simply invert good and evil, nor does it collapse categorical imperatives—morality and purity do not merge with immorality and impurity—rather it materializes their purely reactionary trajectories. In fact, the liquefaction of what Peter Sloterdijk calls "false oppositions" is undermined by a seditious subjugation of the disruptive forces of desire and seduction.[29] This reactionary will to absorb all desires, to control or purify, is predicated on and fueled by a sinister *ressentiment*.[30] In order to curtail the potential *ressentiment* of the other, power is transformed from a Nietzschean will to an imminently paranoid reactionary economy of self-interest (satirized by the libertines).

The insurgency of the libertines, for instance, is always carried out in the name of subjugating the desire of the other to a hyperrationalized model of the self—a model of the patriarchy, the law, sexual and cultural hegemonies. The libertines' orderly self-fashioning is allegorically repeated in the fastidiously symmetrical architectural framing of each scene, as well as the detailed enumeration of the laws that govern their society—not only outlined in a book of laws (*regole*) but visualized in the course of the film. Every act of transgression is made hypervisible (whether sodomy, rape, murder, or coprophagy); there is no room left for arbitrariness or the unexpected. The visual texture of *Salò* repeatedly foregrounds the structural organization and symmetrical order of each scene by continuously centering the subject of the gaze within an architectural space. The architecture of the mise-en-scène itself serves as a framing device, yet this concentration on architectural symmetry is juxtaposed with a series of asymmetrical reverse shots that reveal the unequal distribution of power between the libertines, who move through the various passageways, and their chosen victims, who are fixed within the frame. The immobility of the victims signifies their complete objectification by the libertines: the victims are required to disrobe, at which point they are inspected and selected by the libertines. However, while the camera follows from the viewpoint of the libertines' passing glances from the faces to the genitalia, back to the faces of the victims, it also reveals the excited expressions of the libertines. The most notable difference between the libertines and their victims remains that the libertines are defined by their subjective views, their facial reactions, while the victims are revealed by their bodies, their faces are often expressionless or at most emoting a sense of humiliation.

This sadistic desire of the bourgeois capitalist, as Nietzsche argues, not only becomes the privilege of power but is always already inscribed in every expression of power: every expression of power is also an expression of self-interest whether or not it is disguised by moral or universal law. Pasolini replicates the Sadean mode of parody (hyperrationalization) in order to expose the duplicitous conflation of self-interest with universal ideas. In *Salò*, this mimicry of Sade's own mimetic agenda takes the form of an ironic parody of the anthropocentric (narcissistic) remodeling of natural law in the cult of individualism. Sade's violent parody of reason and individuation provides Pasolini with a textual model for the theatrical play of neocapitalism and consumerism. Pasolini, like Sade before him, forces moral imperatives put forward by bourgeois cultural hegemony to exceed their limit, disclosing the territorialization of enlightened power as always already benefiting only those who already have power—liberty, freedom, property are determined on the basis of protecting privileges that already exist.

While this scandalous force of reactionary purification—pure reason metonymically linked to pure capital, pure consumption, and pure control—infects binary thinking by corroding polarities, it cannot resynthesize what it has already decomposed (a symbolic mode of identification). In order to appear synthetic (productive, progressive, unequivocal, authoritative), neocapitalism simulates visions of scandal, narratives and images of evil, so as to reinforce narratives of good (symbolic meaning). Yet these goodly icons and narratives constantly defer their meaning to a duplicitous sacrificial logic that steers the image of good away from the visage of power. Thus power rests on the masquerade of the good (a universal model in which all men are created equal and therefore have equal exchange value), wherein images of power and their iconic references serve to conceal that pure power is purely consumptive and destructive (singular). The logic of duplicity, the logic of scandal, conceals the disappearance of morality and meaning (metaphysics).

The spectacle of scandal (much like the spectacle of the femme fatale) serves a dual purpose; first to resurrect an image of moral authority and second as a means of deterrence, reinstalling the spectator in the economy of self-censorship. However, this moral panic reflects the need for allusions to morality in order to protect the spectator from witnessing the radical dissimulation of capital—its waging of war on its own immoral phantasms in order to conceal the radical divestment in moral and economic equivalence. Sade declares that "the Republic will preserve itself only by war, and nothing is less moral than war" (*Philosophy of the Bedroom*, 315). This bellicose logic, in which all parties identify themselves with the scandalized, constantly conjoins rhetoric with images that transfer one's own immorality—"its instantaneous cruelty," collateral damage, civilian casualties, "incomprehensible ferocity"—onto "the greater evil" of its opponent. Yet in order to maintain power and at the same time justify its acts of violence, the war machine (ethnic, national, international, and even intergalactic) must manufacture conflicts. This permanent insurrection (which also takes the form of products, science, cold war economies, economic competition), described by both Sade and Baudrillard, results in demands for reassurance (of value and identity) and security (of boundaries and propriety) transforming pure war into pure deterrence. The transmutation of war into deterrence placates the spectators with images and narratives of identification permitting spectators/citizens to reinscribe themselves within the aegis of a moral purpose, yet only as its guilty subjects. Although the cold war economic strategy of deterrence (mutual assured destruction, otherwise known as MAD) precludes conspicuous warlike imperial expansions, it internalizes war in the form of a society of control, invading and programming the microcosm (the community, family, individual, television) so that nothing is left to chance. And it operates on the assumption that all subjects are already guilty; the individual is Oedipalized and the state becomes both the analyst and the symbolic father par excellence. The Orwellian premise of thought policing posits that thoughts are taken for actions and that all citizens and noncitizens are guilty of every crime against the state, and therefore, much like the preemptive strike, it arbitrarily punishes in the name of national security, necessary downsizing, inflation, recession, and so forth. Yet, rather than focus on the unmasking of the social spectacle, Pasolini refutes the simulation of legitimacy or moral purpose by presenting the theatrics of a system of power that knows itself to be illegitimate.

What attracts Pasolini to Sade is his decoding of a priori concepts like normalcy, commonality, equivalence, and morality in order to expose these very concepts as themselves the real scandal, an outrageous emptiness—the unaccountable system of moral and economic isomorphism. This deconstruction of concepts that foster stable social identities causes the collapse of the three-tiered construction of the social apparatus bound by a social contract: first, the conscience and credulity with regard to a supreme being; second, the obligation to fellow man or civil society; and third, self-interest (*Philosophy of the Bedroom*, 308–310). And by subtracting the irrational (a priori) figures of God, good, moral, Sade vindictively unveils reason's own fatal strategy, its own nihilistic will to power that disassembles "other" desire and reassembles desire as a mechanized destructive reaction compulsion.[31] Driving this fatal strategy is the fusion of contradictions, authority that falsifies its own image and discourse, operating outside of the law upon which it derives its power, and acting out its desire for pure control as a desire purely to defile.[32] *Salò* presents both the outbreak of evil as well as the victory over evil, the passing of transgression into law. This film visualizes the Baudrillardian paradigm of the simulated society where every subversion of the system merely promotes its deterrence, which in turn reinforces an insubstantial masquerade of public good. The decoding of this masquerade leads Pasolini to the Sadean axiom, the institutionalization of transgression (a fatal strategy). Within this axiom the law is presented as schizophrenic, speaking in the name of the father, the *patria*, the state in order to completely nullify the discourse of the father, the *patria*, the state—or at least reveal that these discourses are already bankrupt. This manifold law devours meaning, excreting itself in the form of abjection, which is defined by modern critics such as Julia Kristeva as "any crime, since it draws attention to the fragility of the law."[33] Yet, in contrast to thinkers like Kristeva who specifically exclude Sade from the moral politics of abjection on the grounds that "he who denies morality is not abject; there can be grandeur in amorality and even in crime that flaunts its disrespect for the law," Pasolini proposes that the institutionalization of transgression or the aggrandizement of subversion disavows speculative discourses (like Kristeva's) that reserve for the strategy of subversion some sacred or moral purpose. Regardless whether abjection is aggrandized as the law (Sade) or an undermining of law (Kristeva), it conserves a notion of the host as a "pure body" that can be defiled. Yet once Pasolini inveighs against his own Catholic upbringing, unlike Sade, he can no longer maintain an image of purity—evil has already triumphed in the world and purity becomes for Pasolini a nostalgia for lost innocence.

The favorite symbolic victims of the libertines, much like those of Kristeva herself, are the virgin and the mother, both of which hark back to symbolic narratives of sacrifice and sanctity. Klossowski explains that "the virgin is an image of divine purity; at the same time she is a sign of the fall of him who desires her simply as a creature. As an image of the purity of God, the virgin is excluded from possession by man; but

In *Salò*, two of the victims are forced to marry each other symbolically, but they will be raped by the libertines before their "marriage" can be consummated.

man cannot forget that she is possessable. She becomes in Sade a motif of exasperation, and prohibition, of virility" (*Sade mon prochain*, 103). In order to maintain an assemblage of power (perpetual motion, permanent revolution[34]), the abject constantly recalls (pays homage to) some sacred or religious doctrine even if it is only to transgress its moral or ethical principles. Virginity and purity are emphasized in order to reveal their absurd logic or illogic of privileging one part of the body over another, as well as to express the libertine's and the law's complete disregard for their symbolic value. In *Salò*, the libertines stage a heterosexual marriage between two of the victims for the sole purpose of transgressing its moral and religious vows. Coming of age, as a criterion of whether one is mature enough to be married, is parodied by the libertines as determined by the victim's ability to ejaculate. And as a reward for ejaculating to same-sex fellatio and cunnilingus, Sergio and Renata are given the gift of marriage. Their theatrical ceremony is interrupted by the Duke's groping all the spectators, and the act of consummation becomes a spectacle for these fascist fathers, who demand that the couple "get busy." Before the marriage can be consummated, the libertines intervene, halting the couple's heterosexual intercourse so that they can sodomize them, "deflower" the couple in order to devalue the institution of marriage and its supplementary narratives of romantic love and family romance. The mimicry of marriage—and the transgression of marriage—is staged repeatedly. The repetition of the ritual of marriage in each *girone* (circle or level) is contingent on the subject of narration chosen by each *Raconteuse*, beginning with the *girone delle manie* (circle of obsessions), then the *girone di merda* (circle of shit), and finally the *girone di sangue* (circle of blood or death). In the second *girone* (*di merda*), Sergio, one of the male victims, is dressed in drag as a bride. Here the mimicry of the sealing of marriage vows with a kiss is not only disrupted by the cross-dressing of the bride but more vividly by the close-up of this kiss, which reveals that the libertine lips are smeared with feces. In the last enactment of marriage (in the *girone di sangue*), three of the libertines (the fourth acts as a Dionysian priest) dress as women (mimicking or replacing their own daughters) and stage their marriage to their own guards, sealing the guards' vows to collaborate with the libertines. The ritual is underscored by the theatrical drag performance of the libertines and by the fact that they have assumed (consumed) the experience and identity of both their wives and their daughters. Each restaging of the ritual of marriage becomes progressively more grotesque, distorting and carnivalizing clichéd symbols of love, romance, and most importantly the union of the sexes. What is left is only the simulation of the ritual format; the narratives that legitimate marriage are savagely disregarded and undermined as pure theatricality. For the libertines, marriage is purely an exchange—of daughters and sons, that is, victims of a sadistic law. Subsequently, marriage is reduced to an act of sexual domination that only satisfies fathers whose aim is to completely subjugate their children.

While Sade's discourse of subversion requires the predetermined existence of morality (marriage, romance, intimacy, parenting, religion, politics) as defined in opposition to crime and transgression, the distinction between transgression and institutional practice becomes indistinguishable for Pasolini, since transgression as an amoral point of departure is no longer radical once society has been spectacularized. The libertines already have been institutionalized—evil in the form of capital has been hatched. Since radical modernism or society of control acquiesces to the vector of disappearance (comprising its own fatal strategy or line of pure destruction), Pasolini counters the constantly deferred nihilistic effect of disappearing by offering a fatal antibody, escalating this very scandal of disappearance. What has disappeared is the reference to the good or the law, upon which real systems are legitimated and validated. The first glimpse we have of the libertines in *Salò* is their creating laws that are written (democratically) by all four of them, as they congratulate each other on their excessive activity ("tu sei buono quando sei eccessivo" ("you are good when you are excessive"). The emphasis here is not only on the written word of the law as a symbolic authority, which then takes on its own identity (such as Rousseau's legislator, general will, or social contract), but on the complete arbitrariness involved in establishing such a law—the laws serve only the pleasure of the lawmakers. What persists is only the mockery (the spectacle) of the social contract and the bourgeois social system (the family, civil society, the state). Yet in this mockery or soiling of everything considered to be pure or respectable, as Bataille argues, "each one of us is personally implicated. [No matter how slender the human element] the mind still has to reach, if not the absence of desire, at least that despair felt in the reader by the feeling of an ultimate affinity between the desires felt by Sade and his own desires, which are less intense and which are normal."[35]

The Critical Reception of *Salò*

Like many other filmmakers in the sixties and seventies, Pasolini returns to fascism as a symbol of evil desire, and like many intellectuals of the postwar period he turns to Sade's radical challenge to the staging of desire as a struggle between good (as defined by Enlightenment thinking) and evil (as both ingrained in the discourse of purity and goodness and a reaction to the violence of purity and goodness). Yet what distinguishes Pasolini from numerous other filmmakers is that he does not use fascism or nazism to recuperate the language of radical intellectual criticism and the aesthetics of the sublime (the mysterious power of man), nor does he reinstall this cinematic visualization of fascism into a moral narrative as do the neorealist (e.g., Rossellini and De Sica) and neodecadent representations of fascism (i.e., Bob Fosse's *Cabaret* and Luchino Visconti's *The Damned*). Unlike the intellectuals referenced in the preface to *Salò*—Beauvoir, Klossowski, Barthes, Sollers, and Blanchot—Pasolini uses Sade as a model of the extreme manifestation of neocapitalist fascism. He does not attempt to recuperate the radically transgressive qualities of Sadean thinking for the purpose of critiquing neocapitalism and bourgeois hegemony. That is, Pasolini does not disengage the form from the content, nor does he provide for what Barthes would call a "critical middle voice." For Pasolini, Sade is radical only in his parodic gesture of

scandalizing what is already scandalous—the disassociation of capitalism and bourgeois moralism from its fascistic manifestations. Accordingly, the representation of
total contamination (of purity with evil and neocapitalism with neofascism) disables
any form of disengagement, whether critical or moral: no identifiable subject position emerges from these narratives. As Calvino concludes, Pasolini approaches Sade
from the "inside" rather than the "outside" ("Sade Is Within Us," 107). However,
Calvino faults Pasolini for not reestablishing a cognitive distance from which to analyze or contemplate the meaning of the film. Calvino argues that the "Sade within"
Pasolini's film is an impostor since he lacks "internal clarity," a criticism which is left
unsupported since Calvino never bothers to analyze the film. Yet Calvino's self-
proclaimed "outsider" position is caught in its own double bind, caught up in personal
(inside) affronts of Pasolini's sexual and intellectual perspectives. He accuses Pasolini
of using money like a libertine, to "become a successful filmmaker" as well as to "condition his relationship with the subproletariat boys." Ironically, while Calvino claims
that Pasolini has not grasped the "spirit" of Sade, he labels Pasolini a Sadean libertine,
implying that in "real life" Pasolini internalized Sade, but because Pasolini lacked self-
conscious reflection he was unable to establish a cognitive (inauthentic) distance from
the text—the critical middle voice or enlightened consciousness that Calvino claims
for himself.

Criticisms of Pasolini's film that establish "spirits" and "phantasms" as a criteria
for reading Sade both jettison discourses of "internal clarity" and expose their own
ideological hysteria over the preservation of certain notions of objectivity—notions
that maintain categorical imperatives, objectivity, subjectivity, criticality. For example,
while the Sadean philosophy has provided postwar theorists and philosophers with a
purely deconstructive or critical model from which to approach Western cultures and
ideologies, fascism, on the other hand, remains a discourse largely rooted in the discourses of moral indignation, historical realism (social realism), psychoanalysis (sexual perversion), and Marxism (resistances and martyrs). Historians, filmmakers, and
social and cultural theorists have attempted to give closure to, or at least wash their
hands of, fascism and the possibility of the continual existence of a fascist imaginary.
And it is precisely Pasolini's intersecting of these discourses with neocapitalism and
neofascism that questions the stable objectivity of the moral narrative representations
of fascism. Hence *Salò* is largely dismissed: Italo Calvino, Roland Barthes, and
Leonardo Sciascia do not endeavor to analyze the film; rather they protect Sade by
reading Pasolini psychoanalytically.[36] The vehement rejections of *Salò* by critics and
writers including Calvino, Barthes, and Sciascia demonstrate an unequivocal sensitivity
to the representation of fascism and the need to distinguish fascism from intellectual
endeavors (Sade's own radical thought and the numerous postwar reinterpretations of
Sade's radical criticality).[37]

What makes Pasolini so disturbing is that he cannot be consumed, even intellectually, since, he places Western intellectual thinking in a double bind. For Pasolini,
intellectual thought, whether critical or ideological, is completely internalized in the

capitalist system, and therefore it is at once radical and fascist. Pasolini ups the stakes in the game by networking the discourses of neocapitalism, neofascism, and sadism in *Salò* and by pointing to the fact that revised interest in the texts of Sade came at precisely the time when European intellectuals (including Barthes) were trying to make sense, or nonsense, out of nazism and fascism. What distinguishes Pasolini's interpretation of Sade from that of Barthes is Pasolini's fatal strategy: Pasolini refuses to salvage Sade, and maybe himself, from the politics of scandal, in that he refuses to disassociate neofascism and neocapitalism from their critics.[38] The Monsignore (one of the fascist libertines in *Salò*) exemplifies this double bind of postwar intellectualism when he announces that "*noi fascisti sono i veri anarchici*" while claiming that "the principle of greatness is to be bathed in blood"—he attributes this quote to Baudelaire, Nietzsche, St. Paul, and Dada. Since, for Pasolini, there is no undermining the system from within, avant-garde culture as well as intellectual criticism is synonymous with fascism—it is a radical anarchy of the elites. For Pasolini, the twentieth-century avant-garde thinkers are the libertines, they are the ones like the futurists, the fascists, the neorealists, and Wertmüller's depiction of the anarchist Pedro in *Seven Beauties* (see chapter 5) who call for a "new man" to emerge, a new more ideal or pure man. As Barthes himself points out "one cannot be a libertine without money, money proves vice . . . it guarantees the spectacle of poverty . . . [And, he continues] the master is he who speaks, who disposes of the entirety of language, the object is he who is silent, who remains separate, by a mutilation more absolute than any erotic torture from any access to discourse" (*Sade, Fourier, Loyola*, 24). What could be more absolute than the distance between the intellectual and his or her object of study? The critic, like the sadist, is he or she who, as Bataille argues, "points the way to the continuity of crime, yet this continuity transcends nothing."[39]

For Pasolini, survival in the age of neofascism indicates some form of collaboration; even the passivity of the silent majority amounts to a certain type of complicity. Levels of collaboration and conformism warrant different treatments by the neofascist system. In *Salò* Pasolini distinguishes among the levels of collaboration: one group, the libertines, points to the intersections of Western philosophy with bourgeois culture, avant-garde movements, cartel-capitalism, and fascism; a second group, the four raconteuses (otherwise named by Sade "the Fuckers"), though not coconspirators, inspires and encourages the violent sexual acts perpetrated by the libertines; a third group collaborates with the libertines as their militaristic policing force. It is this group that Sade described as ignorant beasts who possess a great sexual prowess. One rank below this group of military *collaboratori* are a group of guards who are selected and coerced to join the ranks of the Salò government. Pasolini makes significant distinctions among this group of characters, whom he translates into *militi*. Claudio, who is first seen being taken away by the fascists, slaps his mother's face and demands that she leave as she follows him pleading for his release; Ezio (who will later disobey the regime by having a heterosexual relationship with an African maid) is seen acknowledging the greetings of neighborhood boys, displaying not only a touch of "kindness" but his established communal connections. Efizio (another one of the *militi*) viciously sodomizes one of the libertines' daughters in front of a dinner gathering, appears abreast with Fabrizio, who becomes the lover of one of the libertines.

Pasolini establishes certain *gironi* (circles or levels of collaboration)—raconteuses, guards, then servants and victims—but also differences within these groups. While questioning their coherence as a group, he rejects any criteria that would allow for excuses or apologies such as "I was just following orders," or "I didn't know what was going on." In fact, the symbolic marriage of the libertines to the *collaboratori* weds them not only to fascist ideology but more importantly to their own responsibility in the dissemination of the fascism. Pasolini's cultural and social indictment is total. There is no "outside" of fascism or neofascism. To put oneself outside means to die, yet always on the terms of the neofascists. Death in and of itself is neither heroic nor tragic. Even Ezio—who when caught sleeping with the North African maid raises his arm with a clenched fist (symbolizing both the communist salute and black solidarity) before he is shot by the reluctant libertines—cannot represent any form of martyrdom, since his gesture refers to neither political allegiance nor racial solidarity nor social opposition. In juxtaposition to Ezio's seemingly heroic gesture before the firing squad of libertines, his lover, the maid, who is dressed as a Westernized or colonized household slave, dies in a gesture of submission. While kneeling before one of the libertines, she is shot point blank in the head, as if she were an animal waiting to be put down. This action not only reflects the bourgeoisie's subhuman treatment of racial and ethnic others but also the Left's privileging of the white male heterosexual in the discourse of heroism and martyrdom. Moreover, the use of the actress Ines Pellegrini, who played Zumurrud in *Arabian Nights* (*Il fiore di mille e una notte*, 1974) and actor Franco Merli, who played her lover (Nur-ed-Din), emphasizes Pasolini's own awareness of the failure of multiculturist politics. The very casting of the protagonists of *Arabian Nights* in the roles of servant (symbolizing both a racial and economic oppression of the North African figure) and victim (reflecting the West's own internal forces of repression and submission) suggests the foreclosure of the celebration of the other and his own mythopoetic strategy in the *dopostoria* of neocapitalism and neofascism. Ezio's gesture, therefore, only remarks the disappearance of the credibility of discourses of opposition. Rather than referring to a collective resistance, what makes his gesture radical is that it is an act of complete singularity, complete defiance—yet a fatal strategy.

Reading *Salò* Literally

Reactions to *Salò* like Calvino's and Barthes's draw attention to what is intellectually and culturally at stake in representing Sade in the context of fascism and fascism in the context of Sade. Like Calvino, Barthes accuses Pasolini of being too literal: Barthes writes, "remaining faithful to the letter of Sadean scenes, Pasolini comes to the point of distorting the object-Sade and the object-fascism." Elsewhere, however, Barthes argues that what makes Sade's work radical is its literalness, the obscene language that renders everything hypervisible.[40] While guarding the sanctity of the text against what they consider to be a "misreading" of what is "unportrayable," unrepresentable (except in academic interpretations of the text), Barthes and Calvino focus on the incommensurability of the visualization process and *écriture*. *Écriture* functions as a radical gesture that disrupts language's smooth surface of understanding—the ability of language to assign ideological meanings, to offer both the security of knowing and the satisfaction of understanding. Therefore this radical gesture, *écriture*, creates the aftereffect of the pure event, the *phantasme* (an event that cannot be analogized or interpreted in terms of conventional understanding or language). Barthes declares that "Sade in no way can be represented," and he continues, "just as there is no Portrait of de Sade there is no possible image of Sade's universe" ("Pasolini-Sade," 100). Barthes privileges the radical text (*écriture*) as the ideal *phantasme* (immaterial, anti-object, a pure event) over what he calls the "descriptive plenitude of the [cinematic] object." He also disengages the obscenity (radical dissemination or deconstruction) of language from the obscenity of the image (that is all-too-real).

Ironically, Barthes implies that Pasolini's film becomes more realistic (mimetic) when treating the subject of fascism than the Sadean text is in its treatment of the French Revolution. This inconsistent treatment of media (literature and film) raises questions: what are the criteria for privileging *écriture* as a *phantasme* and defining something as ephemeral as film as more realistic (mimetic) and therefore less subversive or intrinsically critical, as Barthes seems to imply?[41] Is fascism as Barthes suggests "too serious and too insidious a danger to be treated by *simple* analogy? [and does this seriousness] force us to think about fascism *accurately*, analytically, philosophically?" What Barthes implies in his positing of danger and the accuracy necessary in responding to this danger is that somehow fascism and cinema come closer to the real than the more imaginary and phantasmagoric "object-texts" and "object-de Sades." By dismissing *Salò* as a "simplistic analogy," Barthes denies Pasolini's (although hardly historically accurate) analytic and philosophical readings of the "corporeal state of affairs." When Barthes argues that

> the legal condemnation brought against Sade is therefore based on a certain system of literature, and this system is that of realism: it postulates that literature "represents," "figures," "imitates"; that the conformity of this imitation is what is being offered for judgment, aesthetic if the object is emotive, instructive or penal if it is monstrous; lastly, that to imitate is to persuade, to seduce: a schoolroom view point with which, however, an entire society, and its institutions, agrees (*Sade, Fourier, Loyola*, 37)

he calls attention to not only his contradictory "realist reading" of Pasolini's filmmaking but also the debates over censorship (of both language and the visual image) conducted in the United States by the Edwin Meese Commission (*The Attorney General's Commission on Pornography*, 1986), where it was argued that representations of pornography, like true crime, are instructive and are therefore themselves criminal. As a consequence, pornographic images and pornographic language, as well as images and language of violence, are considered to incite pornographic and violent activity. Somehow the spectator/listener presumably loses consciousness when confronting issues of sex and violence.

Banned in Italy, the United States, the United Kingdom, and various other European countries because of its so-called pornographic content, *Salò* has been read literally; it provokes public fear of what is culturally considered *too real*. This scandalized reaction to what is *too real* recalls Linda Williams's study of media censorship (specifically the interconnections of pornography and violence) and her linking of the logic of censorship to the cinematic and aesthetic theory of André Bazin. In her analysis she points out that for Bazin, "real sex, like real death, is unaesthetic and therefore out of place, yet elsewhere in his writing he has celebrated documentary realism in fictional contexts, and he is honest enough there to acknowledge the inconsistency: to grant the novel the privilege of evoking [emoting] everything, and yet to deny the cinema, which is so similar, the right of showing everything, is a critical contradiction which he consciously notes without resolving."[42] The antiaesthetic categorization of pornography (considered to be both the documentation of sex and death) reveals a larger contradiction at its foundation: the "see and learn" or "see to believe" mentality, which privileges the visual over the literary, at the same time invalidates the imaginary or artificial qualities inscribed in the process of visualization itself.

Since pornography, according to many of its critics, does not participate in the imaginary, it divorces itself from aesthetics (defined as a culture thinking about itself) and enters into the obscene (an ambiguous territory between the real and the spectacle, yet one that is treated as if it were a real crime). Bazin's very labeling of pornographic cinema as spectacle calls into question the social construction of cinema as a form of imaginary projection and its alleged role as the screening of social consciousness. How does the censorship of the visual image—by a not only *personalized* but *cultural* superego—affect the social function of cinema, especially if it is to be simultaneously considered a screen onto which we project our cultural fantasies? Bazin and those who refer to his theoretical distinction between the aesthetic and the antiaesthetic in order to support arguments for censorship imply that film should play the role of a social superego, a screen that at once represents fantasies and censors or represses them. Bazin argues that "we must stay in the realm of imagination: I ought to be able to look upon what takes place on the screen as a simple story, an evocation which never touches the *level of reality*, at least unless I am to be made an *accomplice* after the fact of an action or at least of an emotion which demands secrecy for its realization" (*What Is Cinema 2*, 174, my emphasis). The assumption behind the criminalization or the "realization" of violent and sexual content in film is predicated on a "see and learn" mentality, yet one where the spectator is designated to be an accomplice in the spectacle of the imaginary only by proxy but cannot become an accomplice (after the "fact") in the enactment of sex and violence.[43]

The classification of the *too real*, that which evokes "jealousy and competition," in turn reads the diegetic instance of violence and sex in film as what Metz calls "speaking directly," or directly effectuating the consciousness of the spectator (*Film Language*, 143–44). The spectator can no longer conciously reflect on him- or herself; instead he or she becomes an object to be inscribed upon, to be programmed by the libidinal economy of film. The logic behind this argument is that cinema that signifies or enframes social taboos (sex and violence) transforms itself from an inauthentic form of representation to an authentic event or spectacle. Like Barthes, Bazin devalues the aesthetics of sex and violence in order to revalue the aesthetics of imagination— the allusion to sex and violence rather than the representation of sex and violence— as a form of social consciousness and, in Barthes's case, as an aesthetic disruption.

Cinema, according to Bazin and to many Lacanian film theorists, must present itself as a symptom of social fantasies already censored by social mores. Thus the spectacle must always situate the spectator as a voyeur and itself as a fetish. What transpires in the dark is always the internalization of a spectacularized fantasy (both sexual and violent) and internal censorship of that very fantasy. Baudrillard argues that "the only phantasy in pornography, if there is one, is thus not a phantasy of sex, but of the real, and its absorption into something other than the real, the hyperreal. Pornographic voyeurism is not a sexual voyeurism, but a voyeurism of representation and its perdition, a dizziness born of the loss of the scene and the irruption of the obscene" (*Seduction*, 29). In response to the construction of a voyeuristic cinematic gaze, Pasolini upsets (sets up) the hypocrisy of the discourse of purity and its weapon of disengagement—of the pure text, the pure context, event, *phantasme*, and the pure playing out of the imaginary, which must always touch impurity, but only by proxy. For Pasolini, it is voyeurism that is pornographic, not the supersensuality of the visual object but the process whereby the spectator disengages the object from its form of sensual imagery in order to consume and eradicate its seductive power. His aim is to disrupt the artificial construction of a spatial dividing line between spectator and spectacle that furnishes the spectator with the comfort of becoming an outsider in this very process of consumption. Presenting the libertines as themselves voyeurs who inspect, examine, and objectify the human body for their own disengaged (sadistic, supracarnal) pleasure, Pasolini draws the voyeur into the spotlight, thus dislodging him or her from his or her comfort zone. Hence this hyperconscious representation of voyeurism implicates the spectator in the very act of voyeurism—an act of violence and violation. More than becoming accomplice by proxy, by watching violence, Pasolini questions the spectator's ability to disengage the "sublime object of desire" from the libertines' supracarnal consumption of that visual object, via coprophagy, mutilation, rape, and murder.

What have disappeared are not only political and ideological forms of opposition but sexuality and the seduction of images themselves. Baudrillard argues that pornography is founded on the disappearance of seduction. He posits that "sexuality does not vanish in sublimation, repression and morality. It vanishes more effectively in what is more sexual than sex: pornography. The hypersexual is the contemporary of the hyperreal."[44] The spectacle of hypersex, consequently, reduces sexuality to a hypervisible image, and thus its social, interpersonal, and sacred significance disappears into not only obscurity but obscenity. This *obscene*, however, has no affinity with the discourse of religious morality nor the disgust for the visualization of the body but rather the reduction of sexuality, seduction, and the body to pure power relations.[45] This control or violation of the body of the other commences with the rounding up of victims and the inspection as the negation of the privacy of the parameter of the body, which is met with no resistance by the prisoners. And so, although it engages with images of sadomasochistic pornography, *Salò* is anything but erotic. Rather it reproaches a definition of pornography predicated on the lascivious obscenity of the body and advances the argument that it is the transparency of everything that is itself pornographic—the scientific rendering of everything visible, the psychoanalytic decoding and recoding of sexual and violent fantasies, the media spectacle that in every representation leaves nothing to imagination. Gaylyn Studlar describes this as

In *Salò,* the libertines obscure the identity of their victims as they conduct a competition as to whether a man or a woman has a more beautiful ass.

the discourse of denotation, which is "scientific in its obscene descriptions and cruel imperatives" (*In the Realm of Pleasure*, 21). The Presidente (one of the libertines) demonstrates this type of obscenity when he demands of Signora Viccari (the first raconteuse to provide stimulating narratives for the libertines) that she be more detailed, that she describe the size of the penis, the type of ejaculation, and so forth. Although in his previous films Pasolini presents sex as part of what Deleuze and Guattari call savage, or becoming-animal, this supersensuality is distinctly not grotesque. What becomes grotesque in *Salò* is the circumscription of sex within a (supercarnal) mechanical system of control and consumption.

As Pasolini wrote before the making of *Salò*, "*Salò* will be a film in the genre of the Artaud's theater of cruelty, since it was designed to express that power that transforms individuals into objects, fascist power, the anarchy of power, the power of consumption" ("*Salò* sarà un film 'crudele' quel potere che trasforma gli individui in oggetti, il potere fascista ... il potere che è anarchico ... il potere dei consumi") (*Pasolini*, 391–93). He elaborates, "a film modeled on the theater of cruelty must be directly political (destructive and anarchic) therefore insincere ... it is to make a film on sex in which joyfulness is presented as a compulsion—as is now the case—to repress"[46] ("un film 'crudele' sarebbe direttamente politico (eversivo e anarchico, in quel momento): quindi insincero ... era fare un film su un sesso la cui gioiosità fosse un compenso—come in fatti era—alla repressione"). Pasolini's instrumental use of cruelty, much like his conscious representation of the inherent cruelty of voyeurism is devised to scandalize the incorporation of sex within the discourses of power (patriarchal, moralistic, and capitalistic) and thereby to render sex as a means of consuming and cannibalizing others as objects or bodies. He establishes a link between the phenomena of what Deleuze describes as the "assumption of social desires"—"including the desires of repression and death, people getting hard-ons for Hitler, for the beautiful fascist machine"—and capitalism's "savage repressiveness, its organization of power and its state apparatus." [47] The result of this theatrical combination of chaotic capitalist desire and the desire for control is the disappearance of human intimacy and the emergence of infinite acts of cruelty.

By decoding this economy of evil rather than reifying what is presumed to be its seductive power, Pasolini exposes an implicit political agenda disguised in the re-representation and re-eroticization of fascism—whether in Mosse's, Reich's, Macciocchi's or Theweleit's intellectualizing, or Visconti's, Fosse's, or Bertolucci's visualizing, an ambiguous fluctuation between purity and impurity. He draws attention to the enterprise of turning fascism into fetish, into fashion or style and the reabsorption of this fetish or fashioning in the discourse of sexuality and abjection (usually read as a subversive act). Pasolini enters into the politics of representing fascism by relentlessly unmasking what is considered to be its foundations. He presents a fascist cultural economy as a pure line of destruction, one that wages war against the cultural and intellectual industry that "keeps fascism alive" by constantly reimagining fascist style, rewriting fascist history. By doing so he reveals that the discourse of fascism is riddled with fragmentary and digressive elements; it has only a partial presence, yet it is partially present in a multiplicity of discourses ranging from aesthetics to the sublime to moral purity. Because of its dissemination, fascism cannot be divorced from neofascism nor can it be contained within the aesthetics of sadomasochism—images of men in leather trenchcoats and jack boots, manly men marching in step, Roman salutes and monumental postures. That is, the reconnection of fascism to the basic banalities of neocapitalism causes it to lose its luster of exceptionality. Although Pasolini's resistance to fascism does not present a contiguous narrative evolution, it presents a persistent disruption of the fascist and neofascist (neocapitalist) internalization of models of desire, based on a model of patriarchal authority embodied in the mechanics of the law. Thus, rather than neutralize Pasolini's relentless decodification of this fascist mystique, as does Naomi Greene, by sterilizing the more dangerous implications of what she considers to be "politically incorrect" analogies—associations of Sadean "sexual pathologies" with the Holocaust—I read his delimitation of the discourses of modernity (fascism, sexual politics, the theoretical revisions of Sade, and capitalism) as a process of synecdochic fragmentation. Pasolini represents fascism as a discourse of partial presence that is subject to unlimited revisions (by historians, artists, filmmakers, documentarians, pop and subcultures) and subdivisions (revised images of seduction, sadism, and masochism). His rhizomatic dissemination of images and ideas establishes partial presence (discursive references within discourses, much like Artaud's virus) and interlinks aesthetic images with historical narratives, theoretical interpretations, and cultural studies—a paranoid discourse. As a partial presence this delimited discourse of and about fascism recalls Deleuze's definition of the Aion: a "fragile and delicate mechanism [of] intersection" that is infinitely subdivisible, unlimited.[48] The decoding of the representation—the uncovering of the genealogy of synecdochic fragmentation of fascism and its intersections with the discourses of evil, perverse sexuality, the aesthetics of the sublime, and the cult of sadomasochism—reveals a process of deterritorialization that is no longer presented as a line of flight, nor a metaphoric figure; it is, as Baudrillard argues, "a figure of metastasis; a deprivation of meaning and territory, a lobotomy of the body resulting from the turmoil of the circuits."[49]

Ironic Strategies

Pasolini's own cinematic agenda is one of accelerating this "turmoil of circuits," transforming turmoil into a parody of entangled forces, whereby he multiplies intertextual and historical referents, weaving them into grotesque and hyperbolic antiaesthetic images of violence. This produces the effect of nonsense, or what he sees as cultural entropy, then an intrinsic unconsumability, uncooptability, and finally the crisis of historical meaning. Performative or spectacular mimicry of fascism, capitalism, and bourgeois moralism undercuts economies of credibility—history, morality, political theory—by revealing the disjunction of the historical/moral subjects from historical/moral consciousness. Freed from respecting historical chronology and its moralistic emplotment, this ironic cinema depicts capitalist and fascist discourses of subjectivity as what Baudelaire labeled "lucid madness": the splitting of the subject into empirical subjects that, as de Man explains, "exist in a state of inauthenticity, and [linguistic] subjects that exist only in the form of a language that asserts the knowledge of this inauthenticity. [Yet he stipulates that] this does not, however, make it into an authentic language, for to know inauthenticity is not the same as to be authentic"(*Blindness and Insight*, 214). What I mean by ironic is that *Salò* not only rejects narrative and ideological resolutions (Hayden White) but also presents an increase in self-awareness in the course of demonstrating the impossibility of our being historical (de Man)—the inability to configure self-reflective systems of meaning. *Salò* represents a world of total artificiality (insincerity or bad faith), which consequently challenges both logical and libidinal economies. For Paul de Man, irony "leads to no synthesis ... irony is unrelated vertigo, dizziness to the point of madness. ... Sanity can only exist because we are willing to function within the conventions of duplicity and dissimulation" (*Blindness and Insight*, 215–16). *Salò* ironizes these conventions, reassembling the hyperhistorical narrative of fascism by fastening it to its various supplementary incarnations (aestheticism, sadomasochism, perversion, violence, capitalism, militarism, modernism). As a result, Pasolini delimits these very classifications. This synecdochic mode of representation thereby puts history into crisis, time becomes "Aionic," it passes into *dopostoria*, which clones the synchronic mechanism of *preistoria* and its ability to transmute. Yet unlike the sacred, Dionysian model of *preistoria*, Aionic time maintains the visage of power and the simulation of order and control. Pasolini utilizes the inauthenticity of Aionic time in order to present the ironic disappearance of the present fleeing into the past and future of Dante's *Inferno*, Sade's, Blanchot's, Klossowski's, Nietzsche's, Barthes's, and others' philosophical thinking, and the history of the representation of fascism, which culminates in the disappearance of notions of depth (meaning, substance, corporeality, human passions).[50] For example, Pasolini overlays Dante's textual structuring of his *Inferno* (a systemic layering of concentric circles, *gironi,* which coil into a frozen core, housing Satan and Judas) with Sade's *utopie du mal,* which is then projected into a high modernist mise-en-scène (the modernist decoration of interior sets) in juxtaposition to the pastoral landscape surrounding the libertines' villa.

These visual and textual references are then encoded in the fascist historical context, which is fastened to the philosophical discussions of Nietzsche's concept of mediocrity and the *Übermann*, Huysmans's dandyism, Proust's modernism, dadaism, futurism, the radio broadcasts of Hitler's speeches and Ezra Pound's poetry—Pound reads his cantos, the deleted ones on fascism, in a radio broadcast from the last days of the *Salò* republic as we watch the libertines torture and kill their victims—and finally the silence of the victims who become pure bodies and provide a space on which these humanist or inhumanist grammars can be inscribed. This artificial layering affects the perception of distance: decadent writers, artists, and thinkers become inexorably entwined with modernist, fascist, anarchist, and leftist artists and thinkers.

Everybody is in hell. Pasolini uses this artificial texture, which collapses notions of time and space as an instrument to probe the limits of interpretation, to challenge mechanisms that assign blame even as they disengage their own position from the discourse of responsibility. Unlike the project of postmodernism, which reads the collision of narratives and metanarratives as imploding or subverting discourses of authority, this "becoming-mad of depths" (the collapse of meaningful discourses), as Deleuze argues, does not create fissures in the capitalist system, as Foucault believed (or at least hoped), but shifts the orientation from the depths to the surface. Similarly, *Salò* does not present a chaotic implosion of the infrastructure engendered by the collapse of discourses of legitimacy but what Deleuze calls "the conquest of the surface" or what Baudrillard labels the "triumph of the simulacra." Rather than exploding disciplines, *Salò*'s fragmentation of images, discourses, and counterdiscourses exemplifies the permeation of violence in all social relations: every social act expresses violence, from production to writing, representation, exchange, marriage, reproduction, and knowledge. Yet Pasolini's incessant referencing reveals his obsession with monumentality—with monumental texts, symbols, and intellectual projects—which emerges in the course of making *Salò* as a kind of Dantean *Inferno*, with the same prophetic and absolute value.

Pasolini's ironic strategy, like the fatal strategy, functions as a form of reactionary moralism. As Bataille writes, "Nobody, unless he is totally deaf to it, can finish *Les 120 Journèes de Sodome* without feeling sick: the sickest is he who is sexually excited by the book . . . there was nothing respectable which Sade did not mock, nothing pure which he did not soil, nothing joyful which he did not frighten . . . [the text] appears to us like a skin disease."[51] Hence our engagement or implication in the immoralism of Sade's *l'utopie du mal* provokes at best an antithetical reaction—it is an expression of violence designed to rid itself of violence. Furthermore, for Pasolini the effect of repulsion must also instill, in the viewer, an existential consciousness—a recognition of one's own reactionary moralism, which punishes victims (as the world) for experiencing any type of pleasure outside predetermined cultural parameters, fascist, paternalistic, bourgeois. The depiction of erotic precocity, which Annie Le Brun describes as transforming "acknowledged tastes into the most licentious and revolting festivals of the senses," ensnares the spectator in an existential gaze.[52] Le Brun distinguishes voyeuristic, or disengaged, spectatorship that desires entertainment from an existential, engaged spectatorship: "unlike the theatre of amusement, whose very essence is to take us outside ourselves, the theatre of passions shows us into our own prison and locks the door behind us. It is as if the aim of deviation were to confront one inexorably with the self" (*Sade, A Sudden Abyss*, 96). In fact, rather than reinforce what Sontag perceives as the sublime beauty of the nazi or fascist, Pasolini's libertines resemble the grotesqueness and banality of the bourgeois father and patriarch. For instance, the libertines are representatives of what Pasolini describes as four hyperbolic yet generic figures of power: a duke, a banker, a captain of industry, and a monsignor (*Pasolini*, 394). Thus Pasolini belies the visual pleasure of the image—whether it be the seductive power of evil or the fetishistic dress of nazi regalia as reconstructed by neodecadent artists, filmmakers, and contemporary cultural theorists. He counters the tendency to associate seduction with evil by satirizing both the cultural theories positing that the desire governing the capitalist system is founded on a voyeuristic and sadistic white, Western, male libido and the interpretation of fascism as a symptom of homosocial and homosexual desire gone awry.

But Pasolini does not prescribe any new means of escape nor any line of flight into the revindication of humanity. Instead, he pushes discourses of legitimacy and stability over the edge, returning man to the Unheimlicheit (unhomely). In response to popular theories and representations of fascism, Pasolini carnivalizes the patriarchal power structure by spectacularizing its franchising or prostitution of sexuality: old whores are commended for turning sexually inexperienced young women into "first-class whores," and middle-aged bourgeois men are sexually aroused by consuming narratives that they internalize and act out on bodies, especially those of young men. He emphasizes the ironic affiliation between the omnipresent homosocial discourse of power—which he sees as a closeted sadistic polysexuality—and the fetishistic image or spectacle of the femme fatale—an icon that marks the sexual conjecture of that very homosocial economy. By hyperbolizing heterosexuality, homosociality, and homosexuality in their extreme sadistic or maniacal manifestations, he abrogates the spectacle of ambiguity and discloses that behind the mask of authority, and all of its perverse manifestations (incest, sadism, and masochism), lies the desire for total control, total consumption of all bodily desires, and, hence, the foreclosure of all desire, passion, and intimacy.

Desire Overdetermined by Power

Salò presents a historic closure, the failure of pleasure, or *jouissance*, to rupture the Sadean logic of the law. But instead of presenting an apocalyptic explosion of evil, *Salò* expresses closure by nailing neofascism and neocapitalism into an Oedipal economy. This incestuous continuity is made apparent in the Duke's proposal "cari amici sposando i nostri figle rispitivi" ("dear friends, let us marry each others' daughters"), which, as he continues, "uniremo per sempre i nostri destini" ("will unite us forever in one destiny"). In direct opposition to *Open City*, *The Damned*, *The Conformist*, and *Cabaret*, Pasolini presents the fascist apparatus of power as a form of radical masculinity directed against daughters, sons, and mothers, rather than the infantile masculinity of Fellini's *Amarcord* or the ambiguous, yet feminized sexuality of *The Damned* and *The Conformist*. *Salò*'s extreme masculinity manifests itself as a compulsion to radically eliminate all possible progeny and difference in favor of what Klossowski calls a "monstrous singularity," the extreme expression of sadistic narcissism. Sade defines the objective of this "monstrous singularity" as the "preservation of one's own existence, at no matter whose expense" (*Philosophy of the Bedroom*, 303). Pasolini subsequently replicates this Sadean annihilation of symbolic figures that menace this radical singularity: the mother and the daughter, both of whom represent reproduction, and the son, who threatens the libertines with the replacement of the self. For this reason, the libertines wage war against nature. This revolt of the unnatural, as Blanchot believes, reflects man's deepest need to outrage nature—a need, as he sees it, that is infinitely stronger than the need to offend God (*Sade et Lautrèamont*).

This monstrous singularity is itself a fatal strategy, since it presents not only fascism's last (metastatic) stand but the end of the line, where fathers consume their children. The Monsignore (one of the four libertines) demonstrates this desire to erase any potential threatening or competing desires when he recites the Proustian axiom that "within a budding grove, the girls think of love, hear the radio, drink tea, and to hell with being free, they have no idea that the bourgeoisie has never hesitated to kill its own children."[53] The decontextualization of this quote deflates its critical impact, since this seemingly autocritical cognition of the libertines' abuse of power leaves no space for resistance or opposition. Self-awareness merely suggests the absurdity or obscenity of institutional power structures, that is, that they are predicated on supreme sadistic fantasies. As Klossowski has shown, the sadistic fantasy rests on the desire of the father to destroy his own family. Victims are chosen not only on the basis of their political affiliation with the resistance—their political or symbolic value—but also on the grounds that they present a threat to the libertines' desire for total control or mastery. While the nonconformity to fascist republican law may be one of the principal criteria in determining who will be a victim and who will be a collaborator and *milite*, the subproletariat does not exclusively constitute the ranks of the victims. The libertines' very own daughters are treated by the *collaboratori* and the *militi* as "deboli creature incatenate." For example, Claudio, one of the most aggressive misogynists of the *militi*, spits in the face of one of the libertines' daughters just before leading the group of the four young women in to marry their respective fathers.

The repetition of this act of defilement—again Claudio spits, this time on the buttocks of the same character—draws attention to the fact that the libertines have made their daughters/wives the servants of their sadistic republic. In the next scene in which they appear, they have been stripped, both literally (as they are the only characters who appear nude in this scene) and symbolically, of their bourgeois clothing (status). Denuded of any trace of familial or class affiliation, other than becoming objects of exchange between their fascist/capitalist fathers and objects of the *militi*'s aggression, they undergo a process of dehumanization. As servants, they suffer some of the most violent humiliation at the hands of the *militi*, who represent the lower classes' *ressentiment* of the bourgeoisie. Yet this *ressentiment* is distinctly not revolutionary; it is rather a desire to mimic or assume the identity of the bourgeois fascist fathers and thus consume the power and possessions of the bourgeoisie. While one of the daughters is constantly being spit upon, another is violently sodomized and ridiculed in front of a dinner gathering as she screams in pain, and all of them are forced to behave like dogs: they are collared and put on a leash, only to be fed a handful of dog food containing within it a number of nails. Ultimately, the libertines will not hesitate to kill their own daughters/wives; they select their daughters among the other victims to be awarded "blue ribbon" treatment, torture and execution.

Pasolini presents the family as the primary site of submission to a sadistic father, a sadistic superego or law that consumes and annihilates any possible pleasure outside its own desire to humiliate and destroy. The libertines no longer circumscribe an external enemy, the uncivilized other; instead they *internalize* acts of violence, imprisoning their victims within their very own house. All violence is portrayed as functioning on the personal level, replicating the internal structure of the family and its interpersonal relationships. Pasolini relentlessly confines all relationships to the Freudian model, the pyramid or triangle—fathers and daughters, fathers and sons, fathers and wives, and so forth. Yet, what culminates in Freud as the Electra and Oedipus complexes—the desire of the child to kill the parent of the same sex and marry the one of the opposite sex—and in Sade as the father's inciting the daughter to torture and kill the mother, returns in *Salò* as the simultaneous elimination of both mother and daughter, as well as son. Through the radical elimination of any means of identification, ego formation, and, especially, eradication of the victims' desiring agencies, Pasolini problematizes the Freudian theory of Electra and Oedipus complexes as well as the Sadean essentializing of nature and gender. Rather than returning gender to an essentialist discourse, Pasolini attributes the "primal force of the father" and the "secondary force of the mother" as a product of preexisting social relations. Instead of repeating the Freudian model, which places the father as the ego-ideal and the mother as the victim par excellence, Pasolini focuses on a monstrous egocentric desire whereby the incestuous desire to reproduce the self through the other is consumed by a greater desire for pure self-affirmation. As a result, rather than reinforce the dissemination of power within a familial structure, Pasolini presents the family as possessing its own fatal strategy—the stronger desire for self-affirmation negates the desire for the reproduction of institutionalized power.

As in the neodecadent films of Visconti, Bertolucci, and Fosse, the symbolic apparatus of Christian and humanist arguments for the moral advance of the human species falls apart. Yet Pasolini distinguishes the unreproductivity of the neodecadents, where children consume their parents (*The Damned, Germania anno zero,* and *The Conformist*), from the neofascist or neocapitalist institutionalization of fathers consuming their families. Rather than reading fascism as an "exceptional" outbreak of psychotic homosexuality that refuses to submit to Oedipalization, he reads fascism as a normative psychosis of the law that castrates in the name of the father and to the advantage of the father. The libertines clearly reject humanist notions, including the more narcissistic impulses to reproduce, and so the vision of the child as an extension of the self transforms into the image of the child as a threatening replacement of the self. What Freud articulates in *Civilization and Its Discontents* as the radical desire to "exploit one's neighbor's capacity for work without compensation, to use him sexually without his consent, to seize his possessions, to humiliate him, to cause him pain, to torture and to kill him," is turned loose against every man, especially those within close proximity to the libertine, the members of his own family.[54]

This omnipresent model of *Homo homini lupus*, therefore, undermines the moral and cultural fabric of the nuclear family and denigrates its reproductive and repressive (Oedipal) functions. Deleuze argues that within the Sadean framework "the father can only be a father by overriding the law, by dissolving the family and prostituting its members. The father represents nature as primitive anarchic force that can only be restored to its original state by destroying the laws and the secondary beings that are subject to them" (*Masochism*, 60). The libertines, therefore, articulate the desire for monstrous singularity as a process whereby all possible identifications with the law, with the father, with authority, legitimacy, and justice are debilitated. Pasolini pushes the image of the capitalist/fascist bourgeois father beyond Deleuze's adaptation of Freud's primal horde, the primal nature of man, to an image of anarchic parody of authority and recalcitrant reaction against nature. Instead of returning to an image of purity, a pure anarchic or primal force, Pasolini's vision of capitalist sadism is one of conscious contamination, conscious illegitimacy, and insincerity. Indeed, the authority of the libertines is markedly ironic since the aim of the father is not to re-produce but repeatedly to affirm his own absolute power, by negating any form of existentialism.

In this world of sadistic, incestuous fathers, the role of motherhood is radically rejected: from one of the forced collaborators (Claudio) ordering his mother ("va via") to go away—slapping her face as she runs to give him a scarf—to the libertines' replacement of mothers with their daughters, to the drowning of the mother of one of the female victims when she attempts to save her daughter, and finally to the narration of the second raconteuse (Signora Maggi), who tells matter of factly how she murdered her mother: "non stetti per resistire la tentazione e allora la uccisi" ("I couldn't resist the temptation, so I killed her"). This admission of murder is met with the applause of the libertines, who retort in kind "era la unica cosa da farsi" ("it was the only thing to do"), adding, "è follia supporre che si debba qualcosa alla propria madre. Dovremmo essere sempre grati perchè ha goduto mentre qualcuno l'ha posse-duta una volta?" ("it is crazy to think that one owes something to one's mother. Must we always be indebted to her for having once felt pleasure while being possessed by a man?"). The libertines do not simply reduce (devalue) all familial relations to the physicality or mechanics of sexual reproduction; they parody nineteenth-century sci-entific attempts to equate feminine sexual pleasure with a maternal instinct. Accord-ingly, they mimic the attempts of nineteenth-century thinkers to solve the mystery of female orgasm by applying it to a materialist model, a model that is predicated on physical evidence. In the case of sexual arousal, the evidence (ejaculation) must always be measured in terms of a phallic model. Because of woman's lack of visible ejacula-tion, they equate feminine pleasure to insemination, the production of a child, since it was considered the only physical evidence to substantiate the existence of feminine pleasure.[55] However, what is markedly distinguished is the difference of the two sexual models; while female sexuality remains grounded in a productive or reproductive sexual model, male sexuality is not dependent on the same productive model but instead on a model of enjoyment, a model of expenditure, which nullifies the productive model itself.

Here *Salò* recalls the teachings of Lombroso, Weininger, and Nordau, which distinguish two types of women, the mother and the prostitute. These writers interpret motherhood as instinctive, a mere preservation of the species, therefore intellectually very low; while prostitution is the most highly developed type of femininity, "intellectually speaking" (*Sex and Character*, 226). Pasolini satirizes their sterile, dubious logic in order to demonstrate the preservation of their theoretical premises within neofascism's and neocapitalism's discourses on race and gender, discourses that were popularized in the early twentieth century and later associated with fascist thinking. What Pasolini singles out in this thought is the use of sexual aggressiveness as a barometer to determine who is more masculine and therefore who is the more intelligent species. Regardless of the Platonic prioritizing of intelligence over sensuality (mind over body or matter), the privilege conflates the model of intelligence with that of aggression, resulting in the de-eroticization of male sensuality. Intelligence is measured in opposition to passivity over against activity (production versus reproduction) and to sentimentality (the less emotionalism, the more intelligent the man). Intelligence signifies both the demystification of all love relations and the divestment of amatory relations. Pasolini's aim is not to reveal so much the reactionary degeneracy of pseudoscientific thought as the global permeation of capitalist and protofascist thinking, which cannibalizes natural instincts, and what Pasolini believed to be sacred about those instincts, in favor of a more sterile, consumptive, and intellectual or "scientific" way of regarding sexual instincts. In *Salò* the conflict between the sacred and the profane has disappeared, leaving behind the remains of a tyrannical desire to master nature by becoming purely unnatural. And for Pasolini nothing is more unnatural than complete alliance of capitalism with fascism and patriarchalism.

While the libertines refer to themselves as fathers, women are distinctly *not* mothers. They are all considered whores by the republican government, since even daughters, virgins, and wives no longer symbolize currency in the libertines' sexual economy. Whether victims dressed as little girls, brides, or the aging raconteuses dressed as femme fatales, they function for the libertines as accessories to crimes committed against nature. The femme fatale, the bride, and the virgin lose all their seductive powers, their ability to produce metaphorical ambiguities, to bedazzle instead of being constantly ripped open and exposed. As Baudrillard writes, "[*Salò*] illustrates the truth that in a dominant masculine system ... it is femininity that incarnates reversibility, the possibility of play and symbolic involvement.... Here one perceives that sexual gratification is truly the industrial usufruct of the body, and the opposite of all seduction: it is a product of extraction, a technological product of a machinery of bodies, a logistics of pleasure which goes straight to its objective, on to find its object dead"

(*Seduction*, 21). For Pasolini, *Salò* presents more than the death of femininity and feminine seduction. It heralds the death of the productive (capital) model. Even the "enjoyment of one's symptom" or of one's fetish—defined by Freud as "a penis substitute," yet not a "chance penis" but the "Mother's phallus"[56]—disappears into its own negative vector of anxiety, the cognition of loss and the impossibility of retrieving what would make for an "acceptable object of desire." Pasolini questions the entire scenario of sexuality and psychoanalysis as a mode of simulation—as the simulation of a masculine sadistic model of sexuality. The image of the prostitute therefore becomes the ideal model of controlled or artificial sexuality/nature—a sterile sexual economy, which reproduces desire as a desire to consume pleasure.

The Return of the Femme Fatale

For Pasolini, the desire that the prostitute masks is radically singular. She not only represents the commodification of sex—the containment of sex in the form of exchange value—but the immersion of sexuality in the economy of discharge in which the body itself is reduced to a site of expenditure. The prostitute becomes an emblem of orgasm, which in turn becomes emblematic of sexuality devoid of seduction—she or he makes sexuality visible, without secrets, without uncertainty. Subsequently, each raconteuse/narratrice focuses on specific themes of discharge (sperm, feces, and blood), and each narrative results in the enacting of the expenditure of life-affirming fluids (sperm and blood) and the consumption of waste (feces).

However, Pasolini emphasizes the radical disunion between the raconteuse's emblematic significance and her function within this libidinal economy. The only orgasms they participate in are the pleasure of listening to Hitler's voice on the radio and the coprophilic feast that climaxes in their singing (along with the libertines, *collaboratori*, and the *militi*) the fascist song "Bandiera nera." Similar to the futurists' staging of masculine expenditure of virility (by shrinking woman into a receptacle for man's sexual aggression), as Leo Bersani and Ulysse Dutoit explain, "sex in Sade is, essentially, the loss of come, the coming to a loss, the climactic explosion which confirms the success of an esthetic limited to the madly rigorous schedules of Sade's narrative orders" ("Merde Alors," 92). The libertines, like the futurists, consider sexual partners to be necessary evils—to be repeatedly acted on, used up, or violated—rather than the emblems of unification of self with other, from which one derives the pleasure of becoming other, as for instance Kristeva outlines in her definition of amatory relations.[57] Sexual contact in the age of neocapitalism does not produce any intimate relationships; in fact it radically deconstructs sentimental relationships, unhinging cultural illusions that mask a sadistic sexual economy. Pasolini unmasks the ancillary bonding of the sexual liberation to a Sadean system of phallic machismo.

The more liberal the sexual encounter, the more disengaged it is from any emotional or communal sense. Rather than presenting a new-found freedom, this "liberation" treats sex as a series of alienated sexual encounters between two people who have no social obligation to each other. The result, therefore, is the assimilation of all sexual encounters into an ironic model—sex becomes purely functional, an acting out, or an act of discharge. While the futurists model sexuality on the act of penetration as a lethal means to verify the death of the other—"to prove the other's nothingness"—for Pasolini's libertines sex is equated to nonreproductive ejaculation, thereby "wasting the germ of the species, mixing it with blood and shit." Instead of reacting against woman per se, the libertines defile the symbolic substance that has been attributed to woman's essence, her serving as a model for production and reproduction. Beyond the bachelor machine of futurism and its paranoia about feminine decadence (life bursting forth), which returns woman to some primal nature (cosmic slop) and man to an excessive negative virility, Pasolini's and Sade's libertines' acts of violence cannot be reinterpolated as having some creative or cleansing purpose. Rather, the prostitute provides the libertines with a model of nothingness; she is completely excessive, she represents a waste of semen, pleasure without purpose, nonreproductivity, and the contagion of evil, since it is her narratives that will excite and stimulate the acts of the libertines.

Stripped of their seductive allure, the four raconteuses become emblems of sterility, simultaneously promoting the death of seduction as they employ the victims and the libertines in relentlessly brutal narratives. This erotic bankruptcy of the femme fatale results in the undermining of aesthetic codes, not only of illicit sexuality (feminine decadence) but also the aesthetization of fascism itself. The femme fatale no longer seduces us via visual stimulation nor does she give rise to what Barthes calls the "mystical feelings of perdition." Instead she is asked to "enflame the imagination" ("infiammare l'imaginazione") of the libertines, ironically, by cataloguing minute details of her past sexual encounters (*Mythologies*, 56). Pasolini uses Sade's language of exactitude to disrupt these iconic images of seduction and ambiguous sexuality. What was once the visual pleasure of viewing the surface (the screening of the body of the femme fatale) or the flesh metamorphosizes into the displeasure of extricating and exterminating the mystery of seduction.

The return of the femme fatale in *Salò* no longer fetishizes the smooth "face-object" of Garbo as Barthes described it; instead this return serves to implicate her in the fatal strategy of neocapitalism and neofascism. Unlike Sade's raconteuses, Pasolini's revisionary femme fatales are not missing fingers, teeth, nipples; they do not represent the grotesque in general but the fetid mechanics of consumer society, which eternalizes images of beauty, youth, cold seduction while discarding the woman, since she is subject to decay. Her mortality itself disrupts the seductive power of her image—an image that promises a certain immortality. Therefore, this femme fatale that still looms as an eternal but "ominous image maturing of beauty," and as an aging image of seduction, mocks her previous incarnations, dragging them out into the light to expose them as a series of worn-out fantasies. Like the portrait of Dorian Gray, Pasolini's femmes fatales reveal all the physical traces of spiritual and moral disfiguring, traces that correlate to acts of cruelty and debauchery. Pasolini's juxtaposition of the overly dressed and made-up femmes fatales with the nude bodies of the young victims draws attention to both the worship of youth as a universal symbol of sexiness and beauty and the role of the sex symbol as a mask for the commodification and fetishization of desire. The image of the diva, specifically the femme fatale, simulates sexuality yet masks the fact that it only functions to stimulate more perverse sexual actions that are directed elsewhere, toward the innocent and inexperienced youthful victims. Thus these parodic embodiments of the femme fatale can no longer play the game of seduction/illusion or mystery; they endlessly point to an orgy of realism, the perfidy of their own spectacle of seduction as constructed on the image of violent sexuality. Having already succumbed to the "ominous withering of beauty," the femme fatale becomes a hyperbole of decadent sexuality, yet at the same time her very image conforms to a baroque or kitsch enterprise of oversignification, vivid detail, touching on the grotesque. It is not only their age that makes the raconteuses grotesque but also the fact that they serve as a pretext for a sexual economy where they are considered undesirable. Pasolini takes decadence out of the theoretical and aesthetic context of the beautiful and reestablishes it in the aesthetics of the banal and the grotesque.

Similar to the libertines' exorcising the philosophy of Sade, Nietzsche, Freud, and numerous others, the raconteuses conjure up multiple iconic references ranging from Elenora Duse, Ida Rubenstein, Lyda Borelli, Marlene Dietrich, Jean Harlow, Louise Brooks, Mae West, Isa Miranda, and Greta Garbo to Joel Grey and Helmut Berger. This reciting of drag femmes fatales along with non-drag femmes fatales challenges the sexuality of the femme fatale altogether. Because the femme fatale always appears more feminine than the feminine, it is not clear what exactly is being parodied, whether it is the sexual politics of the 1930s and 1940s star system or the transformation of the sexiness of the female star or image of the femme fatale into an icon of kitsch, or even the drag reimaging of the femme fatale. However, it is clear, that within the matrix of parodic references and carnivalizations of these images of feminine seduction, feminine sexuality disappears. Woman becomes a pure object of parody. Furthermore, the reminiscent glamour of 1930s and 1940s movie stars, awakened by Pasolini—who, like Cavani, uses actresses made famous during the fascist period— raises questions concerning the aesthetization of feminine sexuality and its debt to the aesthetics of fascism. What is the role of the femme fatale in the visualization of neofascism and neocapitalism? Do the perverse desires of the femme fatale warrant her or his coming to represent fascist sexuality itself? For Pasolini, she is the libertines' sexually inactive and undesirable accomplice. The femme fatale becomes a mascot to the libertines' homosocial economy, legitimizing her own objectification.

In radical opposition to Pasolini's sacred image of motherhood, the raconteuses become what Kristeva would call accomplices of the patriarchy: "they wipe out all traces of dependence on the mother's body," and she adds, "the sadistic component of such an economy is so violent [it attempts to] obliterate the vagina."[58] This radical negation of motherhood and feminine sexuality is seen repeatedly in the killing of the mother, the repulsiveness of the female body, especially the genitalia. Pasolini exemplifies the connection of motherhood with the repudiation of female genitalia in a scene that commences with the symbolic "punitive" action taken against a young woman who has been killed for praying to an icon of the Madonna. Signora Viccari, standing over the dead body of the victim, returns to her storytelling; yet this time she recounts the tale of how the man whose name she has taken (Viccari) covered his eyes in horror after viewing her genitals, commenting, "poor whores have only their pussies to display."

Salò merges the death of the mother and the dependency on the mother (whether psychical, spiritual, or symbolical) by dismissing feminine sexuality altogether. The *narratrici* not only recount the murder of their mothers but denigrate genital sex, focusing rather on tales of sodomy, coprophagy, and anthropophagy. Unlike Kristeva, for whom the figure of Electra emblemizes the *necessary* identification of women intellectuals (writers, critics, and artists) with a patriarchal superstructure—preventing them from overidentifying with the mother's "inexhaustible non-symbolic drive," which, she argues, would lead them to psychosis or suicide—Pasolini envisions these gatekeepers of the patriarchy (Electras/eunuchs) as abetting and assisting in the complete de-eroticization of seductive feminine sexuality (the nonsymbolic). In contrast to Electra's alleged attempt to conceal or eradicate all traces of her "non-symbolic femininity," the raconteuse makes a spectacle of her iconic femininity, exposing her artificial construction. For Pasolini, then, the letter of the law and its overdetermined masculine symbolic value is more than a necessary evil that, as Kristeva suggests, can be "subverted" via frequent clashes with the feminine nonsymbolic. It is itself both psychotic and suicidal. Rather than engaging in the masochistic act of sacrificing the female body in exchange for the male intellectual capacity, as in the case of the futurist women, or seducing the sadist into a masochistic contract, as Cavani's *Night Porter* exemplifies (see chapter 4), these feminine figures present themselves as bodies without organs, sexual objects, or fetishes. The raconteuses are only used as parodic veils for the four libertines' pleasure: the women narrate their sexual adventures but do not partake in the Sadean rituals. As Baudrillard insightfully explains, "the *femme fatale* is never *fatale* as a natural element, but as artifice, as seductress or as the projective artifact of male hysteria. The absent woman, ideal or diabolic, object, scoffs at the difference of the sexes. She scoffs at desire and the subject of desire" (*The Perfect Crime*, 119). As an object, she becomes fatal only to herself by disappearing in the spectacle of her own artificiality.

The raconteuses serve purely as a framing device for the narrative. Before each narration, each respective raconteuse is seen admiring herself before the mirror. Each one of the three narrators repeats the same actions, gazing at herself in the mirror, descending the stairs, which marks the descent into the next *girone*, where, by commencing her monologue, she will become the master of ceremonies. The narration spirals downward from the *girone delle manie*, where Signora Viccari is utilized to "turn the victims into first-class whores," to the *girone di merda*, where Signora Maggi excites the libertines' coprophilic fantasies, and finally to the *girone di sangue*, where Signora Castella will narrate the tales of anthropophagy, torture, and mutilation, thereby prefacing the ultimate act of the Salò republic, the consumption of all its victims. These aging femmes fatales change costume as they change face and language: beginning with the French fairylike coquette (a parody of lost youth), to the Italian Dietrichesque cabaret femme fatale (who is too old to excite any sexual attention), to the German ice princess who laughs luridly when she recites tales of Sadean psychical cruelty (the insertion and sewing up of a mouse inside a woman's vagina, the flaying of young women, etc.). The reference to national or ethnic identity serves to emphasize the collaboration and participation of the French, Italians, and Germans in supporting fascism and its atrocities (in the case of the French I am referring to both Vichy and the pervasive anti-Semitism that allowed for the mass transportation of French Jews during the occupation). This ethnic stereotyping spills over into the simulation of national identity as manifested in feminine sexuality: French sexuality is coquettish, Italians master the spectacle of the *diva* (or *divo* in the case of Mussolini), and the Germans remain cold as in Dietrich's portrayal of *The Blue Angel*, becoming "angels of death."

While aesthetically the raconteuses are no longer desirable—they continually offer their sexual services to the libertines, who consistently refuse them—their appearance as well as their role in stimulating the libertines' imagination provides Pasolini with a venue for critiquing the promotion of the image of the femme fatale as an icon for sexual politics. These aging femmes fatales even remark on their own sexual bankruptcy. Indeed, women are consistently rejected as sexual objects: not only, as Barthes points out, is the vagina seen as unworthy in comparison to the phallus; the female anus is seen as inferior to the male. For instance, when given the opportunity to satisfy his desire to perform sodomy, the Eccellenza declares to Signora Castella, "lasciate mi perdere, dovreste sapere che ci sorvo milioni di occasioni che un uomo non desideri l'ano di una donna" ("leave me alone, you should know that there are millions of occasions on which a man does not desire the anus of a woman"). Barthes outlines the Sadean economy whereby the libertines scrupulously shroud the female's sexual organs. And it is this process, he argues, that yields a "threefold profit":

First, morality is overturned by a derisory parody: the same sentence serves both libertine and puritan: "Conceal your cunts, ladies." Next, Woman is destroyed: she is wrapped up, twisted about, veiled, disguised so as to erase every trace of her anterior features (figure, breasts, sexual organs); a kind of surgical and functional doll is produced, a body without a front part (structural horror and flouting), a monstrous bandage, a thing. Finally, in his order of occultation, the libertine contradicts everyday immorality; he takes the opposite tack from sophomoric pornography, which makes the supreme audacity the sexual denudation of Woman. Sade calls for a counter-striptease.... (*Sade, Fourier, Loyola*, 124)

Therefore, unlike Theweleit's recounting of the fantasies of the men of the Freikorps, where the rejection of the female was caused by the fear of female sexuality (an abyss from whence life bursts forth), or the Lacanian attribution of woman's secondary nature to a lack of a spectacular object, or even Sade's privileging of the female victim (since she has two sites of entry), for Pasolini the denunciation of woman is contingent on her *symbolic* value of transgression. Pasolini foregrounds the cultural overvaluing of the phallus and the homosocial nature of sexuality and further emphasizes the disappearance of not only the feminine but all forms of sensuality within an economy where men look at the phallus as a weapon and the vagina as a wound that needs to be not just concealed or clothed but stitched up. This disappearance of feminine difference serves to confine all forms of sexual expression to a singular economy, which Irigaray describes in *This Sex Which Is Not One* as the process of making love to oneself through the other. However, according to Pasolini, this total objectification of all sexual relations does not reinforce gender distinctions, that is, this object through which one loves oneself is not necessarily *feminine* or *feminized*. While the libertines divide the sexes in the process of selecting victims, both sexes are treated in a similar fashion: the young men are lined up and inspected by the libertines; the young girls are presented by the raconteuses as sexual objects in a fashion show; and both are treated as sexless in the scene that stages a competition for the most beautiful ass, where the sex of the victim is disguised.[59] Since sexual interaction in no way corresponds to sexual expression outside of pure self-affirmation, pure destruction, the gender of the victim becomes progressively less important.

The Eradication of Intimacy

Sodomy, the only form of sexual contact between libertine and victim, represents an act of transgression rather than a rebellious annihilation of femininity or heterosexuality.[60] This negative depiction of sodomy led Ben Lawton to argue that "Pasolini's strongest indictment of homosexuality comes in *Salò o le 120 giornate di sodoma*."[61] This argument, which equates sodomy with homosexuality, eclipses the libertines' larger symbolic value as the law or patriarchal authority. For Sade, the sign of sodomy is anti-theist; Pasolini, however, distinguishes the act of sodomy as depicted in the *The Trilogy of Life* (*Trilogia della vita*) film series from its symbolic representation in *Salò*. While in the *The Trilogy of Life* sodomy represents one form of sexual expression, operating within the sensual world of Dionysian passions, in *Salò* all sexual acts are confined to the realm of supercarnal activity, which abnegates any form of sensuality. Thus, the arguments of Naomi Greene, who sees "sodomy as a symbol of revolt and transgression—a dandy's protest against a capitalist world where all is abased on use and exchange" (*Cinema as Heresy*, 211), not only recodes homosexuality as decadent but misses Pasolini's point, that sodomy in the neofascist world of *Salò* is also inscribed in the sexual language of dominance; it is a pure expression of control. Deleuze and Guattari point out that "no gay liberation movement is possible as long as homosexuality is caught up in a relation of exclusive disjunction with heterosexuality, a relation that ascribes them both to a common Oedipal and castrating stock, charged with ensuring only their differentiation in two noncommunicating series, instead of bringing to light their reciprocal inclusion and their transverse communication in the decoded flows of desire" (*Anti-Oedipus*, 350–51). Hence arguments such as Watson's—"the self-destructiveness of the bourgeoisie can be seen in a variety of Italian films of the late 1960's and early 1970's, such as Bertolucci's *Conformist* (1970) Visconti's *Death in Venice*, De Sica's *The Garden of the Finzi-Continis*, *The Night Porter*.... Virtually all the bourgeois protagonists of these films condemn and destroy themselves in some way, as they attempt to internalize the Laius-Oedipus polemic"— will always return to the same point of departure, the castration of all sexualities (*Pier Paolo Pasolini and the Theatre of the Word*, 14). Instead of returning to the psychoanalytic model in order to understand fascism in the light of sexuality, Pasolini implicates psychoanalysis in amplifying the extremely violent masculine sexual politics of fascism and neofascism. For Pasolini, psychoanalysis internalizes the law of castration, thus installing the apparatus of repression universally. In turn, repression punishes humans for desiring and therefore alienates them from their own desiring agency. Pasolini recalls the question raised in Moravia's *The Conformist*: whether murder and fascist atrocities are more or less serious a crime against moral purity than is the act of sodomy. He does not participate in the demonization of the homosexual but in the grotesque parody of patriarchal law itself, a law that castrates desire in the name of repression. For Pasolini, fascist desire performs much like Oedipalized desire; it is a desire for repression, a reactionary desire—one that inveighs against difference and the possibility of becoming different.

As a consequence of this accelerated patriarchal model, all acts of eroticism collapse because of the extreme masculine position of what Foucault calls the isomorphism between sexual relations and social relations. Sexual relations, he posits,

> are always contrived in terms of the model act of penetration, assuming a polarity that opposes activity and passivity where sex can be seen as being of the same type as the relationship between a superior and a subordinate, an individual who dominates and one who is dominated, one who commands and one who complies, one who vanquishes and one who is vanquished (*History of Sexuality 2*, 215).

Replicating the Freudian model in which all victims are feminized, rather than the decadent and neodecadentist models where all illicit sexuality is feminized, Sade's and Pasolini's victims satirize the gender coding of this sexual and social isomorphism. The cross-dressing of the libertines as bourgeois women and the male victims as brides serves to erase feminine sexuality. The ridiculing of gender roles transforms them into pure artifice, costuming, a performance amounting to nothing. Unlike the Freudian who considers the masochist a willing recipient of sadistic performance, Pasolini follows the Deleuzian argument that masochism and sadism constitute two distinctly diverse libidinal economies. While the masochist enters into a contract with his/her dominatrix/dominator, thus controlling the masquerade of punishment, consuming it as pleasure, for the sadist there is no contract. He/she is the law and that law is interpreted as absolute power; therefore, all pleasure outside of those who embody the law is seen as transgressing the law. For Sade this distinction is illustrated by the two sisters, Juliette and Justine: Justine takes pleasure in sadistic orgies. In order to do so, however, she must identify herself with the law of the libertines; Juliette, on the other hand, resists each infliction and is left without any means of identification other than becoming the body of the victim. It is Juliette's suffering that affirms the dominance of the sadist and gives him/her pleasure. An analogy to these two sisters can be seen in Pasolini's juxtaposition of Albertina—who, when asked to disrobe, grins, revealing that she has a missing tooth, that is, she is an imperfect victim, not only physically, but also because she is already contaminated by evil—with Doris, the perfect victim, who enters nude, crying for her dead mother.

The visual display of suffering excites the libertines so much that they are visibly drawn to the young woman. What makes her a perfect victim is that she assumes the role of suffering or self-negation, while Albertina promises to become more of an accomplice in the libertines' acts of debauchery. Barthes elucidates the logic behind these two visceral responses: "The scream is the victim's mark: she makes herself a victim because she chooses to scream, if, under the same vexation, she were to ejaculate, she would cease to be a victim, she would be transformed into a libertine: to scream/to discharge, this paradigm is the beginning of choice, i.e. Sadean meaning" (*Sade, Fourier, Loyola*, 143). Pasolini juxtaposes these reactions that markedly distinguish the libertines from their victims and even daughters: Catalania, one of the libertines' daughters, screams as a result of being brutally sodomized by one of the *collaboratori*; her father then exposes himself, begging Efizio (the *collaboratore*) "a me" ("do me"). Thus the close-up of Catalania's scream is displaced and incorporated into the close-up of the Duke's enjoyment, only to be interrupted by the patriotic singing of "Bandiera nera"—the incorporation into fascist choreography. The scream serves as a threshold forever separating the libertine from the victim. While many screams serve to punctuate scenes, the ultimate death screams of the victims will not be heard. They will be silenced by the music sounding over the radio and the sound of Ezra Pound's voice as he reads his Canto 99. Pasolini emphasizes the irony behind Pound's poetic text by using it to enhance the image of these bourgeois fathers' torture, rape, and murder of their children. As they act we listen to the squeaky voice of the poet: "the whole tribe is from man's body/the father's word is compassion/the sons' filiality."

Yet the libertines' pleasure is also contingent on the victims' despair. Beyond the pleasure principle of discharge, the libertines indulge in the excessive frenzy of death and the concept of commotion. What Bersani and Dutoit call the "vibration" produces recognizable signs of sexual excitement. It is the spectacle of the other person's commotion. Sadism is the consequence of this form of voyeuristic erotic stimulation that is contingent on the witnessed or fantasized commotion of others; the stimulation of the libertines increases in direct proportion to the visible intensification of the victims' suffering. However, this perpetual motion (commotion) or permanent revolution against nature must be repeated, intensified, and accelerated, since, as Baudrillard points out, the unreal *jouissance* of consuming the other's pain, suffering, and even death reduces "sexuality to the actualization of desire in a moment of pleasure" (*Seduction*, 24). The libertines are conscious of the dilemma of repetition but also of the enigma entailed in the process of consumption—in order to consume the suffering and death of the victim one must cross this "limit of love" and appropriate the accomplices' experience, beyond the act of voyeuristic viewing or witnessing. They must reanimate what they have thoroughly dehumanized, the object-victim. While the Duke argues that sodomy is a more perfect form of transgression, since it can be infinitely repeated, the Banker argues that there is something still more *monstruoso*, *il gesto del carneifice*, the role of the executioner. The ecstasy resulting from the act of execution paradoxically means that one must know how to be "allo stesso tempo carnefice e vittima" ("at the same time executioner and victim"). That is, in order to take pleasure from the death throes of the other, the executioner must somehow establish an empathic connection to the other. Or as Deleuze argues, "in Sade it is the victim who speaks through the mouth of the torturer" (*Coldness and Cruelty*, 22). What Pasolini problematizes is the very act of empathy; it is not only a gesture of intrusive intimacy—it also functions as an act of appropriation.

Negative Desires

As if challenged by Heidegger's axiom that death and suffering are singular experiences, the libertines attempt both to usurp the suffering of the victims and to consume their deaths. And while the victims do make some limited attempts at rebellion—Ezio has a heterosexual relationship with the North African servant; Graziella has hidden a picture of her boyfriend; Eva and Antoniska have a lesbian relationship—by and large they cooperate in their own destruction. They accept humiliation, pain, and the exemplary deaths of the other victims rather than rebel against the system that is destroying them. They are guilty not only of turning each other in as a means of survival but also of not defending themselves or, at the very least, for Pasolini, of choosing to subsist under such subhuman conditions. Here Pasolini, like Wertmüller, poses the existential question of responsibility. If death is immanent, as he implies, is it irresponsible to die on the terms of neofascism and neocapitalist law? For Pasolini, this existential question cannot be simplified by "blaming the victims" for collaborating. Victims and libertines are two distinct groups; hence the question of collaboration does not enter into the assigning of blame. By de-eroticizing complicity, Pasolini strips the relationship of libertines to victims to pure power relations. He does not re-eroticize the connection between sex and power. While there may not be a collaboration between torturers and victims nor any compliance with the sadistic libidinal code, the question of collaboration remains an issue for Pasolini; he extends the role of compliance beyond destructive acts of sadistic eroticism to interaction with fascist and capitalist libidinal economies. It is compliance with the laws and institutions of neo-fascism and neocapitalism that challenges the notion that the relationship of the victim to the executioner is purely accidental. Is there a pure evil that exists separate from what it acts on? Is it only in the eyes of the libertine or his law that, as Blanchot describes, "the victim does not exist in and of himself, he is not a distinct being but a mere cipher who can be indefinitely substituted in an immense erotic equation?" (*Lautrèamont et Sade*, 234). If so, what allows for the simultaneous binding of citizens/victims to the law and the completely arbitrary and gratuitously violent treatment the law performs to the disservice of its citizens/victims? And how is it that the frenzy of monstrous singularity can coexist with, if not thrive on, the mechanisms that produce a society of control?

While the neocapitalist/neofascist system runs on speed and velocity, chaos and frenzy, what endures, frozen at its epicenter, is the law of consumption and discharge. For Pasolini, the anarchic frenzy of consumption is supplementary to the law or society of control itself. The law, in order to exist, must uphold its purity, its pure instrumental faculties, by radically rejecting (reacting against and acting on) any contamination or potential contamination. Consequently, it is in their essential relation to the law that the libertines acquire their function as masters and their significance as the law's pure agency. This logic of negation and consumption subverts the moral purpose of the law, and turns Platonic systems upside down. Divorced of its ideological content, the very law that gives the libertines their power, and therefore their identity, is itself revealed as a pure system of functionality, a system of punishment. And it is precisely this encoding of the bourgeois law as a system of punishment devoid of significance, or operating against its own point of reference, that Pasolini depicts as intertwined with the system of neocapitalism and the law of fascism. The convergence of reason and destruction results in the expropriation of the corporeal and the moral. The entrenchment of power in the mechanics of negation of desire (or the will of the other) functions as an equivocal energy that is at the same time a reserve and an expenditure of force. This type of affirmation, Blanchot ascertains, "fulfills itself only by negation, a power which is destruction: it is fact and law, datum and value. [. . . Yet] oddly enough Sade subordinates desire and treats it as suspect. This is because desire militates against solitude and leads to the dangerous recognition of the world of the other."[62] Hence the ecstasy of the libertine, which submits to the controlled economy of consumption, transforms pleasure from a spontaneous force of self-abandonment to a reactionary, impersonal form of acting on—an act of punishing and cannibalizing so as to extract for personal consumption. While the ultimate erotic expression of the libertines will manifest itself as the law's own form of contagion (the excess of evil, the pleasure of consumption), this contagion functions more as a fatal antibody designed to radically purge the other by exterminating his/her desiring agencies.

In contrast to the effects of a communicable, yet unbridled, desire that corrodes, metamorphosizes, and changes the structure of cells, the libertines' scourge spreads like a disease that consumes the vital organs. The logic of this biological warfare unfolds as a process defiling the body so as to oxidize its possibility of hosting a more radical form of impurity, the ability to transmute, to become other. Since, as Airaksinen argues, in the world of otherness "one can only beg for love, like one begs for any other gift, [i.e.] mutual love forms a network of gift-relationships which also entails a strong ethical bond," the libertines inveigh against the principles of a Maussian notion of gift-economy, which is replaced by an economy of consumption and expenditure (*Of Glamour, Sex and de Sade*, 119). They negate not only primitive societies but all forms of social bonding other than the abstraction of that bond in the form of the social contract that gives birth to the law itself. Yet in *Salò* subjective intimacy itself is treated with suspicion, equated not to transgression and, ironically, to contamination. All acts of subjective intimacy, specifically heterosexual love, are punishable by death, since intimacy is the most radical form of contaminating order—it has the potential of reproduction beyond the repetition of pure pleasure, pure discharge. The intimacy of romantic involvement is de-eroticized and made grotesque throughout the libertines' carnivalistic staging of traditional intimate relationships. This staging de-eroticizes the sexual relationship by stripping the victims of their agency, reducing them to objects who now become intimately known in the process of looking, probing, and peeling back the skin. Hence Pasolini implicates the intimate gaze of science as a forced intimacy and objectification of intimacy, which also "arrives at its object to find its object dead."

Reflecting this "suspicion" of desire as always dependent on the other, one of the libertines decries "il limite dell'amore è di sempre avere bisogno di un complice" ("the limit of love is that it is always dependent on an accomplice"). Pasolini uses this suspicion of desire to emphasize the ironic return of sexually demonized figures (libertines, fascists, sadists, etc.) to a discourse of purity (pure law and pure war), what Klossowski calls a "monstrous singularity." It is this monstrous singularity that constitutes the principle of subjectivity: the faculty that exercises it is the same faculty that invents it. Accordingly, it erases not only the object through which it affirms itself but also the authority of the law, since all law is predicated on the preconception of the universal or the homogeneous state of nature (a resemblance used to determine commonality among men). And so Pasolini also implicates the construction of law (moral, legal, or symbolic) in sadism or fascism.

By associating the libertines with generic bourgeois figures of authority and with the framers of the law (those who speak in the name of the universal "we"), Pasolini reveals that morality itself is not as much arbitrary as it is grounded in a system of control. As Slavoj Žižek points out qua Kant, the paradox inscribed in morality and its institutionalization in the law is its lack of an ideal model. What is good is in fact unknowable, and what remains is the desire for purity. Žižek states: "the sadistic superego is the hidden truth behind Kantian ethics. That is to say, is not Kant's rigorist ethics patently 'sadistic'?; is not the agency which pronounces the ethical imperative a sublime version of the sadistic torturer who demands the impossible and finds enjoyment in humiliating the subject, that is, in the subject's failure to comply with his demand?"[63] By the same token, Žižek implicates Lacan and his psychoanalytic theory of modeling normalcy on sadism. He writes, "Lacan 'purifies' Sade: the sadist Will-to-Enjoy is the exemplary case of a pure, nonpathological desire." And he adds, "perhaps therein resides the ultimate cause of all the troubles with so-called modern subjectivity" (*Metastases of Enjoyment*, 173). The desire that the libertines express is not for what they term the "deboli creature incantenate, destinate ai nostri piaceri," ("weak chained creatures destined for our pleasure") but for the consumption of what can only be singularly experienced, what Žižek qua Lacan calls the humiliation and resignation of the other, his or her suffering and death. In the words of Bersani and Dutoit, "slaves are killed so that the masters may, as it were, appropriate their suffering as their own sexuality" ("Merde Alors," 83). The appropriation of suffering as well as suffering by proxy, however, blocks them from the limits of otherness. The pleasure or sexuality of the libertines relentlessly and repeatedly negates the others' desire in an attempt to pierce the intimacy of their being and appropriate their experience of death. And it is for this reason that Pasolini describes these libertines as "uomini che condannano uomini in nome del nulla: perchè le Istituzioni sono nulla, quando hanno perso ogni forza, la forza fanciulla delle rivoluzioni—perchè nulla è la Morale del buon senso, di una comunità passiva, senza più realtà" ("men who condemn men in the name of nothing, because their institutions mean nothing when they have lost the youthful force of revolution—because the morality of common sense coming from a passive community amounts to nothing.")[64]

This bureaucratic parody of Dante's hell as a theater of violent sexuality, where each *girone* is directly related to sadistic sexual torture, does not lead to Dante's frozen devil at its epicenter but to both Sade's anti-orgy of blood and death and the legalization of a neocapitalist society of control. Within the imaginary landscape of the *Inferno*, Sadean tales of debauchery, as narrated by aging women made up to look like drag queens, are told. These Sadean tales serve to disrupt the humanist division of ideology—an ideology that validates the law—from violence, high ideals of culture divorced from the barbarism employed in its service. If these aging parodic visions of fascist sexuality serve as nodal points in the neocapitalist and neofascist network of sexuality to aesthetics and politics, then they expose the artificial coding or coating that conceals the social bankruptcy of a system driven by the desire to control, conquer, and fix markets, to circumscribe others within a global system (a united nations) whose predominant function is to patrol borders, suppress uprisings, and police economies—consuming images, producing otherness as newness in order to cannibalize or to kill it. *Salò* presents the victory of fascism and of the neofascist symbolic, which consequently castrates the will to live as difference or as a will of becoming other. The film itself embodies Pasolini's last attempt to disclose the obscenity and pernicious underside of the society of control. It offers an uncomfortable (*scomodo*) vision of our "passion for abolition." It is a scandal designed to provoke both a sense of social bankruptcy and a profound anger at a system that patrols and consumes our very agency of desire. Since there is no undermining the system from within—"there is no way to escape, even he who refuses to take part, he is that other man, miserable, cruel, stupid, cold, ironical, who makes every serious passion artificial, who does not believe in the passions of others"—Pasolini offers an antibody, a way of unhinging this fatal social contract. He prescribes, "Burn down institutions, this is a hope of those who weep now, it is a hope not foreseen by the real passions that will be born, nor in the new sounds of their words."[65]

4. Mixing Memory with Desire

In diesen heil'gen Hallen
Kennt man die Rache nicht . . .
Weil man dem Feind vergibt
Wen solche Lehren nicht erfreu'n
Verdienet nicht, ein Mensch zu sein.

—Mozart, *Die Zauberflöte*[1]

Every woman adores a fascist
The boot in the face, the brute
Brute heart of a brute like you.

—Sylvia Plath, "Daddy"

Nessuno voleva sentir parlare di colpa. . . . Non volevano sentir parlare di colpa gli innocenti, ma nemmeno i criminali che pretesero di mettere una pietra su quello che era accaduto con il <<befehl ist befehl>>, gli ordini sono ordini. E la tesi della <<Befehlsnotstand>> valse sempre da attenuate presso le giurie che covevano giudicare dei crimini di guerra. È sempre colpa del funzionario che sta sopra e cosí la colpa passa di testa in testa fino ad Hitler. Solo Hitler sarebbe dunque colpevole.[2]

—Liliana Cavani, *Il portiere di notte*

Because *The Night Porter* has been accused of representing a plethora of abjections— "a terrifically decadent X" (Russell Davis); both "sleazy and slow moving" (David Sterritt); "a thinly disguised fascist propaganda film that glorifies sadism, brutality and

149

exaggerated *machismo*, [whose] barbarism rests not only in its audacity to extol fascist principles, but also in its attempt to *legitimize* the death of millions of innocent victims at the hands of the nazi machine" (Henry Giroux)[3]—the film provokes intense emotional, ideological, and moral responses. These reactions in turn attest to the prevalent emotional investment in representations of nazism and the "Final Solution", as well as depictions of sadomasochistic relationships and aestheticizations of sexual politics. Yet given the precedent of depicting nazis and fascists as sexual predators (preying on the weak and morally deprived), decadent hom(m)osexuals, depraved transvestites, and vicious sadists, what makes *The Night Porter* so controversial, as Cavani herself points out, is that it is a complex love story that explores notions of power, guilt, and selflessness.[4] Unlike portrayals of nazis and fascists engaging in acts of violent sexuality, rape, sodomy, and debauchery and expressing enjoyment only at the sight or expense of someone else's pain, Cavani's characters do not conform to binary models of good and evil. In other words, Cavani does not participate in the convenient alliance of nazis and fascists to other socially conceived forms of impurity and immorality—sadism, homosexuality, decadence, disease, feminine sexuality. With the exception of Max (the protagonist), who is said by his former colleagues to be insane and to have a wild imagination, Cavani's depiction of former nazis is almost puritanical. The group of former nazis in *The Night Porter* comprises paranoid professionals, austere doctors, probing lawyers, and closeted homosexuals. They are the epitome of the bourgeosie. And they express their disgust—similar perhaps to the sentiments of some members of the audience—at Max and Lucia's sadomasochistic "love story." By juxtaposing these cardboard nazis—efficient bureaucrats, narcissistic homosexuals, and nostalgic nazis who are indifferent to any form of human suffering—with Max and Lucia, Cavani implodes such conflated one-dimensional symbols of evil, demonstrating how fascist moral constructions dovetail with bourgeois morality. She sets up an uncomfortable alliance of former nazis with bourgeois moralists in order to explore the moral implications of such a convergence. She enframes both ways of seeing into a masculinist (and in this case nazi) sexual economy, in which, as George Mosse describes, "sexual intoxication is viewed as unmanly and anti-social" (*Nationalism and Sexuality*, 10).

Foregrounding the enigmatic intimacy and interdependency of the victim (a non-Aryan daughter of a socialist) and the victimizer (a German SS-man), Cavani incites a tremendous amount of critical scorn, if not outright moral condemnation, not only from many film critics but more importantly from many male survivors of the Holocaust and many feminists.[5] Critics like Giroux, who calls the film "blatant neo-fascism," and Richard Schickel, who proclaims that "the true immorality of *The Night Porter* lies in its implicit trivialization of a historical tragedy," interpret this intimacy as "legitimizing" the atrocities of World War II.[6] Still others see the sadomasochistic relationship between Max and Lucia as validating the abuse of women. Marguerite Waller points out that "Mirto Gaolo Stone and Teresa de Lauretis, among others find the film unbearable," which owes to what Waller sees as the film's ability to "destabiliz[e] the spectator."[7] It is no wonder that the film was banned and confiscated

by Italian censors, resulting in the indictment of Cavani and her producer on criminal charges for its portrayal of sexual torture. Critiques and reactions such as these,
however, imply that the representation of intimacy and the power of seduction alone
interrupt a social desire to reinforce categorical imperatives that distinguish victims
from nazis and fascists. Sadomasochistic scenarios, as Linda Williams's work has
shown, present a difficult problem in the assessment of violence in sexual representation; Williams writes, "for here the violence is depicted not as actual coercion but as
a highly ritualized game in which the participants consent to play predetermined roles
of dominance and submission" (*Hardcore*, 18). Aware of such problems, Cavani clearly
differentiates sadism from masochism: Max and Lucia's memories of nazi Austria,
visualized in the flashback sequences, recall a sadistic economy whereby Max (the nazi
concentration camp official) had absolute power to determine the fate of Lucia (the
concentration camp prisoner). Lucia was, then, left with only one choice, as Molly
Haskell explains, "to survive by surrendering to the 'unspeakable' requirements of her
enemy-guardian," or, as Mario (a fellow survivor) elucidates, "to save your skin, no
price was too high" ("Are Women Directors Different," 73).

Although these flashbacks are highly aestheticized (romanticized), they exemplify
the sadistic distribution of power through which the nazi possesses total agency (self-
affirmation, authority: he embodies the law). The process of aestheticizing such
images also serves to confuse memory with desire. Max's and Lucia's relationship,
predicated on a sadistic economy, does not transform into a masochistic economy but
a masochistic masquerade, in which Max is disempowered as a former nazi war criminal and Lucia is empowered as a witness who could turn him over to the war tribunal.
This shift in power provides Lucia with the agency of choice, whether or not to engage
in a romantic relationship with Max. This transgression of set identities does not
describe a sexual dynamic within the lagers (concentration camps), but postwar eroticized obsession with memory—not only the victims' desire or compulsion to remember
but also the media's fetishization of fascism. *The Night Porter* undermines the theoretical premises that serve to define sadism and masochism by confusing domination
with submission: "the question of passivity is not the question of slavery, but the question of dependency not the plea to be dominated." In fact, what disturbs Hans Vogler
(the nazi professor) more than that Max is hiding a dangerous witness is that she is not
being held captive against her will. Lucia is empowered both as a seductress (inducing
Max's obsession) and an impending threat (to Max and his former-nazi friends); as
Klaus (the former-nazi lawyer) puts it, "even if [a document says someone was responsible for the death of] one thousand or ten thousand persons, it still makes less
impression than one witness in flesh and blood staring at you, that is why they are so
dangerous, my task is to find them wherever they are and see that they are filed away."

By engaging with some of the intricate dialogues involved in the discourse of
nazism and fascism, Cavani deconstructs the binary positioning of the "pure victim"
and "pure evil," yet she does not allow for a reversal of *vittime* and *assassini*, as Levi
accuses her.[8] Instead Cavani's subversion of the moral and sexual subject functions as

a series of ironic refractions, as a play of juxtapositions that ultimately question conventional roles rather than allow for the questioning of subject/object relations in accordance with what Laura Mulvey considers to be the feminine spectacle (the medium of cinema itself) performed for the enjoyment of the male gaze. Cavani deliberately seeks to articulate the sexual as political and to subvert its cinematic rendering through a sustained examination of visual power. Her strategy is to problematize the discursive divisions such as self and other, male gaze and female spectacle. As a result, *The Night Porter* challenges film theory's frequent theoretical investment in Lacan's concept of sexual difference, which in turn promotes what Luce Irigaray criticizes as the "imperialism of Lacan's deterministic cultural and historic codes."[9] For Cavani the dynamic of victim/victimizer opens into a discourse of voyeurism, sadism, and subject identification and locates the very process of disengaging from the visual, racial, sexual, and political other. Returning to the site of disengagement, she reveals that the reenforcing of such divisions functions as a fascistic practice. While she utilizes the premise that cinema, according to film theorists such as Christian Metz, Laura Mulvey, and Mary Ann Doane, is the medium of seduction, fascination, delirium, and utter absorption in the image, she problematizes their locking this cinematic pleasure into an "Oedipal phallic paradigm of vision," exciting secondary pleasure that is a fetishistic scopophilia. By reducing cinema to a gaze that is essentially sadistic, such theoretical interpretations turn against themselves or into what Metz called a "voyeuristic sadism sublimated into epistemophilia."[10]

Unlike Pasolini, who attempts to implode this process of sublimation into "epistemophilia" as another form of sadism, thereby relinquishing the seductive visual pleasure of film, Cavani returns to the aesthetics of seduction. She counteracts what Lacanian film theory exorcises as a form of damage control, a conscious repression of desire designed to retard and neutralize what are perceived as dangerous imaginary distortions. I view *The Night Porter* as critical of "isolating" what Rainer Nägele argues "belongs inseparable together."[11] The key point for Nägele is the intimate connection of sexuality with violence. The constitution of pleasure and pain as oppositional categories bridges diverse thought and political beliefs, from Freud—who believes that pleasure (*Lust*), what Sam Weber defines as a "narcissistic ambivalence," is bound to pain (*Unlust*), a sense of loss or sexual abandon, what Shakespeare labeled "*la petite mort*"—to Andrea Dworkin, who argues that every act of penetration is an act of violence.[12] Yet both these visions, as many others, tend to focus solely on logocentric male subjectivity, which takes pleasure in self-identification, and phallocentric sexuality, in which the penis is transformed into an animate object that acts on passive bodies. Within this binary logic of man and woman, active and passive, something and nothing, I find the most perverse to be imperialistic and despotic notions about gender and sexuality. This binary or dialectical model of interpretation operates on the most rigid moralism (the sacrificial logic of desire) and the most rigid discipline—demanding the repression first of sexual desires, then of social desires, and finally constituting desire as a desire for repression. While Cavani mimics the intrinsic relationship of pleasure to pain, she does not present the connection as necessarily inherent but instead as a political relationship, a relationship of unequal power. In opposition to the notion that all desire is sadistic (a primary desire to consume, or a reactionary desire to destroy) and masculine, Cavani presents power as unstable, in flux.

She explores the inseparable relationship between the desire of the victim and that of the victimizer, which cannot be read as purely sadistic (as the victims argue) nor masochistic (as feminists argue), but as dangerously intimate. This dangerous intimacy challenges certain historical and theoretical notions of power embedded within the discourses of subjectivity, memory, trauma, aesthetics, and sexual politics. Accordingly, I divide my analysis of *The Night Porter* into four thematic sections: (1) reactive memories, an exploration of the politics of memory; (2) traumatic therapies, a questioning of the use-value of psychoanalysis for interpreting sexual ambiguity; (3) the aesthetic fetish, an analysis of the undermining of notions of high culture by implicating them in humanist ideals, which are ultimately used as justifications for racial, ethnic, and class hierarchies; (4) seduction and ambiguous power, investigating Cavani's transgression of boundaries, between self and other, victim and victimizer, memory and fantasy, and the dissipation of the image of the femme fatale.

Reactive Memories

The Night Porter commences with the juxtaposition of the past and present as experienced by Max and Lucia. This juxtaposition results in the blurring of time and space, memory and reality, from postwar Vienna (1957) to a Hungarian concentration camp in the early 1940s. As Cavani writes, 1957 was "l'anno in cui ho datato il film, sono partite da poco le truppe sovietiche d'occupazione e Vienna riprende a vivere come se niente fosse mai accaduto" ("the year that marks the departure of the occupying Soviet troops, and with their departure Vienna began to live again as if nothing had happened").[13] Cavani undercuts this auspicious "return to national autonomy" or return to the prewar cultural and national "ranks they held" by focusing on interiors, what she calls the "sottosuolo" ("basement"). For instance, the banal gray surface of everyday life in the city—as depicted in the establishing shot where Max walks to work through the empty bluish-gray streets of Vienna—peels away, revealing the dark interiors where the inhabitants relive their nazi past. The persistent oscillation between exterior/interior and public/private creates a certain sense of schizophrenia, temporally, visually, and psychologically. *The Night Porter* transverses notions of surface and depth, past and present, the historical debates over memory and forgetting, thereby leaving the protagonists along with the audience in a precarious place— between a desire to forget and a need to remember. Through her use of montage, Cavani maps out the intricate connections of personal memory of the "Final Solution" to aesthetic references of previous filmic representations of nazism or fascism, classical music, Art Nouveau, German Expressionism, and the high humanist ideals of the Enlightenment, German utilitarianism, and functionalism.

The point of creating such an elaborate pastiche is not only to challenge the autonomy and legitimacy of such cultural artifacts but also to foreground the overdetermined aesthetic coding of nazism, fascism, and the "Final Solution." For example, the aestheticized memories of Max and Lucia, which serve as an unreal or fantastic bridging of past to present, are often triggered by musical and visual references. In one case Mozart's opera, *Die Zauberflöte*, evokes the memory of a concentration camp prisoner being sodomized by an SS-man. German opera is integrated into the aesthetic texture of this brutal image, therefore implicating the opera, an emblem of German high culture, in the cultural production of nazism. At the same time, however, the overt theatricality of this image points away from the "real" traumatic experience of memory (as described by Freud and visualized in such films as *The Pawnbroker* and *Sophie's Choice*) toward the popular memory of fascism or nazism that is already buttressed by its own aesthetic code, if not its own cinematic genre. By exaggerating the sadomasochistic (aesthetic) enframing of nazism, Cavani foregrounds the artificiality of conventional devices such as a filtered flashback, sound-over, or nondiegetic sound used in the representation of nazism and the "Final Solution." These technical devices contribute to the construction of the popular memory of fascism. Yet the effect of rendering such devices as intrinsic to representations of the Holocaust disavows their diegetic "reality effect."

The constant aesthetic and diegetic interruptions commence with the opening scene of the film, where a series of reverse shots cut from Max's (the night porter's) face to Lucia's (the wife of the visiting opera conductor) until they establish eye contact. That very moment of recognition triggers the first flashback, a line of clothed prisoners, some with the yellow Star of David pinned to their jackets, the yellow standing out against the blue hue of the film. In the next flashback the same clothed prisoners appear nude, waiting to be incarcerated or killed by the nazis. In this flashback, the juxtaposition of nude, vulnerable prisoners to bureaucratic SS officers in full regalia clearly establishes the relation of victim to victimizer: Max holds a camera, documenting the prisoners, yet his documentary is interrupted by his focusing on Lucia. Within this double voyeuristic spectatorship we are given the eroticized vision of the victimizer as we watch Max film Lucia and watch his filming of Lucia. Cavani juxtaposes Max's subjective point of view with Lucia's: the examining of her body is juxtaposed with the filming of Lucia watching the camera watching her. Memories that represent Lucia's subjective point of view express a more violent reading of the same images. Yet once Max is introduced into the same frame with Lucia (where they appear alone) it becomes unclear whose memory (who invokes the flashback), perspective, or fantasy we are viewing. This emphasis on a confused and eroticized subjectivity renders any clear vision of the nazi past as unrecoverable. Furthermore, the highly aestheticized flashback reminds us that memory is selective. While Lucia's memories of Max are often violent, when asked by Hans Vogler whether she remembers that Max was an "obedient *Sturmbannführer*," she replies that she does not but does remember how many orders Hans gave. The visualized memories of Lucia and

Max become progressively more romanticized and aestheticized, focusing only on their *erotic* relationship. When mixed with the melodramatic language of opera or the sorrowful sound of cabaret, these memories are not only unreliable but abstruse (and in this case surreal). The pronounced aesthetization of memory—the layering of various linguistic, musical, and visual codes—only serves to enforce a general dreamlike quality in the film. *The Night Porter* mimics the stylistic representation of memory as depicted in *The Pawnbroker*: the fluid editing process that bridges the past to the present, demarcated only by the replacement of diegetic sound with non-diegetic sound (the music of Quincy Jones in the case of *The Pawnbroker* and Danièle Paris in *The Night Porter*), the use of slow-motion footage and soft focus. The blue-and-gray hue of Max's and Lucia's memory establishes a mood, a nostalgic, faded image. This attempt to represent mood or emotional sentiment suggests a sense of personal memory rather than a public, popular, or historical documentation of nazism, fascism, and the "Final Solution." The emphasis on aesthetic style stands in contrast to films like *Night and Fog*, which uses documentary footage from the 1940s in order to appeal to history and to promote an image of historical reality (by evoking the discourse of evidence and fact), and *Schindler's List*, which mimics realist modes of narration, simulating documentary footage vis-à-vis the use of black and white film, and deep-focus cinematography.

The juxtaposition of the two cinematic styles (realism as opposed to the psychological narrative) accents the technical devices (the editing process itself) used in order to achieve such (authentic) aesthetic effects. Even as this type of juxtaposition differentiates the two modes of representation, it destroys direct referential illusions used in both documentary and fiction film. *The Night Porter*'s radically contrived and artificial mode of presentation attacks seemingly authentic reconstructions of the past. It does so by stringing together a constellation of memories, fantasies, desires, and reactions to these multilayered memories and desires. By foregrounding aesthetics as a means of manipulation, Cavani challenges the *transparency* of conventional film language used to signify nazism and fascism in popular entertainment—cinematic and narrative syntax as well as canonical cultural and metahistorical texts.

In the film, memory and one's investment in memory (a source of identification) appear as another form of artifice. While Max and Lucia evoke memory as a form narrativizing the present, Erika (the countess) and Bert (the former nazi performer) live only partially in the present, keeping their identification with the past an innermost secret—a sign of intimacy and shame to be protected and to be "locked away." The film continues to introduce characters as split personalities, split between their postwar (often seedy) existence and their wartime identity (which is highly stylized, playing on the various representations of nazism and fascism in postwar cinema). For example, throughout the film Erika remains confined to her hotel bedroom and for the most part confined to her bed. The image of Erika harks back to a decadent image of the femme fatale, an image of reclining (seductive) sickness. This image is only underscored by her self-motivated confinement to the bed, where she is first seen awaiting her "usual assistance," a prearranged (paid) sexual encounter with one of the hotel servants. Surrounded by symbols of wealth and 1940s-style notions of glamour—her mink bedcover, her make-up, jewelry, and demeanor—she is marked as both a faded beauty and a faded socialite. Although Erika does not diegetically recall her involvement in fascism/nazism, Cavani's casting of the fascist film star and sex symbol (a femme fatale) Isa Miranda in the role establishes extradiegetic links not only to fascist film culture but also to the history of the representation of the femme fatale. The very presence of Isa Miranda in an antifascist film about fascism or nazism functions simultaneously as a mimetic (authentic) reference to the popular memory of fascism and a subversive presentation of the inauthentic self-referentiality of cinematic and narrative representation itself. The fact that Miranda can represent both fascist and antifascist ideals, morals, and aesthetics blurs the distinctions between fact and fiction by treating her relationship to history and historical events as a product of both fact (her own personal memory of fascism and her involvement in fascist aesthetic politics) and fiction (what she represents in fascist and postfascist culture). For example, she represents both the (fixed) icon of the 1940s femme fatale and the aging parody of that icon. She reflects not only the disruption of this aesthetic that has undergone many transformations (from the fin-de-siècle to German Expressionism and camp) but also the postwar cultural obsession with that very (self)image of seductive beauty. What has been normalized as a conventional trope, nostalgia for lost youth, is complicated by the fact that this emblem of youth is an integral part of the fascist aesthetic.

Like Erika, who propositions Max, Bert also implies that he desires Max's services in facilitating his erotic or fetishistic relationship to his nazi past. When rebuffed by Max, Erika tells him that he has no imagination—to which Max retorts that it is she who has no imagination—and Bert declares that Max doesn't want to wipe anybody's ass. Ironically, while Bert makes this statement Max is seen doing just that, wiping Bert's ass before he administers a shot. This scene, replete with homosexual innuendoes, suggests not only Max's sexual ambivalence but the permutation of sexual ambiguity throughout the film. Max is objectified as a sexual object not only by the aristocratic Contessa but also by the bourgeois former nazi Bert, Lucia (the survivor), and perhaps the audience as well.

Cavani's choice of male protagonist, Dirk Bogarde, reflects her desire to use an actor who has a preestablished character-type within this very genre. By the time Bogarde made *The Night Porter* he was already famous or infamous as an icon of sexual ambivalence, in *The Servant, The Damned, Death in Venice,* and other films. Similarly, Charlotte Rampling appears in *The Damned,* where she plays the role of a pure victim, the wife of a socialist who dies at Dachau. Playing on Rampling's androgynous physique and Bogarde's known homosexuality as well as his role as the manipulative servant (in the film of the same title), Cavani explodes monolithic notions of film theory, namely, the construction of cinematic looking as an appendage of a sadistic male gaze and the cinematic object as masochistic female spectacle. While Cavani takes issue with the view of sexual difference organized according to a strict binary model, she does not emphasize bisexuality as an alternative, as many feminist film theorists have suggested, most notably Mary Ann Doane, Gertrud Koch, Janet Bergstrom, and Kaja Silverman. The "weakness" with this formulation, as Tania Modleski argues, "lies in its assumption that notions of bisexuality can be considered apart from power relations.... A discussion of bisexuality as it relates to spectatorship ought, then, to be informed by a knowledge of the way male and female responses are rendered asymmetrical by a patriarchal power structure."[14] For Cavani, however, sexuality is not just an expression of power relations but also, as Gaylyn Studlar articulates it, a delimitation of sexual positions, "the mobility of multiple fluid identifications" (*In the Realm of Pleasure*, 16). Because *The Night Porter* treats sexuality as a masquerade (role playing) where Max takes care of Bert's, Erika's, and Lucia's fetishistic desires, the film presents a certain polysexuality of cinema and cinematic desires. For this reason Max's and Lucia's desire, which expresses itself as becoming other, is incongruous with what Silverman calls self-abandonment, the losing of one's sense of self as a return to the past—a necrophiliac obsession.

Unlike Max and Lucia, who rewrite their wartime relationship (transforming it from a monolithic sadistic play to an ambiguous masochistic charade) Bert, Erika, and the former nazis cling to necrophiliac phantasms. For instance, Bert repeatedly performs the same ballets that he danced before his fellow SS-men. Yet what distinguishes his reenactment from Max's and Lucia's acting on their memories is that his desire and his memory are idealized; they are therefore locatable within an absolute past (symbolizing absence or lack) that can be controlled and repeated in the form of a ballet performance. Thus Bert, like Erika and the other former nazis, fixes himself within the unreachable past: he identifies himself in terms of a necrophiliac and at the same time imaginary appeal to history. This causes these characters to appear both morbid and ridiculous. Controverting the view of William Wolf, who claims that "the film's rare and insidious power" derives from the fact that "nobody escapes the past," even for those who harbor nostalgic desires, identifications, or obsessions, the past always escapes them.[15] Their fixation on the past transforms them into parodic figures much like Pirandello's Henry IV, who eternally plays the part of the twenty-six-year-old Holy Roman Emperor even though he is a sixty-year-old modern Italian man. According to Rancière, "there is history because there is a past and a specific passion for the past.... The status of history depends on the treatment of this twofold absence of the 'thing itself' that is no longer there—that is in the past; and that never was—because it never was such as it was told. Historical affect is bound to the personal absence of what the names name" (*The Names of History*, 63). It is for this reason that Max's and Lucia's relationship is not historical. While it might appeal to history, because it is predicated on memory it cannot represent the past nor can it conceive of a stable narrative structure. The very instability (the transgression of boundaries between victims and victimizers, between good and evil, pure and impure, past and present) causes their relationship to be classified as "sick and unhealthy" by both the former nazis and the survivors. The reenactment of such an event destabilizes the symbolic centrality of nazism and the "Final Solution." It threatens not only those who want to remember but those who want to forget, by turning it into something else—something living, and yet something entirely different.

Nazism, however, whether celebrated—by the former nazis who pledge allegiance to the Third Reich—or repudiated for its motivating the mass murder of millions of Jews, Gypsies, Slavs, and homosexuals, becomes the common point of departure, thus the locus of identification for both victim and victimizer. When Max and Lucia actively return to their wartime "relationship," they are hunted down by Max's former-nazi friends who find the presence of such a dynamic both dangerous and disruptive to their sense of order—in terms not only of their racism and political bias but also their desire to conceal their past. Max and Lucia's erotic relationship undermines necessary distinctions in the production of meaning and morality. They threaten to expose former nazis and at the same time pollute the memory of the victims, that is, the intimacy between victim and victimizer questions the ongoing narrative and moral identifications of both former nazis and their victims. Yet when accused by Hans of having a "deranged obsession for the past," and "fishing up the past," Lucia replies that "Max is more than my past." Unlike the former nazis, Max and Lucia engage in more than memory and repetition; they cross many lines, and not only in

In *The Night Porter* (1974), Bert (Amedeo Amodio) performs ballet for a group of SS officers, symbolizing the neoclassical ideal model of the male body.

terms of victim and victimizer, past and present, subject and object identification, self and other—they put morality (both fascist and antifascist) along with historical narrative into crisis. What is at stake is not just a struggle between official history and popular memory but also the struggle between thinking of the historical event as a subjective social drama and more radical notions of thinking that history is itself fictional. This does not mean that these events did not happen but that historical texts are themselves interpretive dramatizations and therefore sites of contention. Memory in the form of repetition (personal or public) comprises what Deleuze calls reflections, echoes, and doubles that "do not belong to the domain of resemblance or equivalence . . . [but] to that of excess " (*Difference and Repetition*, 112). History as repetition performs as a dissembling of memory, identification, and order by reintegrating them into discursive systems of meaning. Yet this means that memory itself cannot be integrated into narrative discourse, only its double (a present value, identity displaced onto history).

While remembrance in the form of linear narrative provides both distance and closure to the past, memory in a nonlinear format transforms the power structure of Max and Lucia's wartime economy by recontextualizing them in terms of postwar politics (specifically the politics of memory and its role in the incrimination of nazi war criminals). Yet the more intimate one's relationship to the past, the less likely it can be narrativized or moralized. For Cavani, neither survivors like Lucia nor the former nazis want to let go of the past or forget. Yet she presents two types of intimacy with the past: (1) the disruptive relationship of Max and Lucia, which reopens what historians have attempted to give closure to by establishing stable and moral subject positions; and (2) the protective relationship of the former nazis with each other as a support group and to their (concealed) self-identification with the Third Reich. While Max and Lucia treat history like a trauma in order to preserve its emotional and personal symbolic value, the former nazis idealize their relationship to the past— Klaus declares that "we are honored to be officials of the most important branch of the Third Reich."

In contrast to *The Pawnbroker*, where memory in the form of flashback interrupts the protagonist's (Nazerman's) sense of the present with a flood of traumatic, uncontrollable (repressed) images of the past that disable his volition to act, in *The Night Porter* both forms of remembering, although not controllable, are often conjured up. What is traumatic for the former nazis is that they cannot relive their past; they can only reclaim their identifications with the past, as Klaus does: "If I were born again I would do it exactly the same way." Therefore the problem with reading memory into a therapeutic or historiotherapeutic (hysterical) model is that therapeutic notions suggest that one must "historicize" memory in order to cleanse or purge oneself of what remains dangerously uncontrollable. And as Cavani demonstrates, this therapy itself becomes dangerous when practiced by the former nazis, for whom Lucia represents the return of the repressed.

Traumatic Therapies

By invoking a therapeutic model, Cavani questions the "healing" process undertaken in order to denazify or *defascistizzare* Europe. She suggests, as Teresa de Lauretis explains (and as Michael Verhoeven's film *The Nasty Girl* [*Das schreckliche Mädchen*, 1991] demonstrates), that "the heritage of fascism remained and festered in the dark tenement houses and luxury hotels of Europe" and, also, that there is no cure for bad history.[16] Yet this does not imply, as does Werner Herzog's *Nosferatu: Phantom der nacht* (1979), that evil festers and lurks within humans like a dormant plague that at any moment is ready to strike again. Instead, for Cavani, former fascists and fascism itself have undergone numerous transformations, mutating more like a virus than a bacteria. By the time Cavani made *The Night Porter*, the resurfacing of neofascism in the popular electorate and the uncovering of neofascist networks linked to government agencies (most notably the secret service) and the economic industries had already been under public scrutiny. Therefore, like *The Nasty Girl*, which commences with the question "Wo ward Ihr zwischen '39–'45?, [und] Wo seid Ihr jetzts?" ("Where were you from 1939 to 1945, [and] where are you now?"), Cavani examines the circumstances that allowed for the reintegration of former nazis, former fascists, neonazis, and neofascists into bourgeois society. Describing the project of *The Night Porter* she writes, "it is 'ignorance' about the events of World War II that may be examined if we are to better understand the ignorance allowed during the war, that same ignorance that allowed for the rise of the dictators," and that made it possible for Kurt Waldheim to become the president of Austria in 1986 (*Il portiere di notte*, x). Like Pasolini, Cavani insinuates that bourgeois culture fomented nazism and fascism and continues to harbor such extreme ideologies—racism, sexism, and a sadistic form of moral puritanism. For this reason she chooses to focus on bourgeois subjects rather than traditional representations of proletariat resistance fighters. Yet, unlike Visconti, Bertolucci, and Fosse in their neodecadent representations of the bourgeoisie and the upper class under fascism and nazism, Cavani presents bourgeois figures as both "moral" and violent.

All of the former nazis portrayed in *The Night Porter* hold prestigious positions, positions of authority, with the exception of Max, who has become the night porter at the Hotel Opera. Klaus retains his position as a lawyer who now has access to the war tribunal archives; Hans remains a professor and a practicing psychoanalyst; Kurt continues to be an established businessman; and even Bert (the ballet dancer) has some "honorable duties." This cell of former stormtroopers represents a larger underground network where former nazis and fascists aid in concealing and destroying evidence that would link them or their colleagues to war crimes and, more importantly, they help establish each other within the legitimate social structure of postwar society. Ironically, this "legitimate" postwar social fabric is inextricably intertwined with (if not run by) this underground network. Although, according to Hans, they have "all gone through their [private] trials, and now they are *cured*," this cure does not entail denazification. They still make gestures that mark their solidarity to the ideology of the Third Reich—they verbally reaffirm their allegiance and symbolically make the sign of the Roman salute. The "cure" that Hans refers to represents a social and cultural readjustment; the refashioning of one's own relation to authority. Cavani's depiction of a "seamless" transference of power from the nazi court system, university, industrial capitalism, and aesthetic culture to postwar reconstruction of the European infrastructure undermines notions of denazification and purification. Furthermore, she challenges historical and political narratives that pronounce a "clean breakage" or "absolute rupture" with Europe's fascist past and its democratic present.

History, according to Michel de Certeau, is anything but clean: it is "cannibalistic, and memory becomes the closed arena of conflict between two contradictory operations: forgetting, which is not something passive, a loss, but an action directed against the past; and the mnemic [*sic*] trace, the return of what is forgotten, in other words, an action by a past that is now forced to disguise itself."[17] In *The Night Porter* the former nazis wield the cannibalistic force of history in an attempt to neutralize the appearance of the past by extricating their names from any official documents and relocating themselves within the newly formed power structure. For Klaus, Hans, Kurt, and Bert, historical narrative functions as a distancing device, a means of depersonalization. Yet the practice of depersonalizing and disengaging is contingent on a process of narrowing the field of vision to a one-dimensional way of seeing history as linear (emblemized by Klaus's monocle), a constant moving away from a point of origin. By limiting their vision and their image to a forward way of looking they can be born again within a new (postwar) historical narrative. These shifting signifiers that frame history in terms of a diegetic narrative as opposed to mimetic representation, in the words of Rancière, "remove the spoken words from the voice of mimesis [in order] to give them *another voice*. It places their meaning on the side, in reserve, under the *shelter* of new imitations and new turns of language" (*The Names of History*, 51). The process of forgetting and disguising, however, is confronted with Max's and Lucia's disruptive, mimetic mode of gazing back, one that intimately bridges former nazis to their victims. Their relationship recalls a traumatic (violent) union between victims and victimizers, one that both survivors and former nazis have "actively" chosen to forget. Hence this "intimacy" threatens to expose the intricate connections of former nazis to a past that they have tried so "carefully" to bury. They reactively repress not only their memory of the other, but the other as a form of popular memory. More than "sheltered," Max and Lucia are imprisoned by the former nazis, condemned to represent and speak in the voice of madness, sickness, and radical impurity. Within this postwar economy, the *pure* is segregated from the *impure* through a process of externalization—narrativizing and grafting oneself to a newly constructed stable subjective identity. What makes Max and Lucia's relationship so impure is that it emotes a radical intimacy that prohibits the solidification of stable subjective identities (narrative positions of victim and victimizer, man and woman, empowered and disempowered).

In *The Night Porter* these conflicting operations of history are manifested in the confrontation of "official history"—which narrativizes in order to neutralize—with personal memory—which attempts to mimic or recapture the past as it was—and aesthetic representation, which refers neither to personal memory nor "official" history but mimics the history of the representation of fascism. Max and Lucia, who represent the coalescence of the latter two, paralyze historical continuity and historical discourse by recalling the inconsistent relationship of the personal and popular memory to official history. While this dichotomy seems to refer to the Freudian model of continuity (tradition or myth) and discontinuity (the return of the repressed) of historical forces, for Cavani it is only the former nazis who adhere to a Freudian model. This model allows them to reaffirm a fixed set (sexual, familial, and symbolic) of positions under the sign of "the Law of the Father," the threat of castration, as well as to relegate the "real" traumatic consequences of their actions to the "unsymbolizable" or the "unrepresentable." *The Night Porter* mimics the Freudian method of interrogating the normativizing law of the father, yet it implicates psychoanalysis in its own process of normativization. Cavani draws attention to the critical practice of psychoanalysis, which is supposed to assure the fluidity and instability of every given discursive formulation, but in fact Oedipalizes and territorializes, installing the "Law of the Father" at every symbolic and discursive juncture where there appears to be a "lack" or absence of representation. The film problematizes Freudian theory's articulation of history as the erection of "delirious phantoms" or myths (men with tragic flaws), which are constructed in the absence or "impossibility" of representing the "real." While the positing of history as myth delegitimizes nazism and fascism, presenting them as a mythic cover-up of the violent suppression of otherness (Jews, Gypsies, homosexuals, women, Slavs, communists), it also returns nazism and fascism to an ontology of equivalent "traumatic kernels."

In her critique of Žižek's argument that "the family, concentration camps, and the Gulag, instantiate the same traumatic kernel," Judith Butler points out that "indeed the historical becomes what is most indifferent to the question of trauma, and the political or historical effort to understand the institution of the family or the formation of concentration camps or Gulags cannot account for the 'traumatic' character of these formations."[18] What makes psychoanalysis so attractive to this group of former nazis is that regardless of the fact that the "Law of the Father" is exposed as inherently violent—it is not only established on a threat of violence (castration) but actively annihilates what Freud calls "the real," what Lacan defines as "the Other," and what Nietzsche attributes to the logic of *ressentiment*—it is perceived as a necessary means of maintaining order. Thus the logic of the law of the superego allows not only the former nazis but also Erika to "file the past away" in the name of stabilizing civic order. The fact that Erika tells Max "be careful before she [Lucia] can testify against you, you should file her away" attests to the postwar complicity in which even those who were not nazis protected former nazis and blamed victims who demanded justice, for "fishing up" what they actively chose to forget. Freud reminds us that "we shall be making a false calculation if we disregard the fact that the Law was originally brute violence and that even today it cannot do without the support of violence."[19] Yet by suggesting that the laws of civil society are both predicated on violence and continually produce violent acts against otherness, he opens the way for ontological interpretations such as Žižek, who claims that all societies are founded on the brotherhood of guilt. Žižek argues that "identification with community is ultimately always based upon some shared guilt or, more precisely, upon the fetishistic disavowal of this guilt" (*Metastases of Enjoyment*, 57). It is not clear, however, what exactly is fetishized in this metaphysical community, whether it is the law itself or humankind's metaphorical refusal to see where it came from. Nonetheless, according to this model it is only in the process of killing the other that the community can identify and define itself; hence such atrocities are trivialized under the sign of the "Ethnic Thing" or the pleasure principle—the pleasure of identifying oneself.

Max and Lucia, then, do not represent the return of the repressed but an internal criticism of this dialectic of identification, an identification based on a process of negation. They represent the intimate touching of what has been construed as a series of dialectical oppositions—man and woman, victim and victimizer, pleasure and pain, memory and immediacy. In a soliloquy Max illustrates this blurring of self/other, memory/presence, material/immaterial: after he has established contact with Lucia, he reflects, "just when all seems lost, something unexpected happens, ghosts take shape in the mind, how can one run away from it, this phantom with a voice and a body, it is a part of oneself." Not only are personal pronouns absent in Max's speech, indicating a lack of positionality, but there is also a breakdown of subject/object relationships—a dynamic opposition that gives symbolic language its grounding. Instead of representing a traumatic seizure of "the real," Max and Lucia present a disruptive force that challenges symbolic modes of identification: identification with new forms of authority, as well as identification with the repressed or the victim, since both of these modes of identification are predicated on acts of disengagement. By exemplifying the callous reaction to Max and Lucia, Cavani emphasizes the consistent severity of fascist thinking and fascist politics that act out or write out not the other but intimacy and desire themselves. However, because Cavani juxtaposes the intimate yet destructive relationship of Max and Lucia with the community of former nazis who violently disengage themselves from that past, she leaves the audience with no clear perspective as to how to read or relate to Europe's fascist past. Both personal memory and official accounts prove to be inadequate forms of representing the past. Since personal narratives are too narrow to comprehend intersubjective or contextual issues, and official accounts are too depersonalized to understand human experience, they are considered equally unreal. Consequently, Cavani questions the ability of language and film to represent anything other than a political present.

The film defies those critics who wish to inscribe it within the context of "historical realities" as opposed to political realities. For example, Foucault denounces *The Sorrow and the Pity*, *The Night Porter*, and *Lacombe Lucien* for supplanting what he

Max (Dirk Bogarde) breaks into Lucia's (Charlotte Rampling) room in his attempt to find out why she came back to Vienna.

considers "the real struggle" or the real history of fascism (the resistance) with the "unreal" history of the bourgeoisie under fascism. Yet he finds Cavani's portrait of the "love for power" or the "erotic charge of power" a key to understanding both the appeal of fascism and the current re-eroticization of nazism and fascism (*Foucault Live*, 89–98). For Cavani there are two registers of power: (1) official power, located within the discursive economies of the law and the bureaucracy (Klaus), science and psychoanalysis (Hans), practical reason (Kurt), and humanism (Bert), which has deep-seated roots within the prefascist and fascist ideologies. Official power operates on the principles of what Foucault describes as a disciplinary society. And (2) the deterritorializing power of seduction that eroticizes and ambiguates the discourse (and image) of power. The flip side of this official or territorializing operation is what Deleuze and Guattari explain as "the 'real inorganization' of the molecular element: partial objects that enter into indirect syntheses or interactions, since they are not partial (*partiels*) in the sense of parts, but *partiaux* like intensities under which a unit of matter always fills space in varying degrees . . . *syntheses operating without a plan*" (*Anti-Oedipus*, 309). While "official" power does not necessarily interfere with the former nazis' identification with nazism, seductive (*inorganizing*) power questions not only the project of nazism, its "Ethnic Thing," but compromises the former nazis' new-found security. In *The Night Porter* these two mutually incompatible forces collide, resulting in the repression (subjugation) of seductive power. Because the repression of desire reproduces the structural unity of official institutions of power, it charges official power with producing, sustaining, and reproducing fascism. What distinguishes the postwar discourses of power from those of nazism and fascism is that they are de-eroticized, demystified, and unspectacular. Consequently they express a sense of cold indifference with regard to human suffering—murder is euphemistically referred to as "filing away," victims are transformed into witnesses, that is, dangerous informers. In Marshall McLuhan's terms the spectacle of power is cold and distant (functional) as opposed to hot (erotic or passionate). *The Night Porter* models official power on a therapeutic paradigm that operates on the need for "cold" discipline—repression of desire, disruptive memories, and bad ego-ideals—and punishment—reclassifying subversive figures as unhealthy or deranged in order to justify filing them away. Yet this discipline is no longer ritualized through the mass spectacle but instead through discursive practices. This discursive apparatus is designed to de-eroticize the organization of power, to desexualize and sublimate its direct means of violence (suppression) in the indirect violence of grammar and semantics. It reduces the production of desire to representation.

Rather than focusing on the postwar amnesia, or what she calls "ignorance," of many Europeans who protect the social fabric of their local communities by "forgetting" key members' involvement in nazism or fascism, Cavani focuses on the larger phenomenon of engaging therapeutic models designed to cleanse the bourgeoisie and the capitalist superstructure of any shred of evidence (written documents or verbal documents of witnesses) that could link them to a nazi or fascist past. Parodying conventional conjectures such as Slavoj Žižek that "postwar Austria is a country whose very existence is based on a refusal to 'work through' its traumatic Nazi past," Cavani presents a scenario of Austrian former nazis "working through" a therapeutic process.[20] Because this therapeutic practice is performed by former nazis who wish to liberate themselves from the trauma of the past, Cavani undermines the social function of "working through" trauma itself. The fact that Max and his nazi colleagues agree to participate in group therapy "to delve together to the very bottom of [their] personal histories, to confront them by speaking without reserve without fear" in order to discern whether they are in fact "victims of guilt complexes or not," turns therapy into a farce or another means of reintegrating (rehabilitating) those guilty of nazi war crimes. The psychoanalytic model offers them the fixed structural logic of the symbolic order that does not differentiate between the real and the imaginary. In fact it trivializes the occurrence of historical events in favor of the metahistorical repetition of the symbolic order. The objective for these former nazis to "work through" the past is to reinscribe themselves within the symbolic order, even if their relationship to the symbolic is fictional. According to Bert this means to "live as peaceful citizens," and for Kurt it means "to take back the ranks they held" (not within a military structure but within the military industrial complex). Thus therapy becomes an editing process, retracing the events that organize the present in order to cut out or erase those traces or residues that link the analysand to a "traumatic past." When used by these former nazis, the language of psychoanalysis itself appears repressive; it merges with the discursive practices found in religious, legal, and political inquisitions. Therapy is even referred to as a "trial." The language of psychoanalytic therapy dovetails with "legal" and "scientific" discourse, whereby the analyst assumes the semantic roles of doctor, archivist, historian, inquisitor, and judge, and the analysand is named a defendant. In fact, legal, medical, and hygienic vocabulary dominate the description of this therapy: those who have undergone the therapeutic process are described as "clean," "pure," "healthy," "normally adjusted," while Max, who refuses this therapy, is seen as "deranged," "sick," and Lucia is called "impure," "neurotic," "unhealthy," and a "whore."

The oscillation and consensus between discursive fields (psychoanalysis, nazism, capitalism, etc.) when dealing with notions of purity and impurity create a sense of conspiracy. For example, Cavani uncovers an intertextual network in which various linguistic, cinematic, and discursive modes of thinking are utilized to justify silencing witnesses (victims) and repressing differences. Terms such as "cleansing" and "purification" evoke the positive affirmation of hygiene, mental sanity, and political health, yet these affirmative values are contingent on murder, destroying documents, and falsifying one's public image. As this conspiracy unfolds it reveals the rhizomatic networking of various discourses of power to repressive agencies: starting with psychoanalysis, which operates as a policing of private desires, linking up to historical discourse, which translates into a patrolling of historical evidence, and governance, which maintains order by "keeping a most particular eye on witnesses," and the destroying of all existing traces of evidence that could incriminate any of the members of the group. All authoritative discourses thereby merge into one (neofascist) force of repression. The designated aim of these forces is to circumvent any possible identification with the position of the victim—the former nazis do not want to suffer from "guilt complexes" or "bad history." Accordingly, they shift between purely subjective analysis and objective or factual analysis. Klaus posits that "we cannot delude ourselves, memory is not made of shadows but of eyes that can stare right at you, and of fingers that point right at you." He argues that in order to effectively free oneself from persecution one must remember, in detail, the past trauma so as to determine, as Hans suggests, "just how far we can defend ourselves." But, as Žižek argues, "such documentation is a priori false, it transforms the trauma into a neutral, objective fact,"[21] which can be externalized, examined, and refuted.

These former nazis understand that although it is by way of a "false interpretation of trauma," society determines guilt and responsibility on the grounds of objective proof and material evidence. By destroying the documented facts, and in some cases "filing away a dangerous eye-witness," they secure their chances of becoming "peaceful citizens." While Bert asserts that "it did me good to speak, to confess, when it was over I felt a great relief," Kurt retorts, "you feel relieved because Klaus burned thirty documents with your name in them." While the burning of documents and evidence alleviates the "defendant's" fear of being persecuted by outside forces, his confession and defense of his actions binds him to this secret community and their codes of behavior. Thus "freedom from fear and a guilt complex"—read by Hans as "a disturbance of the psyche, a neurosis"—comes at a price, the submission to communal law. For instance, Hans's explanation of what it means to "live in peace" (to be a good citizen) can be interpreted as a threat: he states, "one lives in peace only when one is in harmony with one's friends, *when one honors his agreement*," allegedly to the law of the society of former nazis that he has entered. Hence peace must always be in tune with the law. Irigaray identifies Hans as "an agent or servant of repression and censorship, [one who] ensures that this order subsists as though it were the only possible order, that there can be no imaginable speech, desire or language other than that which has already taken place, no culture authorized other than the monocratism of patriarchal discourse" ("The Poverty of Psychoanalysis," 82). By reinstalling the law of the same (patriarchal, logocentric, phallocentric) the former nazis "take back the ranks they held," at the expense of being able to become other or different.

This private trial makes a mockery out of the war tribunal's handling of such "crimes against humanity," questioning not only the metaphysical fallacy of the law (see chapter 3) but also the law's built-in technical inconsistencies. The "trial" simulates the judicial model, in order to find its weak points and to exploit them. The very weakness of the law lies in its binary vision. It sees only in terms of good (innocence) and evil (guilt), yet this polarizing vision is not confined exclusively to defendants; in fact, witnesses and victims are judged by the same criteria. Although Cavani does not directly contest the validity of the law, as Pasolini does, she depicts its malleability, foregrounding the distinction between its discursive practices—simulating the voice of the good by speaking in the name of the good—and its ideological foundation—a model of a singular ideal, civic good. The fact that fascists and antifascists can evoke the same law, speak in the name of good and evil, underscores the law's inconsistent relationship to its own model: it underlines its linguistic rather than ideological function. "In order to speak morality," Butler contends, "one repeats the position of the Law, that which punishes in the name of good or in the name of evil as *interpreted* by those who command the discourse, therefore, I find it necessary to abandon such a discourse not only for its rigidity and singularity, but for its practice of silencing difference" (*Bodies That Matter*, 195, emphasis mine).

By calling the trial "a farce" and a "game for freaks," Max underscores the manipulation contingent on such clear distinctions as "real" and "imaginary," good and evil psyche, and pure and impure as hermetically sealed. Dichotomies such as these silence the voice of the disempowered. Because the law operates on a scientific or objective model, a model that requires evidence, the burden of proof always falls on the witness or the victim. A trial, then, is more than a war of words and a clash of images—between the defendant's present state of "presumed innocence" and the prosecution's ability to "conjure up" an image of his or her immorality—it is also a clash of discursive positions, a battle between the objective depersonalized language of the court and the all-too-personal language of the victim. And since the victim speaks from a position of impurity (by definition he or she has been violated in some manner), the law that stands for purity can neither identify with the victim nor designate justice in the name of the victim. Like Stanley Kramer's *Judgment at Nuremberg* and Roman Polanski's *Death and the Maiden, The Night Porter* depicts the law as incapable of hearing the victims, since their language is too personal, too carnal, and too intimate. In *Judgment at Nuremberg* judges are not only cajoled into "giving lighter sentences because civilization wants these ex-nazi judges off," but the very witnesses/victims brought in to testify against the accused nazi judges themselves become defendants. The witnesses for the prosecution endure more than conventional defaming in an attempt to prove them unreliable. They must hear again the narratives of their victimization, and they are retried for the very "crimes" for which they had been indicted by these nazi judges (who are now themselves on trial).[22] The war tribunal mimics the very process that led to the witnesses' victimization. This mimetic doubling of the courtroom blurs the boundaries between the staging of the war tribunals and the restaging of the actual cases, drawing attention to the impossibility of maintaining stable moral distinctions between fascist and democratic legal systems and, most importantly, between victims and the accused. Paradoxically, in order to indict the judge the prosecution must prove that the victim was undeserving of the punishment incurred—that is, that the victim is morally pure.

Although it does not treat the subject of fascism, *Death and the Maiden* further accentuates this precariously deterritorialized position of the witness: as a survivor of imprisonment, torture, and rape by a "South American death squad," Paulina Escobar cannot even be considered a victim, since she is still alive—the justice system only tries cases of murder; torture and rape are not considered such grave crimes. The living witness to the Holocaust, as Cavani suggests, becomes a pariah, a remainder of what has been condemned and of the social and cultural complicity of such acts of atrocity. Witnessing itself is silenced by the legal system. Paulina's own husband, who has been chosen by the new president to head the tribunal's investigation of illegal imprisonment, torture, and execution of political subversives, explains to her that she is not a "reliable" witness because she has too much "emotional baggage"—she is perceived by her husband (the lawyer) as hysterical, therefore she would "not survive in court." Similarly, Lyotard postulates that the only "pure victim" is a dead victim, and for that reason the witness is perceived as a traitor to both the living and the dead (*The Inhuman*, 204). The witness persists in disrupting the "purity" of the act of total condemnation (ethnic or racial cleansing) and the pure innocence of the dead victim. *Judgment at Nuremberg, Death and the Maiden*, and *The Night Porter* ask why a victim cannot witness to her or his own rape and torture.[23] In the words of Lyotard, "every Jew is a bad 'jew,' a bad witness to what cannot be represented, just like all texts fail to reinscribe what has not been inscribed." (*Heidegger and "the jews,"* 81). The legal or historical process of inscription, which speaks in the name of the people (as victims), intervenes as a third party, translating human experience and witnessing into an objective, homogenous, or inhuman discourse.

Realizing that the law is another form of silencing or blaming the victims, both Cavani and Polanski return justice to a psychical act. Although their relationships with their victimizers are diametrically opposed—Paulina wants revenge, to rape and torture the "doctor who determined just how much torture her body could take," and Lucia reestablishes an erotic relationship with Max (the quack nazi doctor)—they both psychically avenge their victimizers by forcing them to identify with the position of the victim (the object, the woman, the violated, or the impure). Yet in the process of avenging they identify with the victimizer—they know how to torture, to interrogate, and to play sadomasochistic games; as in the Deleuzian paradigm of masochism, "the victim speaks the language of the torturer, with all the hypocrisy of the torturer" (*Coldness and Cruelty*, 17). As a result, revenge is always on the terms of the victimizer; it is a form of repetition, a mimicry of forced intimacy. Justice, according to Hewitt, "is physical, even though its aspirations are meta-physical" (*Radical Evil*, 80). What is so disturbing about the physicality of justice is not only that it reduces the good (morality) to a condition of relativity and contingency but more importantly that it foregrounds a grotesque intimacy forced upon the victim by the victimizer. And in the case of *Death and the Maiden* this "forced intimacy" always threatens to come between Paulina and her husband. Polanski attributes this "violent intimacy" to the "doctor's" own lust for power combined with his own misogyny—he got drunk on the power, he didn't have to seduce his victims, "he could hurt them or he could fuck them." The doctor admits that what makes him keep coming back to his wife is that "she keeps chopping my balls off, and I want them back," yet he does not "get his balls back" from his wife but rather from the helpless victims he rapes and tortures.

What is conceived of as a masochistic form of exchange, however, is articulated as a sadistic economy—acting out on a third party, a victim. This slippage between two different models of intimacy points to the radical exclusion of the victim from attaining any subjective position. Both characters (Lucia and Paulina) take back their subjectivity, their autonomy, and power, yet while Paulina's strategy is to disempower her victimizer by assuming his identity, mimicking his very actions, Lucia's strategy is to mimic her past role as "Max's little girl." By doing so she wields the power of seduction, not of vengeance. While seduction may entail retribution, it does not clearly present itself as such. Instead of entering into an economy of violence, this seductive allure undermines the binary and symbolic economies that reproduce power as a victory or conquest over the other—sexual, cultural, economic, ethnic, and racial. Max and Lucia's reformed relationship ambiguates conventional economies of power; it is not clear whether Lucia conspires in Max's demise, whether he has drawn her down with him, or whether it is accidental. It is not a direct act of revenge on the part of Lucia but an effect of their intimate relationship that causes Max to be hunted down by his former-nazi friends. And the former nazis also assume their old roles and effectively turn Max (ironically this time "one of their own") into Lucia, by shooting at him, entrapping him in his own apartment (concentration camp), starving him to death. They designate him to the impure, since he is considered to be "a freak like his whore." Yet rather than detaching Max from being "one of them," Cavani illustrates that these former nazis also remain one with him, "they are rotten and they will stay rotten." At the same time that the former nazis "other" Max and Lucia (cause them to disappear), they also resort to their "old behavior." For these former nazis there is no real passing away (no cleansing or therapeutic purging of bad ideals and models), only a fascistic reaction to desires that are reconsidered to be impure. The resurfacing of the "residue" of the past, what de Certeau terms the "improper," "filth," and the "obscene," therefore presents a problem beyond that of the trauma of memory and the threatening gaze of the witness. This residue returns the desire for purity (a fascist desire) into a desire for the impure—a desire for what is other, not disempowered, but dangerously seductive.

The Aesthetic Fetish

For Cavani seduction is a transgressive force that disrupts the existing new world order. Seductive desire does not conform to a model predicated on subject/object relations; it succumbs to an economy of dissemination, a "giving in" to an uncontrollable (irrepressible) desire that entices the seduced to cross disciplinary, moral, and gender boundaries, thereby undermining codes of representation, discourses of power, and their aestheticizations. According to Mary Ann Doane, the seductive force embodied in the femme fatale "blurs the opposition between passivity and activity; [since the seductive image] is not the subject of power but its carrier" (*Femmes Fatales*, 2). It blurs subject/object relations that give rise to the institutionalization of power. Instead of solidifying power into discursive and institutional bodies, the disorganizing force of seduction disembodies or deterritorializes traditional constructs of power. For instance, what makes the femme fatale, or Lucia, so appealing is not her objectification or incarnation as a victim or a woman but her transgression of set power relations and gender definitions. Lucia changes from "Max's little girl" to Salome, to a transvestite, performing bare-breasted in long black leather gloves and an SS uniform in a smoky room full of SS officers, resembling a little boy, a femme fatale, or a dragged-out interpretation of cabaret more than a little girl. Her ephemeral nature produces both an aura of mystery and a sense of perpetual motion. Yet this movement is not predicated on a dialectical or synthetic model of "transcendence"; instead it oscillates between images, causing them to converge and diverge.

Seduction inducts a rhythm much like what Deleuze describes as a pulsation: "an anonymous primary order," an "explosion of nomadic singularities," that grumbles under the surface of "the secondary organization of sense," resurfacing when the production of sense collapses" (*The Logic of Sense*, 125). Hence seduction breaks down the various grammars (semiotic, linguistic, logistical) of sense, emitting tactile, sonorous, and visual sensations. It derails desires that conform to set libidinal drives as well as the narratives that give these drives meaning or objectives. For example, *The Night*

Lucia (Charlotte Rampling) performs cabaret bare-breasted in long black leather gloves and an SS uniform in a smoky room full of SS officers.

Porter jettisons linear emplotment by breaking down the diegetic narrative in multiple incompatible directions: primarily following Max's and Lucia's erotic desires on the one hand, while secondarily digressing into the former nazis' paranoid logic of concealment on the other, a logic that manifests itself in the form of clandestine trials, therapeutic purgings of "dangerous others," and the endless repetition, acting out, of unseemly desires. In addition, the film is structured as a constant shuttling between nostalgic images and the present overload of sensations: violence, cruelty, coldness, seduction, passion, opera, cabaret, and ragtime. Consequently, the film appears as a network of spectacles ranging from ballet to opera, cabaret, men in uniform (nazi theatrics), (trans)sexual masquerades, and sadomasochistic plays.

Because seduction appeals to the senses, it attaches itself to the body (as sentient experience) and the aestheticization of the body (the visualization of bodily experience). It recycles previously established aesthetic representations of the body: images of beauty, masculinity, purity, control, morality, and images of sexuality, femininity, decadence, impurity, wildness, and immorality. Seduction functions as a process of mimicry; imitating culturally instantiated aesthetic gestures only to reveal their inherent inauthentic connection to what they allegedly represent or mean. The result of such an explosion of references and gestures, is, according to Deleuze, that "words are no longer anything but affectations of the body" (*The Logic of Sense*, 126). Like simulation, seduction operates beyond references, beyond meaning. The seductive repetition menaces set models by creating a double vision, disclosing the ambivalence of, in this case, logocentric or phallocentric discourse in order to disrupt its authority. Not being grounded in any substance other than visual simulation, the icon or sign of seduction can never have any assurance of existence. Instead it persists as a force of subversion. This aesthetic gesture or sign of passion, as Paul de Man points out, "is precisely the manifestation of a will that exists independently of any specific meaning or intent and that therefore can never be traced back to a cause or origin . . . it is devoid of substance, not because it has to be a transparent indicator that should not mask a plenitude of meaning, but because the meaning itself is empty; the sign should not offer its own sensory richness as a substitute for the void that it signifies" (*Blindness and Insight*, 132). Thus, while the sensory richness of the seductive image marks a site of plenitude (incalculable effects), its inscription within an ideological narrative reduces the image to a negative space, a site of disappearance (a space that marks where a sensory experience once was).

Representation itself neutralizes the image of seduction. "With respect to the liberty of signifieds of the image," Roland Barthes maintains, the representative text "has thus a repressive value, and we can see that it is at this level that the morality and ideology of a society are above all invested."[24] By focusing on the sensual persistence of the image, Cavani problematizes fixed ideological constructions that territorialize the body—anchoring the body to moral and ideological paradigms of control. This paradigmatic order affects the way we read the body and its gestures, translating it into the locus of all territorializing discourses (as for instance psychoanalysis, Hobbesian notions of the "body politic," and corporativism). Cavani's visualization of Max's and Lucia's relationship transgresses such culturally entrenched (bodily) demarcations that distinguish the moral from the immoral, the empowered from the "unhomely," man from woman, seducer from seduced. Their transgressive desires (a desire of the victim for the victimizer, the concentration camp prisoner for the former nazi, and vice versa) result in the short-circuiting of regimes that organize and discipline the body. For example, bodily regimes—represented by uniforms (of concentration camp inmates and SS jailers, night porters, suits, ball gowns, etc.) and the lack thereof, the naked-ness of the prisoners as opposed to the nudity of Bert (as he performs ballet)—lose their symbolic meaning when they become part of Max's and Lucia's masquerade. Max's and Lucia's masquerade of gender, race, and sexual identities, shaped by the rep-etitions of cultural positions, fits within Judith Butler's notion of "performance" "in the sense that the essence or identity that they otherwise purport to express are fabri-cations manufactured and sustained through corporeal signs and other discursive means."[25] While still a prisoner, Lucia wears the SS uniform, and Max, as Rex Reed puts it, "bares only his left nipple." Janet Maslin proclaims that "Bogarde spends most of the film, even the love scenes, in an immaculate three piece suit."[26] Yet, while imi-tating this hagiography of body types (the fully clothed man, the naked woman), Cavani manipulates conventional models, not by defamiliarizing the image within a given context but exaggerating the features of that image in relation to its ideological and moral codings. Rather than disrobing, Max, the epitome of reserve, loses control over his extremely regimented body; with Lucia he becomes both violent and pas-sionate, with the former nazis he becomes ironic, losing his decorum as he mocks their serious allegiance to the now defunct Third Reich—smirking and withdrawing his arm as they all salute the Führer. Lucia, on the other hand, who is first seen standing naked in a line of prisoners, consistently clothes herself (or is clothed) in Max's apparel, from the SS uniform to his sweaters. While he progressively exposes his pas-sion, she disguises hers, appropriating an image of control. She not only puts on his clothes but smokes his pipe, posing as the "man of the house," and Max, in a moment of vulnerability, unpacks the groceries and tells her that he has quit his job in order to be with her.

Further, Cavani's insistent use of extreme close-up—off-centered just enough to cut out part of the face, or in some cases parts of the body—deconstructs conventional images, as for instance the mythic face of the movie star. This skewed framing of shots serves to fracture holistic representations of the body, presenting the body as a series of autonomous parts. Cavani correlates the fragmentation of the body with the disruption of stable subjective positions via tracking shots that move from hands (usu-ally chained, being wrung, or gloved) to faces, which are often out of focus in the fore-front, revealing the images in the background. Moreover, this panning of the body is usually interrupted by a series of shot-reverse-shots that cut from the face of Lucia to the face of Max. Yet these shot-reverse-shots, rather than appearing as a series of stac-cato images, are incorporated into a fluid motion, whereby the camera pulls away from the close-up framing of either Max's or Lucia's face to include the other within the frame, then it cuts either Max or Lucia out of the frame only to zoom back in on the close-up of the original subject. This fluid motion connotes Max's and Lucia's inextricable connection.

These disruptive or fractured images and sensations transport the body from the site (marked territory) or image of control to a deterritorialized system of antibodies, a network of sensations, erogenous zones, obsessions, desires, transformations, flows, and short circuits (ambiguities). For example, static aesthetic images of a pure "sublime" or classical beauty of the male body, and the impure popular theatricality of the femme fatale, do not punctuate the dynamic or fluid relationship between Max and Lucia but are incorporated into their sadomasochistic "play." In fact, these extradiegetic references—classical male beauty worshiped by the nazis and decadent feminine sexuality spurned by the nazis—become gestures and roles, not symbols of certain ideological principles. By multiplying "historical" references to aesthetic representation, Cavani adduces a blurring of icons of purity and impurity, health and sickness, morality and immorality. She pits seduction against representation by strategically situating icons of nazism (SS uniforms, monocles, black leather trench coats), victimhood (the striped uniform of the concentration camp prisoner, short haircuts, nudity of emaciated bodies), the femme fatale (the smoky room, the long black leather gloves, the song, and the texture of the voice), and transvestitism (the appeal to Dietrich, cabaret, the spectacle of nazi sadomasochism, the fetishization of the uniform) as sites of contestation.

At the same time that these images are contradictory, fraught with complexities, ambiguities, and vulnerabilities, they intersect with each other. This is not to say, however, that Cavani creates new synthetic images of gender, sexuality, and history. In an attempt to circumvent the politics of representation she refuses to rename this "seductive otherness" in terms of a designated alternative, what Carol Smith-Rosenberg calls a "third term," what Sandra Gilbert and Susan Gubar define as a "third sex," or Lacan calls "the third order of the symbolic."[27] Instead, Cavani focuses on undermining traditionally conceived binary economies. In *The Night Porter* she hyperbolically literalizes the ideology that equates femininity with passivity, receptivity, masochism, and castration. The obsession with aesthetics of gender, culture (both high and low), morality, strength, nazism, and victimhood emphasizes the artificiality of aesthetic and moral gender codings, which impose restricted economies of sexual representation, moralism, and health onto engendered bodies. These symbolic inscriptions of fixed gender and moral identities reach their limit, that is, they no longer represent the model of social control, in fact they reveal the inconsistencies in that very model.

The collapsing of limits of representation, however, does not translate into the collapsing of difference, as for instance Susan Sontag insinuates when she states that "what is most beautiful about men is something feminine, [and] what is most beautiful in women is something masculine; woman [is seen] as a 'big-playing-role' [hence] the taste for androgynous [the feminized SS officer] merges with excessive *femme*, in the articulation of gesture and pose" (*Against Interpretation*, 29). Rather than merging into a gesture of excessive femininity (camp) or ambiguous sexuality (kitsch), for Cavani, the more these diverse positions continue to comment on each other the more they appear to be irreconcilable. Gender alone does not divide these two aesthetic codes; instead notions of gender embedded within discourses of moral purity, hygiene, and aesthetic perfection infinitely separate the two *feminized* "gestures or poses." The juxtaposition of Bert's (Max's comrade and friend) ballet performance with Lucia's cabaret performance, for example, evokes a multiplicity of aesthetic gestures: Bert's posing as the emblem of monumental effeminate masculine beauty (the pristine beauty of a Kouros statue); his representation of high German culture; Lucia's posing as a series of film femmes fatales; Dietrich's cross-dressing; Rita Hayward's long leather gloves and stylized singing (in *Gilda*); Helmut Berger's performance of the effeminate, sadistic SS officer Martin Von Essenbeck (in *The Damned*). Yet when these images are recontextualized or repeated in the context of nazism, sadomasochism, and the "Final Solution," they emphasize the inherent violence ingrained within aesthetic hierarchies, disengaging high from low culture. By examining the reading of ballet and opera as an expression of high humanism, rather than one of nationalism, violence, and sexual subjugation, Cavani questions the role of aesthetics in harboring some of the most pernicious notions about class, race, and gender.

While Bert's and Lucia's ambiguous sexuality (androgyny) question an anatomical destiny—the "biological necessity of sexual difference"—their iconic relationship to cultural hierarchies remains intact. Just as Bert remains within the aesthetic framework of high humanism that intersects with the fascist idealization of the pure male body, and the postwar reinstitution of such cultural codings, Lucia is reinscribed as an icon of impurity, a hedonistic femme fatale. However, Bert's association with the nazis and Lucia's identification with the victims of the "Final Solution" problematize such aesthetic codings, drawing attention to the embedding of such images (of feminine decadence) within moral discourse. Even if Lucia is identified as a victim, her performance falls into the category of the impure, while Bert presents a "pure" humanist ideal. Hence the nazi is returned to the image of purity and the victim to the aesthetics of the impure. In his interpretation of Richard Strauss's *Der Rosenkavalier*, Bert simulates what George Mosse describes as the sexless beauty of "the classical heroic, or Greek sculpture of the male body" (*Nationalism and Sexuality*, 14). Although he dances nude before a group of SS men, his flesh-colored jockstrap serves to desexualize, or at least remove, his aesthetic image from the context of genital sexuality. It is as if, as Steven Kasher comments, "sexual excitation has been drained from the genitals and used to pump up the limbs and torso."[28] Bert's sexual repression (confining his sexual expression to the closet) ironically manifests itself as the image of racial purity, chaste and self-controlled virility. This image, as Kasher notes, was "erected to stand ready to fight the whole array of those defined by the Nazis as *Untermenschen*, including Jews, Negros, women, homosexuals, moderns, Bolsheviks and urban degenerates" ("The Art of Hitler," 56). This dispassionate love, sublimated into desexualized male bonding, stands in opposition to Lucia's simulation of multiple positionalities of sexual desire. She simulates the ambiguous yet seductive role of Dietrich, performing cabaret for the same group of nazis. Confronting Bert, Lucia's performance is replete with lewd sexual content, sexual innuendoes, erotic gestures, and vulgarity, which, as Adorno expounds, "express the failure of sublimation."[29] Rather than desublimating desire (as Marcuse proposes) or celebrating the monumentality of the female body, Lucia hyperbolizes woman's relationship to conventional fetish items, such as the long black leather gloves used in Gilda's striptease, the SS uniform that has become an icon of sadomasochism, the mask, and the riding crop. Instead of resisting the aesthetics of impurity that link the feminine to sexuality, disease, and evil, Cavani delves into these overdetermined aesthetics of feminine sexuality in order to expose and explode the radical inconsistencies and artificial consistencies of the discourse of purity and masculinity.

By hyperbolizing the excessive determinations of femininity, Cavani forces certain processes of representation to surface, specifically cinematic apparatuses of domination, voyeurism, and fetishism. Teresa de Lauretis argues that voyeurism and fetishism (understood both visually and theoretically) serve as a "political function of cultural domination including, but not limited to the sexual exploitation of women and the repression or containment of female sexuality." She adds that these "apparatuses of social reproduction are directly implicated in a discourse which circumscribes women in the sexual, binds her (in) sexuality, makes her the absolute representation, the phallic scenario" (*Alice Doesn't*, 26). Hence Lucia, as a metaphor of feminine sexuality, also serves as a metaphorical object/fetish for current critical readings of cinema itself. Was it not the very practice of reading cinema as a screen, what Stephen Heath calls "the smooth surface of the visualized body, the sexually charged, and thus, feminine body," that aided in eroticizing if not fetishizing the way we look at cinema and, at the same time, disingenuously replicating the process of distancing critical subjects from the fetishized cinematic object in the name of aesthetic or psychoanalytic interpretation?[30] Even as *The Night Porter* invokes the cultural (visual) codes of fetishism, voyeurism, sadomasochism, and the representation of nazism, it also denaturalizes the filming of fetishism, voyeurism, sadomasochism, and nazism.

Although obsessively envisaged as an object of desire, Lucia cannot be contained or limited to female sexuality nor its cinematic framing. By overdetermining sexual and subsequent moral references Cavani implodes paradigms of power that are predicated on sexual difference. Lucia, who is represented as a cross-dresser—crossing not only gender dress codes but ideological, political, and moral ones—problematizes dominant cinematic codes of representation. While mimicking excessive femininity, she traces this excess to certain masculine references. Kaja Silverman affirms that "the vocal corporealization [of Lucia's cabaret performance] is to be compared with ... sounds emitted by Mae West, Marlene Dietrich or Lauren Bacall.... [T]heir distinctive quality [deposits] a male rather than a female body in the voice" (*The Acoustic Mirror*, 61). Although I disagree with Silverman's insistence on returning to distinct gender classifications (male versus female), I want to point out that the texture of Dietrich's, West's, Bacall's, and Rampling's voices carry certain ambiguities, an attraction that is performative. They represent a masculinity performed by women or men in drag. Hence it is impossible to return such aesthetics to straight politics (male versus female). The fetishization of the female body performing as a phallus (Lacan) or an "imaginary signifier" of masculine virility itself (Metz) reveals a blurring of sexual boundaries. If the fetish supplements what Žižek names the "primordial lack" (the mother's missing phallus) and indeed assists in the evasion or veiling of castration, then, by attributing the fetish to woman, woman becomes an emblem of male sexuality.[31] As a result, feminine sexuality disappears altogether within this model. Žižek illustrates this disappearance as a fusing of woman with the cinematic screen whereby she becomes "that cold, *neutral* screen which opens up the space for possible *projections*, surface functions as a 'black hole,' a mirror whose limit is beyond inaccessible" (*Metastases of Enjoyment*, 91, emphasis mine). Yet, because woman represents male sexuality, she becomes what Žižek calls an impostor, or a male impersonator. And it is this impersonation of male sexuality by someone who does "not exist" that Cavani exploits through not only Lucia but also Max and Bert.

The question is not who possesses the phallus (a repetition of the Freudian *Fort-Da* game) but how is it that the phallus (or lack thereof) supports representation while being contingent on or supported by it—that is, how can it both preexist and exceed systems of meaning? Cavani goes to the very root of the problem by challenging the culturally constituted edifice of sexual difference. Rather than returning to the aesthetics of camp and kitsch, where feminine sexuality is exaggerated, Cavani demonstrates the inconsistencies in converging femininity with sexuality and decadence— usually attributed to the nazi rather than the victim, even if that victim is a woman. For Cavani, camp is no longer the exaggerated femininity played out by a male transvestite; it is a male femininity played out by an androgynous female and a homosexual man who imitate the aesthetics of the sublime or beautiful image of the icon of masculinity. Rather than simply protesting psychoanalytic renderings of sexual difference, Cavani attacks the incursion of the discourse of sexual difference into moral, racial, and ideological discourses—discourses that link masculine sexuality to moral righteousness, racial purity, and the embodiment of ontological ideals.

Although Bert's performance comes across as a sterilized enactment of his (tragic) homosexual desire, it is the concealment and confinement of this desire, his hiding in the dark (closet) hotel room, that problematizes his reference to any discourse of purity. The flashback to Bert's dance demonstrates his obsessive compulsion to cover his genitals, to conceal his homosexuality, which is incompatible with nazi dictate. This concealment connotes a sense of sexual shame that is not necessarily homosexual; in fact it evokes humans' fall from grace, their realization that before God they are naked, sexual beings. But because Bert's genitals are already camouflaged by the flesh-colored jockstrap, this gesture (of covering his genitals with his hands) draws attention to their absence, to the fact that his sexual desire has already been castrated.

Moreover, his compulsive looking at his hands and wiping them on his body recalls the guilt of Lady Macbeth and doubles the sense of sexual guilt, tying it to a bad conscience for acts of physical violence, presumably Bert's participation in the "Final Solution."

Bert's sexual masquerade (his repression of his homosexuality) is mirrored in Erika, who also confines her "voracious" sexual role-playing to the hotel room, where she pays for the "favors" of young men. Yet what makes their sexual identity perverse is not a linkage to their nazi identity but rather the confinement of their present postwar sexual desires to a necrophilic desire to repeat the past. As Marguerite Waller puts it, "Bert [and here I include Erika] [are] made-up to resemble movie vampire[s], the living dead" ("Signifying the Holocaust," 14). Their only means of sexual expression is through recollections, which must be hidden away in their own separate hotel rooms. While Erika and Bert are presented as one-dimensional (backward-looking) characters, Lucia, "Max's little girl" turned bad boy, is reinscribed in his "biblical narrative" as both Salome and potentially John the Baptist. Asked by Erika to recount his love story, Max recalls (via flashback) what he likens to the biblical narrative of Salome. When Lucia asks to have a fellow prisoner (who constantly bothered her because of the preferential treatment Max gave her) "moved"/removed, Max responds by bestowing her with a gift box containing the head of the prisoner. Lucia's terrified reaction to this gift reminds us that she is also subject to Max's writing and reading of the "biblical narrative" in which she will be a player, yet she is also the impetus for Max's subsequent action. Hence Lucia is inscribed in his/her narrative as both the temptress and the victim. Likewise it is the sexualization of Max and Lucia's relationship that causes a similar effect, displacing them from the language of absolutes. Although Max and Lucia act out a variety of roles corresponding to their changing power relations, their sexualities are not static as those of Erika, Bert, or Lucia's husband.

The memory of Bert's dance to *Der Rosenkavalier* (which he constantly replays in the privacy of his hotel room) introduces the depersonalized concept of purity and humanity as a reference to German high humanism. The filmic device of flashback, as Susan Sontag writes, "effectively erases the subject of the enunciation, giving the past presence," and it also undermines the romanticized aesthetics of high humanism (as absolute liberalism) (*Against Interpretation*, 56). Rather than repeating the "romantic" aura (in the sense of heroic masculinity) of Bert's initial dancing before the SS, the repetition of the dance in the dark hotel room instills a sense of hopeless longing for something unreachable (the past) and abject. While the flashback to Bert's dance suggests a certain nostalgic longing for a nazi past, another flashback that weaves in and out of the duet in *Die Zauberflöte* juxtaposes the idealized marriage of Papagena to Papageno with the vision of a male prisoner being raped by a nazi guard. Here the operatic music serves as a bridge linking the theatricality of opera to that of violence. This flashback bars a nostalgic return to the high ideals of German humanism and nationalism by splicing this spectacle of high culture with what Nietzsche calls "its low returns." The nondiegetic sound-over of the opera music as we watch the mute images of the concentration camp radically disrupts the moral content of the opera, especially that of the lyrical text, which promotes the joys of marriage. The image of the concentration camp, set against or within the opera in a series of shot-reverse-shots, doubles the operatic spectacle. Yet the subject of this spectacle radically diverges from the triumphant marriage vows of Papagena and Papageno, who sing of the joys of bearing children. Instead this sequence captures the spectacle of violence, the rape of a male prisoner. This duet is followed by the chorus's exclamation: "Dort wollen wir sie überfallen, die Frömmler tilgen von der Erd' mit Feuersglut und mächt'gem Schwert!" ("We will attack them there, eradicate the bigots from the earth with glowing fire and mighty sword!") Cavani foregrounds the irony of bourgeois (and fascist) moralism that purges and slashes to ensure/secure "humanity." This sadistic morality readily turns into antihuman activity (violent sexuality) when confronted with what it considers to be nonhuman. Hence liberal thought that threatens to "eradicate the bigots from the earth," having pronounced, "Wen solche Lehren nicht erfreu'n verdienet nicht, ein Mensch zu sein" ("He who does not rejoice in such teaching does not deserve to be called a human being," or in the words of Primo Levi, cannot "*considera se questo un'uomo*"/consider if this is a man, since humanism is only an ideal which is dependent on the definition of the term "human" itself—as a totalizing term. The resurfacing of moral values installs Lucia's husband (the American opera conductor) back into the discourse of nazi moralism by visually associating him with acts of violence. It appears as if he is in fact directing both "operas," one public and the other privately hidden within the "not so-sacred walls" of the concentration camp. What he perpetuates is an idealized representation of (Aryan) humanity that, instead of recreating the melodramatic event, legitimizes the sadistic law of purification, upholding heterosexual marriage and rejecting the miscegenation of Pamina with the Moor Monostatos. As Marguerite Waller points out, "if the Viennese opera house and the concentration camp are seen as reverse images of each other, then it becomes more difficult simply to oppose Lucia's husband to Max. Lucia's husband is reproducing and naturalizing the white Aryan male subject position that Nazism, the epitome of the patriarchal repression of women and 'non-Aryans,' tried to solidify to an absurd extent" ("Signifying the Holocaust," 17).

Here Cavani "plays" with the Wagnerian notion of the *Gesamtkunstwerk*, what Philippe Lacoue-Labarthe describes as "the Work in absolute terms, the absolute *organon* of Schelling, or, as Nietzsche will say, the *opus metaphysicum* . . . the *end* of art in the form of the unification and synthesis of all the individual arts."[32] In fact, Wagner's *Gesamtkunstwerk* incorporates music, poetry, and theater with nationalism—a means of unifying disparate forces in *Siegfried*—and sexual difference, especially in the case of Parsifal, who purifies his desire and at the same time rejects Kundry (the woman who is given existence only because she is desired by Parsifal), transforming her into a mute shadow who finally dies. Thus this end (epitome) of art aspires to a synthetic ideal while simultaneously disengaging art from its ugly effects.

By recontexualizing humanism within the discourse of racial superiority, hygiene, sexuality, and their aesthetic renderings, Cavani visualizes the violence performed under the guise of purification. Yet she further explores the connection of endings to systems of meaning and constructions of morality: from the Wagnerian understanding of the ideal, synthetic work of art, to Adorno's famous comment that Auschwitz represents the end of poetry or art. For Cavani both ends (theories of conclusion) create models that are predicated on a binary economy and a certain understanding of humanism. While the very same moral humanism that inscribes the law of legal sexual relationships and moral identifications into the *Gesamtkunstwerk* treats what it considers as inhuman inhumanely, the critical model attaches art to a need to reflect or critique this inhumanity. However, the project of enlightenment is still performed in the name of humanism.[33] At the same time that Cavani imitates Adorno's critical project, illustrating the violence upon which notions such as humanism rest—the translation of discursive silencing, denying the other subjectivity, into a form of silencing the body—she questions the principles upon which consciousness rests. She challenges the equation of high culture (esteemed by Adorno and Wagner) with a higher consciousness, since it excludes all representations of pleasure as manifestations of popular culture, falsely conscious at best.

Seduction and Ambiguous Power

In contrast to the sadistic desire to annihilate the impure, Max and Lucia are cast in a masochistic suprasensual play designed to undermine notions of purity. Their masquerade as victim and victimizer indulges in an array of inversions, projections, and blurring of boundaries—of self and other, man and woman, heterosexual and homosexual, victim and victimizer, good and evil. For Deleuze this type of masochism marks the triumph of "femininity," which has traditionally been conceived of as impure; that is, according to Deleuze, the masochist is a hermaphrodite who "attacks the Law [whether sexual or social] on the level of humor." He qualifies this act of rebellion as a "contradistinction to the upward movement of irony toward a transcendent higher principle, [instead] it is a downward movement from the law to its consequences, a demonstration of the Law's absurdity" (*Coldness and Cruelty*, 88). *The Night Porter* rebels against (1) "the wonders of marriage" that are expounded upon as we watch an anonymous prisoner as well as Lucia being raped; (2) the psychoanalytic cure of former nazis who desire to evade persecution; (3) the notion of justice that files the witnesses away; (4) the beauty of high culture that aestheticizes its own violent response to otherness as a heroic or romantic act; (5) the triumph of democracy that reinstalls former fascists in the same political and economic posts they once held; and (6) the law of sexual difference that merely creates a society of sexually alienated individuals (in other words, rather than define a sexual order, it gives sexual orders). *The Night Porter* manifests this process of tearing down cultural ideals, installed in hierarchical and legal systems, in the sensual blurring of images. The film is structured as a series of rhythmic inversions in which the visualizations of cultural ideals (social, sexual, moral) not only face their consequences but incorporate them, as in the case of the opera that includes the visualization of the concentration camp. Often the camera moves in and out of focus so as to destabilize subjective positions, so that the audience cannot identify with just one subject of the gaze. This is enhanced by a pro-fusion of gazes—Max watching Lucia who watches her husband conducting *Die Zauberflöte*, Max watching Bert who is revisualizing his past performance, or Max being watched by his former-nazi friends. What is of crucial importance here, in Žižek's argument, is "the total self-externalization of the masochist's most intimate pas-sions: the most intimate desires become objects of contract and composed negotia-tion. The nature of the masochistic theatre is therefore thoroughly non-psychological" (*Metastases of Enjoyment*, 92).

Unlike Deleuze's definition of the theatrics of masochism, where the sub-ject/object and gender positions are written in the contract, Max and Lucia's power positions are constantly shifting. For Deleuze, the masochist maintains a reflective dis-tance; he or she never really abandons him- or herself to the game, the contract always allows for the masochist to maintain order and control. Deleuze reads masochism in terms of sacrificial logic; it is a small death, which fends off any experience of pleasure so as to infinitely put off the end of pleasure. Hence masochism is a ritual process that defends itself against the temporality of pleasure and life, that will ultimately result in death. Masochism functions as a form of preservation whose ultimate goal, paradox-ically, is death, yet a pleasureless death. Through pain the masochist attempts to con-trol or disavow any sense of emptiness or meaninglessness. This prolongation of a promised pleasure circumvents the supposed aftereffects of pleasure, a sense of total lack of engagement. However, Deleuze omits one thing from his definition of masochism—love—and for Cavani this is the most destabilizing factor of Max's and Lucia's relationship. Cavani argues, "In every couple there exists a degree of sado-masochism [or at least the tension caused by certain power struggles] . . . this is noth-ing compared to the numberless couples who tear each other apart psychologically"; therefore Max's and Lucia's is "a relationship that is freer than normal." What makes this relationship relatively "free" is that love is constructed as a process of becoming different or other, what Kristeva calls a loss of the sense of parameters of the self (*Tales of Love*, 15).

This process of becoming radically other rejects notions of higher awareness or consciousness of self as both deadly and narcissistic. For this reason Cavani rejects the definition of masochism as a game of coldness and cruelty predicated on a need for distance. For her, power is not static but dynamic and therefore power cannot be contracted in the legal sense nor can it be harnessed; it can only be contracted in the sense of Artaud's *pest* or Deleuze and Guattari's concept of nomadic distribution. Since power is always in flux, positions of power neither conform to rigid models nor do they reinforce culturally established gender roles or historical identities. Instead, as Cavani demonstrates, masculinity and femininity, like victim and victimizer, are culturally produced roles and as such are exchangeable. This does not mean that history can be revised (survivors cannot be repictured as nazis within the context of World War II). It suggests instead that identities and identifications with power are relative to every given situation and are constantly subject to reconstitution with every given permutation. This distinction of relative power from official power dovetails with Lyotard's setting of what he calls "language games" in opposition to master-narratives, and Deleuze's distinguishing of legal from contractual relations. All of these relative or rebellious economies treat power as nomadic and temporary rather than fixed or institutionalized. For instance, even though Max claims that Lucia is still his "little girl, exactly like she was before," the context of the postwar period drastically transforms their relationship, because it radically changes their social status. Whereas under Lucia during the nazi period is considered to be nonhuman as a woman, a daughter of a socialist, and possibly a non-Ayran, in the postwar period it is Max who represents the epitome of inhumanity, the difference being of course that Max has warranted this label. Yet the characteristics (effeminacy, hedonism, perverse sexuality) that serve to distinguish nazis from good citizens are decidedly similar to those qualities the fascists, futurists, and the decadents used to distinguish good from evil, pure from impure. And so, while political institutions have disengaged any social form of identification with the German romantic image of racially and sexually superior heroes, they have replaced the very qualities of heroism with either the tragic victims of the Holocaust, the heroic feats of the partisans, or the triumphant image of the Allies.

Paradoxically, the need for romantic, virile, but unsexed heroes remains detached from the need for moral retribution, that is, these two needs coexist as distinct if not opposing forces rather than as two elements of the same binary logic. The identity of the victim, or of the hero, is contingent on a repeated act of negating their binary antithesis—evil, decadence, woman. *The Night Porter* challenges the production of meaning, by installing this dialectical system within a masochistic economy—an excessive indulgence in carnal sensuality and impurity. What is in question is the very construct of value/meaning (purity, morality, power) that is contingent on a negative double. Cavani reveals that this double is the same for both the nazis and the neofascists: it is a demonized image of feminine sexuality, the femme fatale. Whether she is played by a man or a woman is irrelevant. The difference between Cavani's (and Wertmüller's) representation of this radical evil and its neodecadent incarnations is that, while the victim and the victimizer are understood to be inseparable within this dialectic, their positions are not fixed. If one has once been branded a victim, he or she is not forever fixed within that role in every given situation. As Jacqueline Rose suggests, "being a victim does not stop you from identifying with the aggressor, being an aggressor does not stop you from identifying with the victim. Identification is something that always has to be constructed."[34] Although the victim needs the victimizer in order to be defined as a victim, the translation of this "dependency" into a sexual economy questions the repetition of the romantic and tragic narrative or historic positions. This subsequently questions the translation of the event (absolute sadistic control on the part of the nazi) into its representation (as masochistic play between victim and victimizer, where the sadistic law is no longer present). What disappears in such an unstable economy is the sovereignty of the aesthetics of domination, the law of castration, and the sublime attraction to the *man* in uniform—from the nazi to the opera conductor to the night porter.

By disintegrating this official line that divides good and evil, Cavani blurs the aesthetics of domination, nazism, victimization, and submission. In a departure from neo-decadent cinema as well as neorealism, which already conflate the nazi (the paragon of racist purity, official regimentation, and bureaucratic efficiency) with radical evil (evil incarnate, the symbol for the most vicious atrocities of the century), Cavani rejects the recoding of evil in the misogynist discourse and aesthetics that stem from thinkers such as Otto Weininger, Max Nordeau, Cesare Lombroso, and Sigmund Freud. On the other hand, she does not subscribe to the politics of victimization; that is to say, she does not support identifying with the victims any more than she does with the victimizers. For Cavani both positions are already radically disempowered since they are fixed: they belong to the dead rather than the living. What makes this dissolution of boundaries, identities, and power structures so unpalatable for many viewers, as well as many critics, is that the deconstruction of subjective (patriarchal) identities opens up onto questions of morality that are deeply embedded within historical, sexual, and gender discourses. In the case of *The Night Porter* the audience is left with an "impossible" choice, of identifying with a victim who is no longer a "pure" victim, a victimizer who is not absolutely evil nor in complete control, and a group of former nazis who desire a return to order as the separation of nazi from victim. Most critics of *The Night Porter*, however, find Max's indulgence in sadomasochistic theatrics less offensive than Lucia's. Implicit within such critique is a belief that the victimizer is always completely impure, while the victim, in order to be defined as a victim, must be pure, morally irreproachable. Critics reinforce the alleged "social need" for stable subjective identifications, calling for Max and Lucia to be put in their proper places. It is not only Lucia's reenactment of the erotic play but more importantly her apparent sexual enjoyment that causes feminists and male survivors to react violently to the film. For example, Primo Levi responds to *The Night Porter* calling it "bello e falso," and demanding that the distinction between victims and assassins be maintained.[35] Thomas Quinn Curtis writes, "Lucia is a mad sadist without a trace of conscience; Cavani's 'heroine' seems to be a complacent slut, a singularly weak-willed moron."[36] Ironically, Cavani supports the distinction between victim and victimizer in the context of the war and the "Final Solution". It is only in the representation of the postwar period that such identifications become problematic. The problem for Cavani is not the representation of the "Final Solution" but the maintaining of such rigid moral identifications.

The violent critical reaction (by Levi, Kael, Quinn, and others) to the portrayal of feminized men, former-nazi officials, quack doctors (both past and present), impure victims, and femmes fatales within the context of a love story indicates a demand that the victim be desexualized. Only then can one identify with either the sadistic nazi or his or her absolute victim. What is at stake is the undesirable intimacy between victims and victimizers. The social desire to disavow this intimacy, however, exists in the name of objectifying the victim and subjectifying the victimizer so as to create a relationship of total indifference in which all acts of malevolence are driven solely by sadistic yet narcissistic desires to act out onto innocent objects. This returns us to a futurist economy in which all actions are seen as both acts of violence and acts of self-expression irrespective of any outside influences. Consequently, such readings suggest that the only way to comprehend the dynamic between victims and victimizers is sadistically, hence the only way to represent fascism is through sadism. But Cavani replaces the conventional sadistic representation of the relationship of nazis to their victims—cold indifference—with an enigmatic intimacy. Furthermore, *The Night Porter* challenges critical readings that return Lucia to the conventional discourse of the femme fatale—"a slut," "a moron," "a sadist," "decadent," and even "fascist." Readings such as Pauline Kael's, who describes Rampling's appeal as a "necrophiliac allure" under the sign of "contamination" and "drag," speak in the name of political correctness, while (at the same time) blaming the victims for not remaining "pure victims" but turning into feminized images "with an underlying homosexual feeling" ("The Current Cinema: Stuck in the Fun," 51). Such readings not only conflate the image of the femme fatale with homosexuality, decadence, disease, and death; they reify the discourse of purity by relocating the femme fatale (even if she is a victim) within the discourse of the abject. The problem is, of course, that such criticism seems to justify, if not suggest, that the former nazis were right to want to file Lucia away, since she threatens to contaminate and therefore disrupt the social order. Such thinking dovetails with that of Otto Weininger, who argues that it is the hysterical female, impregnated and penetrated by everything (an image of total corruption), who destroys the community (*Sex and Character*, 145). As a consequence, this line of thinking returns to notions of the healthy male body as the model of purity and community, which were circulating at the turn of the century. For example, Žižek illustrates this (il)logic when he states that "in man the sense of the Good of the community is expressed far more than it is in woman . . . women who are really behind the superego, capitalize on men's guilt, the guilt men possess for having to admit that rather than loving the ideal [man's own self-image of the Good] they love women [sexual corruption, decadence]" (*Metastases of Enjoyment*, 69). For Žižek all women are dangerous femmes fatales who threaten to corrupt men's symbolic order by drawing them into the nothingness and sexual abandon of the Big Other.

Cavani's play of seduction confuses the positioning of subject and object in what may be read as a Lacanian twist, yet it does not necessarily have to return to the deterministic language of repression. Max's and Lucia's relationship—which undermines traditional notions of the masochistic contract in which man sets up the rules of the game, placing woman in the role of the superego so as to undermine the symbolic value of the dead father—escapes symbolic castration. And by escaping the symbolic,

Max and Lucia move beyond the law itself, making a mockery of notions such as the common good that are predicated on an act of repression (submission to symbolic castration) so as to avoid repression (symbolic castration). What distinguishes this dangerously seductive otherness from the Lacanian politics of the Big Other is that the otherness of becoming evades linguistic (logocentric) inscription. Most of the dialogue in *The Night Porter* is reserved for the interaction of the former nazis; Max and Lucia rarely exchange words. Their communication is almost purely visual, if perceivable at all. Rather than visualize communication, Cavani enframes the effects of communication. She underscores the bureaucratic, if not banal, discourse of the former nazis by juxtaposing it with the fantastic imagery of Max and Lucia's sexual desires and interactions. Here the question of emptiness and fullness is reaccessed; the symbolic, rather than representing even a shadow of reality, suffocates all potential meaningful exchanges, silencing desires. Rather than responding to the Freudian question "What does a woman want?" by relegating woman and her desires to the Big Nowhere, Cavani, like Lyotard, retorts, "She wants the man to become neither man nor woman, that he no longer age at all, that she and he, different people, be identical in the insane concoctions of every tissue. It would be more in keeping with the realization of desire, in the afterlife, that one be there finally delivered from sexual difference" (*Libidinal Economies*, 66–67).

5. *Fammi campà*:
Survival without *Omertà*

Your thirst for life disgusts me. Your love is disgusting to me. In Paris a Greek made love to a
goose; he did this to eat, to live. Subhuman Italian larva, you ate and moments later you found
strength for an erection.... That is why you'll survive, and win in the end.

      —*Seven Beauties* (*Pasqualino Settebellezze*)[1]

Considerate se questo è un uomo ...
Che lotta per mezzo pane
Che muore per un si o per un no.
Considerate se questa è una donna, Senza capelli e senza nome
Senza più forza di ricordare.[2]

      —Primo Levi, *Se questo è un uomo*

I proceeded with great faith in the power of laughter and tears, without fearing to be too obvious
or banal, always trying to communicate and entertain problems to think over and analyze.

      —Lina Wertmüller

In an attempt to question how power relations are in fact socially produced—especially the hierarchy of binary oppositions, including gender, race, and class oppositions that persist in the re-representations of nazism and fascism—Lina Wertmüller
thwarts the process of morality and rendering gender, sexuality, and national/regional
identity as functions of ideology. She subverts ideological practices by first reversing
traditional gender coding and then hyperbolizing and exaggerating an array of conventional stereotypes, including political ideologies, Italian and German sexual and
national identities, and images of nazism and fascism. Playing with Felliniesque

images and comedic style, as well as thematic concerns of the *commedia italiana* that emerged in the late 1950s, Wertmüller does not so much lament as satirize positions of power that are codified in terms of gender.[3] In *Seven Beauties* the protagonist's (Pasqualino's) masculinity is constantly challenged by his need to perpetuate his macho self-image to everyone he encounters. And so he dominates: he plays the man of the house with his seven sisters (the *settebellezze*), especially Concettina (the oldest of the seven, who is a cabaret singer and later becomes a prostitute); he plays the role of the good son to enchant the female doctor at the mental institute where he is imprisoned; and after his capture by the nazis for desertion from the Italian Army, he plays the role of the seducer, pretending to be in love with the female concentration camp commandant. While Pasqualino never plays the role of a woman (as, for instance, a transvestite would), he is often out-manned by the women he encounters. The women assume not traditional male roles but positions of power, and Pasqualino inconspicuously submits. Wertmüller pries the masculine gender coding that characterizes power from essentialist discourses, including biological and sexual determinism. The inversions and subversions of masculinity, femininity, and national identity disrupt logical systems by which we standardize and legitimize representations of reality and their underlying visual systems of power.

For Wertmüller, national, sexual, and political identities are largely invested in stereotypical images—in notions of Italian motherhood, machismo, regional and class distinctions, difference between Italian fascism and German nazism—and in the spectacle that produces them—the process of othering that feeds off sexual and national boundaries. Rather than neutralize what is *real*, Wertmüller exaggerates gestures and symbols of power, commenting on the "artifice" inherent in the construction or representation of "reality." Hence she focuses on the unreal, the ideology, morality, and symbolism that typecast and install individuals as well as communities into a prefabricated spectacle or master-narrative of reality. This does not mean that, for Wertmüller, there is no real. She suggests that by submitting to preexisting structures of power we assume stereotypical or caricatured identities, thereby reducing reality to the consequences of such submission. Within the mise-en-scène of Wertmüller's films reality lies strictly in power relations. This understanding of reality as contingent on power alliances and shifts does not exclude alternative realities, ones that reject the terms of submission. Yet, like Pasolini, Wertmüller is highly skeptical of traditional forms of resistance, since they also participate in the spectacular economy that reproduces images of good versus evil. Her bloated form of mimicry, accordingly, exposes normativized understandings of reality as simulations of preexisting ideological, moral, and symbolic economies.

Rather than simplify complex power networks reducing all power relationships to binary economies, Wertmüller multiplies these networks, revealing an intricately layered circuitry that does not conform to the convenient "order" of binary economies but instead to a disorderly profusion of forces. In contrast to Millicent Marcus, who reads Wertmüller as deintellectualizing social issues by reducing and exaggerating them in order to conform to a dialectical model as well as "our comic delight in it," I read Wertmüller's exaggeration of stereotypic images as a disavowal of the overwhelming social desire for real heroes, real villains, true victims, real men, and real women.[4] By reinscribing her characters into binary models Wertmüller does not simply simulate the "politics of polarity": she attempts to make it very difficult to codify Pasqualino. For example, Pasqualino, who is first seen as a Neapolitan *guappo* or Latin lover type, is constantly repictured: he is a mafioso, a murderer (*il mostro di Napoli*), a madman, an orderly in the asylum, a rapist, a deserter from the Italian Army, and a concentration camp inmate who is emasculated by the commandant. His experiences are not simply in conflict with his original image (a lovable buffoon); each event (his murder of Totonno, rape of a bound psychiatric patient, and seduction of the nazi commandant) demands that his image be reframed or recontextualized according to his actions. Thus he falls in and out of various disparate narratives. His relationship to power changes in every given situation, and with every act he loses his sympathetic and even humorous appeal. And so he cannot be read in terms of pure evil or pure good; instead he is a victim who is also implicated in sanctioning the very conditions to which he is later subjected.

In contrast to Cavani, who problematizes the various registers of cultural representations (romantic images of nazis and their victims and the moral self-presentations promoted by former nazis), pushing the limits of identification, Wertmüller facilitates the process of identification by presenting her characters as "readable" stereotypes. Yet as the narrative progresses, the spectator who identifies or sympathizes with Pasqualino, the bumbling Latin lover, is forced to also identify with his acts of violence, immorality, and cruelty. For this reason Jerzy Kosinski reviles the depiction of Pasqualino, believing that Wertmüller "condones despicable moral choices" by making her protagonist a cartoon character. He argues that "laughter tempers our reaction to the monstrosity of his final deeds," his seduction of the nazi commandant, his selection of six anonymous prisoners from his own barracks for execution, and his shooting of his only friend (Francesco) for insubordination against the nazi camp officials.[5] Here I would like to point out that, as Bakhtin argues, the very same laughter that tends to familiarize the character to the audience does not necessarily undermine moral perspectives. What it does undermine, according to Bakhtin, is "all one-sided or dogmatic seriousness and [thus,] it does not permit any single point of view, any single polar extreme of life or of thought, to be absolutized."[6] Wertmüller uses "black comedy" as a means of dismantling what have been construed as clear moral choices, exposing the impossibility of such choices themselves. Unlike Bakhtin, Wertmüller does not situate laughter within a ritualized play of the carnivalesque, one that explodes the existing order only to return once again to order, that is, one that effectively performs as a release of tension. Bakhtin perceives the world as both ordered and disciplined in the form of institutions and social hierarchies. For Wertmüller, the world order itself feeds off laughter's disorganizing principles. Hence this new order neither thrives on a disciplinary model, since it provides spaces for such simulated social disruptions, nor is threatened by such interruptions.

Pasqualino's masquerading as different characters (the *guappo*, mafioso, kapo, madman, victim, rapist) does not disrupt the existing systems of order; these often conflicting economies of systematized order break him down. As a result he loses his ability to role play and, therefore, to procure the audience's laughter. Even Bruno Bettelheim, the film's most adamant critic, suggests that his acts of violence and cruelty "rob Pasqualino of his soul."[7] In fact, the film delineates the metamorphoses of Pasqualino from his animated *guappo* appearance—his slicked back hair, double-breasted white suit and hat with black trim, his cigarette holder, and overemphasized manly gait—to his tattered Italian Army uniform with the hospital bandage wrapped around his head, his dusty concentration camp uniform, and finally to his sedate, dark suit and uncovered head. His image becomes progressively less "laughable" and less animated (or cartoonlike) in correlation to his "deeds," and especially his suffering the consequences for his "deeds." If anything, the film presents what Eli Pfefferkorn calls "the painful ambiguities, deriving from survival in extremity . . . leaving the viewer at loose ends, which are both intellectually confusing and morally disturbing. But such an approach to the subject-matter of survival seems preferable to one that has all the ready-made answers" ("Bettelheim, Wertmüller, and the Morality of Survival," 20). Kosinski leaves out of his criticism these very conditions within which "despicable moral choices" are made, "la vita ambigua del lager" ("ambiguous life of the lager"), about which Primo Levi writes: "the lager offered some individual slaves a privileged position, a premium probability of surviving, demanding in exchange the betrayal of the natural solidarity with their companions, and certainly no-one could refuse."[8] Moral choices in these extreme circumstances, accompanied by Pasqualino's strong desire to survive, illustrate what Pelagia Lewinska saw as a model life inside the lager, which she describes as "a condensed social image of the Third Reich, [where] human-itarian scruples and thoughtfulness became a ridiculous weakness, while the bestial struggle to go on living was intended to produce a camp 'elite' in the image of the one that governed Germany."[9] Rather than "condon[ing] despicable moral choices," Wertmüller questions whether it is more moral to die like a hero or a martyr than to live with the guilt of surviving (by whatever means necessary). Even if the Kapo was "il più odioso e odiato" ("the most hateful and hated"), Ralph Tutt points out that "nowhere in *Seven Beauties* is Pasqualino devoid of moral conscience. . . . Throughout his criminal career, he is an honor-bound, conscience-stricken stumble-bum who ago-nizes over his crimes and pays for them in descending circles of hell, until having learned the price of political apathy."[10]

Bettelheim's criticism of the film derives precisely from this depiction of the sur-vivor as someone who compromises even the most basic human values in order to sur-vive. He inveighs against the "animalizing" of the will to live, accusing Wertmüller of supporting the notion that "all that matters is life in its crudest, merely biological form"

("Reflections: Surviving," 38). Annette Insdorf responds to Bettelheim and Kosinski by writing that "critics who assumed that the director was endorsing her protagonist simply by having him survive tended to ignore the cinematic means through which Wertmüller was examining her hero."[11] But Bettelheim criticizes Wertmüller for misrepresenting the *reality* of the concentration camp. He writes, "in the concentration camp staying alive required a powerful determination. Once one lost it—gave in to the omnipresent despair and let it dominate the wish to live—one was doomed" ("Reflections: Surviving," 47). What Bettelheim assumes is the conflation of survival with moral determinism. In addition he suggests, as Jacqueline Rose comments, "only those who directly experienced the Holocaust have the right to speak of it, to speak of it in what must be by implication, *nonmetaphorical* speech."[12] According to Eli Pfefferkorn, "by suggesting a reciprocal relation between survival and assertion of the self, Bettelheim upholds the faith in the humanistic values of Western culture. He gives comfort by taking the position that individual freedom of action and thought could counteract the cruel coercion of the SS machinery" ("Bettelheim, Wertmüller, and the Morality of Survival," 15). In an attempt to circumvent one-sided or dogmatic readings of inherently problematic and morally ambiguous events, Wertmüller extends her commentary on the survival of individuals to the survival of moral structures, national identities, sexual politics, and power relations that emerge from such economies.

Through Pasqualino, Wertmüller sets out to disprove the "essential" relationships of power, especially the gendering of power. Although she initially mimics conventional relationships of power, Pasqualino's constant shifts from a position of empowerment to one of no power are not consistent with traditionally conceived masculine/feminine roles. In fact, Pasqualino's desire to conform to traditional masculine roles is often at the root of his socio-political and economic disempowerment. In contrast to the futurist celebration of pure masculine agency, Wertmüller depicts Pasqualino's acting-out masculine desires for respect, vengeance, and sexual gratification as acts of pure violence. Rather than reify the legitimacy of masculine authority (or feminine authority for that matter), Wertmüller focuses on the panic of male identity that is entwined with the national imaginary and with "fascist" notions of manliness. Klaus Theweleit describes men's fear of being consumed by an all-pervasive infectious femininity, but Wertmüller represents this panic as a consequence of Pasqualino's realization that masculinity is itself an empty signifier. In other words, masculinity only serves to animate power; it is not powerful in and of itself. And once man realizes that his own resemblance or reference to a masculinized symbol of power is purely artificial or inauthentic, he "falls into lostness." Here the threat of losing one's agency (power or will) cannot be projected onto some unknowable, mystic other but is realized as the impossibility of living up to socially constructed ideals. Wertmüller presents the image of the *Übermensch* as one that only serves to validate those (men and women) who have already assumed power under its name.

Wertmüller's social and political critique, however, does not stop at the implosion of the myths of the *Übermensch* and the *guapo* but continues to unravel other mythic identifications that comply with a binary model. Like Cavani, Wertmüller contests the economy of purity, where she locates a whole range of complex power relations and effects operating in multiple registers throughout the global political economy. The desire for purity permeates, if it does not serve as a structuring agent in, the discourses of morality, sexuality, gender, history, law, medicine, and semiotics, reinstalling at every level of the society a binary economy. This binarist operation, as Lyotard postulates, "is not at all a matter of cleaving instances in two"—cleaving the pure from the impure, man from woman, the victim from the victimizer, or even life from death—instead it is "on the contrary, a matter of rendering their confusion always possible and menacing, or rendering insoluble the question of knowing whether a particular *Gestaltung* is an effect of life rather than death."[13] Moreover, such an operation does not constitute a dialectical order; it does keep preexisting patriarchal economies intact. Like *Salò*, *Seven Beauties* proclaims its own fatal strategy designed to reproduce the effects or consequences of certain technologies of power. This renders the act of conforming or submitting to the existing global order a suicidal one. Pasqualino submits to the southern Italian code of honor, which leads to his being jailed for the murder of his sister's lover; he refuses to engage in politics, thus accepting uncritically the regime's promotion and media's advertisement of the Duce as bringing honor to the image of Italy, building roads and making the trains run on time; he joins the Italian Army as a means of escaping his incarceration, which leads to his being sent to the Russian Front and ultimately his being captured by the Germans for desertion; he seduces the enemy as a means of survival, which leads to his following their orders to select six men for execution and to shoot his only friend in the camp. He too, in essence, just follows orders.

I situate Wertmüller among the dissident film directors who challenge the spectacularization of nazi and fascist theatrics in postwar media and film. Wertmüller calls into question imaginary constructions of masculine virility, feminine seduction, conventional notions of gender-bending, moral economies, and the national and sexual identities that emerge from such images. What makes this assemblage of cinematic representations of fascism and sexual politics unique is that their cinematic treatment is both intertextual, referencing a multiplicity of previous representations of fascism (prefascist, fascist, and postfascist), and satirical. While this collage evokes a range of disparate images, it also disarms their aesthetic appeal and their moral and ideological implications. This accelerated intertextual referencing that gives the film hypertextual, hybrid, and carnivalesque qualities leads to the challenging of stable subjective positions, since it undermines fixed ideological or narrative frameworks. As a result, what Wertmüller calls the "man of disorder" emerges from the wreckage of systems of representation. Yet this disordering of man subsequently problematizes our ability to read such a man without identifiable qualities—a man whose only identifiable will is to survive.

Declassifying Documents

Wertmüller's cinematic style combines the Felliniesque mode of caricaturizing national and sexual stereotypes with widely used documentary footage of the Second World War as well as conventional depictions of personal memory, which are structured as a series of flashbacks. This radical juxtaposition of "nostalgic" or "historic" images, modes of representation, aesthetic references, and discourses results in the disorientation of what had been considered distinct spectacular historical and cultural frameworks. That is, Wertmüller incorporates what seems to be incommensurable modes of representation: the romantic heroism of the mass spectacles of Mussolini and Hitler with the local humor that gives shape to the nostalgic spectacle of the *Amarcord* or "fond memory" of Fellini, the numerous sadomasochistic and eroticized revisions and representations of fascism, and the complex psychological narratives of survival. The opening sequence of *Seven Beauties* evidences this confounding of aesthetics by intercutting disparate elements: (1) the archival footage of Hitler's and Mussolini's famous handshake sealing the Iron Pact of 22 May 1939, with (2) propaganda footage of each regime: newsreel clips used in Leni Riefensthal's *Triumph of the Will*, which film the Nuremberg Rallies, the mass spectacle of the German Army marching in unison, and the impassioned speeches of Hitler; and newsreel clips of the balcony speeches of Mussolini, which focus on the absurdities of his postures—the forward thrust of his jaw, the emphatic placing of his hands on his hips, his inflated chest, his ostentatious uniforms; (3) archival footage taken by the American and British news organizations staging Hitler and Mussolini as the master builders of their respective nations; (4) archival footage taken by the Allies documenting the destruction of war: exploding bombs, dead soldiers on the battlefield, men marching through the snow on the Russian Front, aerial shots of bombed-out buildings, falling bombs; and finally (5) the diegetic narrative of the film itself. These prolific and entangled visions mix political and historical registers from fascism to the Western reverence for fascism in the 1920s and early 1930s, Allied antifascism, and post–1968 European antifascism, foregrounding the relationship of cinematic style to modes of representation and their reality effects. By blending multiple film "genres" used to represent fascism, Wertmüller undermines the acceptance of certain conventional forms as more "real" than others. Instead she presents the layering of incommensurable perspectives and cognitive positions: from the perpetrators (the fascists and national socialists) to the victims and bystanders. Each presents a distinct way of seeing as well as remembering. Wertmüller reflects on what has been considered to be a singular or "truthful" reading of history and memory. Hence she destabilizes what has been constructed as the past (an intelligible narrative) by multiplying and entwining various conflicting historiographical explanations of the past.

In response to such political battles over representation, Wertmüller makes visible not only a hidden agenda but also what Deleuze calls "the hidden ground of time, that is, its differentiation into two flows, that of presents which pass and that of pasts which are preserved" (*Cinema 2*, 98). Rather than present an alternative mode of representation, as a more "transparent" or truthful rendition of historical events, Wertmüller examines narrative modes of representation, drawing attention to their political coding. Because historiography projects and objectifies the past in the sense of an explicable and surveyable nexus of actions and consequences (one only intelligible in the present), Wertmüller criticizes the circumscription of the past and the future within the sphere of perceivable objects.[14] Taking issue with the objectification or compartmentalization of events and time into "meaningful" narratives and logical sequences, Wertmüller structures *Seven Beauties* as a series of flashbacks, both emphasizing the idea of recollection as rupturing a sense of presence and revising a sense of pastness. Her strategy is to underscore the artificiality of historiographic projects themselves. For example, in the opening sequence these two flows—one grounded in the fascist past, the other in the postfascist present—intersect, taking apart narrative constructs that are contingent on time and its passage, that is, official histories (both fascist and antifascist) and personal memories (both fond and traumatic). As a consequence Wertmüller challenges what James Hay calls the "Passage of the Rex," as the passage of one monumental discourse into another—imperial fascist myths into Allied victories, and the "Jewish Question" (a racial and political question) into the "Final Solution" (a question of historiography). For Wertmüller, such monumental discourses maintain not only reactionary understandings of race, sex, and gender but also reactionary notions of purity. Hence the representation of historical "passages" functions more like transference of ideological and moral coding rather than the instantiation of singular events and perspectives.

For Wertmüller this disruption of narratives does not concern the question of reorganizing or prioritizing aesthetic forms, as in the case of Adorno's *Aesthetic Theory*—whereby avant-gardist art that rejects reality is seen as more *real* or valuable than popular forms of representation—but of revealing that each type of representation has its own style and its own political agenda. While documentary and archival footage appeal to "serious" historical constructions, objectivity, and the presentation of visual "documents" as "facts," the comedic encoding of Pasqualino's memories of Napoli appeal to "popular culture" and stereotypic representations of Italian male and female identities. The juxtaposition of the two styles draws attention to modes of reproduction (of events) and their means of transmission. By calling attention to creative processes, Wertmüller tests our ability to read visual images. Such relativizing of artistic visualization problematizes any sort of totalizing conclusion regarding how we look at fascism. This is not to say that Wertmüller does not take nazism, fascism, and the "Final Solution" seriously, as Bettelheim claims, but that she seriously questions the manner in which the "Final Solution" and figures like Mussolini and Hitler are represented. While Mussolini has often been made the subject of comical parody, even by the historians Jonathan Steinberg and Angelo Tasca, who consider him "the stuff that caricatures are made out of," it is still taboo to laugh at Hitler.[15] Depictions of Mussolini and Italian fascism are often comically conveyed in film: Charlie Chaplin's *The*

Great Dictator (1940); the Castle newsreel footage of 1943 (right after the fall of the Italian fascist regime) where Mussolini is labeled a "buffoon," a "saw-dust Caesar," a "balcony dictator"; or Fellini's *Amarcord*, where Mussolini is symbolized by smoke and emblemized as a gigantic head made out of flowers. Even brutal figures such as Attila in Bertolucci's *1900* hyperbolize the absurdity, bordering on the stupidity, of the regime's founding members, the *squadristi* (as for instance Achille Starace).[16] In contrast to Italian and other non-German films, there are almost no films coming out of Germany that depict Hitler in the same light. It is the rhetorical style rather than the figure of Hitler that is subject to ridicule, and this ridicule comes mostly from non-German films, including *The Great Dictator*, Ernst Lubitsch's *To Be or Not To Be* (1942), William Hay's *The Goose Steps Out* (1942), Mel Brooks's *The Producers* (1968), Stanley Kubrick's *Dr. Strangelove* (1964), Woody Allen's *Zelig* (1983), and television shows such as *Hogan's Heroes*. In fact, the very airing of *The Great Dictator* and *To Be or Not To Be*—both created without prior knowledge of the "Final Solution"—instigated a national debate as to whether it is appropriate to use humor in light of the "Final Solution."[17] Unlike *Amarcord* or Gabriele Salvatores's *Mediterraneo* (1991), *Seven Beauties* attempts to address the disassociation of the comedic revisions of Hitler and Mussolini—in films such as *Amarcord*, and *The Great Dictator*—from the serious documentary and neorealist styles used to depict the Holocaust, as in Alain Resnais's

In *The Great Dictator* (1940), Charlie Chaplin plays the double role of Adenoid Hynkel (a parody of Hitler) and his Jewish lookalike.

Night and Fog (1955), Pare Lorentz's and Stuart Schulberg's *Nuremberg* (1946), Max Ophuls's *The Sorrow and the Pity* (1970) and *Hotel Terminus* (1988), and Claude Lanzmann's *Shoah* (1986). I am in no way suggesting that *Seven Beauties* synthesizes the two discourses—the mass spectacle of Mussolini and Hitler on the one hand and the "Final Solution" on the other—rather, I argue that Wertmüller carnivalizes (turns upsidedown) films such as *Amarcord* and *Mediterraneo* for disengaging their humorous vision of fascism from the devastation of the war, which in turn hyperbolizes the "realistic" aestheticization of evil found in these clearly moralistic documentary films. I read *Seven Beauties* as critically responding to comedic representations of fascism and nazism that reduce fascism to what Fellini has called a "prolonged adolescence," and to the docudramatization of the "Final Solution" that calls for new moral men, for new forms of purity.

One of the most disturbing aspects of the film, for Bettelheim, is that Hitler and Mussolini appear as caricatures. Bettelheim argues that Wertmüller's contextualization of archival footage makes fun of Mussolini and Hitler, yet he supports his critique by arguing that "Hitler is shown as the man with the funny mustache as he was in Chaplin's film," and "Mussolini and Hitler are so pompous that we cannot take them seriously" ("Reflections: Surviving," 34). That is, rather than addressing the diegetic narrative of the film (where there are no characterizations of Hitler and Mussolini, as for instance in *The Great Dictator*, only pictures of Mussolini on the wall of a train station and a picture of Hitler on the commandant's wall in the concentration camp), Bettelheim conflates the archival footage and actual rhetoric of each regime with the fictional parody of fascism and nazism appearing in Chaplin's film. Under the auspices of critiquing Wertmüller, Bettelheim, like many of the film's critics, reveals his own aesthetic preference for documentary and neorealistic representations in treating subjects like the "Final Solution," yet ones that exclude representations of Hitler and Mussolini. At the same time Bettelheim denounces the use of archival footage for being "unreal," he implies that nazism, fascism, and the "Final Solution" cannot be "fictionalized" (treated metaphorically), only recorded or documented mimetically. Yet, contrary to Bettelheim's desired aesthetic mode of representing the "Final Solution," the comic irony of the image of the newsreel footage stands in opposition to his own visualization of the past: while the words "nazism" and "fascism" still evoke strong responses, the "real" images and faces of the Duce (which Fellini hyperbolizes in *Amarcord*) and the Führer produce laughter. Hence *Seven Beauties* exemplifies the slippage between the comic image and its "serious" emplotment in narrative history as absolute evil. What makes Mussolini and Hitler seem ridiculous is not any doing of Wertmüller; it is her reference to the "serious" tone of the original newsreel footage that is accompanied by the fascists' and national socialists' hyperbolic and monumental mass orchestration and the aggrandized self-promotion of both dictators.

Wertmüller demonstrates that documenting nazism or fascism in the light of realism or even neorealism produces far more caricature than the caricatured figures she presents. For example, films such as Luciano Salace's *Il federale* (1965) portray Italian fascists as buffoons and German national socialists as natural born killers, and Roberto Rossellini's *Open City* depicts fascists as traitors to their own people and nazis as hyperbolas of evil (homosexual, murderous, and decadent). Even though the mode of representation used to picture Mussolini and Hitler in archival footage itself can no longer compare to what we presently consider "serious" documentation—in fact such footage is often referred to as propaganda—given the outcome of the events of World War II, Hitler and Mussolini can no longer represent anything other than a certain "seriousness." This means, however, that they have also been repictured as "serious," hyperbolic figures or symbols of evil. Wertmüller counteracts both the "comical effect" that these visualizations produce by resituating the (overcoded images of) Hitler and Mussolini within the context of World War II—the mass devastation and atrocities committed by each regime—and the overdetermined postwar re-representations of Hitler and Mussolini by sarcastically mimicking the manner in which fascists and nazis have been popularly spectacularized.

The film begins as an animation of these two figures, situating them, contrary to Bettelheim's belief, not as buffoons but as those responsible (yet not solely) for the mass destruction of Europe and the violence toward European Jews, Gypsies, Slavs, homosexuals, socialists, and others. *Seven Beauties* commences with a freeze frame of what appears to be a still photograph of Mussolini shaking Hitler's hand. The shot lingers about five seconds, just long enough to reveal the smiling faces of both dictators and to establish the following narrative within the context of the Axis powers' alliance. The silence in which this still image appears is suddenly interrupted by a drumbeat, which sets the image into motion—as if the drum were animating the characters (Mussolini and Hitler). Yet the rhythm of the drum does not simply supplement or set Hitler and Mussolini into motion but also enables a series of cinematic interruptions. Wertmüller juxtaposes the establishing shot of Hitler's and Mussolini's friendly handshake with footage of an exploding building, highlighting the ruinous effects or consequences that germinated from such an alliance. Rather than concentrate solely on the images of the two dictators, she splices the footage taken by each regime with the footage taken by the Allies to document the devastation of the war: cutting from Mussolini and Hitler to exploding bombs, army formations in the desert, aerial shots of bombs falling, planes crashing, and buildings exploding, dead soldiers strewn over the battlefield, and images of Pasqualino deserting his regiment bound for the Russian Front.

The weaving together of such discontinuous cinematic modes of representation disavows more simplistic readings that would metonymically link Hitler to Mussolini, the events of World War II, and its participants. Wertmüller reaches beyond the metonymic economy of cause and effect—the association of the images of Hitler and Mussolini with the destruction of Europe—intermingling images of past with those of the present and even ones involving a projected image of the future. This pastiche of chronotopes results in the foregrounding of a "world picture"; the visual, epistemological, and ideological layering of reality present in all modes of representation. The effect of such layering uncovers artificial organizations of time into flows (historical narratives and ideologies), which Deleuze defines as, first, "always already there, [and] second, arriving from an outside always to come." For Deleuze these flows comprise the two cults of death, the two sides of the absolute—"death from the inside or the past and death from the outside or the future"(*Cinema 2*, 209). Not just a limit of consciousness, death signifies the fixing of individual subjects within intelligible, yet determined, historical narratives. Here death signifies a closure; the death of experience that closes one's identity into a predetermined symbolic position, exhausting the possibilities of going beyond the confines of that set position.[18] By juxtaposing these discontinuous master narratives—one of the fascist past and the other of the postwar future—Wertmüller explores the inconsistencies of historical and ideological discourse, which disappear and reappear within these absolute or deadly flows. These cinematic ruptures unhinge what Stephen Heath calls the suturing of "identification with the fiction of the sign" or the "joining of the subject in structures of meaning."[19] Although *Seven Beauties* plays with multiple registers, including social and historical identity formations, it does not present a sutured or unified narrative subject but rather one that absorbs the ideological order or epistemological influences of outside forces—forces that objectify Pasqualino's subjectivity and self-determination. Because this flow of disorienting images consistently undermines stable subjective positions, it does not comprise what Michel Foucault calls "cracks in the system." Wertmüller does not provide a space from which one can establish a critical distance from the film. Her cinematic strategy is not one of resistance or estrangement, as for instance is the case in Pasolini's *Medea*, *Edipo Re*, or *Porcile*, but one of surrender to various preexisting spectacles. Every situation that Pasqualino enters requires that he play a role within a preestablished spectacle or masquerade: from his emulation of the Mafia don (Don Raffaele) to that of a *buffone*, a madman, a soldier, and a lover. Pasqualino has no stable subjective narrative identity nor any "real" moral conviction, so he becomes an object in each narrative role he plays. What makes Wertmüller's style radical is that it reflects the inconstancy or total chaos of conventional roles and their performative spectacularizations of nazism, fascism, and the "Final Solution."

Furthermore, these conflictual and disorienting images are accompanied by the unique voice of Enzo Jannacci, whose song "Quelli che" blends spoken word with popular music. The music that supplements these images oscillates between the emphatic rhythm of the drumbeat that sets the film in motion, punctuates each cut, and mimics the rapid succession of explosions and gunfire, and the saturated sound of the saxophone that resonates, commenting on these historical or documentary images, expressing the political underpinnings of the 1970s (associated with Italian political rock music) and a historical understanding of the past, rather than attempting to represent that past. The lyrics of Jannacci's song further enhance this sensation of disorientation and social commentary since they seem to denounce documentary or "historic footage" as both humorless and ironic. Wertmüller synchronizes the close-up image of Hitler delivering an impassioned speech to the lyrics "Quelli che non si divertono mai neanche quando ridono, oh yeah" ("Those who don't enjoy themselves even when they laugh, oh yeah"); the image of Mussolini speaking to thousands gathered below his balcony on the Via Veneto to "Quelli che dicono, noi italiani siamo i più superuomini del mondo, oh yeah" ("Those who say, we Italians are the greatest he-men on earth, oh yeah"); and the images of the ones who died in battle to "Quelli che credono in tutto anche in Dio, oh yeah" ("Those who believe in everything even in God, oh yeah"). Hence this sound mix serves as a devastating preliminary critique not only of fascism and nazism but, more importantly, of those who blindly followed fascism, nazism, religion, and orders.

The repetitive drumbeat and the repetition of the words "Quelli che" ("Those who"), introducing each line of the song, directly link the images, rhetoric, and atrocities of Mussolini:

Quelli che dicono se evenzo, seguitemi, se indietreggio, uccidetemi, si fa per dire
Quelli che fanno lavoro di Hitler convinti di essere stati assunti da un'alta dittta, oh yeah
Quelli che il sono sempre al bar, quelli che sono sempre in svizzere
Quelli che vota la destra perchè basta con questi scioperi
Quelli che tengono al re
Quelli che amerebbero la patria
Quelli che no si sono mai occupati di politica
Quelli che perdono la guerra per un pelo

Those who say follow me if I move forward, but kill me if I retreat
Those who do the work of Hitler convinced that they are doing the work of
    another army
Those who are always at the bar, those who are still in Switzerland
Those who vote for the right because enough with all of these strikes
Those who support the king
Those who would love their country
Those who have never been interested in politics
Those who lost the war by the skin of their teeth.

The lyrics that accompany the images of the rise and fall of both regimes follow the same chronological order, from the alliance of Hitler and Mussolini, the mass spectacles, the colonization of Africa and Eastern Europe, to the violent images of battle and the mass devastation at the end of the war. As the archival footage dissolves into darkness, the last line of the song, "Quelle che [dicono] facciamoci due risate" ("The ones who say now let's all have a good laugh") trails off into silence. Ironically this silence is not followed by "having a good laugh"; rather it is interrupted by the diegetic sound of bombs exploding, gunfire, and the apparition (now in color) of Pasqualino's bandaged head emerging from the darkness. Thus, contrary to Bettelheim's argument that the dubbing of the song "Quelle che" over the archival clips of Hitler, Mussolini, and various images from World War II renders the "seriousness of the event a farce," the music performs the exact opposite—returning fascism and nazism from their almost comic appearance in archival footage to a political discourse that comments on the sociohistorical significance of these otherwise uninterpretable moving pictures.

The Aesthetics of Discord

This barrage of images—heroic gestures, mass spectacles, destruction and death—coupled with extradiegetic musical commentaries intertwines a variety of discontinuous, anachronistic, and contradictory cinematic and spectacular codes. While pop music serves as an expository text for fascist and antifascist images, fascist songs are made into burlesque performances referencing a comedic revision of fascism and cabaret and at the same time signifying Concettina's dishonoring of the family name; flamenco music parodies Pasqualino's unheroic confrontation with Totonno; and Wagner's *Ride of the Valkyries* (*Die Walküre*) marks Pasqualino's entrance into "Appleplatz," the concentration camp where he is interned.[20] Musical sound-overs accentuate the sense of rupture and discontinuity as they often conflict with, if not criticize, the visual subject (and vice-versa); the visual subject often subverts the sound object.

In *Seven Beauties,* Pasqualino (Giancarlo Giannini) takes lessons from Mafia don Don Raffaele (Enzo Vitale), who forces him to avenge his sister's "degradation."

For example, on the one hand Jannacci's song "Quelle che" invalidates the "seriousness" with which archival images were filmed, linking the fascist spectacle of mythic power and mass unity with postwar antifascist criticism. On the other hand, the images of Pasqualino's and Francesco's capture and entrance into the concentration camp disavows the epic or mythic grandeur of Wagner's *Ring des Nibelungen*.[21] The Wagnerian opera, which delineates the rise and fall of the mythic German gods (the *Götterdämmerung*, the twilight of the gods), supplements and is supplemented by the visualization of Germans as faceless silhouettes yet monumental militaristic figures (shot from a low camera-angle), men in uniform who tower over their victims with machine guns in hand.[22]

The low camera-angle used to shoot the German soldiers contrasts with the high camera-angle used to enframe their captives: men dressed in dusty striped uniforms, disrobed, standing in symmetrical lines, hanging lifeless from the rafters of the concentration camp, and ultimately stacked in piles of bodies as waste products. While the images of the victims are clearly distinguished from those of their nazi captors, the use of Wagnerian music interrupts what could otherwise be read as a simple dichotomy of good versus evil. Here Wertmüller exaggerates the mythic imaging of the *Übermensch*, emerging from both Wagnerian opera and the nazi appropriation of the Wagnerian operatic spectacle in their own pageantry. She turns what has otherwise been considered the aesthetics of kitsch—defined by Saul Friedlander as "an appeal to harmony, to emotional communion and solitude and terror," which amounts to the "neutralization of extreme situations, particularly death, by turning them into some sentimental idyll"—into an ambiguous orchestration of campy theatricality (*Reflections on Nazism*, 2–4). This hyperbolic explosion of what has been associated with the aesthetics of fascism and the "kitschy" re-representation of the regime instantiates an overturning of conventional notions of "reality" in all its "seriousness," promoting in its stead a sense of disorder. *Seven Beauties* highlights what Clement Greenberg calls the "mechanical formulas of Kitsch, its vicarious experience and faked sensations" and "its debased and academicized simulacra of genuine culture."[23] Yet, for Wertmüller, this notion of "genuine culture" is only an effect of kitsch, of popular culture that is academicized, whether by the fascists or the antifascists. And so she ridicules the mass spectacle of fascism and the massive re-representation of fascism as kitsch. Rather than reify the preexisting narrative and aesthetic models, Wertmüller questions the intersections of Wagnerian opera with understandings of narrative or epic history, mythic identity, operatic ornamentation, cinema, and mass spectacle. By synchronizing the music of Wagner, which has become a trademark, if not a sight gag for postwar representations of nazism (both fictional and documentary) or extreme notions of militarism (as in the case of Francis Ford Coppola's *Apocalypse Now*, 1976), Wertmüller links the mythic image of the romantic or heroic German to the violence of mass destruction and mass murder. The music of Wagner comes to represent the antithesis of its designated nationalistic and spiritual effect. Instead it illustrates the grotesque consequences resulting from the emulation of such mythic figures and such "nationalist ideals." Furthermore, this implicit criticism of German Romanticism spills over into the conventional aesthetics of documentary or newsreel footage, which, similar to nazi and fascist "documentaries," glorifies the image of the soldier, narrates military victories with an authoritative male voice-over, and uses music to supplement shots of advancing armies followed by shots of enemy troops surrendering or fleeing—used in, for instance, *Triumph of the Will, Victory at Sea, The Battle of San Pietro*, and *The March of Time*. What Wertmüller resists is the glorification of violence, in which music serves as a contributing factor. By supplementing violent sequences with music that is culturally understood as representing victory, romance, pathos, and, moreover, kitsch aesthetics, Wertmüller upsets cultural codes of verisimilitude.

Whereas music in film is conventionally used to supplement the mise-en-scène or to augment desired emotional effects, Wertmüller uses extradiegetic sound as an "unreality effect," one that points to the artificiality of the cinematic, artistic, historical, and music-editing processes. In addition, the oscillation between sound and image offers another subjective position paralleling the binary dichotomy already depicted by the use of extreme camera angles—those that demarcate the ones in power from the ones subjugated by that power, or the mythic from the comedic. Wertmüller uses the discord between sound and image to produce a sense of mayhem, thereby engaging and exaggerating extradiegetic references to Wagner's nationalist mythos, the idyllic appeal to folklore and peasants made by both regimes, the pageantry of nazi and fascist mass spectacles, and the comic redomestication of fascism. This chaotic intertextuality—which alludes to what Wagner articulated as *Gesamtkunstwerk* (total work of art), and Heidegger called the "world picture" as well as to historical, cinematic, and artistic ways of seeing—multiplies the textual references of the film to the point of incomprehensibility. That is, Wertmüller constructs a complicated nexus of conflicting world pictures, histories, and mythic values. In an attempt to undermine concepts such as master narrative, world picture, epic history, and *Gesamtkunstwerk*, Wertmüller implodes traditional aesthetic strategies designed to represent mythic heroes, master races, glorious nations, sublime martyrs, and victims par excellence. She uses music as another form of hyperbole. And by hyperbolizing the sublime, mystical, and epic qualities of Wagner's operas, which, in *Seven Beauties*, animate the panoramas of the Rhine, foggy German forests, monumental figures of militaristic nazi men and women, romantic images of a German woman playing *Die Walküre* on the piano while singing an aria that expresses *Liebestod* (love-death), Wertmüller undermines what Maria Tartar defines as "assertions of transcendent desire and the spiritualization of Eros, [which] found their most celebrated incarnation in the musical dramas of Richard Wagner" (*Lustmord*, 10). She deconstructs mythic forms and the production of mythic values found in both written history and documentary film. As Hayden White explains, "even in written history, we are often forced to represent some agents only as 'character types,' that is, as individuals known only by their general social attributes or by the kinds of actions that their 'roles' in a given historical event permitted them to play, rather than as full-blown 'characters,' individuals with many known attributes, proper names and a range of known actions that permit us to draw fuller *portraits* of them."[24] Yet films like *Seven Beauties* "subvert the 'realism' we associate with conventional films and conventional historiography," not, as White argues, because they "sacrifice 'accuracy of detail,' but because they show us instead that the criterion for determining what shall count as 'accuracy of detail' depends on the 'way' chosen to represent both 'the past' and our thought about its historical significance" ("Historiography and Historiophoty," 119).

Although the archival footage situates the film within the context of nazism, fascism, and the "Final Solution," the fragmentary images produced by splicing together archival footage from various epistemological frameworks and political points of view counters appeals to "official history." Wertmüller's piecing together of different, if not contradictory, versions of the same historical event orchestrates what Nietzsche called "critical history": "breaking up and dissolving a part of the past ... by scrupulously examining it and finally condemning it."[25] Wertmüller exemplifies this critical mode of visualizing historiographical representations by entwining various historical modes of representation: juxtaposing the monumental posturing of Mussolini and Hitler and their appeal to epic history vis-à-vis nation and empire; the antiquarian spectacle of the preservation of ethnic purity; operatic narratives of blood and soil (*Blut und Boden*) in Germany and *strapaese* in Italy; and the satirical depiction of the effects of such histories on the "common man," who absorbs or is objectified by all of these forms of history. Yet by objectifying the "common man" she does not characterize Pasqualino as disempowered or disenfranchised. He maintains his desiring agency and expresses his desire for fascism on what Deleuze and Guattari call a micropolar level. In fact, Pasqualino participates in the exaltation of the Duce as bringing honor and a manly image to Italy and Italians, as opposed to what was considered to be a dishonorable image of Italy created by the socialists and union movements. While the discourse of socialism, presented by a fellow prisoner, criticizes the regime for its empty nationalist propaganda and its creation of a collective hysteria, it is largely dismissed by Pasqualino, who sees such thinking as threatening to a regime that he perceives as boosting the economy, reabsorbing unemployment, and controlling capital. Hence, rather than advocating a certain political perspective, Wertmüller scrutinizes the competing political models. Far from establishing a suprahistorical position, what Nietzsche describes as giving stable and eternal characteristics to art, religion, and science, or what Hayden White terms metahistory, Wertmüller questions criticism that espouses fixed philosophical deductions.

Wertmüller chooses to objectify her protagonist. In other words, she uncovers the effects of such subjective and suprahistorical discourses rather than presents a new or more "truthful" way of seeing. As the object of "historical" manipulation, Pasqualino becomes the vestige of contradictory appeals to history made under the rubric of the fascist regime and its postwar re-representations, both of which appeal to warrior or military culture; an antiquarian veneration of honor and family; the capitalist mode of production; and the cultural effects of what Mussolini considered his great cultural, political, and economical *sintesi*. Yet *Seven Beauties* does not synthesize aesthetic and narrative "appeals to history" but subverts the conventional encoding of such appeals. Wertmüller achieves this effect of disorientation by challenging conventional modes of representation. For example, while black and white footage usually serves to authenticate a film's appeal to history or the past, in *Seven Beauties* the movement from black and white to color film signals a movement away from the alleged objectivity of official history, treating it as artificial and propagandized discourse. Here Wertmüller questions the "reality" of such documentation, replacing these remote (almost mythic) images of Mussolini, Hitler, and the war with familiar (comic and stereotypical) images of Pasqualino and his family, Francesco, and Pedro. Because Wertmüller breaks down modes of representation into a series of contradictory images—epic nationalism, fascist virility, pomposity, buffoonery, madness, despair—she challenges the position from which histories are told. Furthermore, her multiplication of interpretations, political and philosophical stances defended by one or another character, disrupts the very construction of authorial concepts. This profoundly dialogical style carnivalizes monological thinking required in historical narratives and moral discourse. The effect of Wertmüller's cinematic strategy of layering philosophical stances (anarchist, socialist, existentialist, and fascist), filmic styles (newsreel, documentary, *commedia italiana*, camp, sadomasochist aesthetics), and musical and cultural references is one of disorienting what Judith Mayne calls the "assumed homogeneity of perception"—disorganizing preconceived notions of time, place, genre, political positioning, ideological and moral stances.[26]

The movement through different visual and sound spaces—popular music, cabaret, Wagner's *Ride of the Valkyries*, which echoes Wertmüller's earlier film, *All Screwed Up* (1973), where the music supplements the filming of rows of beef in the slaughterhouse—restages different cultural references "chosen to represent the past" as already inundated with "historical significance." However, by recalling disparate cultural references to nazism, fascism, and the "Final Solution," Wertmüller challenges singular readings of such cultural mediums as well as their ability to reproduce "historical significance." For instance, she juxtaposes Wagner as a point of reference to monumental and mythic nazi aesthetics, cabaret, a postwar association of nazism and fascism, decadence and popular folk music. Although the amalgamation of musical references—of heroic nationalism, decadent sexuality and seduction, along with a celebration of "the People"—replicates stereotypical representations of nazism, fascism, national, regional, and class-oriented characterizations that are already in place, the very juxtapositing of these overdetermined musical references calls forth a series of contradictions. The musical sound-over serves as a device that problematizes binary images of victims and victimizers, Italians and Germans. While there appears to be no middle ground here—both heroes and victims are pictured in the extreme—they are either monuments of brutality and inhumanity or the pathetic objects of such dehumanization. The lowliness, dirtiness, and smallness of the prisoners compared to the monumental stature of the nazis clashes with the tragic (sublime) operatic music of Wagner. Thus it is not clear whether *Ride of the Valkyries*, which represents the death of the German gods in the context of the opera, serves to illustrate the brutality enacted in the name of nazi idealism or the unheroic pathos of "Mediterranean survival." Because, as Lacoue-Labarthe observes, "tragedy has been thought, in any case in the whole tradition of German idealism, to be the political art par excellence," Wertmüller challenges the persistent usage of the tragic mode of representation as the predominant mode of representing nazism, fascism, and the "Final Solution" (*Musica Ficta*, 12).

The question for Wertmüller is not one of relearning the same moral lesson but one of questioning notions of "reality" that arise from tragic and romantic modes of representation. Specifically, she thwarts the sacrificial logic of tragedy and romance as incompatible with the representation of nazism, fascism, and the "Final Solution." In the words of Lyotard, "Auschwitz represents a paradox of faith, the scandal obligation," because it neutralizes notions of transcendence.[27] That is, the victims cannot be read as having a tragic flaw or be offered up in sacrifice. Likewise, when the commandant attempts to locate Germans as victims of a world that is unfit for their heroism, her invocation of tragedy appears completely incredulous. Thus aesthetic politics can no longer assign meaning, tragic or otherwise, to a crime of such proportions when, as Lacoue-Labarthe points out, "it is administered like a production, the exploitation of human bodies as of waste material."[28] But Wertmüller does not simply dismiss tragedy and romance as incompatible forms of representation. Since the moral ideals and narrative modes of representation remain operational in the representation of nazism, fascism, and the "Final Solution," she uses them as a point of departure, invoking tragic and romantic aesthetic models, which prevail as the most common modes of representing and visualizing the events of World War II, in order to challenge their transcendental effects. That is, she resists conforming the representation of nazism, fascism, and the "Final Solution" to written and visual narratives of conventional moral politics, which reduces the meaning of the war to "a fighting of the good fight" or a construction of ethical conflicts in terms of good versus evil, the pure versus the impure. *Seven Beauties* counteracts the confinement of meaning to the triumph of good over evil and the restricting of political agency to the cult of the hero, the great man in history, and the pure victim.

The use of music in *Seven Beauties* serves most importantly as a device that frames the characters as hyperbolic operatic figures; introduces each narrative sequence; contextualizes the narrative sequence in terms of place (German music supplements events that take place in Germany and Italian music supplements Pasqualino's memories of Italy); and demarcates the film's narrative sequences (the same music used at the beginning of a sequence also marks its end). Wertmüller uses music not only to signal a shift in time—designating each flashback of Pasqualino's memories of Italy and Napoli, and each flash-forward to his life in the German concentration camp—but also to denote a transversal of boundaries (national, memory, and reality) and national myths. Music, then, serves to disorient (dissolve into a flashback or flash-forward) and reorient the spectator by indicating that the narrative will follow Pasqualino's thought processes, it will drift in and out of his memories. Consequently, the musical prelude to each narrative sequence suggests that the following action will be enfolded in an artificial parameter—in Pasqualino's personal perspective, which is filtered through his selective memory and "limited" interpretation of the events that lead to his being interned in a concentration camp. Hence the diegetic narrative of the film that begins as entangled in "official" documents or reports on Hitler, Mussolini, and the war is replaced by Pasqualino's personal narrative. This movement away from conventional images and narratives suggests that narratives of survival not only stand in opposition to "official histories" but they undermine the very moral premises upon which official histories are erected.

Musical accompaniments, however, also recall a sense of national feeling (an iden-tification with sound-objects). The parody of nationalist sentiment reflects general stereotypes about differences between Italy and Germany, Italians and Germans. Ger-man soundscapes are distinguished from Italian ones not only in terms of musical selections (Wagner as opposed to popular Italian fascist songs) but also in terms of stereotypical images (Germans are orderly, romantic, yet cold and brutal, while Ital-ians are comical, familiar, and disorderly). Wertmüller sets Italy apart from Germany by distancing Pasqualino's recollection of his past in Italy from his present struggle to survive in the German concentration camp. She synchronizes the filming of foggy mystical landscapes of the Rhine and the technological production as seen in the factories of death with what have been designated as tragic and romantic sounds of Wagnerian opera and Straussian waltzes. Wagner's music supplements the images of submission and death, while a Strauss waltz is played as prisoners are gunned down by their nazi captors. This sharply contrasts with the synchronization of Italian cabaret and folk music with the visualization of the sunny streets of Napoli, where Pasqualino encounters a variety of women who ogle at him, and the mattress factory where Pasqualino's mother and seven sisters work. Yet as the narrative progresses, the alter-nation of "national-music" occurs less frequently and Wagner and Strauss are replaced by Italian music. Although German music is never used to illustrate narrative sequences in Italy, Italian music is imported to Germany, suggesting that music itself serves as a narrative thread, weaving narrative sequences interrupted by flash-back into a unified story. Moreover, music symbolizes Pasqualino's "life-line." The more Pasqualino is forced to compromise his will, his identity, and his desires, the more he turns to music and his memory: memories that always involve music, mem-ories of his mother's singing, the music he associates with his first love Fifi, and the song "Fammi campà" (Let Me Love). Music represents his only link to humanity, his only source of identity and sense of belonging. Paradoxically, the same song that refers to Pasqualino's desire to live, "Fammi campà," supplements the image of hundreds of motionless prisoners bowed in silence and submission immediately after Pasqualino shoots his friend Francesco, and also supplements the last scene of the film, in which Pasqualino stares critically at himself in the mirror. The same music that expresses Pasqualino's will to live also signifies his "death in life."

Even as Wertmüller mimics musical invocations to cultural identities in order to bloat stereotypical images and their subsequent bodily postures, forcing them to appear ludicrous, she also refers to music's ability to transport us beyond our culturally predetermined conceptions, into what Nietzsche called in *The Birth of Tragedy* a "disruption of subjectivity," a "spasmodic rhapsody or an orgiastic abandon." Yet in *Seven Beauties* this rhapsody of abandon that emancipates Pasqualino from his comical (cartoonlike) body also marks his "pathetic metamorphosis" into what Elaine Scarry calls a "pure body," the body in pain. As a consequence, his movement away from his own hyperbolic self-image or his chosen point of origin results in his emergence in what Paul de Man calls an "ironic consciousness." This produces a sense of disjunction between the comical vision of the past—Pasqualino's self-identification as Neapolitan *guappo*—and the "deflated" subjective position from which he evokes that past image. The point of Wertmüller's hyperconscious use of extradiagetic sound and visual sources is not, therefore, as Bettelheim argues, to render "human dignity a sham" or "induce a false sense of security when one is in greatest danger," or what Pauline Kael calls the turning of the "Final Solution" into "vaudeville" but to seriously question the aesthetic modes of representation used to index the past ("Reflections: Surviving," 33–34). It is far more complicated: Wertmüller uses comedy, hyperbole,

Francesco (Piero Di Orio) begs Pasqualino (Giancarlo Giannini) to kill him before he "humiliates himself."

and "vaudeville" in order to inauthenticate what have congenitally been accepted as "serious" narrative topics. By rendering such "realistic" codes and aesthetics artificial and inauthentic, Wertmüller demonstrates that "realist" codes, attached to tragic and romantic narratives, themselves create a "false sense of security," an illusion of the containment of evil within a moral narrative. The defamiliarization of aesthetic codes, therefore, reveals this artificial link of aesthetics to moral discourse. Once this link has been severed we are left with an "ironic consciousness," one that realizes its inauthentic (if not manipulative) relationship to the material it seeks to illuminate.

Hence, like Fellini, rather than reproducing stable and identifiable subjective positions, she hyperbolizes her characters, both visually and through the use of music. And, again like Fellini, Wertmüller evades the politics of binarism that seeks to moralize such historical events. However, in contrast to the narrative of *Seven Beauties*, as James Hay explains, the "title *Amarcord* suggests a fond memory, [and the film itself] satirizes the ritual of the provincial community."[29] Wertmüller, on the other hand, manipulates the myth of the *Amarcord* by placing it in the larger context of European politics. She problematizes the ability of the *Amarcord* to localize or domesticate fascism, by pointing to the fact that memory as *Amarcord* focuses solely on a "fascist imaginary"—the dreams of adolescent boys who hope to gain power and love by attaching themselves to what appears to be the "sexiness" of the regime and the image of the Duce—which refuses to enter into a discourse of victimization. Wertmüller mimics Fellini, who infantilizes fascism as a "prolonged adolescence," yet she reproduces these infantile figures of Italian men and women and incorporates them within the context of the violence and brutality of the war. While there have been numerous other cinematic depictions of wartime violence (as for example Bertolucci's *Strategia del ragno, 1900, The Conformist*; De Sica's *Garden of the Finzi-Continis*, and Scola's *Una giornata particolare*), these narratives, which contain elements of humor, for the most part subscribe to the aesthetics of neorealism or neodecadentism. Further, these narratives never question the discourse of moral righteousness nor the preordained dichotomy of victims and victimizers, good and evil. Instead, Wertmüller embraces carnivalesque images, yet unlike Fellini she forces the caricature of the Italian fascist (as a bungler who is disinterested in politics) into an intertextual play with the mythic image of the puritanically cruel nazi. The result is a delegitimation of the national myth of "failed" fascist virility mixed with Italian machismo, imaging itself as the lesser evil in relation to nazism: less puritanical (or more sexualized), less racist (less anti-Semitic but not less anti-Slav or anti-African), and less militarist and nationalist (less successful in its colonial enterprises). Via her ironic citation of Fellini, and even historians such as Saul Friedländer, who define nazism as a "juvenile fraternity," Wertmüller redresses the question of responsibility shirked by the infantile image of the *Great Dictator*, the "adolescent images of Fellini," and the various infantilizations of Hitler as in the case of Hans-Jürgen Syberberg's *Hitler, a Film from Germany*.[30] She suggests that such readings contribute to the perpetuation of the myth of masculine monumentality as well as the Oedipal myth of the family, revising history in terms of a hierarchy of maturity inscribed in a family economy.

Wertmüller foreshadows questions about the motivation behind the numerous protests made by historians and critics, such as Zeev Sternhell, who argue that "Fascism in no way can be compared to Nazism."[31] But this does not imply that she treats fascism and nazism as the same or equal, rather, that she reestablishes their alliance and sets out to explore the question of responsibility. For example, Francesco—another Italian Army deserter whom we encounter in the first scene of the film—explains to Pasqualino that "noi siamo colpevoli con quella merda li" ("we are as guilty as these shits there")—referring to the nazis who are simultaneously depicted massacring hundreds of Jews. Francesco, who expresses what Millicent Marcus calls "a sense of personal honor and political integrity," confronts Pasqualino's claim that resistance against the fascists and the nazis would have been "inutile" (*Italian Film in the Light of Neorealism*, 317). He retorts to Pasqualino that "non è inutile, un'uomo deve dire no a Mussolini, invece abbiamo detto si a Mussolini, al dovere, alla guerra, ho ucciso uomini che non concoscevo, e per nulla" ("it is not futile, a man must say no to Mussolini, instead we said yes to Mussolini, to duty, to the war, I killed men I didn't even know, and for nothing at all"). Yet, far from presenting a simple dichotomy between the politically correct and the politically incorrect, Francesco's "personal honor" and political perspective are developed as an afterthought to the events he has already witnessed, hence his political point of view seems to come from a historical perspective (a judgment made after the fact). Pasqualino, on the other hand, like many concentration camp survivors reproached by thinkers like Hannah Arendt for not rebelling against the nazis, responds by disassociating himself from the nazis and even from Francesco; he claims that instead of killing as a soldier, "ho ucciso per una femina" ("I killed for a woman")—he killed the man who dishonored his sister Concettina, Don Totonno.[32] According to Eli Pfefferkorn, "the diametrically contrary positions taken by Francesco and Pasqualino point to the double vision of the survival issue ... [while] some watched and withdrew out of apathy or self-interest, like Pasqualino, and some, like Francesco, watched with compassion but withdrew, for they did not have the moral courage to raise their voices, [both] comment on the breakdown of human compassion" ("Bettelheim, Wertmüller, and the Morality of Survival," 18). Furthermore, as Bauman suggests, "seldom was the mere concern with self-survival so close to moral corruption" (*Modernity and the Holocaust*, 146).

In contrast to Francesco, who has killed in the name of fascism, in the name of the state and the Axis powers, Pasqualino's admission to premeditated murder takes him out of the context of the war: he kills in the name of self-interest. In fact, Wertmüller visualizes this travel away from the context of the war by overlaying the sound of fascist music onto the German landscape. In addition, the camera moves in a circular motion creating a sense of dizziness, panning over the images of the forest and progressively shooting upward to the sky. Thus Pasqualino's identification with the act of murder, in comparison to Francesco's, is more personalized yet one not clearly connected to fascism or only vaguely associated by his apathy to fascism and the music played in the nightclub where his sister performs cabaret. Here she appears with a red, white, and green garter, a black fascist cap (a replica of those worn by Mussolini), singing a fascist song only to be ridiculed and derided by the audience of men. Although she emblemizes the omnipresence of fascist nationalist sentiment, she points to her own inability to represent the "glorified aesthetics" of fascism, which are centered on images of manliness, motherhood, cleanliness, strength, and youth. Fascism itself seems to have a precarious relationship with the "average Italian"; while it is taken seriously by the soldier and the socialist who are victims of fascist violence and fascist ideology, it is ridiculed, although unwittingly, by Concettina and the audience who make fun of her "ugliness" as she sings of "the beauty of fascism." She represents the contradictory appeal of the regime, which is simultaneously presented as illicitly sexy—celebrating the sexual triumphs of the Duce and figures like Achille Starace—and family oriented, as well as its double standard with regard to women's sexuality. In addition, Neapolitan life (through the eyes of Pasqualino) seems relatively unaffected by the presence of the fascists. Rather, the monumentality of the regime seems to have been absorbed by men in power, people like the Mafia don, Don Raffaele, who is also always shot with a low camera angle and often shot against the backdrop of monuments, enormous statues of men and horses.

Concettina (Elena Fiore) sings a fascist song as the audience makes fun of her "ugliness."

Seven Beauties explores a variety of interpretations of "the common man's" response to fascism, nazism, and the "Final Solution," juxtaposing arguments like Sternhell's that the fascist revolution was to take place "within the framework of the industrial society" (made by the nameless socialist whom Pasqualino encounters on his way to jail) with Francesco's claim that everyone is responsible for all social conditions, and Pasqualino's own irresponsible reckoning with fascism, in which he simply accepts the assimilation of fascist spectacle to preexisting forms of Italian culture because, as he believes, there is nothing else he could do (*The Birth of Fascist Ideology*, 6). Wertmüller's multiplication of personal responses to fascism serves to complicate what she has already established as an intricate network of entangled forces. The effect of the political, musical, and cinematic pastiche of *Seven Beauties* serves a dual purpose. First, it becomes a thread linking Pasqualino to his past, a narrative thread, interweaving nostalgic popular tunes and spectacular images of the Italian fascist regime with the monumental sounds and mythic images of Wagnerian opera. This weaving together of cultural icons gives rise to a dialogue between the two regimes and the two aesthetic styles used to distinguish nazism from fascism. And second, it serves as a critical antidote to political representations of nazism, fascism, and the "Final Solution," exploding archetypal myths of national, sexual, and political identities. Wertmüller's cinematic strategy of hyperbolizing conventional stereotypes, "proliferating the resemblance" or gesture of power, serves to uproot power from what it identifies as its source. She points to the liquidation of an authorial male subjective agency and the emergence of the reactionary "hysterical male subject."

Masculine or Feminine Machismo

Instead of duplicating the economy of purity, placing and tracing the mass attraction of fascism and nazism as a seduction on the part of the charismatic leader or a wildly decadent femme fatale, *Seven Beauties* restores women to fascism, not simply in the way Maria Antonietta Macciocchi fashions them, as victims of seduction, but as enigmatic figures that tear apart the narratives of both psychosexual politics and nazi eroticism.[33] The fact that nazi brutality and authority is embodied in a female character (the nazi commandant) challenges the masculinist interpretations of fascism and nazism put forward by historians like Macciocchi and Eugen Weber, who argues that "the fascist leader conquers a crowd and subdues it as he would a woman or a horse."[34] Wertmüller goes beyond a critique of the projected self-image of the fascist, castigating the postwar fascist imaginary, which supports the images and the rhetoric of Mussolini and Hitler as icons of charm and virility, even if that means that they are also seen as "subduing," seducing, feminizing, and even "raping" their followers (the masses). If, as Barbara Spackman argues, the "staging of Mussolini's sexual forcefulness may be construed as an interpellation of other men for," what Spackman likens to Irigaray's notion of a "hom(m)o-sexual economy," then does the continued reinterpretation of this extreme masculinist image in fact promote the same hom(m)o-sexual economy?[35] This ideological repositioning of Italian fascism as an expression of aggressive male sexuality is manifest in Macciocchi's interpretation of Mussolini as a seducer of men, appealing to men's "Virilismo fascista," which she distinguishes from the "omosessuale nazista." She goes as far as to claim "I nazisti, essendo per lo piú omosessuali rappresentavano le donne tutte nude (e frigide) come frutti della natura.... La propensione pederastica dei Nazisti é la fame di donne" ("The nazi, being for the most part homosexual, represents women as completely nude and frigid like the fruit of nature.... [The result of this] pederastic propensity of the nazis is the hunger of women.")[36] Macciocchi's division of the aggressive sexuality imbued in the image of the "pure manliness" of the Duce from the feminized, and therefore "sexually perverse," image of Hitler serves to justify conventional distinctions of the two regimes, which place Italian fascism as the lesser evil. However, embedded within these cultural distinctions are also aesthetic, sexual, and moral discriminations that anachronistically reterritorialize nazism within the context of decadence, femininity, and homosexuality, and fascism within the discourse of virility, manliness, and heterosexuality. Hence Macciocchi preserves binary models when addressing and characterizing the nature of fascism.

Rather than engaging in a dispute over such interpretations, Wertmüller parodies the distinction between Italian "virilismo"—by depicting Pasqualino as a ladies' man—and nazi "frigidity"—by depicting the commandant as "perversely" asexual. Yet she rejects the revision of fascism and nazism that seeks to assimilate them to the discourse of "sexual perversity" and moral deviance (particularly that of homosexuality). Nowhere in the film does Wertmüller imply such a linkage exists; rather, she returns to examine the question of "gendering" the "Final Solution," exploring the masses' desire for nazism and fascism. Although the appeal of fascism and nazism draws on the rhetoric of masculinity, virility, purity, and violence, for Wertmüller the allure of such rhetoric is not gender specific. In fact, it is the commandant who epitomizes the ideal fascist man, while Pasqualino and Francesco are failures as fascists and especially failures as men, since they are neither devout fascists nor antifascists. The images of the commandant and Pasqualino contradict what Karen Pinkus calls the "traditional iconography of fascism": the image of the muscular young man and the "bosomy peasant-mother." Although, as Pinkus writes, "the 'true' body of the fascist is the phallic body, existing in a state of preparedness for war. It was possible for women to occupy this position at certain moments in the history of the regime, as long as they were relatively malleable, capable of moving back to the mystical place reserved for maternity."[37] Wertmüller reverses gender roles, suggesting that gender itself appears to be purely a cultural construct. As a result, she scrutinizes the encasing of masculine sexuality within the discourse of "truth," moral and national purity. At the same time she presents gender as a masquerade, she seeks to debunk the reversal of the image of fascism from its self-promoted aggressive masculinity to its postwar revision as perverse and decadent femininity, as in Visconti's *The Damned*, where nazism is encoded in the aesthetics of sadomasochism and kitsch.

In an attempt to expose some of the metaphorical or metonymic associations of femininity with a plethora of contradictory positions—decadence, evil, victimhood, sexuality, and racial and ethical impurity—imbedded in what Susan Sontag calls the "fascination with fascism," Wertmüller inverts and hyperbolizes traditional gender roles associated with fascism and nazism. The nazi commandant is not simply a woman—she is a woman of monumental proportions, who appears as a giant next to Pasqualino and the other male prisoners lined up in rows of anonymous bodies or heaped in piles of emaciated and mangled corpses. Yet aside from her monumental stature, which signifies health, strength, and nazi brutality, she presents an enigma to conventional understandings of gender: she is neither excessively feminine nor excessively masculine; she is neither antisexual—she demands that Pasqualino finish his "game of seduction" by making love to her—nor is she overtly sexual—she is not interested is sexual pleasure, but she wants to know just how far Pasqualino will go to survive. She identifies with the violent purity of the party's racial, moral, and sexual laws, yet she also mimics the seductive and decadent, yet cold and indifferent, allure of Dietrich and recalls the tableaux of Otto Dix's and Georg Grosz's depictions of women. The image of the commandant evokes the Expressionists' cultural obsession with deformed, masculinized, or mutilated women, but like Dietrich in *The Blue Angel*, she exalts the figure of *einen Mann* and the *richtigen Mann* rather than playing out the role of the femme fatale. While in *The Blue Angel* that ideal image of man remains purely imaginary—a challenge to men to conform to what Lola Lola wants—in *Seven Beauties* the model man is emblemized by the picture of Hitler that hangs on the commandant's wall.

Wertmüller responds to the overuse and abuse of the image of Dietrich, which has been transplanted from the context of Weimar Germany to serve as an icon of nazi sadomasochism in postwar media. In the figure of the commandant the images of Dietrich and Hitler (and the SS) once again converge and diverge. They converge in reference to the aesthetics of nazi sadomasochism and diverge in that there is nothing sexy or feminine in the image of the commandant's (and implicitly Hitler's) grotesque parody of Dietrich. What is eradicated from the image is not only the aesthetic appeal of Dietrich but the ambiguous "play" with the aesthetics of sexual identity and sexual power. Instead, this masquerade as Dietrich marks the death of the game of seduction and desire, turning it into a brutal play of force. Furthermore, by mixing identification with Hitler with desire for Hitler, the commandant illustrates the collapse of gender roles from culturally assigned masculine roles of agency, subjectivity, authority, and authenticity to the relegation of feminine roles to passivity, objectivity, submission, and mass culture. What disappears in this model is the notion of the organic body, the human body, that Agamben postulates was "chained to biological destiny, individual biography and theological foundations."[38] As Andreas Huyssen writes, "in the 1920s mass culture shifts from the realm of feminine to masculine technology, reproduction, administration" (*After the Great Divide*, 48). What replaces the decadent, feminine characterization of the body and the masses is a technological and masculinized image of humanity. However, Wertmüller points out that the massification or regimentation of the body conforms to neither the feminizing nor masculinizing of the masses but instead transsexualizing of the body, which fashions itself as both the subject (agency) and the object (receptacle) of fascist and nazi ideology. This play between subjecting oneself to the authority, or surrendering to the seduction of Hitler and the Third Reich and desiring Hitler or Mussolini as authority figures (or as objects of desire) demonstrates the closed circuitry of the fascist libidinal economy. This economy produces and reproduces desire in the form of mass spectacle, yet one that is designed to reinforce the fascist law (a desire for purification, an angry acting out), rather than a seductive desire for transgression in the form of otherness. It is the elimination of subjects and objects in favor of an entropic desire of the machine.

This identification with and desire for the *einen Mann* and the *richtigen Mann* theoretically sets up a libidinal economy where woman (as a subject or object of desire) disappears; however, in *Seven Beauties* this is not the case: it is Pasqualino who disappears, since he can no longer identify with this image of man, while the commandant, who wields "unmeasurable" power, appears to be larger than life. Thus gender itself does not seem to be biologically determined nor does it determine anatomical destiny but is contingent on one's association with power. Because the aesthetics and rhetoric of power and domination are deeply imbedded in the discourse of male "heterosexuality," power remains figuratively associated with phallic symbols, symbols that exude a sense of violence (military weaponry, firmness, etc.) and sexual metaphors of production and reproduction. Yet, as Luce Irigaray professes, "heterosexuality is nothing but the assignment of economic roles—there are producer subjects and agents of exchange (male) on the one hand, productive earth and commodities (female) on the other" (*This Sex Which Is Not One*, 192). The figure of the commandant, however, challenges this symbolic precedent by mixing metaphors: while she wears men's underwear and jackboots she is also reminiscent of a Dietrichesque femme fatale and dominatrix, brandishing a whip, straddling a chair, smoking a cigar. She not only subverts conventional visual codes of the femme fatale (found in *The Damned, Cabaret,* and other films) associated with fetish clothing and aesthetic gestures; but she also disrupts the gender-coding of power itself by devaluing phallic sexual power associated with desire and female pleasure. Contrary to Laura Mulvey's argument that female spectators are forced into a masculinization of vision, Wertmüller returns all forms of voyeurism to acts of violence that are not gender-specific.[39] She demands that Pasqualino undress so that she may inspect and survey his body, especially his genitalia. Unimpressed by what she sees, and impervious to Pasqualino's advances, she turns the game of seduction into a game of survival predicated on submission and performance. She demands: "ora facciamo l'amore, dopo ti ammazerò con le mie mani, se tu non fich, ti ammazerò ... addesso devi fare li gioco dei macellaio, scegli tu sei prigionieri per esecuzione, se no, tutta la barraca sard sparata"("now we'll fuck, after that I will kill you with my own hands, if you don't fuck (stick it in)

I will kill you ... now you must play my game, the game of slaughter, if you don't select six men for execution, everyone in the barrack will be shot").

Hence the sexual act is transformed from a power play to a form of pure exchange: Pasqualino is promised the possibility of surviving in exchange for his becoming an accomplice to murder. In opposition to the economy of seduction, which Baudrillard describes as a process of "withdrawing something from the visible order so as to run counter to production," Wertmüller depicts the commodification of the body as the hypervisibility of the body and thus the triumph of production over all social relations (*Seduction*, 20). In turn, the model of production spectacularizes the illusion of power as a singular force, a force of exchange and a system of values that are predicated on the systematization of values (one that reproduces everywhere the same or equal desire for authority and the law and reinforces the same order, race, nationality, sex). This force of exchangeability and commodification of value (or value of commodities) opposes the force of intensity, which, as Lyotard explains, "liquidates all stases, demanding the abolition of the I/You relation (which is, like the master/slave, reversible) and also the use-relation" (*Libidinal Economies*, 66). Furthermore, the visu-alization of the mechanics of seduction and the designated purpose of seduction, whether it be Pasqualino's desire to survive or the commandant's desire to humiliate and dehumanize her prisoners, demystifies the practice of seduction and renders its allusive power inoperative. Like Pasolini, Wertmüller sees this dissolution of sexual or erotic intimacy, and its reduction to use-value, as not merely a product of fascism but also a consequence of commodity capitalism—which, for the most part, remains sub-ject to traditional patriarchal forms of expression. In fact, in *Seven Beauties* all sexual relations resemble a neocapitalist economic structure: every sexual act is parodied as either an act of prostitution or rape (a hostile takeover). While sex is radically divorced from any sign of pleasure or desire, it gives Pasqualino's sisters, as prostitutes, a means of self-determination and the ability to raise their standard of living. Like soldiers, these prostitutes all have the same uniform, they appear to be commodified, regi-mented; they are even regulated by the fascist state. Yet, unlike the soldier, they do not act in the name of the state but in the name of self-interest—as the state itself acts. It is the mode of the prostitute, who seduces in the name of self-interest and personal gain, that Pasqualino mimics in his attempt to seduce the commandant, while she remains a model image of the good soldier. What is at stake in the dissemination of these sexualized metaphors of power, therefore, is not only numerous essentialist argu-ments, including those of psychoanalysis, that rest on biologically determined sexual difference but a whole tradition of aesthetizing women, decadence, impurity, and evil.

In addition, rather than masquerading nazism and fascism as a form of decadent sexuality, Wertmüller presents them as intolerant of any desire that conflicts with the reification of the ideology of the regime. The commandant even finds Pasqualino's "unheroic" desire to survive immoral and impure, since it is not motivated by moral or ideological conviction. And his unheroic means of survival verifies the commandant's racist beliefs that Italians are "brutti, schiffosi macaroni … italiani di merda" ("ugly, disgusting macaroni, shitty Italians"), thereby justifying her inhuman treatment of what she considers to be an inferior and immoral people. The commandant exemplifies the logic of the camp that Pelagia Lewinska describes: "the idea which governed the way the camp was organized had been well and consciously thought out. . . . They wanted to debase and humiliate the human dignity within us, to eradicate every trace of humanity from us, to make us feel horrified and disgusted with ourselves," which in turn was used to justify the everyday atrocities committed in the camp.[40] By linking the commandant and nazi idealism to a radical moral economy, Wertmüller questions our ability to overcome fascism by adopting its very principles, idolizing male heroes who make the world a "safer place" by violently purifying and morally cleansing it of "the forces of evil."

Instead of returning to the politics of propaganda—a logic in which the victor smears the image of the enemy—Wertmüller ridicules the obsessive inscription of the discourse and aesthetic representations of nazism, fascism, and the "Final Solution" in the discourse of sexuality. *Seven Beauties* mimics (so as to instill a sense of irony) readings like Susan Sontag's profile of Hitler, where she reports that he considered public speech like rape, a rape that would make "the feminized masses come,"[41] or Friedländer's recollection that "under nazism, Hitler was indeed the object of desire."[42] This image of Hitler, however, was not one of an excessively sexualized rapist, who makes the "feminine masses come," but as Friedländer concludes, "a cultivated image of the petty bourgeois Mr. Everyman, the middle class common denominator."[43] Hence it seems unlikely that he could return as an icon of sexual attraction, to be mimicked in the cults of the nazi pageantry. It is more likely, as Sontag describes, that the SS proved to be the site of sexual attraction since it was "the ideal incarnation of fascism's overt assertion of the righteousness of violence. They were supremely violent, but also supremely beautiful" (*Under the Sign of Saturn*, 97). Wertmüller's characterization of nazism, then, responds to the growing desire to reinstall fascism and nazism in the aesthetics of the sublime or more subversive economies. She counters the spectacular aesthetic return to fascist imaginary, which visually explores the desire for fascism, by visualizing the impact or effects of nazism, fascism, and the "Final Solution" on the common man. Instead of focusing on the "supreme violence" that is (re)considered to be "beautiful," Wertmüller pictures the ugliness of violence—a violence divorced from sublime or romantic aesthetic codes. By de-eroticizing the postwar spectacularization of fascism and nazism, Wertmüller strips away the appealing image of "supreme violence" to reveal, lying under the surface, a desire for control, repression, purification, and, ultimately abolition of desire itself.

Seven Beauties thematically converges with *The Night Porter* in its questioning and ultimately undermining the heroic image of *einen Mann* as well as the *richtigen Mann*. By disputing conventional notions of gender, Cavani and Wertmüller challenge the ironic revisualization and reinterpretation of this decadent image of woman in neodecadentist films such as *The Damned* and in psychoanalytic readings of history.

They demonstrate the paradox of reestablishing a heterosexual economy in light of eroticizing or desiring a man who fits the mold of Hitler, Mussolini, or the "beauty of the SS-man," since it was men like these who conducted antifeminist campaigns, legislated antifeminist laws, and espoused misogynist beliefs. The question is, just whose desire is sparked by such images of violence and violation? Instead of sexualizing the spectacle of masculine militancy, Cavani and Wertmüller explore the practice that continues to enframe the manly man within a moral image. They present manly images that sustain notions of nationalism, racial purity, and technological virility as deriving from fascist spectacles of superior firepower and images of man as fused with the machine, generated by, for instance, the mass spectacles of nazi choreography and the futurist images of the bachelor machine. While for Cavani this image of the "real" or moral man is embodied in the group of former nazis who wish to eradicate those who transgress moral boundaries, Wertmüller portrays the moral or ethical man as a political man or woman (Pedro, Francesco, the commandant, and the socialist whom Pasqualino encounters in a train station). Although each of these characters represents a different political and ethical perspective, they all believe in their own version of a "new world order" and a new man who represents "civilization" and moral order. Wertmüller's juxtaposition of competing militant or revolutionary discourses highlights their dependency on moral models and laws that are put into place by action that is defined in terms of violence, even murder. In an attempt to dismantle the politics, rhetoric, and aesthetics of aggressive masculinity, Cavani destabilizes male/female subjective positions by "blending memory with desire" in a series of flashbacks where it is not clear whether the spectator is "subjected" to Max's or to Lucia's memory or sexual fantasy. Hence the *richtigen Mann*'s identity is bound (both ideologically and erotically) to the victim of the Reich, thereby delegitimizing its definition. For Wertmüller, on the other hand, images of the *richtigen Mann* and the *einen Mann* are embodied in the character of the nazi commandant, a woman who "un-mans" the film's protagonist, a small-time Neapolitan mafioso, Pasqualino. By contrast, Wertmüller dwells on the panic of male identity entwined with not only the imaginary constructions of national identity but also the continuing fascist notions of manliness. Hence Wertmüller problematizes subjectivity, not as a blending of one subject into another but as a questioning of those social constructs that define Pasqualino, his machismo, his *italianità*, his family, and his class consciousness.

Wertmüller directly confronts notions of Italian machismo and its incorporation into the national imaginary by ironically mimicking these notions via Pasqualino, who in turn mimics the Duce in order to convince a jury that he is indeed insane. His role-playing as the Duce verifies his plea that he is the madman of Napoli rather than the monster of Napoli, and accordingly he is committed to an insane asylum rather than given capital punishment. Although Pasqualino mocks the bodily gestures of the Duce, suggesting that the Duce and those that emulate him are deranged, Pasqualino is allowed to live precisely because of this emulation. But, far from living up to the image of the virile fascist leader, his mimicking of Mussolini marks

Pasqualino's departure from narratives and images of manliness and honor. Like Mussolini, however, he is presented as both a "family man" and at the same time he is a "ladies' man" (or at least attempts to be perceived as such). He also represents the "common man's" admiration for Mussolini and men like Mussolini, for what Fellini's character Ciccio describes as being perceived as "having big balls." And since, for Pasqualino, Mussolini embodies all the attributes of manliness—an enigmatic presence, a strong will to action, and an ability to bring respect to the image of Italy—Mussolini's mandate will remain present in his thinking. In fact, even when stripped of his identity, his various roles as a mafioso, a family man, and a ladies' man, Pasqualino holds on to the notion of masculine virility as a sign of vitality. And when he finally returns to Napoli after the war he expresses his paranoid desire to "fare figli, molti figli perchè il numero è potenza" ("have children, many children, because there is power in numbers"), recalling once again Mussolini's infamous dictate that was predicated on the fear of the consequences of a declining population.

As a caricature of "virilismo fascista," Pasqualino encounters a variety of obstacles that threaten his masculine identity: not only the "frigid sadistic" nazi commandant but also a series of what Bettelheim labels "ridiculously fat and grotesque" women—for example, his sisters, who become prostitutes in order to pay for Pasqualino's lawyer but whose standard of living is considerably higher when they are not under the protection and provision of their brother. Wertmüller de-eroticizes both the image of the virile man of the house and the sadomasochistic cult of nazi aesthetics (the beauty of the violent fascist) by returning them to the aesthetics of the grotesque. Ironically, it is Bettelheim who is offended by the grotesqueness of the depictions of feminine seductiveness. He cannot help but comment that "the closer she [the commandant] gets to being a woman the more grotesque this mass of flesh becomes." ("Reflections: Surviving," 48). Although I find Bettelheim's response dubious in terms of sexual politics, his comment serves to point out the film's "play" on the notions of excessive sexuality (the obsessive looking at women's bodies) in relationship to the mythological status of both genders and nations.

Wertmüller reflects on the fear of the grotesque (as exemplified by Bettelheim's reaction) as directed primarily at feminine sexuality, not as a symptom of the fear of the sexually potent woman, as Klaus Theweleit argues, but as the fear of performative inadequacy. And this fear that Pasqualino experiences carries him outside of his highly coded and invested identification with masculine gender. Since woman can no longer be considered, as Slavoj Žižek suggests, as "a determining negativity," "that cold, neutral screen which opens up a space for possible projections, that surface which functions as a black hole" (*Metastases of Enjoyment*, 91). Pasqualino can no longer use woman's desire for him as a mirror that reaffirms his masculine identity and his sense of self-worth, which is bound to that very identity. Not only does the commandant appear to be uninterested in Pasqualino's seductive gestures and amorous overtures — she is repulsed by the fact that he "manages an erection in order to survive." Here the commandant actualizes his humiliation by drawing attention to the inadequacy (the inability to give sexual pleasure) of Pasqualino's sexual performance. During their alleged copulation, the commandant yawns and looks off into the corner at the Bronzino painting, then throws Pasqualino off her body, in scorn for what she calls his "erezione di maschio." This scene, which Bettelheim reads as "the rape of mankind," underscores another social enigma. The alleged rape recalls the previous rape scene, where Pasqualino rapes a bound woman patient in the asylum, calling her a "rotten whore" and a "stinking bitch" as she resists his force. By comparison, this "rape of mankind," which the commandant justifies as a struggle for survival, uncovers a series of gender-related problems. Bettelheim distinguishes the two rape scenes by the intent of the victim: whereas the rape of the woman is a "passive" rape, Pasqualino's is "active." It seems odd, however, that Bettelheim would use the Freudian, and later fascist, notion of agency as opposed to receptivity in order to classify gender distinctions of rape. Wertmüller seems to suggest that such a gender division is not necessary here, that victimhood does not require that Pasqualino's body become feminized in order to be considered "victimized" or violated. Since, according to the narrative, Pasqualino "willfully" contrives this scheme of seduction as a means of survival, this act of violation exceeds the definition of rape. Pasqualino seems to use sex in exchange for survival, thereby requalifying this "rape of mankind" as the "prostitution of man." In fact, like a prostitute Pasqualino must feign attraction and sexual excitement. Whether read as the rape of his manhood or the rape of his soul, contrary to Bettelheim's analysis that the commandant dehumanizes the victim, Wertmüller problematizes this very notion of "humanity." According to Bettelheim's own definition, Pasqualino has no humanity to lose. By depicting Pasqualino as a "ladies' man," a murderer, and a rapist, Wertmüller questions our ability to sympathize with him and simultaneously judge him.

What commences as an image of feminine seduction as seen through the perspective of the male gaze is transformed into a process of desexualization, in which Pasqualino loses control over the gaze and is himself reduced to an object that is subjected (both psychically and visually) to the commandant's way of seeing. These hyperbolic and discontent visualizations of macho men (who are stripped of the trappings of masculinity) and mythic women therefore reduce the classifications of gender to the effects of the politics of theatricality, impersonation, and the imitation of bloated sexual and social ideals. The bloated sexual encoding of characters in *Seven Beauties* subverts notions that gender can be given a proper sexual index or sexual identification: gender appears as a carnivalistic play. *Seven Beauties* turns the discourse about fascism from psychosexual readings of the charismatic leader to the psychosexual problems of the "mythical normal man" who is forced to assimilate to this aggressively masculinized "compulsory system."

Wertmüller's exaggeration or hyperbolization of this sexually charged way of seeing serves to make it visible so as to subject it to public scrutiny. With the exception of Carolina, the young girl Pasqualino will ultimately marry, all the female characters are depicted as excessively "fleshy" (not only corpulent but scantily clothed): his sister Concettina, who performs cabaret dressed in a black brassiere; his mother and sisters, who make themselves up as prostitutes; the Wagnerian German woman he encounters in the forest who dons a white satin dress that reveals her derriere; his memory of his first love Fifi, who is also a cabaret dancer; and the commandant, who strips down to boxer shorts and a tank-top. Wertmüller endeavors to make fun of the way Pasqualino sees women's bodies. These corpulent visions of womanhood resemble those "bosomy" depictions of heroic motherhood and earthy femininity put forward in fascist iconography. This stereotypical masculine (fascist) way of seeing, however, is constantly interrupted or upset: first by the fact that it is Pasqualino's sister who is the object of the gaze, yet instead of eliciting desire she is ridiculed; second because Pasqualino's desire to eat is greater than his desire for the romantic or mythical image projected by the German woman who sits alone at the piano singing an aria from Wagner's *Die Walküre* as her dress slips from her arm; and lastly because the vision of the commandant is so threatening that Pasqualino has to close his eyes.

While in Pasqualino's sexual imagination woman represents suprasensual sexuality, promising excessive pleasure, his actual sexual coupling with the commandant, this monumental image of woman, transforms into the opposite of sensuality, becoming what Deleuze calls supercarnal, that is, sadistic and cruel. She represents not just the grotesque, as Bettelheim claims, but also a sadistic castrating law—that is, she

Pasqualino (Giancarlo Giannini) conjures up the parodic image of Fifi to get in the mood for "seducing" the nazi commandant, played by Shirly Stoler.

takes the place of the father, Hitler, or Mussolini. In addition, the commandant, as an emblem of the law, presents high humanism in its coldest "purity." Not only does she encode herself and the German race in a romantic-tragic narrative (as the ultimate failure of the master race that strove for ideological purity), but she is also presented as a connoisseur of the arts—prisoners play the violin when others are about to die, she acquires Bronzino's *Venus, Cupid, Folly and Time*, which hangs behind her as Pasqualino attempts to seduce her. She mixes metaphors, from Dietrich to Bronzino, the grotesque, and the aesthetics of nazi sadomasochism, spinning them all into an image of coldness and cruelty, yet one that is not only antifeminine but also antihumane and anti-sexual. Hence it is a pure formality that this image of the femme fatale is embodied in a woman.

Seduction as a Means of Survival

Although the commandant is dehumanized as a castrating (paternal/femme fatale) nazi female, she is rehumanized in her relationship with Pasqualino. She is aware that he is using her and she is empowered by his desire for survival—not to use him for sexual satisfaction, as Bettelheim proclaims, since it is obvious she has none, but to test his ability to degrade himself in order to live. Therefore, by entering into a "discourse" with the victimizer, Pasqualino as a victim becomes part of the process of victimization, using the terms of the victimizer for personal gain, in this case, increasing his life expectancy. Bettelheim calls Wertmüller's depictions a "disturbing debasement of life, inside and outside of the concentration camp" ("Reflections: Surviving," 34). He mistakes Pasqualino as the symbolic (everyman) survivor. I want to stress that Pasqualino is distinctly not a Jewish survivor but a caricature of the Italian male who becomes a fascist deserter and then a survivor.[44] Bettelheim's (and Levi's) disgust for the notion of survival at any cost causes him to argue that there is no heroic position in *Seven Beauties*. The real question, however, is whether it is possible to locate heroism in the "Final Solution," and if so, is it possible to continue to model the hero on the same Western notions used by both the fascists and the national socialists? What Bettelheim calls for is the reconstitution of the narrative position of *einen Mann/richtigen Mann*—the romantic hero. Ironically, this calling for a hero does not problematize prefascist or fascist constructions of heroism.

Instead of perpetuating a romantic narrative where good triumphs over evil—which seems almost absurd in relation to the "Final Solution"—Wertmüller opens up a narrative space for an ideological discourse of moral obligation through the character of the anarchist (Pedro) and the apolitical soldier (Francesco). Although Marcus believes that *Seven Beauties* offers the spectator only two choices—identify with Mediterranean survivalism or with nazi idealism—she points out that "there is the *hint* of an alternative in the character of Pedro, the Spanish anarchist who advocates man in disorder in contrast to nazi orderliness, and Francesco, Pasqualino's accomplice in deserting the army, who also has a sense of personal honor and political integrity." However Marcus, like Bettelheim, argues that Wertmüller "undercuts these options by making Pedro and Francesco such minor characters that we have little time to identify with them, and by dying she discounts any *heroic stature in death*—Pedro drowns in excrement and Francesco pleads to be shot before he becomes incontinent with fear" (*Italian Film in the Light of Neorealism*, 317). Even as Pedro calls for a "new man to be born, a civilized man, not a beast, a man with values, nature's value, a new man who can rediscover harmony within," presenting an alternative way of living, he recalls fascist propaganda that also called for a "new man." Although Pedro differentiates this "new man in disorder" from the rhetoric of both regimes, by disassociating the "new man" from the he-man, he also propagates a master race of men who focus on the mind rather than the regimentation of the body.

While I do not read Pedro's leap into the brine as nihilistic nor as expressing the futility of heroic action but instead as an open-ended narrative, a challenge leaving the position of the "new man" as a space that has not yet been filled, I find Marcus's and Bettelheim's responses to the film questionable and even nihilistic in their advocacy of "heroic stature in death." Eli Pfefferkorn inveighs against such assertions because, first, they imply that there is "a reciprocal relation between survival and assertion of the self"; and, second, "in the death camps, death was never a triumph. What might have elevated the recalcitrant inmate to the status of martyrdom or heroism in the eyes of his fellow inmates was an act that supported them in their struggle to get through another day's suffering. . . . In contrast, acts of defiance for the mere purpose of self-assertion not only were not regarded as heroic behavior by the inmates, but were usually condemned, for they incurred the wrath of the SS." ("Bettelheim, Wertmüller, and the Morality of Survival," 19). Thus, contrary to Marcus's and Bettelheim's belief, Wertmüller does not undercut Pedro and Francesco; rather they serve to illustrate alternative ideological and ethical ways of interpreting as well as responding to fascism, ways which conflict with and even criticize Pasqualino's own desire to survive.[45] Just because Pasqualino survives does not mean that Wertmüller supports his way of thinking: she pictures him as a suffering, guilt-ridden survivor who is left with the burden of remorse for his actions. Yet, on the other hand, she does not support the positions of Pedro or Francesco; rather she examines the alternatives and follows them to their logical ends. If she were to represent either Francesco or Pedro as surviving, she would also have to endorse a certain way of historicizing the Holocaust, thus revising the Holocaust to fit contemporary political needs. Instead, Pasqualino as the hyperbole of Italian male machismo, anti-intellectualism, anti-idealism, and amorality serves as a model for the "common man" who can be manipulated by political power and stripped of his (subjective) identification with that power.

Through Pasqualino, Wertmüller explores the inconsistencies and what Pfefferkorn calls "the moral ambiguities" in the historiography of the Holocaust. Pasqualino, primarily a figure who stands in opposition to the resurrection of the Western hero, contradicts Arendt's, Marcus's, Bettelheim's, and even Betty Friedan's measure of a man or a woman as someone who always resists subjugation, oppression, and annihilation. Following Arendt's inquiry as to why the European Jews did not revolt against the nazis even when they were assured of their own imminent death, and Bettelheim's argument that the crucial element in surviving was maintaining a sense of self, Friedan, in her ludicrous comparison of the suburban housewife to the concentration camp victim, writes that

> the guns of the SS were not powerful enough to keep all those prisoners subdued. They were manipulated to trap themselves; they imprisoned themselves by making the concentration camp the whole world, by blinding themselves to the larger world of *the past*, their responsibility for the *present* and their possibilities for the *future*. The ones who survived, who neither died nor were exterminated, were the ones who retained in some essential degree the adult values and interests which had been the essence of their past identity.[46]

Ironically, Pasqualino's attempts to hold on to his Neapolitan past as well as his present self-image as a seducer—depicting not an adult past but a childlike or adolescent past much like that portrayed in *Amarcord*—succeed in helping him seduce the commandant but fail to protect him from being dehumanized and degraded by her subsequent demands that he become a kapo and that he ultimately kill his only friend, Francesco. Primo Levi recounts "that within the camps the [world view] of prisoners became very limited, as they did not have access to the outside world, in fact their life revolved around what would otherwise be considered banal issues" (*I sommersi e i salvati*, 712). Pierre Cortade writes: "one of the characteristics of Hitlerian sadism is to rob things of their meaning, to plunge its victims live into a disorientating world."[47] And Pelagia Lewinska explains her break with a moral way of thinking: "Men with a developed social sense, people with a certain cultural or ideological standard, had to perish crushed beneath a blind and primitive animality" (*Vingt mois à Auschwitz*, 129). If anything was heroic, according to Pfefferkorn, it was "holding out" rather than "releasing oneself of the prison of a miserable life." These accounts of surviving attest to the fierce competition required just to live, but they also dispel arguments that "victims imprisoned themselves" by failing to maintain a sense of their past, present, and future subjective identifications. The problems they point to are the difficulty of coping with the feeling of guilt for surviving (as dramatized in *The Pawnbroker*) and the guilt of turning against each other instead of the nazis (as *Seven Beauties* illustrates). In these accounts degradation indeed amounted to what Bettelheim rebuffs as "a preoccupation with the simplest animal needs."

While *Seven Beauties* intersects with discourses of survival and the aestheticization of survival as well as fascism and nazism, it makes no claim to truth-value and should not be judged by the criteria of historical representation. It offers a critical perspective on the postwar fascist cultural industry, the remanufacturing of fascism as a historical reality, a performative site for sexuality and gender politics. By choosing to explore "moral ambiguities"—impure places where humans become animal—Wertmüller challenges the viability of master narratives of truth, which emplot the great battles between the pure and the impure (good and evil). Rather than pitting "Mediterranean survival against nazi idealism," she disturbs both the notion of basic survival and that of righteous violence, since both seem to amount to extremes—extreme moral convictions and the extreme lack thereof. What she makes clear is that demands for "historical correctness" directly translate into demands to maintain the language of absolute purity and impurity, allowing discourse of purity (which is qualified in terms of race, gender, and sexual preference) itself to remain intact.

Like *Salò* and *The Night Porter*, *Seven Beauties* does not offer a resolution or a narrative closure that would support any moral model. Rather, it ends with a reflection: the last shot of the film enframes Pasqualino, the protagonist, looking at himself in the mirror, replying to his mother, "si son vivo" ("yes, I'm alive"). However, his hesitation and vacuous look suggest otherwise, that he has endured many deaths—the deaths of his family's honor, his pride as a ladies'man, his conscience, and ultimately his soul. He (like the audience) is left to ponder the price of his surviving the war and the concentration camp where he was interned/interred. Pasqualino's bad conscience reflects that in order to survive he became an accomplice to the fascists and the national socialists: he joined the Italian army, he seduced the nazi commandant in order to become the kapo of his barrack, and he followed orders even when he was

In *Seven Beauties,* Pasqualino attempts to seduce Carolina (Francesca Marciano), the figure of virginal innocence who will later become his prostitute fiancée.

asked to choose six random prisoners for execution. Far from representing the heroic survivor or the tragic victim, Pasqualino emblemizes the petty criminal (the suffering sinner) whose preoccupation with survival constantly compromises his "humanity." Yet, while Wertmüller strips Pasqualino of any possible linkage to the image of the pure or innocent victim, she does not associate him with absolute evil either. Pasqualino is neither moral nor completely immoral; rather he is motivated by a desire to live, not a malevolent desire to destroy nor a seemingly benevolent desire to cleanse society of evil. Pasqualino, a lower-class Southern Italian, represents a man without qualities—without a legitimate profession, political or moral convictions, and economic stature. Maurice Merleau-Ponty characterizes the socioeconomic paradox of purity to which Pasqualino is bound: while "the moral man does not want to dirty his hands, because he usually has enough time, talent, or money to stand back from enterprises of which he disapproves and to prepare a good conscience for himself, the common people do not have that freedom: the garage mechanic had to repair German cars if he wanted to live." As a result, Merleau-Ponty adds, "We have unlearned 'pure morality' and learned a kind of vulgar immoralism, which is health."[48] Although *Seven Beauties* demonstrates this process of "unlearning," Wertmüller does not present Pasqualino's subsistence as an example of "health" but rather a morally ambiguous effect of both "vulgar immoralism" and an overdetermined sense of "moral purity." She seems to chastise characters who do not actively participate in politics—resist fascism—but it is unclear whether she supports the existentialist point of view put forward by her character Francesco, which stipulates that we are all responsible for allowing atrocities to happen, or the anarchist demand for a "new man of disorder" touted by her character Pedro. In fact, she reproaches both the ethos of existentialism for its adherence to the nazi dictate that "no-one is innocent" and the anarchist moral model for cleaving to the prefascist demand for a "new man." According to Wertmüller, this "new man" of disorder (as opposed to the nazi man of order) already exists in Pasqualino, which means that the "new man of disorder" cannot fortify himself or herself against fascism but will surrender to hegemonic power and its cultural and political influences.

Conclusion

I must confess that even in *Salò* I do not arrive at the heart of violence . . . the real violence is that of television. . . . For me, the maximum of violence is a television announcer. In my films, violence is a mechanism, never a real fact.[1]

—Pier Paolo Pasolini

Since the making of *Salò*, *The Night Porter*, and *Seven Beauties*, hundreds of films have been produced on the subject of fascism, nazism, and the "Final Solution", yet many tend to emulate historical modes of interpretation (for example, the American docudrama *Holocaust* [1978], Claude Lanzmann's *Shoah* [1985], and Francesco Rosi's *The Truce* [*La Treuga*, 1997]), often reinstalling historical narratives into the project of Enlightenment or humanist discourses (Steven Spielberg's *Schindler's List* [1993], Michael Verhoeven's *My Mother's Courage* [*Mutters Courage*, 1995], and Roberto Benigni's *Life Is Beautiful* [*La vita è bella*, 1997]) or returning to the debauched images of nazi and fascist eroticism, surrealism, and decadence (Rainer Werner Fassbinder's *Die Sehnsucht der Veronika Voss* [1982] and Lars Von Trier's *Zentropa* [1991]). What distinguishes the films of Pier Paolo Pasolini, Liliana Cavani, and Lina Wertmüller is their refusal to disengage nazi or fascist idealism from moral humanism. Instead Pasolini, Cavani, and Wertmüller accuse pre- and postwar (bourgeois) moral humanism of continuing to support a fascist ethos by resurrecting the same mythic figures—real men who are at the same time national heroes—and installing them in the same epic narratives, the same call to arms against what are considered to be inhuman enemies. Hence they find at the heart of such moralism an appeal to the rhetoric of violence in the form of the rhetoric of division (of good versus evil), which is used to justify fascist political maneuvers: "subduing," "neutralizing," or even "filing away" potential adversaries. For these filmmakers, fascism cannot be filed away, subdued, or neutralized when it reemerges in the very same repressive processes. As Félix Guattari explains, "we are led to believe that fascism was just a bad moment we had to go through, a sort of historical error, but also a beautiful page in history for the good heroes. We are further led to believe that there were real antagonistic contradictions between the fascist Axis and the Allies. [Yet] fascism is inseparable from the evolution of productive forces"(*Chaosophy*, 239–40).

Thus, rather than restoring a belief in the world, reassuring the viewer of the triumph of the forces of good over the forces of evil and the reinstitution of ethical values, these filmmakers confound the binary oppositions that produce clear (in the sense of pure or absolute) and identifiable heroes and villains. They provide a forum for what Friedrich Nietzsche names "critical history" and what Martin Heidegger calls "reflection," "the courage to make the truth of our own presuppositions and the realm of our own goals into the things that most deserve to be called into question."[2] Heidegger argues that "the flight into tradition, out of a combination of humility and presumption, can bring about nothing in itself other than self-deception and blindness in relation to the historical moment" (*The Question Concerning Technology*, 120). I use the term "reflection" to illustrate Pasolini's, Cavani's and Wertmüller's strategy of subverting preconceived notions of good and evil and their subsequent inscription in the discourse of nazism and fascism. As these filmmakers *reflect* on cultural presumptions regarding nazism, fascism, and the "Final Solution," they undermine conventional safeguards touching on that which belongs to the self-deception and blindness of critical and historical thinkers. Pasolini, Cavani, and Wertmüller evidence this act of *reflection* in their cinema by interrupting the transmission of moral models into historical and ideological discourses. Their genealogical tracing of these moral models to fascist ideals leads to their rejection of the vindication of bourgeois morality operating in such films as *Schindler's List, Judgment at Nuremberg, Victory at Sea, Victory*, and *Night of the Shooting Stars*, or even the moralistic tone of *1900* and *The Conformist*. What is at stake in deconstructing such a moral economy is the dismantling of the binary construction of the good subject set in opposition to its evil other. The cinema of Pasolini, Cavani, and Wertmüller inculpates the rhetoric of good, pure, and clean in the rhetoric of fascism and fascist violence against what it considers to be other—evil, impure, and unclean.

Yet in doing so these filmmakers realize that they cannot make another stand for radical purity, so they adopt a model much like that of Artaud's *Pest*, a radical impurity, that is, a radical destruction. They adopt a fatal strategy for what they see as a fascist war machine impossible to implode. Therefore their cinematic strategy of revealing the inherent discontinuities in the rhetoric of moral purity functions much like what Gilles Deleuze calls "thought cinema"—"producing a shock to thought" by "mixing-up images which express holistic notions" such as moral ethos, logical continuity, narrative sequence, and history (*Cinema 2*, 157–60). While Pasolini outright rejects the existence of the hero and his or her emplotment within a moral narrative as another form of fascism—insinuating that only "evil" posing as good exists in the world—and Cavani explores the erotic and intimate relationship of the "evil" nazi and the "good" victim, Wertmüller undermines conventional modes of reimaging good (surviving) and evil (fascism and nazism) by hyperbolizing their ideological implications.

More than polluting the image or "bastardizing the memory of the victim," what scandalizes some viewers of these films is the implication of historical, moral, and sexual frameworks in displacing fascism so that it always returns. Consequently Pasolini, Cavani, and Wertmüller envision what appears to be a moral gesture—disengaging good from evil, pure from impure, victim from victimizer, bourgeois from nazi or fascist, or West from East, and democracy from terrorism—as a political action whose significance does not emanate from essential moral and ideological categories but hinges on contemporary realignments or shifts in power, image power, and its textual and visual support systems. Pasolini, Cavani, and Wertmüller inveigh against the spectacle of history, which Siegfried Kracauer argued was perfected by the nazi regime continuing with the bourgeois moral drama and its connections to military culture.[3] The spectacle of bourgeois morality is therefore used by neoliberals and neohumanists as a reactive weapon that squelches ambiguous or unruly desires (what Pasolini calls *diversità* and Cavani labels "free amorous relations"). The moral order represses desires by concealing its own violence behind the masks of law, the common good, national security, and so forth. Ironically, the same repression that Enlightenment as well as psychoanalytic thinkers deemed necessary to ensure humanity's survival (social order) ensured humanity's submission to repressive regimes. Pasolini, Cavani, and Wertmüller focus on the reinstallation of the trope of moral deviance in postwar discourses of sexuality, racism, and nationalism because it is in the image of the impure, evil, or unclean that the language of purity reinstalls itself. That is, the image of deviance becomes a moving target for moral discourse and the reactionary practices of filmmakers and critics who believe that their text/film is clean (promotes a moral message).

The most radical interpretation of these three directors is their equation of bourgeois moralism with indirect forms of violence operating much like massive global networks of control, as for instance the special intelligence services and secret police (modeled on the Gestapo and the SS), since bourgeois moralism, similar to clandestine organizations, is considered to be autonomous, neither accountable to popular opinion nor subject to minimal public scrutiny. Instead, bourgeois morals are established and ordained on the grounds of "communal security" (the common good), "national security," or the securing of personal property. The notion of "securing" directly translates into snuffing out wildly nomadic and disorganizing desires and destroying those who perpetrate them, as in the case of the former nazis filing Max and Lucia away (*The Night Porter*), or the libertines' decree to kill anyone who acts on his or her own desires (*Salò*). Moral law sometimes manifests itself as a preemptive

Pasqualino (Giancarlo Giannini) is arrested after he butchers his sister's lover.

strike against any possible resistance, rebellion, or difference, processing repression after repression by installing a mechanism of control on a personal level—a desire for repression expressed by the emulation of repressive models—and a social level, through the establishment of what Paul Virilio calls a military class whose sole function is to police civil society in the name of national security.[4] Hence Pasolini, Cavani, and Wertmüller equate the violent policing and border controlling of the nazis and the fascists with postwar democratic and global economies and find the same apparatus of distortion operating between what discourse says and what a society does with it. Liberal, democratic, humanitarian, liberating discourses also function as a manifestation of violence. Multiple examples exist: the American B-52 carpet-bombing in North Vietnam was not interpreted as violent but as a declaration of justice, liberty, and peace; similarly, the carpet-bombing of Panama City was presented as "flushing out Noriega"; the Chilean military police who beat and massacred the nation's citizens justified their actions under the rubric of "national security"; the Gulf War and subsequent bombings in Sudan and Afghanistan appealed to "kicking the Vietnam syndrome," "making the world safer for democracy"; and the Yugoslavian civil war has recast the United Nations as a "peace-keeping force" that deters "ethnic cleansing" by "strategic bombings." Terms like "population control," "economic sanctions," and "austerity programs" conceal their agendas to ethnically cleanse, control, and police the peoples of the world.

These films of Pasolini, Cavani, and Wertmüller implicitly argue that the return to moral economies serves to protect the "new order," the form of existing social structures. What appears to rehabilitate national models for Germans and Italians, allowing them to purge themselves of a nazi or fascist past in order to reaffirm moral identities, is in fact a process of editing—a change of ideals and a change of uniforms. The strategy of mimicking this superficial transformation serves to denude otherwise disguised desires for control. Hence, in order to analyze the deployment of historical and symbolic understandings of fascism and the "Final Solution" by current moral discourses and institutions of power, Pasolini, Cavani, and Wertmüller problematize the process through which current political agents identify themselves with such historical figures as antifascists, victims, and survivors. They hyperbolize the construction of subjective identities, thus questioning in particular the formation of resemblances (metonymic or synecdochic) that allow the spectator to identify with a character or an ideal. Their object is to disavow catharsis, that is, the sentiment of redemption—the very sentiment that Steven Spielberg, in his acceptance speech for the Academy Award for Best Picture, has offered as the "right" response to *Schindler's List*. In contrast, the hyperbolic images in *Salò*—sadistic bourgeois fathers and aging femmes fatales made to look like drag queens—*The Night Porter*—repressed homosexual ballet dancers and former nazis with monocles and SS uniforms hidden away in their closets—and *Seven Beauties*—bumbling macho mafiosi and extremely cold and cruel nazi women—cripple attempts to reemploy representations, monuments, and historical emblems in order to make a new collective subjectivity. Instead they compel the images of *einen Mann* (one man) and *richtigen Mann* (right man), as well as what Saul Friedländer calls the Mr. Everyman (in reference to the self-fashioned image of Hitler), to appear ridiculous. As a result, they disavow collective subjectivities that rise out of the ashes of the traditional subjective communities predicated on moral values and national heroes, since these communities reinstigate xenophobic passions—that is, hierarchies, segregations, racism, and the erosion of singularities.

These three films can be read as belonging to the critical thinking that, as Giorgio Agamben has suggested, regards national and moral values of the bourgeoisie as "still attached to a false popular identity," that is, "from a political point of view, fascism and nazism have not been overcome, we still live under their sign" (*The Coming Community*, 63). Pasolini, Cavani, and Wertmüller critique moral projects that judge the inhumanity of fascism and nazism vis-à-vis the same bourgeois model that the nazis and the fascists once used to judge those whom they considered sexually, racially, and ideologically inferior. Because their practice of critiquing conventional (bourgeois) moral models does not aim at dialectical transcendence but at the undermining of such models of repression or suppression, they do not put forward a new moral model. Instead they reveal that the cultural reliance on such a model itself perpetuates blindness to certain fascist notions and practices that have become nearly ubiquitous (cleansing, securing, containing, deterring). Yet this moral or binary model remains culturally ambiguous and thus continues to operate within a multiplicity of ideological and political discourses. Pasolini, Cavani, and Wertmüller do not advocate a *clear* antifascist position—they do not provide the audience with a cathartic release from their possible or potential implication in fascism—they are in turn subjected to the very judgments they set out to critique.

Let me restate the above suggestions by examples from my readings of the films. *Salò*, *The Night Porter*, and *Seven Beauties* present a historic closure—fascism defeated humanist models and revolutionary desires, yet it continues to spread via a desire for control in the name of "civil society," "justice," and the law—in the form of the failure of pleasure or *jouissance*, a complete capitulation to the Sadean logic of the law. This is shocking to many intellectuals on the Left, liberals, and conservatives who desire to overcome fascism, even if it means attempting to graft the democratic ideals of Rousseau and Locke and the ethics of Kant to global corporatization and militarization. As Jean François Lyotard explains, in the context of discussing the failure of Enlightenment ideals, "a republican government is always menaced by the despots surrounding it, and must have as its sole morality its maintenance by any means, [thus] it is ruled out that the means are all moral, that on the contrary it must be immoral men who by their movement of perpetual insurrection keep the republican government on the alert" (*Libidinal Economy*, 90). For example, Pasolini's libertines and Cavani's bureaucrats are meticulous functionaries whose sexual gratifications are, as Baudrillard puts it, "the industrial usufruct of the body, the opposite of all seduction: a product of extraction, a technological product of a machinery of bodies, a logistics of pleasure which goes straight to its objective, only to find its object dead"

(*Seduction*, 20). Within this bureaucratic parody of Dante's hell all human relations are reduced to a sadistic model of power; they are, therefore, manifested as a theatrical form of acting out violent sexuality. Yet each *girone* (circle/act), directly related to sadistic sexual torture, does not lead to a frozen devil at its epicenter (a model of supreme evil) but to an anti-orgy of blood and death (pure articulations of the power of the self over the other). Thus *Salò* returns not only to fascism as the ultimate end of history and continuous site of present violence but also to conventional representations of domination (sexual, economic, patriarchal, legal, etc.). This reproduction of Sade's *A Hundred and Twenty Days of Sodom* relocates the sadistic sexual events to "the last stand" of fascism in *Salò* (the republic of Salò at Lago di Garda), yet Pasolini situates the femme fatale as an accomplice to the institutionalization of sadistic sexual politics.

Shockingly, the victim becomes what Bauman calls a "necessary accomplice," which in turn defamiliarizes the treatment of seduction, as demonstrated in *The Night Porter* and *Seven Beauties*. While both *The Night Porter* and *Seven Beauties* mimic Marlene Dietrich's role of Lola Lola in *The Blue Angel*, their depictions are far less transparent and more ironic than those of the transvestite or the lesbian in Luchino Visconti's *The Damned*, Bernardo Bertolucci's *The Conformist*, and Bob Fosse's *Cabaret*. They subvert the aesthetic reading of fascism as the cult of the visual, in order to render illegible both historical and psychological readings of fascist sexual politics and the Holocaust. Once again, what is at stake here is the inseparability of fascism, representations, and morality.

The battle waged by Pasolini, Cavani, and Wertmüller is not one of equality or establishing a political platform but one of delegitimation of the modernizing process and its narrativizing project, which, they argue, reduces a profusion of entangled events to a unitary narrative, false and misleading. Pasolini, Cavani, and Wertmüller, do not however, endorse what Herbert Marcuse called art's "Great Refusal," since they do not support a heroic consciousness to overcome a repressive discipline's reality principles.[5] Unlike Marcuse's and Heidegger's suspicion of modernity (its one-dimensionality) and Adorno's notion of the negative dialectic, Pasolini, Cavani, and Wertmüller reject the nostalgia for high culture precisely because it advocates a dialectical model of transcendence that is falsely rational and primarily eurocentric (as one can find in Adorno's discussion of jazz). They denounce the neorealist (as well as Marxist) nostalgia (or romantic desire) for a heroic and moral proletariat or peasantry, and the neodecadent nostalgia for aestheticism. It is important, therefore, to examine their cinematic strategy: its endless dissimulation, which draws us into its disruption of authorial gestures, yet at the same time forces us to recognize that this enframing will be unable to escape from the rhetorical deceit it denounces. What Pasolini construes in his "cinema di poesia" is a model of free indirect discourse—a cinematic formalism—that is designed to suspend subjectivity. As Deleuze describes, this cinema of pure form "sets itself up as an autonomous vision of the content perception image and a camera consciousness" (*Cinema 2*, 74). The irony of this pure formalism, this celebration of rupture with subjectivity and creation of art as the truth, is, as Nietzsche points out, that "everything which is good and beautiful depends upon illusion: truth kills, indeed kills itself insofar it realizes its own foundation in error."[6] Thus all art or critical truth must also be self-destructive. The effect of interruption, therefore, is also one of self-destruction. It is for this reason that Pasolini sees modernity as fascism, a process that reacts to criticism and rupture by incessantly historicizing and mastering technology, information, communication, and economies that reduce art (life) to purely an act of scandal—a false pretense of choice, diversity, multiculturalism, and difference in well-ordered, policed, and programmed societies. Modernity presents the turning of lines of escape (subversion, resistance, difference) into lines of disappearance (consumption, absorption, homogenization, globalization, insulation) and the return of fascist order in the form of societies of control. As Pasolini wrote: "il Neo-capitalismo ha vinto sono sul marciapiede" : "Neocapitalism has won, I am out on the street" (*Le Ceneri di Gramsci*, 76). Hence these films ask us to consider what it means to say that we have conquered fascism.

Notes

Introduction

1. Friedrich Holländer, (music) and Robert Liebmann (lyrics), "Ich bin von Kopf bis Fuss auf Liebe eingestellt." My interest in this song is its reference to Josef von Sternberg's 1929 adaptation of Heinrich Mann's novel *Professor Unrat* and *Der Blaue Engel*, especially the character of Lola Lola played by Marlene Dietrich. The original reads "Ich bin von Kopf bis Fuss auf Liebe eingestellt / Denn das ist meine/Welt und sonst garnichts / Das ist- was soll ich machen meine Natur /Ich kann halt lieben nur und sonst garnichts /Männer umschwirren mich wie Motten um das Licht / Und wenn sie verbrennen dafür kann ich nichts /Ich bin von Kopf bis Fuss auf Liebe eingestellt /Denn das ist meine/Welt und sonst garnichts."

2. Michel Foucault, *Cahiers du cinéma*, nos. 251–52 (July–August 1974): 33. Although Foucault's biography seems to implicate him in this "fascinating fascism," here he makes the distinction between nazi moralism and the "pornographic" cult of sadomasochism. While Foucault's position could also be read as presenting a totalizing view of nazism (as possessing an extreme "Victorian" morality, one whose ultimate aim was the annihilation of what it contrived as unhygienic and impure), it is important to note that this moral attitude was an essential part of both nazi and fascist rhetoric, aesthetics, and philosophy. What Foucault draws attention to is the re-representation of nazism as a part of an "erotic," cultural imaginary divorced from its own contextual referents.

3. In *The Unmasterable Past: History, Holocaust, and German National Identity* (Cambridge: Harvard University Press, 1988) 62, Charles Maier observes that Jürgen Habermas (one of the leading figures in the *Historikerstreit*) does not offer "a historical reconstruction of Nazism or the Holocaust but writes a political response to conservative [most notably Ernst Nolte's and Andreas Hilgruber's] mobilization of historical rhetoric for political ends."

4. William Spanos, *Heidegger and Criticism: Retrieving the Cultural Politics of Destruction* (Minneapolis: University of Minnesota Press, 1993) 233. In his analysis of

Lacoue-Labarthe's reference to Auschwitz as a "pure event," Spanos points out that such an interpretation "precludes contextual readings," thereby problematizing interpretation itself.

5. *The Unmasterable Past* 165. Like Spanos, Maier questions the legacy of the Holocaust. He asks, "If the Holocaust must be a debt for Germans, is it automatically an asset for Jews? And if it is an asset must it be shared with other claimants to suffering?"

6. Saul Friedländer, *Reflections on Nazism: An Essay on Kitsch and Death*, trans. Thomas Weyr (Bloomington: Indiana University Press, 1993) 14.

7. Ernst Nolte argues that fascism is complicit with capitalism. He writes, "No Fascist system has been anti-capitalist except in a verbal sense" (*Three Faces of Fascism*, trans. Leila Vennewitz [New York: Holt Rinehart and Winston, 1966] 104).

8. Janet Staiger, *Bad Women* (Minneapolis: University of Minnesota Press, 1995) 13.

9. Theodor W. Adorno and Max Horkheimer, *The Dialectic of Enlightenment*, trans. John Cummings (New York: Continuum, 1989) 168.

10. Zygmunt Bauman, *Modernity and the Holocaust* (Ithaca: Cornell University Press, 1989) 6.

11. Jean-François Lyotard, *Heidegger and "the jews,"* trans. Andreas Michel and Mark Roberts (Minneapolis: University of Minnesota Press, 1990) 77. Lyotard argues that politics never consists in anything but "in taking up again, according to some new model, the task of fashioning." And it is not merely the model of an ideal with which to form the community "that it needs; but also a model of 'how it should be fashioned.... [Yet in the present] 'age of nihilism,' political fashioning can no longer invoke the authority of a metaphysical model, of 'ideas,' 'nature,' of divine truthfulness or goodness, of rational ideals. The philosophical sources are exhausted while a growing anxiety in the face of nothingness strikes and sterilizes modern Europe." And in *The Differend* (trans. George Van Den Abbele [Minneapolis: University of Minnesota Press, 1988] 88) he states: "Auschwitz is a model, not an example.... The 'Auschwitz model' would designate an experience of language that brings speculative discourse to a halt."

12. *Heidegger and Criticism* 233. Spanos argues that the discourse of radical singularity, which makes nazism and the "Final Solution" unreadable, "lends itself to onerous political purposes," such as relativizing other suffering, that of the Vietnamese at the hands of the Americans and the Palestinians at the hands of the Israelis.

13. Omer Bartov, *Murder in Our Midst: The Holocaust, Industrial Killing, and Representation* (New York: Oxford University Press, 1996) 136.

14. *New Conservatism: Cultural Criticism and the Historians' Debate* (Cambridge: MIT University Press, 1989) 229–30.

15. Primo Levi, *I Sommersi e i salvati* (Turin: Einaudi, 1986) 685.

16. Sande Cohen, *Passive Nihilism: Cultural Historiography and the Rhetorics of Scholarship* (New York: St. Martin's Press, 1998) 2. Cohen defines passive nihilism as the "supplying of 'brakeshoes' on the production of sense and meaning, using concepts against the proliferation of concepts. Such texts eliminate improprieties of thinking. They bring 'must' to the status of encoding the unsupervised, the discrepant, the errant, the 'floating', and insofar as such texts support transforming existing contentions into necessities, they belong to genealogies of conflict between the affirmation of nihilism—the logic of affirming the least negative of choices—and resistance to nihilism's presently powerful intuitions." See also Friedrich Nietzsche's *The Will to Power* (trans. Walter Kaufmann and R. J. Hollingdale [New York: Random House, 1967 § 1–37]), where he distinguishes radical nihilism from passive nihilism on the grounds that radical nihilism is purely critical, while passive nihilism is an incomplete form of nihilism, which "attempts to escape nihilism

without reevaluating our values so far: producing the opposite, making the problem more acute."

17. Andrew Hewitt, *Political Inversions* (Stanford: Stanford University Press, 1996) 38–39.

18. Paul de Man, *The Resistance to Theory* (Minneapolis: University of Minnesota Press, 1987) 58.

19. Pasolini argues: "La continuità (dei codici, la violenza poliziesca, il disprezzo per la Costituzione) tra fascismo fascista e fascismo democristiano è completa e asoluta ... In tale universo i <<valori>> che contavano erano gli stessi che per il fascismo: il Chiesa, la patria, la famiglia, l'obbedienza, la disciplina, l'ordine, il risparmio, la moralità." ("The continuity (of codes, police violence, the despair over the Constitution) from fascism to the fascism of the Christian Democrats is complete and absolute. In this sort of universe the values that are important are the same as the fascists': the Church, *patria*, family, obedience, discipline, order, thrift, morality.") *Scritti Corsari* (Milano: Garzanti, 1990) 129.

20. *Modernity and the Holocaust* 23. Bauman argues that this "participation" was a gradual process of dehumanization, a process of stripping away rights, forcing Jews to compete with each other for the basics of survival: it was "a complex system of interaction and distancing of the unsightly or morally repelling outcomes of action to the point of rendering them invisible to the actor, making invisible the very humanity of the victims." Yet Bauman also points out that class differences still operated in the Jewish Ghetto: "The poor died first, and in droves, so did the unresourceful, meek, naive, honest, unpushing ... seldom was the mere concern with self-survival so close to moral corruption."

21. Marguerite Waller, "Signifying the Holocaust: Liliana Cavani's *Portiere di Notte*," in *Feminism in the Cinema*, ed. Laura Pietropalo and Ada Testafferri (Bloomington: Indiana University Press, 1995) 199.

22. See Nancy Harrowitz's essay "Representations of the Holocaust: Levi, Bassani, and the Commemorative Mode," in *Reason and Light: Essays on Primo Levi*, ed. Susan Tarrow (Ithaca: Cornell University Press, 1990), where she argues that "the Holocaust text illustrates simultaneously the survival of the writer and the failure of the text to adequately represent."

1. Between Remembering and Surviving

1. Liliana Cavani, *The Night Porter* (*Il portiere di notte*) (Turin: Einaudi, 1974) introduction, x. The original reads "L'ambiguità della natura umana e quindi della sua storia è il punto dal quale, secondo la mia opinione, occorre patire per cercare di capire. Infatti, è l'analisi dell'ignoranza che si riscontra nel dopoguerra che ci fa capire meglio l'ignoranza che ha permesso la guerra, che ha permesso le dittature. Aveva ragione a scadalizzarsi la sopravvissuta milanese: il mondo allora non vuole sapere! Allora non vuole prevenire, ci ricasherà."

2. Jean-François Lyotard, *Libidinal Economy*, trans. Ian Hamilton Grant (Bloomington: University of Indiana Press, 1993) 60–64. Lyotard points out that the correlation of power to sexual relations is purely a construct predicated on surplus value, on the concept of prostitution.

3. For an analysis of the student movements see Rossana Rossanda's *L'anno degli studenti* (Bari: De Donato, 1986); Giuseppe Bocca's *Noi terroristi: Dodici anni di lotta armata ricostruiti e discussi con i protagonisti* (Milan: Garzanti, 1985); Todd Gitlin's *The Sixties: Years of Hope, Days of Rage* (New York: Bantam, 1987); George Katsiaficas's *The Imagination of the New Left: A Global Analysis of 1968* (Boston: South End Press, 1987); Tom

Vague's *Televisionaries: The Red Army Faction 1963–1980* (Edinburgh: AK Press, 1994); and Stefan Aust's *The Baader-Meinhof Group: The Inside Story of a Phenomenon*, trans. Anthea Bell (London: Bodley Head, 1987).

4. Student movements proclaimed an antiauthoritarian stature; however, militancy against authority on many levels turns inward on the family. This renewed rejection of all forms of authority recalls the principal manifestos of the futurists, in which the family was also attacked as a source of repression and oppression, the only difference being that the discourse of the student manifestos was not laden with misogyny. In addition, these movements were deeply committed to leftist revolutionary politics. Unlike France, where student politics clashed with those of the French working class, in Italy students allied with workers—a role traditionally reserved for the PCI and the PSI. This provided them with a considerable amount of political influence. However, the militancy of these movements caused prominent leftist intellectuals such as Jürgen Habermas to fear the rise of a "fascism of the Left." As Luciano Castillano remarks, the violence caused by militancy was "a positive affirmation of new and powerful productive subjects, born out of the decline of the centrality of the factory and exposed to the full pressure of the economic crisis (quoted in Antonio Negri, *Revolution Retrieved* [London: Red Notes, 1988]).

5. Both the official Left and Right reacted to these movements via traditional means of repression—dismissal, armed suppression, repudiation. Although the PCI did not officially physically participate in the suppression of the students' movement nor the rallies of the radical Left, the party leaders made their position very clear by not coming to the defense of the protesters, nor appealing to civil liberties, rather, Berlinguer even suggested that the students were fascists.

6. Ronald Reagan's statement illustrates his solidarity with the center-Right German Chancellor Helmut Kohl, whose disclaimer was that he was lucky enough to have been born after the rise of nazism: "Die Gnade der späten Geburt." Does this imply, however, that he is entitled to forget? The politics of forgetting in this case appeal to widespread psychological notions present in the defense of criminal cases, creating a culture of victims that diffuses accusations of responsibility. (Reported in the *New York Times*, 19 April 1985). For analysis of the political implications of Bitburg and the politics of forgetfulness, see *Bitburg in Moral and Political Perspective*, ed. Geoffrey Hartman (Bloomington: University of Indiana Press, 1986).

7. Andreas Hillgruber, *Zweierle: Untergang* (Berlin: Siedler, 1986).

8. I am not only referring to the political instability in Europe during these years of armed conflict and multiple terrorist acts but also the crisis of representation, what Habermas calls the "legitimation crisis" and Fredric Jameson the "de-realization of modernity." It is the dilemma of construing a historical subject in lieu of fragmentation of narrative forms. Similar to the modernist questioning of master-narratives and ideological generalizations, post-1968 intellectuals saw the collapse of distinctions such as truth and lie, fact and fiction, official history and popular culture.

9. In December 1997 Le Pen was indicted for "belittling" nazi war crimes by claiming that "the Nazi concentration camps were a detail in the history of the Second World War" (see the *New York Times*, 7 October 1998). The indictment only boosted his popularity.

10. *Reflections on Nazism* 12. Second quote from Michel Foucault's *Foucault Live*, trans. John Johnston (New York: Semiotext(e), 1989) 93.

11. Lanzmann claims that *Shoah* is neither a documentary nor "representational at all" but rather a fiction of the real. "Seminar with Claude Lanzmann, April 11, 1990," *Yale French Studies*, no. 79, 1991.

12. Thomas Elsaesser, "Subject Positions, Speaking Positions: From *Holocaust, Our Hitler,* and *Heimat* to *Shoah* and *Schindler's List*," in *The Persistence of History: Cinema, Television, and the Modern Event,* ed. Vivian Sobchack (London: Routledge, 1996) 145.

13. Michael Geyer, "The Politics of Memory in Contemporary Germany," in *Radical Evil,* ed. Joan Copjec (London: Verso, 1996) 186.

14. Dominick LaCapra, *Representing The Holocaust: History, Theory, Trauma* (Ithaca: Cornell University Press, 1994) 92.

15. Ibid. 93–102.

16. In *The Unmasterable Past* Maier argues that the "[Klaus] Barbie trial suggested that victimhood was prized. This fact brings us to one of the most problematic legacies of the Holocaust" (164).

17. For an analysis of the Heidegger controversy of the mid-eighties see Victor Farías, *Heidegger et le nazisme* (Paris: Lagrasse, 1987), which starts the European debate over the postwar reading of Heidegger; "Symposium on Heidegger and Nazism," in *Critical Inquiry* (winter 1988), which, like Richard Wolin's *The Politics of Being: The Political Thought of Martin Heidegger* (New York: Columbia University Press, 1992), turned the debate over Heidegger into a debate over deconstruction and posthumanist theory; and William Spanos's chapter "Heidegger, Nazism, and the Repressive Hypothesis," in *Heidegger and Criticism,* where he links the renewed interest in Heidegger's affiliation with the nazi party to a political maneuver of the liberal Left against deconstruction and postmodern theory. He argues that Arnold Davidson's critique of Heidegger (appearing in the winter 1989 issue of *Critical Inquiry*) exhibits a "discursive slippage, suggesting it is intended rather to engage the ideological frame of reference … Davidson's ultimate purpose is not simply to undermine Heidegger's argument against humanism as such—his displacement of Man from the center—but also to recuperate the lost authority of humanism." See also Jacques Derrida's *Memories for Paul de Man,* (New York: Columbia University Press, 1988). Derrida points out that the violent condemnation of both de Man and Heidegger reached beyond nazism and the postwar work of both thinkers to include the deconstructive discourse.

18. *Murder in Our Midst* 133. In the chapter "Just One Witness," Carlo Ginzburg argues that in "normal historiographical practice, the value of each document will be tested by the way of comparison, that is, by constructing a series including at least two documents." And it is these "documents" that he equates to *preuves* (proofs) without questioning the validity of the document, or who it was that recorded such a document. Here the document stands in for proof, providing clues as to how to read a certain historical event.

19. Sande Cohen, *Historical Culture: On the Recording of an Academic Discipline* (Berkeley: University of California Press, 1986) 128.

20. Hayden White, "The Modernist Event," in *The Persistence of History: Cinema, Television, and the Modern Event,* ed. Vivian Sobchack (London: Routledge, 1996) 20–22.

21. "The Modernist Event" 21. Here White argues that the discrepancy between fact and meaning "is usually taken to be a basis of historical relativism," which "distinguishes modernism in the arts from all previous forms of realism." Hence he views the "modernist event" as a distinct treatment of "historical reality."

22. For a discussion of the issue of historical revisionism as pertaining to the Faurisson case see Pierre Vidal-Naquet's *Assassins of Memory: Essays on the Denial of the Holocaust,* trans. Jeffrey Mehlman (New York: Columbia University Press, 1992).

23. Perry Anderson, "On Emplotment: Two Kinds of Ruin," in *Probing the Limits of Representation,* ed. Saul Friedländer (Cambridge: Harvard University Press, 1992) 65.

24. Dominick LaCapra, "Lanzmann's *Shoah*: Here There Is No Why," *Critical Inquiry*, no. 23 (winter 1997). What I am getting at is that historians are accusing popular media of not being historical at the same time they express reservations about historicizing such events as the "Final Solution." Hence this crisis or trauma is complicated by the trauma or crisis of historical discourse and its uneasy relationship (inauthentic) to its subject matter.

25. By invoking "Radical Evil" I am referring to Hannah Arendt and the neo-Kantian reappropriation of the term, rather than Kant, who coined the term, since the neo-Kantians apply radical evil to the nazis (specifically the Holocaust). Arendt describes radical evil in *The Origins of Totalitarianism* (Cleveland: Meridian, 1958) as "unforgivable absolute evil which could no longer be understood by the evil motives of self-interest, greed, covetousness, resentment, lust for power, and cowardice; and which therefore anger could not revenge, love could not endure, friendship could not forgive. Just as the victims in the death factories or the holes of oblivion are no longer 'human' in the eyes of their executioners, so this newest species of criminals is beyond the pale even of solidarity in human sinfulness. It is inherent in our entire philosophical tradition that we cannot conceive of a 'radical evil'.... There is only one thing that seems to be discernible: we may say that radical evil has emerged in connection with a system in which all men have become equally superfluous."

26. Etienne Balibar and Immanuel Wallerstein, *Race, Nation, Class: Ambiguous Identities*, trans. Chris Turner (London: Verso, 1992) 51.

27. *Representing the Holocaust* 75. See also Adorno, *Negative Dialectics* (New York: Continuum, 1973) 365. Adorno argues that Auschwitz represents the limits of the Enlightenment since "its sneering mockery of truth may be more true than the superior consciousness." I want to point out that LaCapra and even Adorno distinguish themselves from the criticism of Hannah Arendt, who, as Steven E. Aschheim points out, emphasized the "absolute centrality of the Jews in the creation and maintenance of the modern state economy, their instinctive alliances with the ruling elites and concomitant deep alienation from 'society' and the implication that the Jews bore some responsibility for their predicament, that indeed their actions and roles were not disconnected from the emergence of modern antisemitism" ("Hannah Arendt and the Discourse of Evil," *New German Critique* no. 79 [winter 1997]): 127. For an argument that questions the responsibility or the lack of rebellion by the European Jews during World War II, see Arendt's *A Report on the Banality of Evil: Eichmann in Jerusalem* (New York: Penguin, 1963; hereafter *Eichmann in Jerusalem*) and Raul Hilberg's *The Destruction of the European Jews* (Chicago: Quadrangle, 1961).

28. Maurice Merleau-Ponty, *Sense and Non-Sense*, trans. Hubert L. Dreyfus and Patricia Allen Dreyfus (Evanston: Northwestern University Press, 1964) 141.

29. Jacques Rancière, *The Names of History: On the Poetics of Knowledge*, trans. Hassan Melehy (Minneapolis: University of Minnesota Press, 1994) 51.

30. Hannah Arendt, *Eichmann in Jerusalem* 135–36. See also Andrew Hewitt's discussion of Arendt, Kant, and the "Final Solution" in "The Bad Seed: Auschwitz and the Physiology of Evil," in *Radical Evil*.

31. Sande Cohen, *Academia and the Luster of Capital* (Minneapolis: University of Minnesota Press) 78.

32. In fact, the first phase of nazi war crimes tribunals, the Nuremberg Trials (1950s), was considered a complete failure, unlike the second phase of trials (1960s), in which Eichmann was tried.

33. "Cavani's *The Night Porter*: A Woman's Film?" *Film Quarterly* 30 (1976–77): 36. De Lauretis points out that many Europeans who grew up during the era of "la dolce vita"

or the economic miracle of the 1950s witnessed the conscious and institutional dismissal of their fascist past. Yet, as she argues, "the heritage of fascism remained and festered."

34. Hewitt, "The Bad Seed: Auschwitz and the Physiology of Evil" 92.

35. Ella Taylor, "Fatuous Fascism," *LA Weekly* (22 October 1998): 47.

36. Millicent Marcus, *Italian Film in the Light of Neorealism* (Princeton: Princeton University Press, 1986). See specifically her chapter on *Love and Anarchy*.

37. In her introduction to *The Night Porter* Cavani reveals that the source and inspiration for the making of the film came from information she obtained during the making of *La donna della Resistenza* (a documentary film made for television, 1965).

38. Eli Pfefferkorn, "Bettelheim, Wertmüller, and the Morality of Survival," in *Postscript: Essays in Film and the Humanities*, vol. 1, no. 2 (winter 1982): 15–26.

39. "Sade Is Within Us," trans. Mark Pietralunga, *Stanford Italian Review*, vol. 2, 2 (fall 1982) 108. Calvino's thinking, as Lucia Re explains, is "deeply marked by the vibrant atmosphere of the postwar Reconstruction and the neorealist movement in the arts that accompanied it. The sense of political commitment found in his work of this period is inseparable from his experience as a partisan in the anti-Fascist Resistance during World War II and as a militant member of the Italian Communist Party." (*Calvino and the Age of Neorealism: Fables of Entanglement* [Stanford: Stanford University Press, 1990] 2).

40. Naomi Greene, *Pier Paolo Pasolini: Cinema as Heresy* (Princeton: Princeton University Press, 1990) 202.

41. Alvin Rosenfeld, "Another Revisionism: Popular Culture and the Unchanging Image of the Holocaust," in *Bitburg in Moral and Political Perspective*, ed. Geoffrey Hartman (Bloomington: University of Indiana Press, 1986).

42. Pauline Kael, "The Current Cinema: Stuck in the Fun," *The New Yorker* (7 October 1974): 51–52.

43. Jean Baudrillard, *The Evil Demon of Images*, trans. Philippe Tanguy (Sydney: Power Publications, 1988) 43.

44. Roland Barthes, *Mythologies*, trans. Annette Lavers (New York: Hill and Wang, 1972) 152.

45. The incentive for Herdhitze (whose name means "heat of the furnace," a pun on his role in the death camps) to merge with Klotz (whose name "millstone round one's neck" [stump or handicap]) satirizes both the fact that he is in a wheelchair and the "crippled consciousness" of the postwar generation of German capitalist/bourgeoisie) is blackmail. Each knows the other's darkest secret: Herdhitze exterminated many Jews, while Klotz's son practices bestiality with pigs.

46. For a discussion of the involvement of capitalist industries in the Holocaust see Christopher Simpson's *Splendid Blond Beast* (Monroe, Maine: Common Courage Press, 1995), which discusses the affinity of European criminals, American big business, and intelligence organizations (specifically the CIA) for former nazi war criminals. See also Henry Ashby Turner's *German Big Business and the Rise of Hitler* (New York: Oxford University Press, 1985), which outlines the continual involvement of capitalist enterprise in the formation of the nazi state; and Charles Maier's *Recasting Bourgeois Europe* (Princeton: Princeton University Press, 1975), which explores the reconstruction of the image of the bourgeoisie.

47. For an analysis of the relationship of science to modernity and the "Final Solution" see Mario Biagioli's "Science, Modernity, and the Final Solution" in *Probing the Limits of Representation*, ed. Friedländer, 185–205, where he argues that nazi scientific method was not exceptional; it is only after the fact that historians and cultural critics have denounced nazi doctors. However, he points out that the scientific method and the "belief

in the symbiosis between science and the values of modernity as expressed in the culture of Western democracy, are seriously threatened by [having to account for nazi scientists]." As he suggests: "Holocaust scholars are struggling with the interpretive problems posed by an event like the Final Solution, which took place within the framework of modernity and yet seemed to subvert all the values commonly associated with that culture."

48. The advent of what the Left called "Strategia della Tensione" was set off by the bomb that exploded in the Banca Nazionale dell'Agricoltura in Milano's Piazza Fontana. The media in compliance with the police accused the extreme Left (anarchists in particular, helped and covered by the PCI) of the bombings (in Milan as well as two other bombings that took place on the same day, 12 December 1969); however, evidence that the police had chosen to ignore pointed not to the anarchists but to a neofascist group based in Veneto (under the command of Giovanni Ventura, who was closely associated with Guido Giannettini, a colonel in the SID, the Italian secret service). Because Giannettini was also closely linked to the MSI, as were other members of the SID, an investigation of the SID ensued. The blaming of the anarchists could not have happened without the splintering of the Left into faction groups, some more militant than others. Leftist political thinkers like Quazza saw the bombings as the reaction of the Right to the wave of change that swept all of Europe after May 1968. In Italy, however, contrary to France, the student movement was not made of two separate and hostile parts, the students and the workers. By 1969 the unions had obtained the "Statuto dei Lavoratori," a charter of workers' rights, which the factory councils, modeled on Gramscian theory, had real power, and the students had obtained a series of radical changes in the school system. The country was crossed by waves of strikes. On the Left, however, many people started thinking that the PCI was too soft and not revolutionary enough to succeed in changing the sociopolitical system. In the period of the late sixties to the early seventies many movements emerged from the Left: some of them were splinter groups from the PCI (il Manifesto, for instance); others were more Marxist-Leninists, or Maoists (centered on the vogue of the Chinese Cultural Revolution). Movements including Servire il Popolo and *PC-ML* (Maoists), Lotta Continua (Sofri, Bobbio, the more social Marxist, *moimentisti*), Potere Operaio (lead by Toni Negri, Oresete Scalzone, Franco Piperno), and Collettivi Politici Metropolitani, which then became Brigate Rosse, were born. Theses groups ranged from radical-chic intellectual, to *operaisti* to *trotzkisti* to *neo-terzinternazionalisti* (often modeled on the Fueguistas of Che Guevara). Many groups preached and even started to practice forms of armed struggle. For an analysis of the student movements and the politics of the Left see Antonio Negri's *Revolution Retrieved* (London: Red Notes, 1988); Rossana Rossanda's *L'anno degli studenti* (Bari: De Donato, 1986); Mario Moretti's *Brigate rosse: Una storia italiana* (Milan: Anabasi, 1994); and Giuseppe Bocca's *Noi terroristi: Dodici anni di lotta armata ricostruiti e discussi con i protagonisti* (Milan: Garzanti, 1985) and *Il terrorismo italiano, 1970–1978* (Milan: Rizzoli, 1978). For a study of the secret service see Giuseppe De Lutiis's *Storia dei servizi segreti* (Rome: Editori Riuniti, 1984); Giorgio Bocca's *Il filo nero* (Milan: Mondadori, 1995); and Giorgio Galli's *Storia del partito armato* (Milan: Rizzoli, 1986), *La destra in Italia* (Milan: Gammalibri, 1983), *La crisi italiana e la destra internazionale* (Milan: Mondadori, 1974), and *La sfida perduta: Biografia politica di Enrico Mattei* (Milan: Bompiani, 1976).

49. *Heidegger and "the jews"* 58.

50. Otto Weininger, *Sex and Character*, trans. W. Heinemann (London: Putnam, 1906) 22.

51. For a reading of cabaret, see Peter Jelavich's *Berlin Cabaret* (Cambridge: Harvard University Press, 1993), where he describes the forum of *The Blue Angel* as a "third rate

variety show that was a direct precursor of cabaret." Jelavich explains that the cabaret mixed different issues, specifically sex, race, politics, fashion, and sexuality, hence it was a place (albeit often censored) of liberal thinking and political satire.

2. Feminizing Fascism

1. *The Blue Angel* opens with Dietrich singing in a cabaret; one of the songs is this one. The voice of Dietrich emphasizes the erotic masculinization of excessive feminine sexuality in the sentimental content of many of Dietrich's songs; this song is anomalous as it lacks the sentimental and even tragic qualities of the majority of Dietrich's recordings. It can also be conceived as a challenge to a man who wants to fashion himself as a he-man, and at the same time it plays with the politics of the time.

2. Benedetto Croce, *Scritti e discorsi politica* (Bari: Bompani, 1956). Croce's statement serves two purposes: first, to reflect the desire to forget, to bracket fascism as an aberration, yet also to erase the monumental traces of the conversion of the fascists to nonfascists. Although I do not in any way suggest that Croce was part of this process of defascisizing the intelligencia, his statement suggests a willing dismissal. Ironically, it was made at the same time that popular culture, as well as academic culture, attempted to represent fascism. Hence, while the image of Mussolini may not have appeared in Italian films and television until 1994, when Berlusconi allowed the documentary footage of Mussolini's death to be shown for the first time on national television (Rai uno), the allegorical and metaphorical image of Mussolini appears in almost every re-representation of fascism, from the character Spatoletti in Wertmüller's *Love and Anarchy* to Magnello in *The Conformist*. In addition, Berlusconi's interview with the *Washington Post* suggests that Mussolini was a figure to be revered, in "certain respects" (26 April 1995, A25).

3. Marshall McLuhan, *Understanding Media: The Extensions of Man* (New York: Signet, 1964) 41–44.

4. Pier Paolo Pasolini, *Empirismo eretico* (Milano: Garzanti, 1972) 145. The original reads "E a questa forza negativa-positiva (nella sua violenza anarchiaca, nella sua rabbia pacifista, nella sua religione del misticismo democratico ecc.) si aggiunge la forza *puramente negativa* della rinascita nazista? Ma si può parlare di rinascita nazista. È mai morto il nazismo? Non siamo stati dei pazzi a crederlo un episodio? Non è esso che ha definito la piccola borgehesia <<normale>> e che continua a definirla? C'è qualche ragione per cui i massacri in massa razzistici debbano essere finiti, coi loro lager, le loro camere a gas ecc.?" And he continues: "Le forze nuove, che si scatenano come negative rispetto al razionalismo di questa borghesia <<normale>> che massacra gli ebrei a millioni ecc., son forse un specie di anticorpi di salvezza? Il loro desiderio di morte è salutare?"

5. For a discussion of the function of the dialectic in terms of the identification and the constitution of the law, the nation, and the individual, see Hegel's *Philosophy of Right*, trans. T. M. Knox (London: Oxford University Press, 1952). The Hegelian subject, which is dependent on the nonidentical, takes form from the popular spirit forming both nation-state and individual, which are identical models of "ethical life." My interest is in Hegel's addressing sexuality and sexual difference in terms of the dialectic, in which he designs the destiny of the sexes in terms of public and private spheres. Although for Hegel "civil-society" and the state are masculine spheres, in the private or family sphere the sexes become one. In her *This Sex Which Is Not One* (trans. Catherine Porter [Ithaca: Cornell University Press, 1985]), Luce Irigaray provides a seminal analysis of the Hegelian ontological construction and its replication by Freud and then Lacan, and their grounding of it in sexual difference.

6. *The Unmasterable Past* 1–21. Maier argues that the point of such representations of victims is not whether they are correct or false, "but that they correspond to the historians' ideological starting point." More important than the "historical truth," for Maier, is the understanding of the "choices that historical actors faced to convey the objective and the perceived alternatives confronting his protagonists" (22).

7. Omer Bartov, *Murderers in Our Midst* 82–84. Bartov writes: "even the heavy emphasis on 'rape' and 'orgy' was characteristic, as we have seen, of contemporary linguistic usage; depraved sex and Satan went well together in both the practice and the propaganda of the Third Reich. The 'male fantasies' of the Freikorps' commanders seem to have traveled a long way." He points out Hillgruber's references to Russian women as capable of terribly mutilating a soldier, infecting him with venereal or other infectious diseases, and making unscrupulous use of their sexual advances for the purposes of espionage.

8. For a critical analysis of the circularity of the dialectic see Theodor Adorno's critique of Hegel (in particular) in *Negative Dialectics*.

9. Miriam Hansen argues in "Adventures of Goldilocks: Spectatorship, Consumerism, and Public Life" (*Camera Obscura*, no. 22 [January 1990]: 56) that "women's status within the public sphere shifted from a discourse of domesticity to an updated ideology of consumption, superimposing models of feminine virtue and female skills with appeals of pleasure, glamour and leisure, of sensuality, eroticism and exoticism."

10. Sandra Gilbert and Susan Gubar, *No Man's Land: The Place of the Woman Writer in the Twentieth Century, War of the Words*, vol. 1 (New Haven: Yale University Press, 1988) 22. See also Janet Staiger's *Bad Women* (Minneapolis: University of Minnesota Press, 1995).

11. For an analysis of the connection of Freud to Weininger see Misha Kavka's "The 'Alluring Abyss of Nothingness': Misogyny and (Male) Hysteria in Otto Weininger," *New German Critique* no. 66 (fall 1995): 124.

12. Ibid. In response to the debate as to whether Weininger can be read representative of a cultural milieu present at the turn of the century, or whether he must be considered as an individual, Kavka argues that "the impact of Weininger's study suggests that a large, implicitly male intellectual audience identified with Weininger's hatred of women, and, through the vehicle of misogyny, his hatred of Jews. . . . *Sex and Character* went through 28 editions between the years 1903 and 1947—twelve editions in the first seven years after publication, with four in 1904 alone."

13. F. T. Marinetti, "Contro la Spagna Passatista," from *Teoria e invenzione futurista* a cura di Lucian De Maria (Milan: Arnoldo Mondadori Editore, 1990) 43.

14. F. T. Marinetti, "Abasso il tango e Parsifal!," in *Teoria e invenzione futurista*, a cura di Luciano De Maria (Milan: Arnoldo Mondadori Editore, 1968) 95–96.

15. Jean Baudrillard, *Seduction*, trans. Brian Singer (New York: St. Martins, 1990) 8.

16. Simonetta Falasca-Zamponi, *Fascist Spectacle: The Aesthetics of Power in Mussolini's Italy* (Berkeley: University of California Press, 1997).

17. Although many of the distinctions among the decadents, symbolists, primitivists, futurists, and vorticists are unclear—for example, Wilde and D'Annunzio contribute not only to the "disprezzo della donna" but also to the worship of male youth—their sensual encoding of masculine sexuality in particular and their celebration of the leisure class, disgust for popular culture, and distrust of industrialization marked their disdain. For a literary and theoretical analysis of D'Annunzio, Nietzsche, Lombroso, and Nordeau and the politics of decadence, see Barbara Spackman's *Decadent Genealogies: The Rhetoric of Sickness from Baudelaire to D'Annunzio* (Ithaca: Cornell University Press, 1989) and Nancy Harrowitz's studies of Cesare Lombroso (*Anti-Semitism, Misogyny, and the Logic of*

Cultural Difference in Cesare Lombroso and Matilde Serao [Lincoln: University of Nebraska Press, 1995]) and Otto Weininger (*Jews and Gender: Response to Otto Weininger*, ed. Nancy Harrowitz [Philadelphia: Temple University Press, 1995]).

18. Emilio Gentile, "The Conquest of Modernity: From Modernist Nationalism to Fascism," trans. Lawrence Rainey, *Modernism/Modernity*, vol. 1, no. 3 (September 1994): 57.

19. Raymond Williams, *The Politics of Modernism* (London: Verso, 1989) 52. Williams's interest in the notion of revolution such as the "futurists' call to destroy tradition" was in its "overlapping with socialist calls to destroy the whole existing social order." He distinguishes the futurists, who he argues are "worlds away from the socialists" since they did not have a "tightly organized party which would use scientific socialism to destroy the hitherto powerful and emancipate the hitherto powerless." See also Guy Debord, *Society of the Spectacle* (Detroit: Black and Red Press, 1983).

20. In her seminal biography on Mussolini, *Dux* (Milano: Mondadori, 1926), Margherita Sarfatti clarifies the connection of Mussolini to the futurists as a certain revolutionary nationalist idealism that positioned itself as a Nietzschean force of the Überman against the mediocrity of the herd or the mass, yet it was precisely the mobilization of the masses that sustained Mussolini's popularity. In *Dux*, Sarfatti greatly contributes to the transcendental myth of Mussolini as the Duce: "Il Mussolini come idealista rivoluzionaro contro il Giolitti piccolo-borghese conservatore (mediocre)."

21. In *Lustmord: Sexual Murder in Weimar Germany* ([Princeton: Princeton University Press, 1995] 149), Maria Tartar points out that in the fourth volume of Alfred Döblin's tetralogy *November 1918*, he sexualizes the assassination of Rosa Luxemburg by "presenting Luxemburg as the victim of sexual hysteria and even placing the devil to whom she becomes a sexual slave at the site of her shooting . . . she becomes more or less a victim of unrestrained sexual desires."

22. Here I would include not only the aesthetics of the femme fatale as she is presented in German Expressionist films—Lola Lola; "the woman from the city" in Friedrich Wilhelm Murneau's *Sunrise* (*Die Nacht der Regisseure*, 1927); as well as the mechanical vamp/good Christian (Maria) as portrayed by Brigette Helm in Fritz Lang's *Metropolis* (1926)—but also public images of Clara Bow, Marlene Dietrich, Greta Garbo, and Louise Brooks. While remaining sexualized objects, these actresses and characters make sex into a gesture, a sensual and iconic game of masks and surfaces, as opposed to the weak seductive fatale images of Pastrone's Cabiria and Sofonisba, who can only draw their suitors into their own helplessness.

23. With "ironic," I am directly referring to Hayden White's adaptation of Vladmir Propp's narrative categories and White's analysis and application of these narrative strategies to various ideological forms of representation as outlined in the introductory chapter of *Metahistory* (Baltimore: Johns Hopkins University Press, 1973).

24. For a Deleuzian reading of Dietrich's roles, see Gaylyn Studlar's *In the Realm of Pleasure* (New York: Columbia University Press, 1988). Studlar adopts Deleuze's distinction of masochism as a separate discourse from that of sadism, modeling her argument on Deleuze's *Masochism: Coldness and Cruelty* (New York: Zone Books, 1988).

25. Theodor Adorno criticizes the film for misusing the book, turning its social critique into a commodity by selling Dietrich's legs. He sees the film as a product of the "cultural industry" rather than a poignant social critique (*Gesammelte Schriften* [Frankfurt, Suhrkamp, 1974] 656–57).

26. Siegfried Kracauer, *From Caligari to Hitler: A Psychological History of the German Film* (Princeton: Princeton University Press, 1947) 217.

27. John Orr, *Cinema and Modernity* (Oxford: Polity Press, 1993) 89.

28. Georges Bataille, *The Accursed Share*, trans. Robert Hurley (New York: Zone Books, 1991) vols. 2 and 3.

29. Slogan from Mussolini's fascist regime in the 1930s.

30. Victoria De Grazia, *How Fascism Ruled Women* (Berkeley: University of California Press, 1992) 5. De Grazia argues that the biological politics stemmed from an "ideology of scarcity" that was designed to create an artificial boost in the economy during the period of economic depression. Hence the decline in fertility served two functions: to enact a social disciplining of women and to prepare Italy for a colonial war in North Africa.

31. Klaus Theweleit, *Male Fantasies*, vol. 1, trans. Stephen Conway (Minneapolis: University of Minnesota Press, 1987). Theweleit analyzes the vagina as a "sea of delights," a "garden, drenched in the dew of voluptuousness," a utopian site that is not lacking, yet at the same time it is a mouth that "sucks the marrow from men's bones." As a utopian sea of voluptuousness, woman receives male sexuality without recourse, yet as a mouth, woman, metonymically reduced to the vagina, is sexualized, hence she is masculinized, and hence there is not only the fear of sexual impotence in the face of a sexual challenge, but the fear that she is in fact more masculine than man based on her ability to desire. In *Divine Decadence: Fascism, Female Spectacle, and the Makings of Sally Bowles* (Princeton: Princeton University Press, 1992), Mizejewski claims that this impotence is derived from the nervous "disavowal of what is unknowable about the female body." Although the female body is made into a spectacle and fetishized as such it simultaneously challenges male subjectivity—"female sexuality is posited in a tension between the blatant visibility of female spectacle and fear of the unknown" (9).

32. For a discussion of the connections of Italian cinema of the fascist era to the filmic stylization and cinematic space of German Expressionist cinema, see the chapter titled "The Myth of the Grand Hotel" in James Hay, *Popular Film Culture in Fascist Italy: The Passing of the Rex* (Bloomington: Indiana University Press, 1987).

33. *Birth of Tragedy*, trans. Walter Kaufmann (New York: Modern Library, 1966) § 18.

34. Randy Rutsky, "The Mediation of Technology and Gender: *Metropolis*, Nazism, Modernism," *New German Critique* no. 60 (1993): 51–55.

35. For an analysis of portrayals of Jack the Ripper, see Sander Gilman's "I'm Down on Whores: Race and Gender in Victorian London" in *The Anatomy of Racism*, ed. David Goldberg (Minneapolis: University of Minnesota Press, 1990), and for a discussion of the relationship of anti-Semitism to antifeminism in the work of Lombroso, see Nancy Harrowitz's *Anti-Semitism, Misogyny and the Logic of Cultural Difference* (Lincoln: University of Nebraska Press, 1994).

36. Gertrud Koch, in her essay "Between Two Worlds: Von Sternberg's *The Blue Angel* (1930)," *German Film and Literature: Adaptations and Transformations*, ed. Eric Rentschler (New York: Methuen, 1986), points to Siegfried Kracauer's "socio-psychological critique" of the film (in *From Caligari to Hitler*) as one of the sources that recodify *The Blue Angel* as an "a posteriori apocalyptic prophecy."

37. Susan Sontag, "Notes on Camp," in *Against Interpretation* (New York: Farrar Straus Giroux, 1966) 275, and Andrew Ross, *No Respect: Intellectuals and Popular Culture* (New York: Routledge, 1989) 140.

38. Mizejewski, *Divine Decadence* 25.

39. For an analysis of the masculinist image of Mussolini see Karen Pinkus's *Bodily Regimes: Italian Advertising Under Fascism* (Minneapolis: University of Minnesota Press, 1995) and Simonetta Falasca-Zamponi's *Fascist Spectacle: The Aesthetics of Power in Mussolini's*

Italy (Berkeley: University of California Press, 1997). For an analysis of the rhetoric of the regime see Barbara Spackman's *Fascist Virilities* (Minneapolis: University of Minnesota Press, 1996).

40. Leonardo Paggi, "Antifascism and the Reshaping of Democratic Consensus in Post–1945 Italy," *New German Critique* no. 67 (winter 1996): 102–107.

41. "The End of the Avant-garde" 13. He continues: "The problematical individual, the acceptance of whom had provided the bourgeoisie with an alibi behind which to hide its own poor conscience, had had a right to citizenship in Italy for a while by presenting himself as 'committed,' and it was precisely the bourgeoisie that wanted and accepted him this way: alibi upon alibi, the alibi of commitment upon the alibi of the problematical. Today, commitment has become useless to the Italian bourgeois consciousness, which has overcome poverty and has crossed industrialization's first finish-line. Now, it is the problematical individual who objects to the abnormal, the Different, etc."

42. "Antifascism and the Reshaping of Democratic Consensus in Post–1945 Italy" 102.

43. Millicent Marcus, *Italian Film in the Light of Neorealism* xiv, 23. Here Marcus establishes neorealism as a stylistic movement whose aim is verisimilitude, and a film movement, the "vehicle for a new national identity, and as the conscience of a country coming to terms with its recent historical past." As a means of legitimizing neorealism as an ethical movement, Roberto Rossellini declares "my own personal neorealism is nothing but a moral stance that can be expressed in four words: love of one's neighbor." (*My Method*, trans. Anna Paola Cancogni [New York: Marsilio, 1992] 44.)

44. André Bazin, *What Is Cinema?* vol. 1, trans. Hugh Gray (Berkeley: University of California Press, 1967) 29.

45. Lucia Re, *Calvino and the Age of Neorealism: Fables of Estrangement* (Stanford: Stanford University Press, 1990).

46. For an account of the resistance in Italy see Roberto Battaglia's *Storia della Resistenza italiana* (Turin: Einaudi, 1964); Laura Conti's *La Resistenza in Italia: 25 luglio 1943–25 aprile 1945* (Milan: Feltrinelli, 1961); Claudio Pavone's *Resistenza e storia d'Italia* (*Belfagor* 32, no. 2, 1977); chapter 1 of Paul Ginsborg's *A History of Contemporary Italy* (London: Penguin, 1990); and C. R. S. Harris's *Allied Military Administration in Italy 1943–1945* (London, 1957).

47. In *Film, Politics, and Gramsci* (Minneapolis: University of Minnesota Press, 1994), Marcia Landy defines neorealism as an opposition to the "epic representations of monumental history with their glorification of the past ... the neorealists sought to redefine politics as well as history. In reaction to the public sphere of politics and spectacle characteristic of the Fascist regime, the postwar filmmakers identified politics in more personal terms."

48. Peter Brunette, *Roberto Rossellini* (New York: Oxford University Press, 1987) 45.

49. Angela Dalle Vacche, *The Body in the Mirror: Shapes of History in Italian Cinema* (Princeton: Princeton University Press, 1992) 196.

50. *Fascist Modernism: Aesthetics, Politics, and the Avant-Garde* (Stanford: Stanford University Press, 1993) 70. Hewitt explains Lukács's model of decadence as a "holding that historical periods follow on in a cycle of decay or—stated more positively—that prior to the emergence of the proletariat as the objective subject of history, decadence and progress are indivisible. The decadent self-liquidation of the bourgeoisie is progressive, active, destructive—but ultimately constructive in its unleashing of concrete historical forces."

51. Bram Dijkstra, *Idols of Perversity: Fantasies of Feminine Evil in Fin-de-Siècle Culture* (Oxford: Oxford University Press, 1986) 29.

52. For a description and analysis of *strapaese* and *stracittà*, see James Hay's *Popular*

Film Culture in Fascist Italy, where he argues that "*strapaese* proponents desired more popular and social myths about the machine and industry than those offered by the futurists," whom he labels proponents of *stracittà* and the aestheticization of the industrial revolution.

53. Pierre Sorlin, *Italian National Cinema: 1896–1996* (New York: Routledge, 1996) 97.

54. For a reading of the symbolism of pagan, Christian, and Renaissance myth in *Open City*, see Marcus's reading of the film in *Italian Film in the Light of Neorealism* 33–53.

55. Barbara Spackman, *Fascist Virilities* 24–25.

56. Homi Bhabha, "Of Mimicry and Man: The Ambivalence of Colonial Discourse," *October* 28 (spring 1984): 126.

57. In *Against Interpretation* Susan Sontag attempts to qualify the postwar return to the decadent as a modern version of dandyism: "Detachment is the prerogative of an elite; and as the dandy is the nineteenth century's surrogate for the aristocrat in matters of culture, so Camp is the modern dandyism" (288). She also argues, erroneously I believe, that "it goes without saying that camp sensibility is disengaged, de-politicized, or at least apolitical" (277).

58. Jean Baudrillard, *Simulations*, trans. Paul Foss, Paul Patton, and Philip Beitchman (New York: Semiotext(e), 1983).

59. *Reflections on Nazism* 19.

60. Wilhelm Reich, *Character Analysis*, trans. Vincent Carfagno (New York: Farrar, Straus, Giroux, 1949) 222–23. Reich argues that within this maldeveloped economy, the phallic-narcissistic-sadist fantasizes the woman as having a penis and his own penis becomes associated with the breast. Hence identification with woman causes the male not only to become a narcissist but also a sadist. Similarly, Marcuse argues in *Eros and Civilization* (Boston: Beacon Press, 1966) that "Narcissistic Eros engulfs the reality in libidinal relations which transform the individual and his environment; but this transformation is the isolated deed of unique individuals, and as such, it generates death ... as an isolated individual phenomenon, the reactivating of narcissistic libido is not culture-building but neurotic."

61. Eve Kosofsky Sedgwick, *Epistemology of the Closet* (Berkeley: University of California Press, 1990) 62. Sedgwick argues, "The emphasis on the Homo-, on the dimension of sameness, built into modern understanding of relations of sexual desire within a given gender, has had a sustained and active power to expose that fractiousness, to show how close may be the difference or even the melting between identification and desire."

62. Jean Baudrillard, *Simulacra and Simulation*, trans. Sheila Faria Glaser (Ann Arbor: University of Michigan Press, 1994) 46.

63. Caryl Flinn, "The Deaths of Camp," *New German Critique* 67 (winter 1996): 59. Flinn adds that this critique is "a typically 1970s approach but one that by no means has run its course."

64. Wilhelm Reich, *Character Analysis* 219. Sigmund Freud, "A Child Is Being Beaten," in *The Complete Works of Freud* (London: Hogarth Press, vol. 17, 1955), 107. Here Freud argues that homosexuality is a form of masochism, hysteria, and obsessional neurosis, thus underlining the notion that homosexuality is a sexual inversion.

65. See Judith Butler's *Bodies That Matter: On the Discursive Limits of "Sex"* (New York: Routledge, 1993) 190. In Butler's analysis of the work of Slavoj Žižek, she argues that "the production of the unsymbolizable, the unspeakable, the illegible is also always a strategy of social abjection." She points out that in Žižek's theoretical adaptation of the Lacanian model of language, the socially contingent rules of subject return to the model of sexual difference.

66. Anton Kaes, "History, Fiction, Memory": Fassbinder's *The Marriage of Maria Braun*, in *German Film and Literature*, ed. Eric Rentschler (New York: Methuen, 1979) 283. Kaes notes that when Maria recognizes that she is not the agent of her own fate but an object of financial transaction between her lover and her husband, "the gesture of betrayal is projected and magnified from the private onto the public sphere: the German nation, if one follows the film's logic, was betrayed when Adenauer, despite painful memories of military past, made a secret deal to rearm Germany."

67. David Bathrick, "Inscribing History, Prohibiting and Producing Desire: Fassbinder's *Lili Marleen*," *New German Critique* no. 63 (fall 1994): 37.

68. Slavoj Žižek, *Enjoy Your Symptom* (London: Routledge, 1992) 114.

69. Ibid 127. I would like to clarify that this convergence of the Jew with the feminine pertains to both nazism and fascism, as both parties merely utilized a ready-made category of impurity. In fascism, racism (in terms of anti-Semitism) is only a late development.

70. Jean-François Lyotard, *The Differend* 103.

71. Slavoj Žižek, *The Metastases of Enjoyment* (London: Verso, 1994) 148.

72. *Modernity and the Holocaust* 90–91. Bauman argues that "rage and fury are pitiably primitive and inefficient as tools of mass annihilation. They normally peter out before the job is done. Modern Genocide is an element of social engineering, meant to bring about as social order conforming to the design of the perfect society."

73. Sigmund Freud, *Sexuality and the Psychology of Love* (New York: Macmillan, 1963) 217.

74. Jean-François Lyotard, *Libidinal Economy*, trans. Iain Hamilton Grant (Bloomington: Indiana University Press, 1993) 80.

75. Maria Antonietta Macciocchi, *La dona "nera": "Consenso femminile e fascismo* (Milan: Feltrinelli, 1976) 100.

76. Gilles Deleuze, *Masochism: Coldness and Cruelty* 59.

3. *Salò*

1. Georges Bataille, "Reflections on the Executioner and the Victim," trans. Elizabeth Rottenberg, ed. Claire Nouvet, *Yale French Studies, Literature and the Ethical Question*, 1991, 18–19. Bataille argues, vis-à-vis the novels of David Rousset, that the concentration camps delimited suffering: "never can we establish a limit once a man advances far into suffering; he cannot be assured that a barrier which resisted in the past will not be broken. And what precisely can be admired in the event of a trial survived and in the victory of life is that life, discovering itself to be in the hands of horror and knowing itself to be at the mercy of physical affliction."

2. Italo Calvino, "Sade Is Within Us" 110.

3. Giuseppe Zigaina, "Total Contamination in Pasolini," trans. Giuseppe Zigaina and James Carolan, *Stanford Italian Review* 4, no. 2 (fall 1984): 270.

4. Enzo Siciliano, *Vita di Pasolini* (Milan: Rizzoli, 1978) 389. He proceeds by asking, "Did Pasolini ask himself to die?" The implication here is of course that *Salò* was a suicidal film. This interpretation is echoed in Naomi Greene's analysis as well as the writings of Roland Barthes and numerous others who read the film as Pasolini's own despair over his homosexuality and his inability to create a utopian discourse out of gay politics. The problem with these readings is that they assume Pasolini was naive, as Barthes often does, thereby insinuating that it was not until *Salò* that Pasolini realized that utopian politics were doomed to fail.

5. Maria Antonietta Macciocchi, *Pasolini* (Paris: Bernard Grasset, 1980) 56. More specifically than "society" taking its revenge (as Macciocchi claims), it was the social apparatus patrolling its parameters. Pasolini's relentless implications about the participation of institutions (capitalism, moralism, bourgeois aestheticism, communism, socialism) in what Deleuze and Guattari call the fascist war machine led to the institutions taking their revenge on Pasolini.

6. Beverly Allen, "Poetics of Heresy: Introduction" *Stanford Italian Review* 4, no. 2 (fall 1984): 1. Giuseppe Zigaina, "Total Contamination in Pasolini": 270. Zigaina assesses Pasolini's methodology as one of "contamination," stating, "this contamination does not exclude from its mixture of various languages the language of his physical being, or of his political and social acts, or in short of his general behavior, including the very last moments of his life, that is his death."

7. Millicent Marcus, in the foreword to William Van Watson's *Pier Paolo Pasolini and the Theatre of the Word* (Ann Arbor: UMI Press, 1989) xi. Watson, *Pier Paolo Pasolini* 12–16. Alberto Moravia, "Pasolini Poeta Civile," *Italian Quarterly* 21–22, no. 81–83 (fall-winter 1980–1981): 11. Moravia argues, "il marxismo è sempre molto razionale, anzi scientifico. In Pasolini invece c'era questo sentimentalismo, questo comunismo sentimentale . . . Pasolini si accostò al terzo mondo, si accostò alle civiltà passata, si accostò anche al dramma antico."

8. Paolo Valesio, "Pasolini Come Sintomo," *Italian Quarterly* 21–22: 31–43.

9. Pier Paolo Pasolini, interview with Philippe Bouvard, in a program called *Dix de Der*, cited in Barth David Schwartz, *Pasolini Requiem* (New York: Pantheon, 1992) 662.

10. In *A Thousand Plateaus* Deleuze and Guattari argue that fascism is distinctly not totalitarian in nature since "unlike the totalitarian State, which does its utmost to seal all possible lines of flight, fascism is constructed on an intense line of flight, which it transforms into a line of pure destruction and abolition."

11. Franco Ferrucci, "Il J'accuse di Pasolini," *Italian Quarterly* 21–22, no. 82–83 (fall-winter 1980–1981): 14. The original reads: "Senza contare la parola 'fascista,' completamente inflazionata per tutti gli anni settanta. Pasolini la applica a tutto quello che non gli piace. In ogni caso, è sempre la borghesia alle origini del male."

12. For readings on the continued presence of fascist leaders in Italian politics see Petra Rosenbaum's *Il nuovo fascismo: Da Salò ad Almirante: Storia del MSI*, intro. Carlo Rossella (Milan: Feltrinelli, 1975); S. Colarizi's, *La seconda guerra monidale* (Turin: UTET, 1984); S. Setta's *L'Uomo qualunque, 1944–1948* (Bari: Laterza, 1975); and Guido Quazza's *Resistenza e storia d'Italia: Problemi e ipotesi di ricerca* (Milan: Feltrinelli, 1976). The presence of former fascist leaders and the popular support for such figures was not only a cause for alarm for Pasolini but also proof of the existence of neofascism outside of its historical context. For Pasolini, fascism pre- and postdated Mussolini. More importantly, the newly formed government under De Gaspari (a Vatican librarian) was perceived as the dawn of a new fascist era, since by 1947 De Gasperi made his political agenda clear: he was to align himself with the neocapitalists (what he called the "fourth party, the nation's wealth and economic power") and to delegitimize the communists and socialists on the grounds that they were "paralysing and rendering vain every effort by organizing the sabotage of the national loan, the flight of capital, inflation and the diffusion of scandal campaigns." (Article of 2 June 1949 by R. De Caterini, quoted in Paul Ginsborg's *A History of Contemporary Italy*.) The exclusion of the communists and socialists from the newly formed government directly corresponded to a movement toward the extreme right, toward the *L'Uomo qualunque* and the *monarchisti*. Demographically, a large portion of the supporters of the former fascists came from the south (especially in the ranks of the *L'Uomo qualunque*, which would later form the MSI).

13. In addition, Togliatti was reproached by the Left for making no serious effort to prosecute and purge the Italian government of fascist elements during his term as Minister of Justice (1945–46). De Gaspari's denunciation of the Left was accompanied by pressure from U.S. Secretary of State George Marshall to govern without the communists, and a progressive taxation designed by Einaudi to slow down the rate of inflation, although its effects were credit restrictions, which squeezed small business and amounted to widespread unemployment, especially within the factories, where the Left had its popular foothold.

14. Gilles Deleuze, "Postscript on the Societies of Control," *October* (winter 1992): 3–7. Michel Foucault, *Discipline and Punish: The Birth of the Prison,* trans. Allan Sheridan (Middlesex: Penguin Books, 1977). Pasolini takes a cue from the early forties' Marxist and sixties' leftist and controversial interpretations of fascism: that it was a general phenomenon (Karl Otten, *A Combine of Aggression: Masses, Elites, and Dictatorship in Germany,* London: G. Allen & Unwin, 1942); an explosion of "industrial crisis," "a part of 'modern pathology'" (Detlev Peukert, *Inside Nazi Germany,* trans. Richard Devenson, New Haven: Yale University Press, 1982); a fascist epoch comprising Italian fascism, the French *Action Française,* and National Socialism (Ersnt Nolte, *Der Fachismus in seiner Epoche,* Munich: R. Piper, 1963); that it ambiguously combined modernizing and reactionary influences (Karl-Dietrich Bracher, *Turning Points in Modern Times: Essays on German and European History,* trans. Thomas Dunlap (Cambridge: Harvard University Press, 1995) and that it was schizophrenic (Detlev Peukert).

15. Paul Virilio, *Speed and Politics,* trans. Mark Polizzotti (New York: Semiotext(e), 1986).

16. I am thinking of Paul de Man's definition of irony, in which he argues that irony is beyond the discontinuity of sign and meaning. Irony dislocates the narrative from its temporality and is context, rendering the making of history impossible. For de Man, the ironic trope is self-conscious of its own inability to be historical. Irony, therefore, calls into question interpretive apparatuses—historical, ideological, etc. (*Blindness and Insight: Essays in the Rhetoric of Contemporary Criticism* [Minneapolis: University of Minnesota Press, 1971] 209–28). For a discussion of irony in relation to historiography see Hayden White's *Metahistory,* and in relation to cultural theory see Linda Hutcheon's *Irony's Edge: The Theory and Politics of Irony* (New York: Routledge, 1995).

17. *Sade mon prochain: La philosophie scélèrat* (Paris: Aux Editions du Seuil, 1967) 24.

18. See Carlo Ginzburg, "Just One Witness"; Hayden White, "Historical Emplotment and the Problem of Truth"; Martin Jay, "Of Plots, Witnesses, and Judgments"; and Amos Funkenstein, "History, Counter-history, and Narrative," all in *Probing the Limits of Representation: Nazism and the "Final Solution,"* ed. Saul Friedländer; Jürgen Habermas, "Concerning the Public Use of History," *New German Critique* 44 (1988), and his *The New Conservatism: Cultural Criticism and the Historians' Debate,* ed. and trans. Shierry Nicholsen (Cambridge: MIT University Press, 1989); and Martin Boszat and Saul Friedländer, "A Controversy About the Historicization of National Socialism," *New German Critique* 44 (1988).

19. Barthes, *Sade, Fourier, Loyola,* trans. Richard Miller (Berkeley: University of California Press, 1989) 151.

20. Jean-Luc Nancy, "The Unsacrificeable," trans. Allan Stoekl, *Yale French Studies* 79 (1991): 32.

21. Reinhart Koselleck, *Futures Past: On the Semantics of Historical Time,* trans. Keith Tribe (Cambridge: MIT University Press, 1985) 216.

22. *Vita di Pasolini* 383. The original reads "sono corpi, questi che Pasolini ci storta in

Salò, senza il povero e casto splendore della Trilogia della vita. Sono corpi che il colore fa grigi, certamente belli, ben proporzionati, ma annientati, cancellati nella loro bellezza, dall'inferno in cui sono stati rapiti."

23. Sade perceives pleas for retribution as irrational, therefore they fall outside of the law. That is, the law does not intervene in terms of personal revenge. Only the libertine law would permit the reaction to transgression, but this would entail the complete submersion in the sadistic logic of the republic.

24. As Kant explains, "it can only give as a Law, form, and to itself a transcendental principle" (*Critique of Judgment*, 19 § 16).

25. Blanchot explains that according to Sade "man's sovereignty is based on a transcendental power of negation, a power that does not depend on the objects it destroys; for their destruction does not even need to suppose their previous existence, because, at the moment in which it destroys them it has already, in advance and at all times, considered them as nonexistent (*Lautrèamont et Sade* [Paris: Les Editions de Minuit, 1949] 245). The original reads "l'originalité de Sade nous semble dans la prétention extrêmement ferme de fonder la souveraineté de l'homme sur un pouvoir transcendant de négation, pouvoir qui ne dépend en rien des objets qu'il détruit, qui, pour les détruire, ne suppose même pas leur existence antérieure, parce que, au moment où il les détruit, il les toujours, déja, antérieurement, nuls pour nuls."

26. Although Locke, Montesquieu, Kant, Hobbes, Rousseau and many others are also implicated in constructing natural law to legitimize the law itself, I am thinking here of Hegel's *Philosophy of Right*, where he predicates the "philosophical science of right" on the definition of "what is legal." This "positive right or law" is defined only in opposition to "inclination, caprice, and the sentiments of the heart." Hence law is divided from the will (as passions) and realigned with reason, yet a reason that is only defined as a process of negation, negating that which does not divest in its passion, in its self-interest or singularity and does not conform to a universal will of reason itself. The problem for Sade, and later for Pasolini, is the disjuncture of the desire for moral purity and the desire for rationality. Since it is precisely the extreme will of reason to replace the mystical belief in God with itself, in the process it discounts the moral purity espoused by Christianity in respect to God, by delegitimizing the moral (Christian model itself). Once this model is deconstructed, reason belies its own enlightened implication, since it no longer can justifiably use morality as a means to legitimation.

27. See Sade's *Philosophy of the Bedroom*, trans. Richard Seaver and Austryn Wainhouse (New York: Grove Press, 1965) 308. Here he is directly responding to social contract theories as outlined by Rousseau (*The Social Contract*), Locke (*Two Treatises of Government*), Hegel (*Philosophy of Right*), and Hobbes (*Leviathan*), since they predicate their models of the social contract and civil society on a state of nature that is completely separate from the social obligation (i.e., a self-determined state of nature). Sade points to the enigma that plagues these theories, the slippage between absolute authority (the unmovable mover) that is outside the law (also outside civil society), and the subjugation of self-determined individuals to a common good that is represented by the uncommon, that speaks in their name. For Sade, governors that emerge from these theoretical apparatuses, like libertines, know their own authority to be illegitimate, that is, they do not comply with the very laws they represent. See also Hegel's *Philosophy of Right*, where he discusses freedom of the will as solely a concept, based upon self-mediation (23–25).

28. Similar to Paul Feyerabend's argument in *Farewell to Reason* (London: Verso, 1987), xi, where he presents reason as a distorting agency of objectivity, and rationality its process of normalization or the effect of a forced accommodation, Pasolini and Sade

focus less on the decoding of reason than on representing its effects. Their concern, like Feyerabend's, is "neither rationality, nor science, nor freedom—[since] abstractions such as these have done more harm than good—but the quality of the lives of individuals." Feyerabend continues by arguing, "Reason has been a great success among philosophers who dislike complicity and among politicians (technologists, bankers etc.) who don't mind adding a little class to their struggle for world domination. It is a disaster for the rest, i.e. practically all of us. It is time we bid it farewell."

29. Peter Sloterdijk, *Critique of Cynical Reason*, trans. Michael Eldred (Minneapolis: University of Minnesota Press, 1987) 237.

30. I am referring to Nietzsche's use of the word *ressentiment* in *Thus Spake Zarathustra* (see chapter 1).

31. If reason is unleashed on the transcendental model of the common good (Rousseau), which constantly defers man's identity onto a futuristic narrative of becoming (striving to perfection, Rousseau's reason, Hegel's ideal, Plato's form of the good), then it undermines not only the mythic or irrational genealogy of the common will but also the forward-looking projection of man. This rational negation, therefore, exterminates the humanist idea of man.

32. Klossowski explains the republican state's ironic play on Enlightenment logic: "The republican state pretends to exist for the public good; but if it is clear that it cannot bring about the reign of the good, no one suspects that in its depths lurks the germs of evil; under the pretext of preventing the germs of evil from hatching, the new social order claims itself victorious over evil. A constant threat lies in the depths of this order: the evil that never breaks out but can do so at any moment. This chance for evil to break out is the object of de Sade's constant anxiety; evil has to break out once and for all. It is necessary to make evil reign in the world in order that it destroy itself ... Liberty refuses to recognize that it lives only through evil and claims to exist for the state of good." The original reads "L'État républicain prétend exister pour le bien public: mais, s'il est évident qu'il ne peut faire régner le bien, personne ne soupçonne qu'en son fond il entretient les germes du mal; sous prétexte d'empêcher les germes du mal d'éclore, le nouveau régime social se prétend victorieux du mal; et c'est là précisément ce qui constitue une meance perpétuelle: le mal qui peut éclater à tout instant bien qu'il n'éclate jamais. Cette chance du mal qui n'éclate jamais mais qui peut éclater à tout instant, cette chance est l'angoisse perpétuelle de Sade; il faut donc que le mal éclate une fois pur toutes, il faut que l'ivraie foisonne afin l'esprit l'arrache et le consume. En un mor, il fout faire régner le mal une fois pour toutes dans le monde, afin qu'il se détruise lui-même et que l'esprit de Sade trouve enfin as paix. Mais il n'est pas question de penser à cette paix, il est impossible d'y songer un instant puisque chaque instant est rempli de la meance du mal, alors que la Liberté se refuse à reconnaître qu'elle ne vit que par le mal et prétend exister pour le bien" (*Sade mon prochain* 64).

In his *Of Glamor, Sex, and De Sade* (Wakefield, New Hampshire: Longwood Academic, 1991) Timo Airaksinen argues that Sade's version of utopia is the establishment of a new social contract "between his libertine heroes in order to make injustice and cruelty artificial, for when it is artificial it can be controlled and enjoyed without bitterness of mind" (13).

33. Julia Kristeva, *The Powers of Horror: An Essay on Abjection*, trans. Leon S. Roudiez (New York: Columbia University Press, 1982) 4, 27.

34. Here Sade inverts both the concept of the Platonic ideal and Thomas Hobbes' construction of the body politic. Hobbes, returning to the dilemma of the question of being in relationship to the notion of becoming, constitutes the body politic on scientific principles of motion. Ironically Hobbes attempts, theoretically, to bridle this motion so that politics will function like a machine rather than face another British revolutionary

war. Sade adopts the very notion of permanent motion and applies it to revolution, undermining Hobbes' plea for civil society. See chapters 1 and 2 in "Of Man" in *Leviathan* (New York: Penguin Books, 1968).

35. Georges Bataille, *Literature and Evil,* trans. Alastair Hamilton (London: Marion Boyars Press, 1973) 123–24.

36. The blatant disapproval of *Salò* on the part of Sade scholars calls up a number of questions: What is at stake in Sade's texts? What makes Barthes, the great semiotic and cultural theorist, protect the written word (Sadean style of writing) against visualized interpretation? And what makes Calvino, the postmodern Italian writer and friend of Pasolini, defend the "real" symbolic significance of Sade's transgressive literature and the real political significance of World War II that cannot be transgressed?

37. While Sciascia places himself as a victim at the hands of the film—it attacked his "Christian love for Pasolini" and plunged him into a "moral and intellectual darkness"—Calvino interprets this darkness as Pasolini's own pedagogical desperation, which proves Pasolini's inability to make critical points. That is, Pasolini is too caught up in his own personal tragedies to make any critical statements. Barthes, on the other hand, reacts to the film by protecting Sade from being read as a fascist: "if there were some fascism in Sade, some fascism does not mean fascism."

38. Barthes' own reading of Sade decontextualizes as well as analogizes the text to modern contexts in an attempt to show the present significance of Sade: "the Sadean practices appear to us today to be totally improbable; however, we need only travel in any underdeveloped country (analogous, all in all, to eighteenth-century France) to understand that they are still operable there: the same social division, the same opportunities for recruitment, the same availability of subjects, the same conditions for seclusion, and the same impunity, so to speak" (*Sade, Fourier, Loyola,* 132). Similarly, he interprets fascism as a product of bourgeois culture, yet he rejects the connection of the two contexts, since he maintains Sadean thought as radically subversive thinking that can still be used to critique (from the inside) bourgeois cultural hegemony. Thus it seems rather disingenuous to critique Pasolini for misreading Sade and to object to his use of the historical context of fascism as an analogy for an extreme model for sexual politics or as a limit of transgression, given the popularization and precedent of readings by Wilhelm Reich (*Character Analysis*), Klaus Theweleit (*Male Fantasies*), Maria Antonietta Macciocchi, and George Mosse in which the origin of fascism and nazism is returned to the Freudian discourse of sexual perversion closely linked to sadism as a manifestation of repressed homosexuality.

39. Georges Bataille, *Eroticism: Death and Sensuality,* trans. Mary Dalwood (San Francisco: City Lights, 1986) 176.

40. Roland Barthes, "Pasolini-Sade," *Stanford Italian Review* (fall 1984): 101.

41. For a discussion of the semiotics of film see Christian Metz's *Film Language: A Semiotics of Cinema* (New York: Oxford University Press, 1974), which attempts to establish a system of analytic tools in order to read film language, and Pasolini's own discussion of film in "The Cinema of Poetry" (*Cahiers du cinéma* no. 6, December 1966), in which he argues that "language of poetry in cinema is bound to a particular form of free indirect cinematic discourse."

42. Linda Williams, *Hard Core: Power, Pleasure, and the "Frenzy of the Visible"* (Berkeley: University of California Press, 1989) 184–88. The second section of the quote is a paraphrase of Bazin in *What Is Cinema?* vol. 2, where he discusses eroticism and the cinema, arguing that "actual sexual emotion by performers is contradictory to the exigencies of art" (173).

43. For example, the spectator can sexually fantasize about Marilyn Monroe by watching her skirt blow in the air in *Seven Year Itch*, since she is offered as a sexual object for general consumption (projection, fantasy), but cannot participate (become a secretive accomplice) in the viewing of the sexual violence of *Salò* because in the film these objects of sexual violence are already consumed, thus causing the possibility of jealousy, competition, or lack of interest. The film breaks the taboo of visualizing what cannot be seen, thus revealing the hypocrisy of voyeurism itself, which causes a crisis for social repression, where it becomes a crime for the spectator to mimic what is considered a mimicry of reality. That is, the visualization of the all-too-real becomes hyperreal and more criminal than simply reading or knowing about murder or sex. This "see and learn" mentality, therefore, is connected to the territorialization of the object of seduction.

44. Jean Baudrillard, *Stratégies fatales* (Paris: Grasset, 1983).

45. In "Merde Alors" (*Stanford Italian Review* 2, no. 2 [fall 1982]: 85) Leo Bersani and Ulysse Dutoit write that "capitalism operates under the law of destruction, it is a return to chaos, yet not a ritualistic supra-sensual, but a supra-carnal, a sadistic mastery over bodies and others as objects of consumption."

46. *Pasolini* 401. Here he connects his critique of modern sexuality to the progressive politics and referendum, especially the referendum on abortion. The reason for all of this emptiness is the death of notions of the sacred and their intersections with the discourse of sexuality, which thereby renders sexuality *la soddisfazione di un obbligo sociale* ("the satisfaction of a social obligation") rather than an act of intimacy.

47. Gilles Deleuze, *Chaosophy*, trans. Sylvève Lotringer (New York: Semiotext(e), 1995).

48. *The Logic of Sense* 165–67. Deleuze defines the Aion as opposed to Chronos, which is "an encasement, a coiling up of relative presents, with God as the extreme circle or the external envelope.... Inside Chronos, the present is in some manner corporeal. It is the time of mixtures, of blendings, the very process of blending; to temper or to temporalize is to mix. The present measures out the action of bodies and cause. The future and past are rather what is left of passion in a body."

49. Jean Baudrillard, *The Ecstasy of Communication*, trans. Bernard and Caroline Schutze (New York: Semiotext(e), 1987) 50.

50. Here I am using "inauthentic" to refer back to Heidegger's connection of inauthentic time to cognition. The Aion is also set up as a time outside of time, an ironic or inauthentic time of cognition that is divorced of chronological time.

51. Georges Bataille, *Literature and Evil* 120–23.

52. Annie Le Brun, *Sade: A Sudden Abyss*, trans. Camille Naish (San Francisco: City Lights, 1990) 88.

53. The quotation as cited in *Salò* is from Marcel Proust's *A la recherche du temps perdu*, the section titled "A l'ombre des jeunes filles en fleur." For a reading of Proust's dandyism, see Walter Benjamin's "The image of Proust," in *Illuminations* (New York: Schocken, 1969).

54. Sigmund Freud, *Civilization and Its Discontents*, trans. James Strachey (New York: Macmillan, 1961) 65.

55. Hence the answer to Freud's question "What does woman want?" is a child. Yet Lombroso, Weininger, and Nordeau distinguish this desire as a maternal desire, differing from the desire of the prostitute, which is always for masculine power. Here Pasolini ridicules and connects the thinking of Lombroso, Weininger, Nordeau, and even Freud to sadism.

56. Sigmund Freud, "Fetishismus," in *Sexuality and the Psychology of Love*, trans. James Stachey (New York: Macmillan, 1927) 373. For Freud, the fetish serves a dual purpose: it is a "token or triumph over the threat of castration, and it also saves the fetishist from being a homosexual by endowing women with the attribute which makes them acceptable as a sexual object." That is, women become acceptable when they have a penis, which would, even in a disguised form, make them men.

57. Julia Kristeva, *Tales of Love*, trans. Leon S. Roudiez (New York: Columbia University of Press, 1987).

58. Julia Kristeva, *Des Chinoises, des femmes* (Paris, 1977) in *The Kristeva Reader*, trans. Marion Boyars (New York: Columbia University Press, 1986) 139.

59. One of the raconteuse demands, "Eva, su, vieni, tu, cara, fai vedere quello nascosto" ("Eva, come here and show us what you have hidden"). The raconteuse undresses Eva, exposing her breasts and her genitalia. Then, attempting to sell her merchandise, she solicits the libertines, "guardate che meraviglia, il culleto delizioso, sordo come non sono mai visti, due pettini" ("look what a marvel, what a delicious ass, firm like you have never seen, two small breasts").

60. Ben Lawton, "The Evolving Rejection of Homosexuality," The Sub-Proletariat, and the Third World in the Films of Pier Paolo Pasolini," *Italian Quarterly* 21–22, no. 82–83 (fall-winter 1980–1981): 171–72. See also Alphonso Linguis's argument in the introduction to his translation of Klossowski's *Sade mon prochain*, where he states, "sodomy is an act done to gore the partner and release the germ of the species in his excrement."

61. "The Evolving Rejection of Homosexuality," 172. Here I wish to question Pasolini's alleged rejection of homosexuality in particular. This argument reads Pasolini back into his work, and in doing so it decontextualizes the more radical implications about sexuality.

62. *Lautrèamont et Sade*, 255. The original reads "L'énergie est, en effet, une notion parfaitement équivoque. Elle est à la fois réserve de forces et dépense de forces, affirmation qui ne s'accomplit qu'avec la négation, puissance qui est destruction. En outre, elle est fait et loi, donnée et valeur. Il est très frappant que, dans cet univers de l'effervescence et de la passion, Sade, loin de mettre au premier plan le désir, l'ait subordonné et jugé suspect. C'est que le désir nie le solitude et condiut à une dangereuse reconnaissance du monde d'autrui."

63. Slavoj Žižek, *The Indivisible Remainder: An Essay on Schelling and Related Matters* (London: Verso, 1996) 172–73.

64. Pier Paolo Pasolini, "La Realtà" *Poesia in forma di rosa* (Milan: Garzuati, 1964).

65. Pier Paolo Pasolini, "Stylistic Reaction," trans. Paul Vangelisti, in *Stanford Italian Review* 2, no. 2 (fall 1982): 22.

4. Mixing Memory with Desire

1. "Within These sacred halls / vengeance is unknown / Since one forgives the enemy/ He/she who does not rejoice in such teachings / Does not deserve to be called a human being" The importance or intersection of Mozart in my text is in reference to Liliana Cavani's *The Night Porter*. In the film, the playing of the opera is juxtaposed with and overlaps the protagonist's (Lucia's) memory of being in a concentration camp, watching a male prisoner be sodomized by a nazi guard. The question of humanity not only intersects with the notion of the high art that Wertmüller's nazi commandant (in *Seven Beauties*) collects (which, according to high cultural values, would afford her a position among the humanists, in their love for human excellence and artistic production) and the writing of Primo Levi, which does not draw on the ideology of what it means to be human in "classical"

terms but speaks from the position of the victims and their encoding in the nazi discourse on humanity.

2. "Nobody wants to speak about responsibility. The innocent don't feel like talking about blame, but neither do the criminals that have subscribed to the pretense that 'What has happened has happened'; orders are orders, the thesis of the necessity of following orders that mitigates the juries at hand to brood over judging the criminals of war. It is always the fault of some functionary who was superior; this is how blame passes from head to head, arriving finally at Hitler. Only Hitler must therefore be guilty."

Cavani argues that it is the victims who are most interested in preserving the memory of their own victimization, and the *carnefice*/victimizer who desires to escape into the darkness. Both Lucia, who seems to want to hide in some type of obscurity by becoming the bourgeois wife of an American conductor, and Max express the desire to live in the darkness, to live "like a mouse" (*un topo*) as Max suggests. Yet all of the characters in *The Night Porter* are drawn to the past as the site of communal binding and also a place of unshakable fascination.

3. Russell Davis, "The Night Porter," *The London Observer*, cinema section, 27 October 1974: 29. Davis's critique is an aesthetic one situating *The Night Porter* within the context of neodecadent films. He writes, "these steel heels, that squeaky leather coat, that monocle! The all-singing, all-dancing, sexy old SS men are back in *The Night Porter* . . . I know the SS were awful, but they were rather gorgeous . . . Liliana Cavani's film offers the familiar litanies of sexual ambivalence, plus two ponderous hours of special pleading on behalf of sadomasochistic relationships. . . . The atmosphere of Cabaret is pure Lesbian night-club. Even on the men the uniforms are drag." David Sterritt, "The Night Porter," *Christian Science Monitor*, 30 December 1974: 16. Sterritt takes Cavani to task for failing to achieve a moralistic reading of humanity: "Miss Cavani attempts to make some kind of statement about the meanness of the human condition but the message gets lost amid its extremely foul surroundings. *The Night Porter* pretends a great seriousness, but actually wallows in what it sets out to condemn." Henry Giroux, "The Challenge of Neo-Fascist Culture," *Cinéaste* 6, no. 4 (1975): 31. Giroux's critique is much more scathing in its morally righteous approach, which points to its own aesthetic criteria as a "realist" and binary model—he refers to both "historical truth" and moral legitimacy. He argues that Cavani's character Lucia "unleashes her 'repressed' sexual yearnings and turns her into a willing apprentice . . . she acts out her masochistic character in a fittingly complementary fashion. . . . It is difficult to imagine that only thirty years after Dachau and Auschwitz a film can be made which suggests that millions of people murdered by the nazis invited their own destruction by responding favorably to the virtues of nazi sadism and pseudo-strength, class hegemony—decadence."

4. Interview with Grace Lichtenstein, "In Liliana Cavani's Love Story, Love Means Always Having to Say Ouch," *New York Times*, 13 October 1974. Lichtenstein notes that when Cavani describes the film's narrative as a love story, "she is totally sincere in her belief that the sado-masochistic duo is neither shocking nor terribly unusual." She adds, "Maybe Bogarde and Rampling do seem to be having a swell time as they force one another to step on broken glass . . . as she slithers around his apartment in chains . . . as he uncorks an occasional left hook to her jaw when he's feeling low." Her criticism attests more to the disgust for certain preconceptions of abusive relationships rather than the intimacy between former nazi and his victim.

5. Ruth McCormick, in "Fascism a la mode or Radical Chic?," *Cinéaste* 6, no. 4, (1975): 32, acknowledges that the "*Night Porter* is highly critical of fascism and other forms of authoritarian class rule, [yet disavows its anti-fascist politics since, it] seems obsessed

with bizarre sexual analogies and dwells almost lovingly on the decadence of the upper classes." The focus on sexual obsession, according to McCormick, pulls it from the ranks of "serious political intentions." Molly Haskell, in "Are Women Directors Different?" (*The Village Voice*, 3 February 1975), argues that "both directors [Cavani and Wertmüller] deal with sex in scenes as gamey and explicit as anything concocted in this department by men (which of course is why these films, and not their directors' previous ones, are box office successes).... [Yet, she distinguishes her argument] moreover, while both films place women in what at first glance might be thought degraded positions—the baroquely monumental nude who engulfs Giancarlo Giannini in their lovers' tryst, Charlotte Rampling as the pale and emotionally stunted 'little girl' who must obey her Nazi Keeper—a closer look reveals that neither film performs the ultimate act of degradation, which is to rob women of their autonomy, and both equalize, in subtle ways, the position and responsibilities of their men and women."

6. Richard Schickel, "Out of the Night," *Time*, 21 October 1974: 9. He adds that she "turns the mass holocaust into a convenient 'explanation' for a psychopathic horror show as unedifying as one is ever likely to witness at the movies."

7. "Signifying the Holocaust: Liliana Cavani's *Portiere di notte*" 220.

8. *I sommersi e i salvati* 685. Levi states "La Regista Liliana Cavani, a cui era stato chiesto di esprimere in breve il senso di un suo film bello e falso, ha dichiarato: 'siamo tutti vittime o assassini e accettiamo questi ruoli volontariamente. Sola Sade e Dosteoevskij l'hanno compreso bene.'" (The director, Liliana Cavani, when asked to briefly explain her beautiful and false film, responded, "We are all victims or victimizers and we accept these roles voluntarily. Only Sade and Dostoevsky understand this well.")

To which he responds, "so che vittima incolpevole sono stato ed assassino no; so che gli assassini sono esistiti, non solo in Germania, e ancora esistono, a riposo o in servizio, e che confonderli con le lore vittime è una malattia morale o un vezzo estetico o un sinistro segnale di complicitá, sopratutto, è un prezioso servizio reso (volutamente o no) ai negatori della veritá." ("I know that I was an innocent victim, not a victimizer. I know victimizers exist, not only in Germany. They continue to exist dormantly or actively. To confuse them with their victims is a moral sickness, an aesthetic veil, a sinister sign of complicity, and most of all a costly act designed to (voluntarily or not) negate the truth.")

9. Luce Irigaray, "The Poverty of Psychoanalysis," in *This Sex Which Is Not One*, 87.

10. Christian Metz, *The Imaginary Signifier: Psychoanalysis and the Cinema*, trans. Celia Britton, Annwyl Williams, Ben Brewster, and Alfred Guzzetti (Bloomington: Indiana University Press, 1982) 16.

11. Rainer Nägele, *Reading After Freud: Essays on Goethe, Hölderlin, Habermas, Nietzsche, Brecht, Celan, and Freud* (New York: Columbia University Press, 1987) 117.

12. Sam Weber, *The Legend of Freud* (Minneapolis: University of Minnesota Press, 1982) 132–33. Andrea Dworkin, *Intercourse* (New York: Free Press, 1987). Dworkin describes heterosexual intercourse as the penetration-invasion of one passive female object by an active male subject and identifies this as the cause of sexual violence. Dworkin implies that men are carnal violent beings who look at every form of interaction as an act of murder, while women are asexual lesbian beings.

13. *Il portiere di notte* xiv. She continues, "I ciminali piccoli e medi (l'Austria registra il piú alto numero di criminali nazisti) hanno ripreso le lor abituali professioni, anche se tengono gli occhi aperti per non cadere nella rete di un'indagine; stanno in contatto tra di lor, tra ex-camerati, per proteggersi." (The small-time war criminals [Austria ranked the highest in numbers of Nazi war criminals] had returned to their normal professions. They

also kept their eyes wide open so as not to fall into any danger; they were in contact with their former comrades for protection.)

14. Tania Modleski, *The Women Who Knew Too Much: Hitchcock and Feminist Theory* (New York: Routledge, 1988) 6–7.

15. William Wolf, "Sadistic Games," *Cue*, 7 October 1974: 17. He calls *The Night Porter* a "hypnotically repellent film," a "ritual of private war crimes."

16. Teresa de Lauretis, "Cavani's *Night Porter*: A Woman's Film?": 36.

17. Michel de Certeau, *Heterologies: Discourse on the Other*, trans. Brian Massumi (Minneapolis: University of Minnesota Press, 1986) 4.

18. The quote from Žižek is taken from *The Sublime Object of Desire* (New York: Verso, 1989) 50, and from Butler's *Bodies That Matter* (202).

19. Sigmund Freud, *Character and Culture*, trans. James Strachey (New York: Macmillan, 1963) 140.

20. Slavoj Žižek, *The Sublime Object of Desire* (New York: Verso, 1989) 106. Although Žižek has contextualized this statement by addressing the election of Kurt Waldheim to the Austrian presidency, he does not support this notion any longer.

21. Slavoj Žižek, *For They Know Not What They Do: Enjoyment as a Political Factor* (New York: Verso, 1991) 273. Instead of this objectivist approach Žižek argues in favor of "protecting the *essence* of the trauma [which] is precisely that it is too horrible to be remembered, to be integrated into our symbolic universe." Hence the symbolic is also protected from embracing the horror of nazism.

22. *Judgment at Nuremberg* depicts two separate cases: forced sterilization and miscegenation. In the case where Rudolf Peterson was sterilized on the grounds that he was an imbecile, the defense sets out to prove that not only is the witness an imbecile but that forced sterilization is (and was) legal in many Western countries at the time; the defense attorney often refers to Supreme Court Justice Oliver Wendell Holmes Jr. in defense of the nazi policies of sterilization. The most disturbing scene occurs when the defense attorney forces the victim to go through the same intelligence test that the nazis had used in order to determine whether defendants were in fact imbeciles. Hence the question shifts from whether the accused judges violated human rights to whether the witness has the right to progenerate, which represents as well a shift in discursive practices when dealing with the question of morality: it is first a question of individual human rights and second a question of protecting the species (a scientific discourse as opposed to a liberal discourse). The second case, in which Irene Hoffman had been sent to a forced labor camp for having had a "sexual relationship" with a Jewish man who was condemned to death in that very courtroom by one of the accused judges, considers not the question of miscegenation but of statutory rape, since the witness was a minor at the time. A dead man is, in effect, being reaccused of a disproved "crime" for which he paid with his life. The problem with the legal system is that it can identify with nazi law, since both effectively speak the same language, and yet cannot identify with the victim; instead, it perpetuates the pattern of blaming the victims.

23. Because Paulina was blindfolded during her torture and rape she must rely on her senses of smell and hearing and her recognition of speech patterns in order to identify her assailant (Dr. Miranda, whose very name means "seeing"). The senses, however, do not count as evidence in a court of law, or at least not the imaginary court that Paulina sets up, appointing her husband as Dr. Miranda's defense attorney. Yet the question of identification spills over into the question of victimization: has Paulina found her true assailant or is she "victimizing"/accusing an innocent man? By repeating her torturer's methods of

interrogation (an act of revenge), she becomes a victimizer. Furthermore, as Gerardo (her husband) points out, the court can only evaluate documents and the accounts of "eyewitnesses." Therefore, as in *Judgment at Nuremberg*, the justice system must rely on the confessed guilt of the defendant, which, in the case of Dr. Miranda, appears to be forced. Even though we are led to believe that Dr. Miranda is indeed confessing his crimes—his abject desires to control, possess, abuse, rape, and own his victims—the problem remains: what kind of punishment is he to have? Paulina wants to kill him; however, as Dr. Miranda points out, "that is not justice, you are not dead." Her reply, "I wasn't so lucky," brings up another dilemma: does the survivor warrant the same retribution as the dead victim? Polanski points out that there is no justice; Gerardo cannot carry out just punishment even though, by the end, he believes Dr. Miranda to be guilty. The final scene of the film conveys the tension created by the realization that victims live side-by-side with their torturers, who in turn are known to the law yet are nonetheless untouchable.

24. Roland Barthes, *Image—Music—Text*, trans. Stephen Heath (New York: Hill and Wang, 1977) 40–41.

25. Judith Butler, *Gender Trouble: Feminism and the Subversion of Identity* (New York: Routledge, 1990) 136.

26. Rex Reed, "The Night Porter Yuck Sick Demented Junk," New York *Daily News*, 4 October 1974: 76. Janet Maslin, *Boston Phoenix*, 22 October 1974: 3. While other critics such as Primo Levi were appalled by the representation of sexual intimacy between survivors and former nazis, these critics chastised the film for not conforming to the Hollywood code of sexiness. Reed argues, "The sex act in movies has become a matter of mutual degradation, it expresses no sense of pleasure." To express pleasure in this situation would not take into consideration the degradation from which Max's and Lucia's relationship originated. Reed also takes issue with the "seedy hotel (it is obviously the kind of gloomy place that smells of cat urine)." It seems Reed and Maslin dismiss *The Night Porter* for not living up to the standards of a Hollywood romance, regardless of the historical and political implications of such a rendition. This type of criticism in and of itself suggests a radical divestment in reading nazism and the "Final Solution" as what LaCapra calls the "pinnacle of the twentieth century."

27. Caroll Smith-Rosenberg, *Disorderly Conduct: Visions of Gender in Victorian America* (New York: Oxford University Press, 1985). Susan Gubar, "Blessings in Disguise: Cross-Dressing as Re-Dressing for Female Modernists," *Massachusetts Review* (Autumn 1981). Sandra M. Gilbert, "Costumes of the Mind: Transvestitism as Metaphor in Modern Literature," *Critical Inquiry* 7: 2 (winter, 1980). Jacques Lacan, "The Agency of the Letter in the Unconscious, in *Ecrits: A Selection*, trans. Alan Sheridan (New York: Norton, 1977).

28. Steven Kasher, "The Art of Hitler," *October* no. 59 (winter 1992): 57.

29. Theodor Adorno, *Theory of Aesthetics*, trans. E. B. Aston (New York: Continuum, 1984) 340.

30. *Questions of Cinema*, 33. Heath also describes this screen as empty space, a place of pleasure and imagination: a place for projections.

31. Slavoj Žižek, *Tarrying with the Negative: Kant, Hegel, and the Critique of Ideology* (Durham: Duke University Press, 1993) 161.

32. Philippe Lacoue-Labarthe, *Musica Ficta: Figures of Wagner*, trans. Felicia McCarren (Stanford: Stanford University Press, 1994) 7.

33. In *Theory of Aesthetics*, Adorno argues that "art is not being for itself"; instead it is "a language of suffering," a critical praxis that has social influence "not by haranguing, but by changing consciousness in ways that are ever so difficult to pin down." Hence Adorno

equates art with a commitment to radical criticism that provides a "higher stage of reflection and aims at changing social ills" (235). Art is only art when it is committed to critique.

34. Jacqueline Rose, *The Haunting of Sylvia Plath* (Cambridge: Harvard University Press, 1992). In her last chapter Rose discusses the politics of who can speak as a victim, who is a legitimate voice of the victims of the Holocaust. She concludes that the most credible or accepted speakers are men "who directly suffered the Holocaust, they speak of it in what must be, by implication, non-metaphorical speech." She argues that any identification with the victims is patrolled by those who claim to be "authentic" victims. That is, the work must comply with the self-image of the victim in order to be sanctioned as "historically and politically correct." See also Robert von Dassanowky's "Wherever you may run, you cannot escape him: Leni Riefenstahl's Self-Reflection and Romantic Transcendence of Nazism in Tiefland," *New German Critique* no. 63 (fall 1994): 107–28, where he argues that the absence of women in the list of artists who did not sustain the taint of fascism is "glaringly obvious." He writes, "It is a fact that cannot be denied in even the most contrived arguments on talent, fame, and political favoritism that male directors, actors, and writers continued to work in postwar Germany and Europe, whereas the end of the Reich was also the career fade-out for many female cinema artists of equal popularity: the director Riefenstahl, but also such popular German-language icons as Zarah Leander, Lilian Harvery, Marika Rökk, Lil Dagover, and Veit Harlan's wife, Kristina Söderbaum."

35. *I sommersi e i salvati* 661. Levi explains that "il discorse di privilegio è delicato, la zona grigia, quella da prigioniere che in qualche misura, magari a fin di bene, hanno collaborato con l'autorità perchè in questo mundo gravido di minacce, almeno questa minaccia venga vanificata?" (The discourse of privilege is a delicate one, a gray zone, where a prisoner, at the end of all hope, collaborated with the authorities in some measure or capacity. Why in this world of severe transgression should the least transgression be thwarted?)

36. Thomas Quinn Curtis, "*The Night Porter*," *International Herald Tribune*, 11 October 1973.

5. *Fammi campà*

1. Lina Wertmüller, *Seven Beauties* (*Pasqualino settebellezze*, 1976).These words, spoken by the female nazi commandant of the concentration camp, reveal a multiplicity of different ideological understandings of the "human condition." Wertmüller parodies national and sexual stereotypes by presenting a masculinized German woman who speaks of racial purity to an Italian fascist deserter. The irony of this "seduction scene," which Bruno Bettelheim labels as a "rape," is that it undermines the notion of survival at any cost (which implicates not the Jews but the Italians). It inculpates the survival of the patriarchal order as a macho reactionary ideology: in the film the need for reproduction becomes only a defense of the self against the masses.

2. Primo Levi, *Se Questo e un uomo*, (Turin: Giulio Einaudi Editore, 1958) 15. This poem, which precedes one of the most eloquent accounts of a death camp (Auschwitz), provides my analysis with a political understanding of what is at stake in representing the experience of the concentration camp. It is a reminder of the limits of representation—calling into question memory and survival.

3. Pierre Sorlin, *Italian National Cinema* 122. Sorlin argues that these films exude a vision of Italy as corrupt, revealing circuits of bribery and corruption, by dragging them into the foreground.

4. *Italian Film in the Light of Neorealism* 314. While Marcus notes that Wertmüller's satirical cinematic style is an "effective method of registering social criticism in the arts," she concludes that Wertmüller's professed desire for political and social commitment "is subverted by her comic technique which is founded on . . . the politics of polarity."

5. Jerzy Kosinsky, "*Seven Beauties*—A Cartoon Trying To Be a Tragedy," *New York Times*, 7 March 1976, section 2.

6. Mikhail Bakhtin, *Problems of Dostoevsky's Poetics*, ed. and trans. Caryl Emerson (Minneapolis: University of Minnesota Press, 1984) 164–65.

7. Bruno Bettelheim, "Reflections: Surviving," *The New Yorker*, 2 August 1976.

8. *Se Questo e un uomo* 122. The original reads "Essi sono il tipico prodotto della struttura del Lager tedesco: si offra ad alcuni individui in stato di schiavitú una posizione privilegiata, un certo agio e una buona probabilità di sporavvivere, esigendone in cambio il tradimento della naturale solidarietà co 'loro compagni, e certamente vi sarà chi accetterà." Here Levi points out that not only are these kapos the most hated individuals but probably the most cruel, since in order to retain their sought-after positions they were "crudele e tirannico, perché capirà che se non lo fosse abbastanza, un altro, giudicato piú idoneo, subentenerebbe al suo posto" ("cruel and tyrannical, because you understand that if they were not cruel enough, another, deemed more fit, would subsume their post").

9. Pelagia Lewinska, *Vignt mois a Auschwitz* (Paris: Minuit, 1945) 40–41. She continues, "Men with a standard, had to perish crushed beneath a blind and primitive animality paying the price for having subtler minds, for a generosity of spirit which in Hitler's book meant nothing but weakness and inferiority."

10. Ralph Tutt, "Seven Beauties and the Beast: Bettelheim, Wertmüller, and the Uses of Enchantment," 194. Tutt adds, "Pasqualino is banal in this sense, to be sure, but he is no Eichmann. He is not a bureaucrat for whom genocide is all in a day's work. He is equivocally reborn at the end of the film." Pasqualino represents what Arendt calls the banality of evil, the complicity of the common man, the everyman, that has so befuddled critical theorists and philosophers in their attempts to make sense of the Holocaust.

11. Annette Insdorf, *Indelible Shadows: Film and the Holocaust* (New York: Cambridge University Press, 1983) 77.

12. *The Haunting of Sylvia Plath* 206. In her analysis of survivors' criticism of Plath's writings about nazism, Rose points out that "Plath is being criticized for not being objective," hence "stealing historic events in order to aggrandize the self."

13. *Libidinal Economies* 28. Here, in his analysis and critique of Freud's setting *eros* against *thanatos*, or the life drive against the death drive, Lyotard postulates that "Freud introduced the instance of the death drives, precisely in order to keep not only such a sign, but libidinal economy in its entirety, in the shelter of the concept and of binarist discrimination."

14. For a discussion of the historiographical process of objectifying the past, see Heidegger's essay "The Age of the World Picture" in *The Question Concerning Technology*, where he argues that "what is stable in what is past is decided on the basis of which historiographical explanation reckons up the solitary and the diverse in history, is the always-has-been-once-already, the comparable." Historiography, or history, is contingent on what is intelligible yet "what is great in history, is the exception." And so history is formed as a discourse of exceptionality, a discourse of limits that can be objectified or understood in narrative terms.

15. Bettelheim, in "Reflections: Surviving" (34) argues that in *Seven Beauties* "Mussolini and Hitler are presented partly as comic figures . . . they are funny, and this quality

simultaneously adds to the rejection and takes the sting of true seriousness out of it." In contrast see Jonathan Steinberg's *All or Nothing* (New York: Routledge, 1990) 181, where he argues that "the cult of personality which required that the Duce know everything, see everything, hear everything, understand everything, which required that the light be on in his office so that passers-by would note that at any hour of the day or night the Duce was at work, provide the stuff of caricatures and gave Charlie Chaplin one of his most effective inspirations." And see Angelo Tasca's *Nascita e avvento del fascismo*, 2 vols. (Bari: Laterza, 1974).

16. In his book *Starace* (Milan: Montadori, 1980) 39–40, Antonio Spinosa notes that Achille Starace, the secretary of the fascist party and uniform designer of the regime, would boast of his exploits and the brutality with which he treated Italian prostitutes. He was allegedly picked for the position because of his feeblemindedness and his violence.

17. *The Great Dictator* and *To Be or Not To Be* have been carefully introduced on German television. They are preceded by a prologue explaining that Chaplin and Lubitsch could make fun of Hitler only because they had no knowledge of the "Final Solution." The films were also preceded by an intellectual debate as to the effect of such representations on the memory of both Hitler and the Holocaust. In 1997 the *New York Times* published in its 20 July issue the results of a survey of the popularity of the TV series *Hogan's Heroes*, which may indicate a change in policy of the treatment of national socialism by the German government. However, the show is aired only on private or pay-per-view (cable) television.

18. In *Posthumous People* (Stanford: Stanford University Press, 1996) 97, Massimo Cacciari argues that "the story or narrative is singularity, and singularly accounts for the death of experience." The narrative rendering drags the survivor back into that experience.

19. Stephen Heath, "On Suture," *Questions of Cinema* (Bloomington: Indiana University Press, 1981).

20. Contrary to Pauline Kael's section "Seven Fatties" in *When the Lights Go Down* (New York: Holt, Rinehart and Winston, 1980) 139, which maintains that "Wertmüller turns suffering into vaudeville not as part of a Brechtian technique, but rather, as an expression of a roller-coaster temperament. The suffering is reduced to fun-house games, vociferously attacked by Jerzy Kosinski and Bruno Bettelheim." Wertmüller's use of music and silence is far more complex than agitprop or vaudeville since it plays with music genres as much as with film genres. For an analysis of Wagner's *Ring* see Nietzsche's *Richard Wagner in Bayreuth*, trans. R. J. Hollingdale (London: Cambridge University Press, 1983).

21. The *Ring des Nibelungen* is the tetralogy for which Wagner designed and erected the Festival Theater at Bayreuth in Bavaria; the cycle was first performed on 13, 14, 16, and 17 August 1876, inaugurating the Bayreuth Festival. *The Ring*, a stage drama designed to last three days, comprises four sections: *Das Rheingold* (*The Rhine Gold*) (one act and four scenes), which serves as a prologue; *Die Walküre* (*The Valkyrie*) (three acts); *Siegfried* (three acts); and *Götterdämmerung* (*The Twilight of the Gods*) (three acts and a prologue). The whole work takes between fifteen and sixteen hours to perform.

22. Albert Speer likens the death of Hitler to the staging of the last act of *Götterdämmerung*: "The last act of *Götterdämmerung* could not have been more effectively staged. The same red light bathed our faces and our hands. The display produced a curiously pensive mood among us. Abruptly turning to one of his military adjutants, Hitler said "looks like a great deal of blood. This time we won't bring it off without violence" *Inside the Third Reich*, trans. Richard and Clara Winston (New York: Macmillan, 1970) 488–89.

23. Clement Greenberg, "The Avant-Garde and Kitsch," in *Pollock and After: The Critical Debate*, ed. Francis Frascina (New York: Harper and Row, 1985) 25.

24. Hayden White, "Historiography and Historiophoty," *American Historical Review* no. 108 (December 1991).

25. *Untimely Meditations*, trans. R. J. Hollingdale (Cambridge: Cambridge University Press, 1993) 75–77. For Nietzsche "critical history" deconstructs the two preexisting forms of history: (1) monumental history, a worshiping of great men and great deeds designed to "masquerade or costume the hatred of the great and powerful of their own age"; and (2) antiquarian history, a veneration of the past.

26. Judith Mayne, "Dietrich, *The Blue Angel*, and Female Performance," in *Seduction and Theory: Readings of Gender, Representation, and Rhetoric*, ed. Dianne Hunter (Urbana: University of Illinois Press, 1989) 32.

27. *The Differend* 107–10. Lyotard argues that "the question is not one of obedience, but of obligation. The question is to know whether, when one hears something that might resemble a call, one is held to be held by it. One can resist it or answer it, but it will first have to be received as a call, rather than, for instance, as a fantasy. One must find oneself placed in the position of addressee of a prescription.... [And to apply this obligation to the] Holocaust is to signify that God commanded the hands of the Nazi butcher, [putting] the Jewish people in the place of Isaac.... Did God want to test the SS's faithfulness to Him? Was there an alliance between them? And did the SS love the Jew as a father does his son? If not, how could crime have the value of a sacrifice in the eyes of its victim?... The only way you can make a 'beautiful death' out of 'Auschwitz death' is by means of a rhetoric."

28. Philippe Lacoue-Labarthe, *La Fiction du politique* (Paris: Christian Bourgeois, 1987) 67. For Lacoue-Labarthe politics transforms into the pure agency of technology.

29. James Hay, *Popular Film Culture in Fascist Italy* xii. Here Hay claims that *Amarcord* presents fascism as antiheroic, and fascists not as "just goodhearted buffoons as nazis are brutes."

30. Friedländer argues in *Reflections on Nazism* that "no matter what their actual age, this is the world of boys, with its pranks (the master, incognito, out at night with his valet) but also its nostalgia and above all the loyalty of a juvenile fraternity to its own norms, to the one among them who becomes the chief. Hitler remained an eternal adolescent" (12).

31. *The Birth of Fascist Ideology* 4. Sternhell grounds his argument on the fascists' disassociation of cultural practices from those of the nazis. His argument attempts to counter the work of Ernst Nolte (*The Faces of Fascism*), who links the Action française to Italian fascism and German nazism through their use of revolutionary revisionist discourse and political strategies.

32. I am referring to Hannah Arendt's argument that if it were not for the deeds of the Jewish collaborators and for the zeal of the *Judenräte* the number of victims would have been considerably reduced. *Eichmann in Jerusalem* (New York: Viking, 1963).

33. In *La Donna Nera* Macciocchi pictures women as victims of not only seduction but the logic of sacrifice. She points out that the regime called for sacrifice, "i fascisti le chiedono ostinatamente sacrificio: potere-gioa-sacrificio = nel sacrificio la gioia; la sesualità del fascimo mussliniano rimpiazza l'eros dell' uomo (o caduto in guerra, o marito, o un inesistente per le zitelle)." Hence the Duce became their surrogate husband.

34. Eugen Weber, *Varieties of Fascism* (New York: Von Nostrand Reinhold, 1964) 35. Weber, like Macciocchi, replicates arguments made by thinkers like Gustav Le Bon at the turn of the century. Le Bon, like many other fin-de-siècle thinkers, uses the feminine as a metaphor for both the masses and popular culture. What I find most problematic with this line of thinking is the need to turn the masses into a feminine body yet at the same

time preserve the identity of both the leader and the followers of nazism and fascism as aggressively masculine.

35. Barbara Spackman, *Fascist Virilities*. Spackman traces this rhetorical (metaphorical) assimilation of the crowd to a woman, specifically to Machiavelli's notion of the rape of Fortuna by Virtue.

36. *La Donna Nera* 96–100. I would like to point out that Macciocchi is not alone in her interpretation; in fact many of the critics I have previously cited hold the same opinion.

37. *Bodily Regimes* 86. Pinkus argues that under the regime men's identification maintains a singular position—"it is absolutely fixed or legislated"—yet women's identity is subject to change.

38. Georgio Agamben, *The Coming Community*, trans. Michael Hardt (Minneapolis: University of Minnesota Press, 1993) 48. Agamben sees the commodification of the body as emancipating the body from its cultural and theological foundations. The effect of such commodification is two-fold: while the body is liberated from the constraints of gender, it is also manipulated, technologized.

39. Laura Mulvey, *Visual and Other Pleasures* (Bloomington: Indiana University Press, 1989). Mulvey argues that cinema reproduces a fetishistic economy whereby "women are simply the scenery onto which men project their narcissistic fantasies." Yet this feminine "to-be-looked-at-ness" is only one dimension of cinematic seeing, which reproduces a sense of violation. In fact, this scene reflects the humiliation of being looked at by force, yet it is man's humiliation in front of a woman who treats his sexual prowess indifferently and is even bored by it.

40. *Vignt mois a Auschwitz* 70. Although she expresses awe at what she calls "the skill with which the Germans had introduced the modern science of man into the way they organized life in the camp, [she notes that] not only had they applied a system of conditions which killed people, but also, with great precision, they had used the science of psychology in order to disorganize the human soul, to destroy the human being morally."

41. What is at stake here is a certain rhetorical complicity with fascism, a reinvestment in the spectacle of masculine virility, both as a point of departure and a "fascinating" return. In pointing to the SS as the model for sadomasochistic eroticism, Sontag returns fascism to another level, beyond its emphatically heterosexual agenda and platform to a more ambiguous yet distinctly masculinist agenda. In other words, while it implies a certain homosexual aesthetic, it contains this aesthetic within the discourse of misogyny, promulgating the man's man.

42. *Reflections on Nazism* 40. Friedländer qualifies this statement by adding that Hitler was indeed an object of desire, yet "not necessarily the actual person—but the idealized image of the chief expressing both a universal sentimentality and the attraction to nothingness that sometimes seizes contemporary crowds."

43. Ibid. 66. This, however, seems to be in conflict with Friedländer's previous assertion that Hitler was a seductive or desirable figure. The implication is that Hitler not only changed the image of the national hero or mythic image of the ideal man from an epic hero to a bourgeois hero, but that he participated in the desire to identify with the natural German man.

44. The Italian army, under the king and Marshal Badoglio (after the meeting of the *grand consiglio*), was abandoned, left to disperse, and many military men (over five hundred thousand) were arrested and deported by the then-occupying nazis. I further want to point out that it was not the fascist regime's policy to deport Jews; it was the nazis'.

While many Italian Jews were deported, and there was even a concentration camp set up in Trieste, the deportations did not occur until the nazis occupied northern and central Italy. Moreover, there was not only forced conscription for able-bodied men but deportations of antifascist subversives—deserters, as the case of Pasqualino, partisans, as the case of Pedro, other radicals, collaborators, and strikers. Few survived the concentration camps. Italian agricultural and industrial labor was also deported to Germany to aid the war economy.

45. See Marcus's discussion of *Love and Anarchy* in *Italian Film in the Light of Neorealism*, where she argues that "inadvertently Tipolina becomes an intensely political character whose final act of love—her decision not to awaken Tunin—politically disenfranchises him as surely as any Fascist dictatorship would. Freedom and harmonious social intercourse, the anarchist ideals to which Tunin's desperate mission is directed, are categorically denied by Tripolina's decision to set her desires above her lover's and obstruct the dictates of his free will" (315).

46. Betty Friedan, *The Feminine Mystique* (New York: Norton, 1963) 307, emphasis mine. Similarly, in *The Informed Heart: Autonomy in a Mass Age* (New York: Glencoe, 1960), Bettelheim, who calls prisoners "docile robots," recounts a story of how a woman dancer is asked to dance by an SS man before she enters the gas chamber, and while she dances she grabs his gun and kills him only to be in turn gunned down. Bettelheim reads the act of dancing as memory of former self, autonomy, individuality—"transformed however momentarily she responded like her old self destroying the enemy bent on her destruction even if she had to die in the process. Despite the hundreds of thousands of living dead men who moved quietly to their graves, this one example shows that in an instant, the old personality can be regained, its destruction undone, once we decide on our own that we wish to cease being units in a system. . . . the dancer threw off her real prison."

47. Pierre Cortade, *Action*, 25 April 1945, quoted in Henri Lefebvre *Critique of Everyday Life*, trans. John Moore (London: Verso, 1947).

48. *Sense and Non-Sense* 147. In his analysis of the question of responsibility, Merleau-Ponty argues that "when we look closely at things, we find culprits nowhere but accomplices everywhere; so it is that we all played a part in the events of 1939." Similarly, Wertmüller depicts Pasqualino as an apolitical figure who, because of his impassive reaction to fascism, becomes more and more implicated in and affected by fascism.

Conclusion

1. From an interview with Philippe Bouvard on *Dix de Der*, quoted in *Pasolini Requiem* 662–63. Here Pasolini comes close to Arendt's argument on the banality of radical evil: that radical evil instead of conforming to a model of impurity conforms to a model of total indifference, total relativity, and narcissism. However, Pasolini adds that radical evil is the replication of morality as a form of purity itself.

2. *The Question Concerning Technology and Other Essays* 120. Heidegger likens the method of inquiry, reflection, to a scientific model, genealogical tracing rules, and laws that are "safeguarded" or rendered incalculable. He points out that "reflection transports the man of the future into that between in which he belongs to Being and yet remains a stranger amid that which is."

3. Siegfried Kracauer, *From Caligari to Hitler: A Psychological History of the German Film* (Princeton: Princeton University Press, 1947) 287. Kracauer argues that newsreel

footage made under the national socialists presented history as immediate. That is, it became the precedent for the spectacularization of the news that touts events as "history in the making." This "historical effect" was also achieved through Hitler's speeches, since he "encouraged people to think in terms of centuries" and analogized the present in terms of the mythic past, therefore imbedding the present within an epic narrative.

4. Paul Virilio, *Pure War* (New York: Semiotext(e), 1983).

5. Herbert Marcuse, *One-Dimensional Man* (Boston: Beacon Press, 1964) 68–74.

6. *Philosophy and Truth* 92. For an analysis of Nietzsche's use of tropes and his language of persuasion, see Paul de Man's *Allegories of Reading: Figural Language in Rousseau, Nietzsche, Rilke, and Proust* (New Haven: Yale University Press, 1979) chapters 4–6.

Bibliography

Adamson, Walter. "Futurism, Mass Culture, and Women: The Reshaping of the Artistic Vocation, 1909–1920." In *Modernism/Modernity* 3 (winter 1997).

———. *Avant-Garde Florence: From Modernism to Fascism.* Cambridge: Harvard University Press, 1993.

Adorno, Theodor. *Prisms.* Trans. Samuel Weber and Shierry Weber. Cambridge: MIT Press, 1986.

———. *Theory of Aesthetics.* Trans. E. B. Aston. New York: Continuum, 1984.

———. *Negative Dialectics.* New York: Continuum, 1973.

Adorno, Theodor W. and Max Horkheimer. *The Dialectic of Enlightenment.* Trans. John Cummings. New York: Continuum, 1989.

Agamben, Giorgio. *The Coming Community.* Trans. Michael Hardt. Minneapolis: University of Minnesota Press, 1993.

———. *Il linguaggio e la morte: Un seminario sul luogo della negatività.* Turin: Einaudi, 1982.

Airaksinen, Timo. *Of Glamour, Sex and de Sade.* Wakefield, N.H.: Longwood Academic Press, 1991.

Allen, Beverly. "Poetics of Heresy: Introduction." In *Stanford Italian Review* 4, no. 2 (fall 1984).

Anderson, Perry. "On Emplotment: Two Kinds of Ruin." In *Probing the Limits of Representation.* Ed. Saul Friedländer. Cambridge: Harvard University Press, 1992.

Armes, Roy. *Patterns of Realism.* New York: A. S. Barnes, 1971.

Artaud, Antonin. *Le téâtre et son double.* Paris: Gallimard, 1964.

Arendt, Hannah. *A Report on the Banality of Evil: Eichmann in Jerusalem.* New York: Penguin, 1963.

———. *On Revolution.* New York: Penguin, 1963.

———. *The Human Condition.* Chicago: University of Chicago Press, 1958.

———. *The Origins of Totalitarianism.* Cleveland: Meridian, 1958.

Aschheim, Steven E. "Hannah Arendt and the Discourse of Evil." In *New German Critique* no. 79 (winter 1997):117–39.

Bachmann, Gideon. "Look Gideon … A Talk with Lina Wertmüller." In *Film Quarterly* no. 30, (spring 1977).

Bakhtin, M. M. *Problems of Dostoevsky's Poetics.* Ed. and trans. Caryl Emerson. Minneapolis: University of Minnesota Press, 1984.

———. *The Dialogic Imagination.* Trans. Michael Holquist and Caryl Emerson. Austin: University of Texas Press, 1981.

Balibar, Etienne, and Immanuel Wallerstein. *Race, Nation, Class: Ambiguous Identities.* Trans. Chris Turner. London: Verso, 1992.

Barthes, Roland. *Sade, Fourier, Loyola.* Trans. Richard Miller. Berkeley: University of California Press, 1989.

———. *Camera Lucida.* Trans. Richard Howard. New York: Noonday Press, 1989.

———. *Image - Music - Text.* Trans. Stephen Heath. New York: Hill and Wang, 1977.

———. *Mythologies.* Trans. Annette Lavers. New York: Hill and Wang, 1972.

Bartov, Omer. *Murder in Our Midst: The Holocaust, Industrial Killing, and Representation.* New York: Oxford University Press, 1996.

Bathrick, David. "Inscribing History, Prohibiting and Producing Desire: Fassbinder's *Lili Marleen.*" In *New German Critique* no. 63 (fall 1994).

Bataille, Georges. *The Accursed Share.* Vols. 1, 2, 3. Trans. Robert Hurley. New York: Zone Books, 1991.

———. "Reflections on the Executioner and the Victim." Trans. Elizabeth Rottenberg. Ed. Claire Nouvet. *Yale French Studies.* 1991.

———. *Eroticism: Death and Sensuality.* Trans. Mary Dalwood. San Francisco: City Lights, 1986.

———. *Visions of Excess: Selected Writings 1927–1939.* Trans. Allan Stoekl. Minneapolis: University of Minnesota Press, 1985.

———. *Literature and Evil.* Trans. Alastair Hamilton. London: Marion Boyars Press, 1973.

Battaglia, Roberto. *Storia della resistenza italiana.* Turin: Einaudi, 1964.

Baudrillard, Jean. *The Perfect Crime.* Trans. Chris Turner. London: Verso, 1995.

———. *Simulacra and Simulation.* Trans. Sheila Faria Glaser. Ann Arbor: University of Michigan Press, 1994.

———. *Seduction.* Trans. Brian Singer. New York: St. Martin's, 1990.

———. *The Evil Demon of Images.* Trans. Philippe Tanguy. Sydney: Power Publications, 1988.

———. *On Seduction, Selected Writings.* Trans. Mark Poster. Stanford: Stanford University Press, 1988.

———. "The System of Objects." In *Selected Writings.*

———. *The Ecstasy of Communication.* Trans. Bernard Schutze and Caroline Schutze. New York: Semiotext(e), 1987.

———. *Simulations.* Trans. Paul Foss, Paul Patton, and Philip Beitchman. New York: Semiotext(e), 1983.

———. *For a Critique of the Political Economy of the Sign.* Trans. Charles Levin. St. Louis: Telos Press, 1981.

———. *The Mirror of Production.* Trans. Mark Poster. St. Louis: Telos Press, 1975.

Bazin, André. *What Is Cinema?* Vols. 1 and 2. Trans. Hugh Gray. Berkeley: University of California Press, 1967.

Ben-Ghiat, Ruth. "Fascism, Writing, and Memory: The Realist Aesthetic in Italy 1930 to 1950." In *The Journal of Modern History* 69 (September 1995).

Benjamin, Walter. "The Image of Proust." In *Illuminations.* New York: Schocken, 1969.

———. "Art in the Age of Mechanical Reproduction." In *Reflections.* New York: Harcourt, Brace, Jovanovich, 1966.

Bersani, Leo and Ulysse Dutoit. "Merde Alors." In *Stanford Italian Review* 2, no.2 (fall 1982).

Bettelheim, Bruno. *Freud and Man's Soul.* New York: Vintage, 1982.

———. "Refections: Surviving." *The New Yorker,* 2 August 1976.

———. *The Informed Heart.* New York: Free Press, 1960.

Bhabha, Homi. *Location of Culture.* New York: Routledge, 1994.

———. "The World and the Home." In *Social Text,* 31/32 (1992).

———. "Of Mimicry and Man: The Ambivalence of Colonial Discourse." In *October* 28 (spring 1984).

Biagioli, Mario. "Science, Modernity, and the Final Solution." In *Probing the Limits of Representation.* Ed. Saul Friedläder, 185–205. Cambridge: Harvard University Press, 1992.

Blanchot, Maurice. *The Infinite Conversation.* Trans. Susan Hanson. Minneapolis: University of Minnesota Press, 1993.

———. *The Gaze of Orphesus.* Trans. Lydia Davis. Barrytown, New York: Station Hill, 1981.

———. *Lautrèamont et Sade.* Paris: Les Editions de Minuit, 1949.

Bloch, Iwan. *Marquis de Sade.* Trans. James Bruce. New York: Castle Books, 1948.

Blumenfeld, Gina. "The (Next to) Last Word on Lina Wertmüller." In *Cinéaste* no. 7 (spring 1976).

Bocca, Giorgio. *Il filo nero.* Milan: A. Mondadori, 1995.

———. *Noi terroristi : Dodici anni di lotta armata ricostruiti e discussi con i protagonisti.* Milan: Garzanti, 1985.

———. *Storia della repubblica italiana : Dalla caduta del fascismo a oggi.* Milan: Rizzoli, 1982.

———. *Il terrorismo italiano, 1970–1978.* Milan: Rizzoli, 1979.

Bondanella, Peter. *The Films of Roberto Rossellini.* Cambridge: Cambridge University Press, 1993.

———. ed. *Federico Fellini: Essays in Criticism.* New York: Oxford University Press, 1978.

Boszat, Martin and Saul Friedländer. "A Controversy about the Historicization of National Socialism." In *New German Critique* 44 (spring/summer 1988).

Bracher, Karl Dietrich. *Turning Points in Modern Times: Essays on German and European History.* Trans. Thomas Dunlap. Cambridge: Harvard University Press, 1995.

Braidotti, Rosi. *Nomadic Subjects: Embodiment and Sexual Difference in Contemporary Feminist Theory.* New York: Columbia University Press, 1994.

Brunette, Peter. *Roberto Rossellini.* New York: Oxford Press, 1987.

Bruno, Giuliana. *Streetwalking on a Ruined Map: Cultural Theory and the City Films of Elvia Notari.* Princeton: Princeton University Press, 1993.

Butler, Judith. *Bodies that Matter: On the Discursive Limits of "Sex".* New York: Routledge, 1993.

———. "Imitation and Gender Insubordination." In *Inside/Out: Lesbian Theories, Gay Theories.* Ed. Diana Fuss. New York: Routledge, 1991.

———. *Gender Trouble: Feminism and the Subversion of Identity.* New York: Routledge, 1990.

Cacciari, Massimo. *Dallo Steinhof.* Milan: Adelphi Edizioni, 1980.

Calvino, Italo. "Sade Is within Us." Trans. Mark Pietralunga. In *Stanford Italian Review* 2, no. 2 (fall 1982).

Carroll, David. "The Temptation of Fascism." In *Cultural Critique* no. 15 (spring 1990).

Caserino, Cesare. "Oedipus Exploded: Pasolini and the Myth of Modernization." In *October* 59 (winter 1992).

Cavani, Liliana. *Il portiere di notte.* Turin: Einaudi, 1974.

Cesare, Tony. "Pasolini's Theorem." In *Film Criticism* 14, no. 1 (fall 1989).

Chomsky, Noam. *Deterring Democracy.* New York: Farrar, Straus and Giroux, 1992.

Cixous, Hélène. "Castration or Decapitation?" In *Out There.* Ed. Russell Ferguson, Martha Gever, Trinh T. Minh-ha, and Cornel West. The New Museum of Contemporary Art Series. Cambridge: MIT University Press, 1990.

Cohen, Sande. *Passive Nihilism: Culture, Historiography, and the Rhetorics of Scholarship.* New York: St. Martin's, 1998.

————. *Academia and the Luster for Capital.* Minneapolis: University of Minnesota Press, 1991.

————. *Historical Culture: On the Recoding of an Academic Discipline.* Berkeley: University of California Press, 1986.

Colarizi, S. *La seconda guerra mondiale.* Turin: UTET, 1984.

Conti, Laura. *La Resistenza in Italia: 25 luglio 1943–25 aprile 1945.* Milan: Feltrinelli, 1961.

Corradini, Enrico. *La Riforma Politica in Europa.* Milan: Mondadori, 1929.

————. *La Rinascita nazionale.* Florence: Felice Le Monnier, 1929.

————. *La Marcia Del soldato ignoto.* Rome: Giorgio Berlutti Editore, 1923.

Croce, Benedetto. *Elementi di Politica.* Bari: Gius. Lerza & Figli, 1946.

Curtis, Thomas Quinn. "*The Night Porter.*" *International Herald Tribune,* 11 October 1973.

Dalle Vacche, Angela. *The Body in the Mirror: Shapes of History in Italian Cinema.* Princeton: Princeton University Press, 1992.

Davis, Russell. "The Night Porter." *The London Observer,* 27 October 1974.

de Certeau, Michel. *The Writing of History.* Trans. Tom Conley. New York: Columbia University Press, 1988.

————. *Heterologies: Discourse on the Other.* Trans. Brian Massumi. Minneapolis: University of Minnesota Press, 1986.

de Felice, Renzo. *Le interpretazioni del fascismo.* Bari: Laterza, 1983.

————. *D'Annunzio politico 1918–1938.* Rome: Laterza, 1978.

de Felice, Renzo and Luigi Goglia. *Storia Fotografica del fascismo.* Rome: Laterze, 1982.

De Grazia, Victoria. *How Fascism Ruled Women: Italy, 1922–1945.* Berkeley: University of California Press, 1992.

————. "The Arts of Purchase: How American Publicity Subverted the European Poster, 1920–1940." In *Remaking History.* Ed. Barbara Kruger and Phil Mariani. Seattle: Bay Press, 1989.

————. *The Culture of Consent.* Cambridge: Cambridge University Press, 1981.

de Lauretis, Teresa. *Technologies of Gender.* Bloomington: Indiana University Press, 1987.

————. *Alice Doesn't: Feminism, Semiotics, Cinema.* Bloomington: Indiana University Press, 1984.

————. "Cavani's *Night Porter:* A Woman's Film?" In *Film Quarterly* 30 (1976–77).

De Lutiis, Guiseppe. *Storia dei servizi segreti.* Rome: Editori Riuniti, 1984.

de Man, Paul. *The Resistance to Theory.* Minneapolis: University of Minnesota Press, 1987.

————. *Allegories of Reading: Figural Language in Rousseau, Nietzsche, Rilke, and Proust.* New Haven: Yale University Press, 1979.

————. *Blindness and Insight: Essays in the Rhetoric of Contemporary Criticism.* Minneapolis: University of Minnesota Press, 1971.

de Saint-Point, Valentine. "Manifesto della Donna Futurista." Reprinted in *Le Futuriste: Donne e Letteratura d'Avanguardia in Italia.* Milan: Claudia Solaris, Edizioni delle Donne, 1982.

Debord, Guy. *Society of the Spectacle.* Detroit: Black and Red Press, 1983.

Deleuze, Gilles. *Difference and Repetition.* Trans. Paul Patton. New York: Columbia University Press, 1994.

————. "Postscript on the Societies of Control." In *October* (winter 1992).

————. *Logic of Sense.* Trans. Mark Lester. New York: Columbia University Press, 1990.

————. *Cinema 2: The Time Image.* Trans. Hugh Tomlinson and Robert Galeta. Minneapolis: University of Minnesota Press, 1989.

————. *Masochism: Coldness and Cruelty.* Trans. Jean McNeil. New York: Zone Books, 1989.

————. *Nietzsche and Philosophy.* Trans. Hugh Tomlinson. New York: Columbia University Press, 1983.

Deleuze, Gilles, and Félix Guattari. *A Thousand Plateaus: Capitalism and Schizophrenia.* Trans. Brian Massumi. Minneapolis: University of Minnesota Press, 1987.

———. *Kafka: Toward a Minor Literature.* Trans. Dana Polan. Minneapolis: University of Minnesota Press, 1986.

———. *Anti-Oedipus: Capitalism and Schizophrenia.* Trans. Robert Hurley, Mark Seem, and Helen R. Lane. Minneapolis: University of Minnesota Press, 1983.

Derrida, Jacques. *Specters of Marx: The State of the Debt, the Work of Mourning, and the New International.* Trans. Peggy Kamuf. New York: Routledge, 1993.

———. *Aporias.* Trans. Thomas Dutoit. Stanford: Stanford University Press, 1993.

———. *Memoirs for Paul de Man.* Trans. Cecile Lindsay, Jonathan Culler, Eduardo Cadava, and Peggy Kamuf. New York: Columbia University Press, 1986.

———. *Dissemination.* Trans. Barbara Johnson. Chicago: University of Chicago Press, 1981.

———. *Of Grammatology.* Trans. Gayatri Chakravorty Spivak. Baltimore: Johns Hopkins University Press, 1974.

Dijkstra, Bram. *Idols of Perversity: Fantasies of Feminine Evil in Fin-de-Siècle Culture.* Oxford: Oxford University Press, 1986.

Doane, Mary Ann. *Femmes Fatales: Feminism, Film Theory, Psychoanalysis.* New York: Routledge, 1991.

———. *The Desire to Desire: The Woman's Film of the 1940s.* Bloomington: Indiana University Press, 1987.

Dworkin, Andrea. *Intercourse.* New York: Free Press, 1987.

Elsaesser, Thomas. "Subject Positions, Speaking Positions: From *Holocaust, Our Hitler,* and *Heimat* to *Shoah* and *Schindler's list.* In *The Persistence of History: Cinema, Television, and the Modern Event.* Ed. Vivian Sobchack. London: Routledge, 1996.

Falasca-Zamponi, Simonetta. *Fascist Spectacle: The Aesthetics of Power in Mussolini's Italy.* Berkeley: University of California Press, 1997.

Felman, Shoshana. "In an Era of Testimony: Claude Lanzmann's *Shoah.*" In *Yale French Studies* no. 79 (1990).

Ferretti, Gian Carlo. *In Pasolini: L'universo orrendo.* Rome: Editori Riuniti, 1976.

Ferrucci, Franco. "Il J'accuse di Pasolini." In *Italian Quarterly* 21–22 (fall-winter 1980–1981).

Feyerabend, Paul. *Farewell to Reason.* London: Verso, 1987.

Flinn, Caryl. "The Deaths of Camp." In *New German Critique* no. 67 (winter 1996).

Foucault, Michel. *Foucault Live.* Trans. John Johnston. New York: Semiotext(e), 1989.

———. *The History of Sexuality.* Vol. 2. Trans. Robert Hurley. New York: Vintage, 1985.

———. *The History of Sexuality.* Vol. 1. Trans. Robert Hurley. New York: Vintage, 1980.

———. *Discipline and Punish: The Birth of the Prison.* Trans. Allan Sheridan. Middlesex: Penguin, 1977.

———. *Language, Counter-Memory, Practice.* Trans. Donald F. Bouchard and Sherry Simon. Ithaca: Cornell University Press, 1977.

———. *Cahiers du Cinéma* nos. 251–52 (July-August 1974).

———. *Power/Knowledge: Selected Interviews and Other Writings.* Ed. and trans. Colin Gordon. New York: Pantheon, 1972.

Freud, Sigmund. *Sexuality and the Psychology of Love.* Trans. James Stachey. New York: Macmillan, 1963.

———. *Character and Culture.* Trans. James Stachey. New York: Macmillan, 1963.

———. *The Sexual Enlightenment of Children.* Trans. James Stachey. New York: Macmillan, 1963.

———. *Civilization and Its Discontents.* Trans. James Stachey. New York: Macmillan, 1961.

———. *The Future of an Illusion.* Trans. James Stachey. New York: Norton, 1961.

————. *Beyond the Pleasure Principle.* Trans. James Stachey. New York: Norton, 1961.

————. *Totem and Taboo.* Trans. James Stachey. New York: Norton, 1950.

————. *New Introductory Lectures on Psychoanalysis.* New York: Norton, 1933.

Friedländer, Saul. *Reflections on Nazism: An Essay on Kitsch and Death.* Trans. Thomas Weyr. Bloomington: Indiana University Press, 1993.

Funkenstein, Amos. "History, Counterhistory, and Narrative." In *Probing the Limits of Representation: Nazism and the "Final Solution."* Ed. Saul Friedländer. Cambridge: Harvard University Press, 1992.

Gadamer, Hans-Georg. *Truth and Method.* Trans. Garret Barden and John Cumming. New York: Crossroads Press, 1984.

Gadda, Carlo Emilio. *Eros e Priapo.* Milan: Garzanti, 1967.

————. *Quer pasticciaccio brutto de via merulana.* Milan: Garzanti, 1957.

————. *La madonna dei filosofi.* Turin: Einaudi, 1955.

Galli, Giorgio. *Storia del partito armato, 1968–1982.* Milan: Rizzoli, 1986.

————. *La destra in Italia.* Milan: Gammalibri, 1983.

————. *La sfida perduta.* Milan: Bompiani, 1976.

————. *La crisi italiana e la destra internazionale.* Milan: Mondadori, 1974.

Gallop, Jane. *Intersections: A Reading of Sade with Bataille, Blanchot, and Klossowski.* Lincoln: University of Nebraska Press, 1981.

Garber, Marjorie. *Vested Interests: Cross-Dressing and Cultural Anxiety.* New York: Routledge, 1992.

Gentile, Emilio. "The Conquest of Modernity: From Modernist Nationalism to Fascism." Trans. Lawrence Rainey. In *Modernism/Modernity* 1, no. 3 (September 1994).

Geyer, Michael. "The Politics of Memory in Contemporary Germany." In *Radical Evil.* Ed. Joan Copjec. London: Verso, 1996.

Gilbert, Sandra M. "Costumes of the Mind: Transvestitism as Metaphor in Modern Literature." In *Critical Inquiry* 7 (winter 1980).

Gilman, Sander. "I'm Down on Whores: Race and Gender in Victorian London." In *The Anatomy of Racism.* Ed. David Goldberg. Minneapolis: University of Minnesota Press, 1990.

Ginsborg, Paul. *A History of Contemporary Italy.* London: Penguin, 1990.

Ginzburg, Carlo. "Just One Witness." In *Probing the Limits of Representation: Nazism and the "Final Solution."* Ed. Saul Friedländer. Cambridge: Harvard University Press, 1992.

Girard, René. *Violence and the Sacred.* Trans. Patrick Gregory. Baltimore: Johns Hopkins University Press, 1972.

Giroux, Henry. "The Challenge of Neo-Fascist Culture." In *Cinéaste* 7, no. 4. (1975).

Gobetti, Piero. *La rivoluzione liberale.* Turin: Einaudi, 1969.

Golino, Enzo. "Pasolini, Politico Esistenziale." In *Italian Quarterly* (fall-winter 1984): 19–29.

Greenberg, Clement. "The Avant-Garde and Kitsch." In *Pollock and After: The Critical Debate.* Ed. Francis Frascina. New York: Harper and Row, 1985.

Greene, Naomi. *Pier Paolo Pasolini: Cinema as Heresy.* Princeton: Princeton University Press, 1990.

————. "Pasolini: 'Organic Intellectual'?" In *Italian Quarterly* 119–20 (winter/spring 1990).

Groz, Elizabeth. *Space, Time, and Perversion.* New York: Routledge, 1995.

Guattari, Félix. *Chaosophy.* Trans. Sylvère Lotringer. New York: Semiotext(e), 1995.

————. *Chaosmosis: An Ethico-Aesthetic Paradigm.* Trans. Paul Bains and Julian Pefanis. Bloomington: Indiana University Press, 1995.

Gubar, Susan. "Blessings in Disguise: Cross-Dressing as Re-Dressing for Female Modernists." In *Massachusetts Review* (autumn 1981).

Guéhenno, Jean-Marie. *The End of The Nation-State.* Trans. Victoria Elliott. Minneapolis: University of Minnesota Press, 1995.

Habermas, Jürgen. *New Conservatism: Cultural Criticism and the Historians' Debate.* Trans. Shierry Nicholsen. Cambridge: MIT University Press, 1989.

———. "Concerning the Public Use of History." In *New German Critique* 44 (1988).

———. *Legitimation Crisis.* Trans. Thomas McCarthy. Boston: Beacon Press, 1973.

Hansen, Miriam. *Babel and Babylon: Spectatorship in American Silent Film.* Cambridge: Harvard University Press, 1991.

———. "Adventures of Goldilocks: Spectatorship, Consumerism, and Public Life." In *Camera Obscura* no. 22 (January 1990).

Harris, C. R. S. *Allied Military Administration in Italy 1943–1945.* London, 1957.

Harrowitz, Nancy. *Anti-Semitism, Misogyny, and the Logic of Cultural Difference in Cesare Lombroso and Matilde Serao.* Lincoln: University of Nebraska Press, 1994.

———, ed. *Jews and Gender: Response to Otto Weininger.* Philadelphia: Temple University Press, 1995.

———. "Representations of the Holocaust: Levi, Bassani, and the Commemorative Mode." In *Reason and Light: Essays on Primo Levi.* Ed. Susan Tarrow. Ithaca: Cornell University Press, 1990.

Hartman, Geoffrey, ed. *Bitburg in Moral and Political Perspective.* Bloomington: University of Indiana Press, 1986.

Haskell, Molly. "Are Women Directors Different?" *The Village Voice,* 3 February 1975.

Hay, James. *Popular Film Culture in Fascist Italy: The Passing of the Rex.* Bloomington: Indiana University Press, 1987.

Heath, Stephen. *Questions of Cinema.* Bloomington: Indiana University Press, 1981.

Heidegger, Martin. *The Question Concerning Technology.* Trans. William Lovitt. New York: Harper Books, 1977.

———. *Being and Time.* Trans. John Macquarrie and Edward Robinson. New York: Harper and Row, 1962.

Hegel, Friedrich. *Philosophy of Right.* Trans. T. M. Knox. London: Oxford University Press, 1952.

Hewitt, Andrew. "The Bad Seed: 'Auschwitz' and the Physiology of Evil." In *Radical Evil.* Ed. Joan Copjec. London: Verso, 1996.

———. *Political Inversions.* Stanford: Stanford University Press, 1996.

———. *Fascist Modernism: Asethetics, Politics, and the Avant-Garde.* Stanford: Stanford University Press, 1993.

Hilberg, Raul. *The Destruction of the European Jews.* Chicago: Quadrangle, 1961.

Hobbes, Thomas. *Leviathan.* New York: Penguin, 1968.

hooks, bell. *Yearnings: Race, Gender, and Cultural Politics.* Boston: South End Press, 1990.

Hutchenson, Linda. *Irony's Edge: The Theory and Politics of Irony.* New York: Routledge, 1995.

Huyssen, Andreas. *After the Great Divide: Modernism, Mass Culture, Postmodernism.* Bloomington, Indiana University Press, 1986.

Insdorf, Annette. *Indelible Shadows: Film and the Holocaust.* New York: Cambridge University Press, 1983.

Irigaray, Luce. *An Ethics of Sexual Difference.* Trans. Carolyn Burke and Gillian C. Gill. Ithaca: Cornell University Press, 1993.

———. *Marine Lover of Friedrich Nietzsche.* Trans. Gillian Gill. New York: Columbia University Press, 1991.

———. *This Sex Which Is Not One.* Trans. Catherine Porter. New York: Cornell University Press, 1985.

———. *Speculum of the Other Woman.* Trans. Gillian C. Gill. Ithaca: Cornell University Press, 1974.

Jay, Martin. "Of Plots, Witnesses, and Judgments. In *Probing the Limits of Representation:*

Nazism and the "Final Solution." Ed. Saul Friedländer. Cambridge: Harvard University Press, 1992.

Jelavich, Peter. *Berlin Cabaret.* Cambridge: Harvard University Press, 1993.

Jewell, Keala. *The Poeisis of History: Experimenting with Genre in Postwar Italy.* Ithaca: Cornell University Press, 1992.

Kael, Pauline. "Seven Beauties." In *The New Yorker,* 16 February 1976.

———. "The Current Cinema: Stuck in the Fun." *The New Yorker,* 7 October 1974.

Kaes, Anton. "History, Fiction, Memory: Fassbinder's *The Marriage of Maria Braun.* In *German Film and Literature.* Ed. Eric Rentschler. New York: Methuen, 1979.

Kaplan, Ann E., ed. *Psychoanalysis and Cinema.* New York: Routledge, 1990.

Kasher, Steven. "The Art of Hitler." In *October* no. 59 (winter 1992).

Kavka, Misha. "The 'Alluring Abyss of Nothingness': Misogyny and (Male) Hysteria in Otto Weininger." In *New German Critique* no. 66 (fall 1995).

Klossowski, Pierre. *Sade mon prochain: Le philosophe scèlèrat.* Paris: Aux Èditions du Seuil, 1967.

Koch, Gertrud. "Between Two Worlds: Von Sternberg's *The Blue Angel* (1930)." In *German Film and Literature: Adaptations and Transformations.* Ed. Eric Rentschler. New York: Methuen, 1986.

Koselleck, Reinhart. *Futures Past: On the Semantics of Historical Time.* Trans. Keith Tribe. Cambridge: MIT University Press, 1985.

Kosinski, Jerzy. "Seven Beauties—A Cartoon Trying to be a Tragedy." In the *New York Times* 7 March 1976).

Kracauer, Siegfried. *The Mass Ornament: Weimar Essays.* Trans. Thomas Y. Levin. Cambridge: Harvard University Press, 1995.

———. *From Caligari to Hitler: A Psychological History of the German Film.* Princeton: Princeton University Press, 1947.

Krauss, Rosalind. *The Originality of the Avant-Garde and Other Modernist Myths.* Cambridge: MIT University Press, 1988.

Kristeva, Julia. *Tales of Love.* Trans. Leon S. Roudiez. New York: Columbia University Press, 1987.

———. *The Kristeva Reader.* Ed. Toril Moi. New York: Columbia University Press, 1986.

———. *The Powers of Horror: An Essay on Abjection.* Trans. Leon S. Roudiez. New York: Columbia University Press, 1982.

LaCapra, Dominick. "Lanzmann's *Shoah*: Here There Is No Why." In *Critical Inquiry* 23 (winter 1997).

———. *Representing the Holocaust: History, Theory, Trauma.* Ithaca: Cornell University Press, 1994.

Lacan, Jacques. *Feminine Sexuality.* Trans. Jacqueline Rose. New York: Norton, 1982.

———. *Ecrits: A Selection.* Trans. Alan Sheridan. New York: Norton, 1977.

———. *Le seminaire livre* XX. Paris: Seuil, 1975.

Lacoue-Labarthe, Philippe. *Musica Ficta: Figures of Wagner.* Trans. Felicia McCarren. Stanford: Stanford University Press, 1994.

———. *La Fiction du politique.* Paris: Christian Bourgeois, 1987.

Landy, Marcia. *Fascism in Film: Italian Commercial Cinema 1931–43.* Princeton: Princeton University Press, 1983.

Lanzmann, Claude. "Seminar with Claude Lanzmann, April 11, 1990." In *Yale French Studies* no. 79 (1991).

Lawton, Ben. "The Evolving Rejection of Homosexuality: The Sub-Proletariat and the Third World in the Films of Pier Paolo Pasolini." In *Italian Quarterly* 21–22 (fall-winter 1980–81).

Le Bon, Gustav. *The Crowd: A Study of the Popular Mind*. New York: Macmillan, 1925.

Le Brun, Annie. *Sade: A Sudden Abyss*. San Francisco: City Lights Books, 1990.

Leehem, Mira. *Passion and Defiance: Film in Italy from 1942 to the Present*. Berkeley: University of California Press, 1984.

———. *The Psychology of Socialism*. New York: Macmillan, 1899.

Lefebvre, Henri. *Critique of Everyday Life*. Trans. John Moore. London: Verso, 1947.

Levi, Primo. *I Sommersi e i salvati*. Turin: Einaudi, 1986.

———. *Se questo e un uomo*. Turin: Einaudi, 1967.

Levinas, Emmanuel. *Outside the Subject*. Trans. Michael B. Smith. Stanford: Stanford University Press, 1994.

Lewinska, Pelagia. *Vignt mois a Auschwitz*. Paris: Minuit, 1945.

Lichtenstein, Grace. "In Liliana Cavani's Love Story, Love Means Always Having to Say Ouch." *New York Times*, 13 October 1974.

Lizzani, Carlo. *Il cinema italiano 1895–1979*. 2 vols. Rome: Riuniti, 1979.

Lyotard, Jean-François. *Lessons on the Analytic of the Sublime*. Trans. Elizabeth Rottenberg. Stanford: Stanford University Press, 1994.

———. *Libidinal Economy*. Trans. Iain Hamilton Grant. Bloomington: Indiana University Press, 1993.

———. *Heidegger and "the jews."* Trans. Andreas Michel and Mark Roberts. Minneapolis: University of Minnesota Press, 1990.

———. *The Differend*. Trans. Georges Van Den Abbeele. Minneapolis: University of Minnesota Press, 1988.

———. *The Inhuman*. Trans. Geoffrey Bennington and Rachel Bowlby. Stanford: Stanford University Press, 1988.

———. *Driftworks*. Trans. Susan Hanson, Richard Lockwood, and Joseph Maier. New York: Semiotext(e), 1984.

Lyotard, Jean-François, and Jean Paul Thébaud. *Just Gaming*. Minneapolis: University of Minnesota Press, 1985.

Macciocchi, Maria Antonietta. *Pasolini*. Paris: Bernard Grasset, 1980.

———. *La donna "nera": "Consenso" femminile e fascismo*. Milan: Feltrinelli, 1976.

Maier, Charles S. *The Unmasterable Past: History, Holocaust, and German National Identity*. Cambridge: Harvard University Press, 1988.

Mannheim, Karl. *Ideology and Utopia*. Trans. Louis Wirth and Edward Shils. New York: Harcourt Brace Jovanovich, 1936.

Marcus, Millicent. *Filmmaking by the Book: Italian Cinema and Literary Adaptation*. Baltimore: Johns Hopkins University Press, 1993.

———. *Italian Film in the Light of Neorealism*. Princeton: Princeton University Press, 1986.

Marcuse, Herbert. *From Luther to Popper*. Trans. Doris De Bres. London: Verso, 1972.

———. *One-Dimensional Man*. Boston: Beacon Press, 1964.

———. *Reason and Revolution*. Oxford: Oxford University Press, 1941.

Marinetti, F. T. "Contro la Spagna Passatista." In *Teoria e invenzione futurista*. Milan: Mondadori Editore, 1990.

———. *Teoria e invenzione futurista*. Milan: A. Mondadori Editore, 1968.

———. *Mafarka*. Trans. Decio Cinti. Milan: Edizioni Futuriste di "Poiesia," 1910.

Marx, Karl, and Friedrich Engles. "The Manifesto of the Communist Party." In *The Marx-Engles Reader*. Ed. Robert C. Tucker. New York: Norton, 1978.

———. *Capital* Vol. 1. Trans. Ben Fowkes. New York: Vintage, 1977.

———. *Economic and Philosophic Manuscripts of 1844*. USSR: Progress Publishers, 1977.

Maslin, Janet. "Film Reviews." *Boston Phoenix*, 22 October 1974.

Mayne, Judith. *The Woman at the Keyhole: Feminism and Women's Cinema*. Bloomington: Indiana University Press, 1990.

———. "Dietrich, The Blue Angel, and Female Performance." In *Seduction and Theory: Readings of Gender, Representation, and Rhetoric*. Ed. Dianne Hunter. Urbana: University of Illinois Press, 1989.

McBean, James Roy. "Between Kitsch and Fascism." In *Cinéaste* 13, no. 4 (1984).

McCormick, Ruth. "Fascism a la Mode or Radical Chic?" In *Cinéaste* 6, no. 4 (1975).

McLuhan, Marshall. *Understanding Media: The Extensions of Man*. New York: Signet, 1964.

Merleau-Ponty, Maurice. *Sense and Non-Sense*. Trans. Hubert L. Dreyfus and Patricia Allen Dreyfus. Evanston: Northwestern University Press, 1964.

Metz, Christian. *The Imaginary Signifier: Psychoanalysis and the Cinema*. Trans. Celia Britton, Annwyl Williams, Ben Brewster, and Alfred Guzzetti. Bloomington: Indiana University Press, 1982.

———. *Film Language*. Trans. Michael Taylor. London: Oxford University Press, 1974.

Mizejewski, Linda. *Divine Decadence: Fascism, Female Spectacle, and the Makings of Sally Bowles*. Princeton: Princeton University Press, 1992.

Modleski, Tania. *The Women Who Knew Too Much: Hitchcock and Feminist Theory*. New York: Routledge, 1988.

———. *Loving with a Vengeance: Mass-Produced Fantasies for Women*. New York: Routledge, 1984.

Moravia, Alberto. *La noia*. Milan: Bompiani, 1960.

———. *La Ciociara*. Milan: Bompiani, 1957.

———. *I Racoonti, 1927–1951*, 2 vols. Milan: Bompiani, 1952.

———. *Il conformista*. Milan: Bompiani, 1951.

———. *Gli indifferenti*. Milan: Bompiani, 1949.

Mosca, Gaetano. *Storia delle dottrine politiche*. Bari: Laterza, 1962.

———. *Partiti e sindacti nella crisi del regime parlamentare*. Bari: Laterza, 1949.

———. *Ruling Class*. Trans. Hannah D. Kahn. New York: McGraw-Hill, 1939.

Mosse, George L. *Germans and Jews: The Right, the Left, and the Search for a "Third Force" in Pre-Nazi Germany*. Detroit: Wayne State University Press, 1987.

———. *Nationalism and Sexuality: Middle-Class Morality and Sexual Norms in Modern Europe*. Madison: University of Wisconsin Press, 1985.

———. *The Nationalization of the Masses: Political Symbolism and Mass Movements in Germany from the Napoleonic Wars through the Third Reich*. Ithaca: Cornell University Press, 1975.

Mulvey, Laura. *Visual and Other Pleasures*. Bloomington: Indiana University Press, 1989.

Nägele, Rainer. *Reading After Freud: Essays on Goethe, Hölderlin, Habermas, Nietzsche, Brecht, Celan, and Freud*. New York: Columbia University Press, 1987.

Naldini, Nico. *Pasolini, una vita*. Turin: Einaudi, 1989.

Nancy, Jean-Luc. "The Unsacrificeable." Trans. Allan Stoekl. In *Yale French Studies* no. 79 (1991).

Negri, Antonio. *Revolution Retrieved*. London: Red Notes, 1988.

Nietzsche, Friedrich. *Philosophy and Truth: Selections from Nietzsche's Notebooks of the Early 1870s*. Trans. Daniel Breazeale. New York: Humanities Press, 1979.

———. *Twilight of the Idols*. Trans. Walter Kaufmann. New York: Penguin, 1968.

———. *The Will to Power*. Trans. Walter Kaufmann and R. J. Hollingdale. New York: Vintage, 1967.

———. *Beyond Good and Evil*. Trans. Walter Kaufmann. New York: Modern Library, 1966.

————. *Birth of Tragedy*. Trans. Walter Kaufmann. New York: Modern Library, 1966.

————. *The Genealogy of Morals*. Trans. Walter Kaufmann. New York: Modern Library, 1966.

————. *The Wanderer and His Shadow*. Trans. Walter Kaufmann. New York: Modern Library, 1966.

Newton, Esther. *Mother Camp: Female Impersonators in America*. Chicago: University of Chicago Press, 1972.

Nolte, Ernst. *Three Faces of Fascism*. Trans. Leila Vennewitz. New York: Holt Rinehart and Winston, 1966.

Nowell-Smith, Geoffrey. "Pasolini's Originality." In *Pier Paolo Pasolini*. Ed. Paul Willemen. London: BFI, 1977.

Orr, John. *Cinema and Modernity*. Oxford: Polity Press, Blackwell, 1993.

Otten, Karl. *A Combine of Aggression: Masses, Elites, and Dictatorship in Germany*. London, 1942.

Paggi, Leonardo. "Antifascism and the Reshaping of Democratic Consensus in Post–1945 Italy." In *New German Critique* no. 67 (winter 1996).

Panofsky, Erwin. *Perspective as Symbolic Form*. Trans. Christopher S. Wood. New York: Zone Books, 1991.

Pasolini, Pier Paolo. *Scritti Corsari*. Milan: Garzanti, 1990.

————. "Porcile." In *Teatro*. Milan: Garzanti, 1988.

————. *Pasolini: Selected Poems*. Eds. Norman MacAfee and Luciano Martinengo. London: John Calder, 1984.

————. "Stylistic Reaction." Trans. Paul Vangelisti. In *Stanford Italian Review* 2, no. 2 (fall 1982).

————. *Passione e ideologia*. Milan: Garzanti, 1977.

————. *Empirismo eretico*. Milan: Garzanti, 1972.

————. *Teorema*. Milan: Garzanti, 1986.

————. "Le Cenere di Gramsci." In *Operere di Pier Paolo Pasolini*. Milan: Garzanti, 1957.

Pavone, Claudio. *Resistenza e storia d'Italia*. *Belfagor* 32, no. 2 (1977).

Perfetti, Francesco. *Il nazionalismo italiano dalle origini alla fusione col fascismo*. Bologna: Capelli, 1977.

Petraglia, Sandro. *Pier Paolo Pasolini*. Florence: La Nuova Italia, 1974.

Peukert, Detlev. *The Weimar Republic: The Crisis of Classical Modernity*. Trans. Richard Deveson. New York: Hill and Wang, 1987.

————. *Inside Nazi Germany: Conformity, Opposition, and Racism in Everyday Life*. Trans. Richard Deveson. New Haven: Yale University Press, 1987.

Pfefferkorn, Eli. "Bettelheim, Wertmüller, and the Morality of Survival." In *Postscript: Essays in Film and the Humanities* 1, no. 2 (winter 1982).

Pinkus, Karen. *Bodily Regimes: Italian Advertising Under Fascism*. Minneapolis: University of Minnesota Press, 1995.

Plant, Richard. *The Pink Triangle: The Nazi War Against Homosexuals*. New York: Henry Holt, 1986.

Quazza, Guido. *Resistenza e storia d'Italia: Problemi e ipotesi di ricerca*. Milan: Feltrinelli, 1976.

Rancière, Jacques. *The Names of History: On the Poetics of Knowledge*. Trans. Hassan Melehy. Minneapolis: University of Minnesota Press, 1994.

Re, Lucia. *Calvino and the Age of Neorealism: Fables of Estrangement*. Stanford: Stanford University Press, 1990.

Reed, Rex. "The Night Porter Yuck Sick Demented Junk." New York *Daily News*, 4 October 1974.

Reich, Wilhelm. *Character Analysis*. Trans. Vincent Carfagno. New York: Farrar, Strauss and Giroux, 1949.

Rohdie, Sam. *The Passion of Pier Paolo Pasolini*. London: BFI, 1995.

Rosa, Rosa. *Una Donna con tre anime*. Milan: Facchi Editore, 1919.

Rosen, Marjorie. "Laughing All the Way to the Gallows." *New York Times*, 5 March 1976.

Rosenbaum, Petra. *Il nuovo fascismo : Da Salò ad Almirante : Storia del MSI*. Milan: Feltrinelli, 1975.

Rosenstone, Robert A., ed. *Revisioning History: Film and the Construction of a New Past*. Princeton: Princeton University Press, 1995.

———. *Visions of the Past: The Challenge of Film to Our Idea of History*. Cambridge: Harvard University Press, 1995.

Ross, Andrew. "Baudrillard's Bad Attitude." In *Seduction and Theory: Readings of Gender, Representation and Rhetoric*. Ed. Dianne Hunter. Urbana: University of Illinois Press, 1989.

———. *No Respect: Intellectuals and Popular Culture*. New York: Routledge, 1989.

Rossanda, Rossana. *L'anno degli studenti*. Bari: De Donato, 1986.

Rosselli, Carlo. *Socialismo liberale*. Milan, 1945.

Rossellini, Roberto. *My Method*. Trans. Anna Paola Cancogni. New York: Marsilio, 1992.

Roth, Michael. "*Hiroshima Mon Amour*: You Must Remember This." In *Revisioning History: Film and the Construction of a New Past*. Ed. Robert Rosenstone. Princeton: Princeton University Press, 1995.

Sade, Marquis de. *120 days of Sodom*. Trans. Richard Seaver and Austryn Wainhouse. New York: Grove Press, 1966.

———. *The Complete Justine, Philosophy in the Bedroom, and Other Writings*. Trans. Richard Seaver and Austryn Wainhouse. New York: Grove Press, 1965.

Santarelli, Enzo. *Storia del movimento e del regime fascista*. 2 vols. Rome: Editori Riuniti, 1967.

Sarfatti, Margherita. *Dvx*. Milan: Mondadori, 1926.

Sarti, Roland. *Fascism and the Industrial Leadership in Italy 1919–1940*. Berkeley: University of California Press, 1971.

Scarry, Elaine. *The Body in Pain: The Making and Unmaking of the World*. New York: Oxford University Press, 1985.

Scheibler, Ingrid. "Heidegger and the Rhetoric of Submission: Technology and Passivity." In *Re-Thinking Technologies*. Ed. Verena Andermatt Conley. Minneapolis: University of Minnesota Press, 1993.

Schorske, Carl E. *Fin-de-Siècle Vienna: Politics and Culture*. New York: Vintage, 1961.

———. *German Social Democracy 1905–1917*. Cambridge: Harvard University Press, 1955.

Sciascia, Leonardo. "God Behind Sade." Trans. Paul Psoinos. In *Stanford Italian Review* 4, no. 2 (fall 1984).

Sedgwick, Eve Kosofsky. *Epistemology of the Closet*. Berkeley: University of California Press, 1990.

———. *Between Men: English Literature and Male Homosocial Desire*. New York: Columbia University Press, 1985.

Serres, Michel. *The Parasite*. Trans. Lawrence R. Schehr. Baltimore: Johns Hopkins University Press, 1982.

Setta, S. *L'Uomo qualunque, 1944–1948*. Bari: Laterza, 1975.

Shaviro, Steven. *The Cinematic Body*. Minneapolis: University of Minnesota Press, 1993.

Siciliano, Enzo. *Vita di Pasolini*. Milan: Rizzoli, 1978.

Silone, Ignazio. *Vino e pane*. Milan: A. Montadori, 1955.

Silverman, Kaja. *The Acoustic Mirror: The Female Voice in Psychoanalysis and Cinema*. Bloomington: Indiana University Press, 1988.

Sloterdijk, Peter. *Critique of Cynical Reason.* Trans. Michael Eldred. Minneapolis: University of Minnesota Press, 1987.

Smith-Rosenberg, Caroll. *Disorderly Conduct: Visions of Gender in Victorian America.* New York: Oxford University Press, 1985.

Sobchack, Vivian, ed. *The Persistence of History: Cinema, Television, and the Modern Event.* New York: Routledge, 1996.

Sontag, Susan. "Fascinating Fascism." In *The Susan Sontag Reader.* New York: Farrar, Strauss and Giroux, 1982.

————. *Against Interpretation.* New York: Farrar, Strauss and Giroux, 1966.

Sorlin, Pierre. *Italian National Cinema: 1896–1996.* New York: Routledge, 1996.

Spackman, Barbara. *Fascist Virilities.* Minneapolis: University of Minnesota Press, 1996.

————. *Decadent Genealogies: The Rhetoric of Sickness from Baudelaire to D'Annunzio.* Ithaca: Cornell University Press, 1989.

Spanos, William. *Heidegger and Criticism: Retrieving the Cultural Politics of Destruction.* Minneapolis: University of Minnesota Press, 1993.

Speer, Albert. *Inside the Third Reich.* Trans. Richard Winston and Clara Winston. New York: Macmillan, 1970.

Spinosa, Antonio. *Starace.* Milan: Mondadori, 1980.

Stack, Oswald. *Pier Paolo Pasolini.* Ed. Paul Willemen. London: BFI, 1977.

Staiger, Janet. "Cinematic Shots: The Narration of Violence." In *The Persistence of History.* Ed. Vivian Sobchack. New York: Routledge, 1996.

————. *Bad Women.* Minneapolis: University of Minnesota Press, 1995.

Sternhell, Zeev. *Neither Right nor Left: Fascist Ideology in France.* Trans. David Maisel. Berkeley: University of California Press, 1986.

————. *The Birth of Fascist Ideology.* Trans. David Maisel. Princeton: Princeton University Press, 1989.

Sterritt, David. "The Night Porter." In *Christian Science Monitor,* 30 December 1974.

Studlar, Gaylyn. *This Mad Masquerade: Stardom and Masculinity in the Jazz Age.* New York: Columbia University Press, 1996.

————. *In the Realm of Pleasure: Von Sternberg, Dietrich, and the Masochistic Aesthetic.* New York: Columbia University Press, 1988.

Tasca, Angelo. *Nascita e avvento del fascismo.* 2 vols. Bari: Laterza, 1974.

Tatar, Maria. *Lustmord: Sexual Murder in Weimar Germany.* Princeton: Princeton University Press, 1995.

Tasker, Yvonne. *Spectacular Bodies: Gender, Genre and the Action Cinema.* New York: Routledge, 1993.

Taussig, Michael. *Mimesis and Alterity: A Particular History of the Senses.* New York: Routledge, 1993.

————. *The Nervous System.* New York: Routledge, 1992.

Tisdall, Caroline, and Angelo Bozzolla. *Futurism.* London: Thames and Hudson, 1977.

Theweleit, Klaus. *Male Fantasies.* Vols. 1 and 2. Trans. Stephen Conway. Minneapolis: University of Minnesota Press, 1987.

Tyler, Carole-Anne. "Decking Out: Performing Identities." In *Inside/Out: Lesbian Theories, Gay Theories.* Ed. Diana Fuss. New York: Routledge, 1991.

Valesio, Paolo. "Pasolini Come Sintomo." In *Italian Quarterly* 21–22 (fall-winter 1980–81).

Vattimo, Gianni. *The End of Modernity.* Trans. Jon Snyder. Baltimore: Johns Hopkins University Press, 1985.

————. *Poesia e ontologia.* Milan: Mursia, 1967–1985.

Verdicchio, Pasquale. "Censoring the Body of Ideology: The Films of Pier Paolo Pasolini." In *Fictional International* (San Diego, 1992), vol. 22: 369–79.

Viano, Maurizio. *A Certain Realism: Making Use of Pasolini's Film Theory and Practice.* Berkeley: University of California Press, 1993.

Vidal-Naquet, Pierre. *Assassins of Memory: Essays on the Denial of the Holocaust.* Trans. Jeffrey Mehlman. New York: Columbia University Press, 1992.

Virilio, Paul. *The Vision Machine.* Trans. Julie Rose. Bloomington: Indiana University Press, 1994.

———. *The Aesthetics of Disappearance.* Trans. Philip Beitchman. New York: Semiotext(e), 1991.

———. *Popular Defense and Ecological Struggles.* Trans. Mark Polizzotti. New York: Semiotext(e), 1990.

———. *War and Cinema: The Logistics of Perception.* Trans. Patrick Camiler. London: Verso, 1989.

———. *Speed and Politics.* Trans. Mark Polizzotti. New York: Semiotext(e), 1986.

———. "The Third Interval: A Critical Transition." In *Re-Thinking Technologies.* Minneapolis: University of Minnesota Press, 1993.

von Dassanowky, Robert. "Wherever you may run, you cannot escape him: Leni Riefenstahl's Self-Reflection and Romantic Transcendence of Nazism in Tiefland." In *New German Critique* no. 63 (fall 1994).

Waller, Marguerite. "Signifying the Holocaust: Liliana Cavani's *Portiere di Notte.*" In *Feminism in the Cinema.* Ed. Laura Pietropalo and Ada Testafferri. Bloomington: Indiana University Press, 1995.

Watson, William Van. *Pier Paolo Pasolini and the Theatre of the Word.* Ann Arbor: UMI Press, 1989.

Weber, Eugen. *Varieties of Fascism.* New York: Von Nostrand Reinhold, 1964.

Weber, Samuel. *Institution and Interpretation.* Minneapolis: University of Minnesota Press, 1987.

———. *The Legend of Freud.* Minneapolis: University of Minnesota Press, 1982.

Weininger, Otto. *Sex and Character.* Trans. W. Heinemann. London: Putnam, 1906.

White, Hayden. "The Modernist Event." In *The Persistence of History: Cinema, Television, and the Modern Event.* Ed. Vivian Sobchack. London: AFI, 1996.

———. "Historical Emplotment and the Problem of Truth." In *Probing the Limits of Representation: Nazism and the "Final Solution."* Ed. Saul Friedländer. Cambridge: Harvard University Press, 1992.

———. "Historiography and Historiophoty." In *American Historical Review* no. 108 (December 1991).

———. *The Content and the Form: Narrative Discourse and Historical Representation.* Baltimore: Johns Hopkins University Press, 1987.

———. *Metahistory.* Baltimore: Johns Hopkins University Press, 1973.

Willemen, Paul, ed. *Pier Paolo Pasolini.* London: BFI, 1977.

Williams, Linda. *Hard Core: Power, Pleasure, and the "Frenzy of the Visible"* Berkeley: University of California Press, 1989.

Williams, Raymond. *The Politics of Modernism.* London: Verso, 1989.

Wippermann, Wolfgang, and Michael Burleigh. *The Racial State: Germany 1933–1945.* Cambridge: Cambridge University Press, 1991.

Wolf, William. "Sadistic Games." In *Cue* 7 October 1974.

Wollen, Peter. *Signs and Meaning in the Cinema.* Bloomington: Indiana University Press, 1969.

Zigaina, Giuseppe. "Total Contamination in Pasolini." Trans. Giuseppe Zigaina and James Carolan. In *Stanford Italian Review* 4, no. 2 (fall 1984).

Zimmerman, Michael. *Heidegger's Confrontation with Modernity: Technology, Politics, Art.* Bloomington: Indiana University Press, 1987.

Žižek, Slavoj. *The Indivisible Remainder: An Essay on Schelling and Related Matters.* London: Verso, 1996.

———. *The Metastases of Enjoyment.* London: Verso, 1994.

———. *Tarrying with the Negative: Kant, Hegel, and the Critique of Ideology.* Durham: Duke University Press, 1993.

———. *Enjoy Your Symptom!* New York: Routledge, 1992.

———. *For They Know Not What They Do: Enjoyment as a Political Factor.* New York: Verso, 1991.

———. *The Sublime Object of Desire.* New York: Verso, 1989.

Index

285

Kriss Ravetto teaches at Emerson College in Boston, Massachusetts.